Why Populism?

The rise to power of populists like Donald Trump is usually attributed to the shifting values and policy preferences of voters – the demand side. *Why Populism* shifts the public debate on populism and examines the other half of the equation – the supply side. Kenny argues that to understand the rise of populism is to understand the cost of different strategies for winning and keeping power. For the aspiring leader, populism – appealing directly to the people through mass communication – can be a quicker, cheaper, and more effective strategy than working through a political party.

Probing the long history of populism in the West from its Ancient Greek roots to the present, this highly readable book shows that the "economic laws of populism are constant." "Forget ideology. Forget resentment. Forget racism or sexism." Populism, the author writes, is the result of a hidden strategic calculus.

PAUL D. KENNY is an award-winning author of two previous books, *Populism and Patronage: Why Populists Win Elections in India, Asia, and Beyond* and *Populism in Southeast Asia*. He holds a PhD in political science from Yale University and degrees in economics and political economy from Trinity College Dublin and the London School of Economics.

Why Populism?

Political Strategy from Ancient Greece to the Present

PAUL D. KENNY
Australian Catholic University

 CAMBRIDGE
UNIVERSITY PRESS

CAMBRIDGE
UNIVERSITY PRESS

Shaftesbury Road, Cambridge CB2 8EA, United Kingdom

One Liberty Plaza, 20th Floor, New York, NY 10006, USA

477 Williamstown Road, Port Melbourne, VIC 3207, Australia

314–321, 3rd Floor, Plot 3, Splendor Forum, Jasola District Centre, New Delhi – 110025, India

103 Penang Road, #05–06/07, Visioncrest Commercial, Singapore 238467

Cambridge University Press is part of Cambridge University Press & Assessment,
a department of the University of Cambridge.

We share the University's mission to contribute to society through the pursuit of
education, learning and research at the highest international levels of excellence.

www.cambridge.org
Information on this title: www.cambridge.org/9781009275293

DOI: 10.1017/9781009275262

First published 2023

Printed in the United Kingdom by TJ Books Limited, Padstow Cornwall

A catalogue record for this publication is available from the British Library.

Library of Congress Cataloging-in-Publication Data
NAMES: Kenny, Paul, 1981– author.
TITLE: Why populism? : political strategy from ancient Greece to the present / Paul Kenny,
    Australian Catholic University, Melbourne.
DESCRIPTION: First Edition. | New York : Cambridge University Press, 2023. | Includes
    bibliographical references and index.
IDENTIFIERS: LCCN 2022043282 (print) | LCCN 2022043283 (ebook) | ISBN 9781009275293
    (Hardback) | ISBN 9781009275309 (Paperback) | ISBN 9781009275262 (epub)
SUBJECTS: LCSH: Populism–History.
CLASSIFICATION: LCC JC423 .K384 2023 (print) | LCC JC423 (ebook) | DDC 320.56/62–dc23/
    eng/20220930
LC record available at https://lccn.loc.gov/2022043282
LC ebook record available at https://lccn.loc.gov/2022043283

ISBN 978-1-009-27529-3 Hardback

For Kate

Contents

Preface

Men love power.

Alexander Hamilton[1]

[H]e who neglects what is done for what ought to be done, sooner effects his ruin than his preservation.

Niccolò Machiavelli[2]

POLITICS IS ABOUT POWER

"Men," said the inimitable Alexander Hamilton, "love power." Politicians seek the highest office that their talents and resources will allow, and they seek as much authority as that office makes possible. Of course, we shouldn't assume that politicians *only* want power or that they are devoid of other goals. No doubt, some politicians have a genuine desire to help (or harm) others. Yet whatever it is that politicians *want* to accomplish, they *need* power to do so. As the preeminent student of political power, Niccolò Machiavelli, wrote in his manual for government, *The Prince*, "[h]e who neglects what is done for what ought to be done, sooner effects his ruin than his preservation." Power first, ideals later. Or in the words of Huey Long, governor of Louisiana and then United States senator, "First you must come into power – POWER – and then you can do things."[3]

Populism, as Long himself knew well, is a strategy in this essential quest for power. This book seeks to explain why politicians choose populism rather than its alternatives. In its most naked form, the competition for power comes down to a clash of arms; assassinations, arrests, coups, bombs, and battles are its means. But if, as Mao Zedong said, "politics is war without bloodshed," we can think about the recruitment of a mass political party membership, vote buying, and social media communication as different sorts of weapons in an aspiring leader's strategic arsenal. Should a politician try to dominate elective office through a disciplined party machine? Or try to gain a following by handing out gifts to supporters? Or try to mobilize support by direct communication with the masses? Putting the recourse to arms aside, these *programmatic*, *patronage*, and *populist* strategies are the three main options from which a politician must choose.[4]

From the politician's perspective, in an ideal world, he might use elements of all these strategies. The more resources he has, the more he'll do, and just as in war, those with the most resources will usually be victorious. God, Napoleon quipped, is on the side with the heaviest artillery. In the 2008 US presidential race, Barack Obama raised and spent more than twice as much as his opponent, John McCain. In 1896, Republican stalwart William McKinley was even better endowed, with more than ten times the funds available to the charismatic William Jennings Bryan. On remarkably few occasions has an outspent candidate won the presidency. Yet because politicians typically compete with closely matched foes, they can ill afford to waste their resources. In any case, no politician has unlimited reserves to throw into the battle. For the politician, money spent on an excessively large personal victory today is money that can't be used to fund the campaigns of allies tomorrow. A landslide victory, according to the esteemed political scientist E. E. Schattschneider, "*is simply political extravagance.*" The ambitious politician must maximize his chances of winning and keeping power given constraints on his money, time, and talents. Good political strategists must be efficient. They must *economize.*[5]

Although my argument in this book is very much "economic," the explanation I offer is not one of how financial crises, unemployment, inflation, or inequality – the subjects of *macroeconomics* – have made populism more or less likely. This territory has been well covered by other writers. My approach is economic in a different sense. Nineteenth–century Scottish writer Thomas Carlyle famously called economics the "*dismal science.*" For modern economists, it is, as I recall learning in my very first weeks as an undergraduate, "the science of scarcity." This doesn't mean that economics should be a source of anxiety. Rather, it means that economics can be understood as the science of how trade-offs are weighed in a world where money, time, and energy are finite. Economics – or more precisely, *microeconomics* – as Nobel Prize–winner Ronald H. Coase put it, "is the science of human choice." Rather than being a specialized academic niche concerned with "the economy," economics is an approach to understanding human behavior in the most general sense.[6]

This "economic approach," as Gary Becker, another Nobel Prize winner termed it, is ideally suited to explaining why a political leader would choose one strategy rather than another to win and keep power. The economic approach takes as fundamental the idea that every choice entails *opportunity costs* – the hidden cost of the investment not made, the good not consumed, the path not taken. Political strategy, as much as any commercial activity, represents a choice in a world of limited resources. Any money, time, or effort expended pursuing one strategy cannot be spent on others. For anyone who has ground their way through ECON 101, many of the concepts and ideas used in this book will be quite familiar, but no prior reading in economics is necessary to understand its main argument: Populism is a political strategy that relies on the use of a personalistic political organization and mass communication to mobilize support in the quest for power; it will be most successful when it is more cost effective than its alternatives.[7]

This sense for the economic logic of populism grew out of my doctoral dissertation research on the political development of post-independence India. Unlike most of its former colonial counterparts, India remained democratic for more than two decades after independence, thanks in large part to the deft distribution of patronage to regional elites by the country's first prime minister and leader of the Indian National Congress party, Jawaharlal Nehru. However, by the time Nehru's daughter, Indira Gandhi, became prime minister in 1966, regional power brokers had the ability to extract ever higher payments for the delivery of their vote banks to the national Congress party. For Mrs. Gandhi, "going once more direct to the people" over the heads of a cabal of these regional elites ominously known as *The Syndicate* was the economically rational choice. I soon found that my explanation for the Indian experience made sense of other well-known cases such as Venezuela and Peru, where the populist strategies of Hugo Chávez and Alberto Fujimori, respectively, were winning propositions amid their countries fraying party systems.[8]

The Asian and Latin American cases I examined in my first two books, *Populism and Patronage* and *Populism in Southeast Asia*, showed that the more costly it becomes to rule through patronage, the more likely populism is to emerge as a successful alternative. However, whenever I talked to Western audiences about my research on populism in these mostly poor and middle-income states, one of the first questions I inevitably received was about how this approach would travel to America or Europe: How, in particular, would it explain the rise of Donald Trump? *Why Populism?* is my attempt to answer that question.

Although Trump features prominently in this book, to really understand why populism has become increasingly prevalent in modern-day North America and Western Europe, I believe we have to put the present in its proper historical context. It is only by taking a longer view, all the way from the ancient world through to the rise of mass democracy in the twentieth century, that we can appreciate what is special about the present – that we can fully explain why Trump succeeded in 2016 whereas most other populists before him in American history have failed. What this historical perspective shows is that the economic laws of populism are constant; when the conditions that affect the cost of different types of political strategy change, so too does effectiveness of populism.

Acknowledgments

Given that I had little interest in, or knowledge of, populism as I began my academic career, I find myself looking back with some surprise that I've now completed yet another book on the subject. Populism has a way of sucking you in. If ten years and three books seem like a lot to dedicate to a single problem, I haven't done it alone. I owe most appreciation to Kate, my partner in everything. Amid illnesses and lockdowns, the last few years have made it even harder for us all to leave work at the "office," but Kate has shared my attention with Roosevelt, Churchill, De Gaulle, and others with equanimity and humor.

About halfway through the writing of this book, we moved from Canberra to Melbourne, as I left my position at the Australian National University (ANU) to join the new Institute for Humanities and Social Sciences at the Australian Catholic University (ACU). I thank the academic and professional staff at both ANU and ACU for providing such supportive research environments and making that transition as smooth as possible.

One of the reasons for my sustained interest in populism has been the amazing engagement I've had from colleagues and friends over the years. Once people learn that I study and write about people like Trump for a living, they're never short of a question or an opinion. I am grateful for all of those conversations. I've benefited from lots of direct and indirect engagement with fellow political scientists and economists on this book. I received valuable feedback from presentations of this project at Johns Hopkins University, the University of Canberra, Dublin City University, Korea University, and the Academia Sinica. I particularly want to thank Jan Werner Müller, Kurt Weyland, and Andrew Leigh, who read all or part of the manuscript, and provided me with very useful criticisms. I also thank the anonymous reviewers solicited by Cambridge University Press for their thoughtful comments.

Finally, I'd like to thank my editor at Cambridge University Press, Robert Dreesen, as well as Lucy Rhymer, the editor of a previous book of mine, who connected us for this project. They and the rest of the team at Cambridge did a fantastic job in bringing this book to fruition.

I

The Price of Power

Give me a balcony and I will become president.
José María Velasco Ibarra, five time president of Ecuador

To govern through a party is sooner or later to make yourself dependent on it.
Napoleon Bonaparte[1]

THE POLITICAL MARKETPLACE

In November 2020, Donald Trump became America's first one-term president for nearly three decades. True, he didn't vacate the White House without an ugly fight, and American politics have probably been left more polarized as a result of his presidency. But, even if only just, the American electorate delivered Trump a rebuke that is unusual in recent political history. In the postwar era, George H. W. Bush, Jimmy Carter, and Gerald Ford are the only sitting presidents to have lost their bid for reelection. Before that, we'd have to go back to Herbert Hoover's Depression-era loss to Franklin Delano Roosevelt in 1932. One interpretation of Trump's defeat might be that Americans got to have a good look at what populism has to offer and said "thanks, but no thanks." Another is that despite a catastrophic twin public health and economic crisis that would normally have devastated an incumbent's reelection hopes, Trump only lost by the narrowest of margins, with more votes than any losing presidential candidate in history. It could well be, in other words, that whatever kind of politics he represented is here to stay.

Was the Trump presidency just a blip best consigned to the history books? Or was his election the harbinger of a more fundamental shift in politics in America, and perhaps, beyond? To answer these questions, we need to better understand why populists like Trump are successful in the first place. And to do that, this book proposes that we should follow Trump's lead and think less like political philosophers and more like CEOs. Populism, as I see it – and as I think Trump would see it too – is not a set of moral values or specific policies, but a low-cost political strategy based on direct communication with voters. This strategic approach to understanding populism may not be everybody's cup of tea. But what we'll see is that it provides a parsimonious explanation for when politicians will use populism to win and keep power: Populism will be most prolific when it is a more cost-effective strategy than its alternatives.

In June 2015, when Trump made his way down one of the lobby escalators at his eponymous New York skyscraper to announce his presidential candidacy, I was pulling long hours trying to finish up my first book on populism. Populism in the economically advanced West wasn't my main focus back then, but this potential bit of political theatre had my interest piqued. What could Donald J. Trump – real estate magnate, celebrity game show host, propagator of the Obama "Birther" myth, a man with zero experience in government – possibly say to make himself look like a viable presidential contender? As he labored through his speech, there was little on show to convince me that I was watching the future Republican candidate, never mind the future president. He had neither the easy, folksy charm of a George W. Bush, nor the infectious optimism of a Barack Obama. Trump was pugnacious. He was dark; nasty, even. In his heavily improvised speech, he painted a world of economic desperation, looming terrorism, and rising crime. He called Mexicans rapists and promised to build a wall to keep them out. All politicians like to talk about their accomplishments, but Trump's self-puffery smacked more of insecurity than authenticity: "I'm really rich, I'll show you that in a second," he said.[2]

This combination of negativity and braggadocio hardly seemed likely to win him many supporters. Unsurprisingly, the mainstream media lampooned his controversial – and frankly inarticulate – speech. However, it was precisely because what Trump said was so outrageous, so beyond the pale, that his candidacy would become such a sensation. Trump was portraying himself as the outsider, the man on horseback, who would fix a broken political system. Trump would be the *anti-politician*. He launched into the Democrats, of course, but he didn't have many kind words for his own party either. He set out his stall against a political establishment he said was failing the people on trade, on immigration, on jobs, and on security. "How stupid are our leaders? How stupid are these politicians to allow this to happen? How stupid are they?" he said.

Trump beat this antiestablishment drum again and again on the campaign trail over the next fifteen months, turning the liability of his total lack of experience in government into an asset. Made for the Twitter age, Trump had – and has – a way with one-liners. He fired off epithets for Republicans and Democrats alike: "Liddle Marco" (Rubio), "Low energy Jeb" (Bush), "Lyin' Ted" (Cruz). He dispatched Kentucky senator Rand Paul at the first televised Republican primary debate with a summary shot of condescension:

"You're having a hard time tonight," he said. When Rubio and Cruz retaliated, the latter suggesting links between Trump and the mob, and the former repeatedly calling Trump a "con man," the maestro of insults had the perfect comeback for an age of mass distrust in the political class: "They can say what they want; at the end of the day, they're just *establishment* guys." Goodbye Rubio and Cruz. "*Establishment*" former Republican governor of Ohio, "1 for 38" John Kasich, got the same treatment. The objections of Republican Party operatives and conservative public intellectuals under the Never Trump banner bounced off the Trump juggernaut like BBs from the hull of a Panzer. "Crooked Hillary" Clinton, the consummate beltway insider, was the perfect foil for his marauding campaign.[3]

Trump's policy agenda was notoriously vague on details and his campaign lacked the sophisticated "ground game" of more seasoned candidates. Yet his trademarked pledge to Make America Great Again resonated. Although it later emerged that his campaign spent millions of dollars on a social media operation developed by the consultancy firm Cambridge Analytica, the bread and butter of his bid for office was the old-school mass rally. Trump's rambling, parenthetical speeches are made to be seen and heard in the flesh, not read in a press release. Even though Trump trailed Clinton in fundraising, he held twice as many rallies as she did, often in the kinds of less densely populated places neglected by other candidates. Donning their red baseball caps, Trump devotees chanted in support of his pledges to "Build that wall!," to "Drain the swamp!," and to "Lock her [Clinton] up!" It didn't matter whether he made fun of the disabled, mocked former POWs like John McCain, or even disparaged the Gold Star mother of an American Muslim soldier; nothing or no one was sacred. Confirming the aphorism that any publicity is good publicity, no matter what Trump said, to his supporters he could do no wrong. "I don't, frankly, have time for political correctness," he declared at a 2015 GOP primary debate. When the infamous Access Hollywood tape – a 2005 off-camera recording in which Trump boasted that when you're a celebrity, women will let you do "anything," even "grab them by the pussy" – hit the airways just a month before the election, the normal laws of political gravity didn't seem to apply. Thumbing his nose so openly at polite society only bolstered his outsider status. Trump beat the odds and the establishment to take the Republican Party nomination and the presidency itself.[4]

DEMANDING POPULISM

We hardly lack explanations of the Trump phenomenon or of the rise of populism in general. For sure, each account has its own slant, but a kind of consensus has emerged: Trump's success, like that of other populists, was based on a long-simmering conservative-authoritarian backlash by voters against liberal democracy and the economic and cultural globalization that has gone with it. Over the past three or four decades, technological change, international trade, and increasing inequality have pushed the working and lower middle classes into ever more precarious economic straits. At the same time, mass immigration and the growing political assertiveness of long-marginalized ethnic minorities have raised the anxiety of working- and lower-middle-class white majorities who fear greater competition over an ever-shrinking economic pie and resent the associated decline in their relative social status. According to this version of events, populism is on the rise because of mass disenchantment with a political establishment that has forced through this agenda of economic and cultural globalization against their wishes. The liberal democratic values that undergirded the postwar political order no longer hold sway. As a result, resentful voters have turned to populists like Trump in droves.[5]

Populism, according to this interpretation, is a distinct way of understanding the political and economic world. It is a political ideology reducible to a simple dictum: *the people versus the elite*. This idea, philosophy, or worldview – whatever you want to call it – underlies people's political preferences. And what the people demand, astute political leaders will deliver. According to this view, which we might call the "product differentiation" model of politics, success is determined by the ideas and policies – the qualities of the product – offered by competing political leaders and parties. When parties of the left or right gain power in a democracy, that's because this is what the people, or at least what a majority of the electorate, wants. If populists are successful, they too must be offering something that the people desire.[6]

In part, the ascendency of this approach stems from our reliance on the omnipresent public opinion poll. Like the drunk searching for his keys under the streetlight even though he probably lost them somewhere else, political analysts are drawn to where the data are available. Because we have mountains of figures on voters' preferences, popular demands are an obvious basis to look to explain the rise of populism. However, the prevalence of this approach is not solely due to biases in modern research design. It has a much longer lineage in political thought that goes all the way back to classical Greece and Rome. If the masses want grain, or peace, or war, well then that is what the political elite should deliver. Philosophers like Aristotle and Cicero dismissed such popular appeals as crass, even dangerous pandering, but each conceded that political leaders needed to be cognizant of something we'd now call public opinion. If this approach to understanding politics is correct, it follows that the greater the number of people who adhere to the populist worldview, and the more intensely they do so, the more likely we are to see populists in power. Populism, by this way of thinking, is successful because voters want it; or in economic terms, what matters is the *demand side*.[7]

Intuitive as this kind of explanation may be, it has several pitfalls. First, it is unclear what exactly the populist ideology is, or how it works to affect political outcomes. The most common efforts to define populism as an ideology either make it so ordinary as to be indistinguishable from democratic politics in general, or they make it so egregious as to equate it with dictatorship.

If populism simply means being *for* "the people" and against whoever is *not* "the people," how many democratic politicians would not be populist? If instead populism is understood as *illiberalism* or *anti-pluralism*, given that the ability of the opposition to freely contest elections is a minimal requirement of democracy, how different is this meaning of populism from outright dictatorship? Second, even if we did agree on an understanding of populism as a set of values or attitudes, measuring them is extraordinarily difficult. Is populism a single coherent belief, or an amalgam of several different attitudes together? If it's the latter, how should these distinct attitudes be aggregated? If populism is manifest in appeals to "the people" against "the elite," is a single speech appealing to "the people" enough? If not, how often must a politician invoke "the people" to qualify as populist? How can we reconcile populism as a coherent set of values when it can take such wildly different forms as Trump's xenophobia on the one hand and Chávez's redistribution of wealth on the other? Third, the best evidence shows that when factors like a voter's personality, policy preferences, and other political attitudes are taken into account, so-called populist values have at best a marginal effect on vote choice. What exactly is it that populist beliefs by themselves *do*? If populism is just being used as a synonym for nativism or socialism, what is the concept adding to our understanding of politics? Last, even if we put these conceptual and measurement issues aside and accepted that populist attitudes or policy preferences might explain why one person is more likely than another to vote for a populist, this still would not account for change in the relative success of populists over time and in different countries. Given that people's values change slowly, how can we account for the swift and sometimes erratic shifts in populists' vote shares? Why do similar grievances not produce the same degree of populist success in different cases?[8]

In this book, I'm largely going to set aside the worries, beliefs, ideologies, and policy preferences of voters – the *demand side* – that animate most accounts of populism. Following that well-known principle of economic analysis, *ceteris paribus* – all else equal – my approach is to hold the demand side constant and see just how much can be explained by looking at what happens when there are changes to the *supply side* of the equation. In other words, rather than asking why people supposedly want populism, I think we can learn a great deal by examining changes in the options that political leaders supply voters with instead. If, as a result, this book appears one-sided in its focus on *populists* rather than their supporters, this is not because I believe the demand side is irrelevant. In the concluding chapter, I'll suggest how we could develop what economists would call a "general equilibrium model" that brings together both the supply and demand sides. My main aim, however, is to restore balance to a field that has become excessively focused on just one side of a complex problem. By examining the supply side, this book will show that populism has a clear economic logic. But before we get there, we need to be clear about just what it is we're trying to explain. What exactly is *populism*?

POPULISM AS STRATEGY

Populism is a famously, frustratingly disputed concept. Although it would be tempting to believe that disagreement over the meaning of populism is due to the post–Trump surge in interest in the subject, the problem of definition has been around for a long time. Back in 1967, a group of prominent social scientists got together at the London School of Economics to try to distill from a wide range of national and historical experiences a shared understanding of populism. The published collection of papers that emerged from that conference is full of insights and still repays reading, but as the editors of the volume acknowledged, they could not establish the conceptual common ground on which future writing on populism would build. In his contribution, Peter Wiles wrote "to each his own definition of populism, according to the academic axe he grinds." Fast forward half a century and the fact that one of the best-selling books on the subject is entitled *What Is Populism?* is telling of how little agreement there still is on what populism actually means and on who or what qualifies as populist.[9]

The reality is that there is no *true* definition of populism. It is, like democracy or justice, one of those essentially contested concepts about which philosophers will forever argue. Yet this doesn't mean that we should just pick a definition at random. Ask a poet and a neuroscientist to define love and you'll get two equally true but very different answers. What we need is a definition of populism that is useful, and fortunately, there are ways of deciding what this would look like – at least for the purposes of political scientists and economists if not philologists. Obviously – but I would also say, trivially – a useful definition of populism should allow us to distinguish populists from non-populists, to separate full populists from partial populists, or to say whether one politician or party is more or less populist than another. But just as importantly, a useful definition should facilitate a better understanding of populism's causes and consequences. It should help us to make clear, testable predictions about the conditions under which it will be successful, the effects it will have on democracy or the economy, and so on; even better, a useful definition will lead to policy remedies. It is with these purposes in mind that I define populism as a *political strategy, in which the leader of a personalistic political movement appeals directly to the people through mass communication to win and/or keep power.* Populism, in short, refers to certain actions or practices, rather than to a set of beliefs or doctrines. It is something that politicians *do* rather than something they *believe.*[10]

Although this understanding of populism as a political strategy is not currently the predominant approach in academia or mainstream punditry, it has a dignified pedigree, going back to one of the fathers of political economy, Max Weber. Weber famously argued that there are three main sources of political authority: the bureaucratic, the patrimonial, and the charismatic. Bureaucratic authority derives from its dependence on rules and procedures, which are, at least in theory, open and unbiased. This kind of authority is viewed as legitimate because of its procedural fairness. Patrimonial authority instead is based on tradition; the authority of kings, for instance, depends not on talent or justice, but on heredity. Such a system may be less open, but it has the benefit of being predictable. In contrast, charismatic leaders depend on neither rules nor tradition for their authority. Charismatic authority instead rests on a direct relationship between leader and follower, where mass belief in the unique qualities of the leader forms the basis of his power.[11]

In what remains for me one of the most insightful analyses of populism published to date, Greek sociologist Nicos Mouzelis wrote that populism is best understood as a type of relationship between party leaders and voters – or what he called a "mode of incorporation." Mouzelis argued that the people don't just exist as some abstract mass of humanity that shows up at the ballot box of their own volition come election time. The public is deliberately "incorporated" or brought into the system by political leaders. Politicians, as we well know, persuade, cajole, and even coerce. Drawing on Weber's three sources of authority, Mouzelis argued – as I do here – that there are basically just three ways of organizing the pursuit of power in a democracy: programmatic, patronage, and populist incorporation. Mouzelis stresses that populists communicate directly with the people, rather than working through intermediaries as in the case of programmatic and patronage-based party leaders. He put it like this: "As a rule, populist leaders are hostile to strongly institutionalized intermediary levels … The emphasis on the leader's charisma, on the necessity for direct, nonmediated rapport between the leader and 'his people' as well as the relatively sudden process of political incorporation all lead to a fluidity of organizational forms." Within the movement or organization, power is vested in the person of the leader. The leader's authority is essentially arbitrary, in that it is only minimally constrained by rules, roles, or procedures – populist parties are organizationally "fluid." Outside of the party, populism implies a direct relationship between leader and supporter, which, as much as possible, is unfiltered by party officials, local elites and bosses, newspaper editors, and other intermediaries. The way in which political movements are organized, or what we might call their corporate structure, is critically important to understanding the utility of these *programmatic, patronage*, and *populist* strategies.[12]

Programmatic parties are complex and usually large bureaucratic organizations, with regular procedures governing internal promotion and candidate selection, professional staffs, permanent offices, and a generally high level of institutionalization. Internally, authority in the bureaucratic party rests in roles or offices – party chairman, whip etc. – rather than persons. As much as any firm, programmatic parties are professional organizations. Programmatic parties provide career paths open to talent – including, of course, the talents of scheming and manipulation. Programmatic parties typically have well-established links with social and economic organizations such as unions, farmers associations, and churches. As a result, they're often identified with particular interest groups and policies. Party leaders' links with voters are also heavily mediated by a dense organizational ecosystem that includes party workers, civil society organizations, and the state bureaucracy itself. Additionally, bureaucratic parties have often been mass membership organizations, funded by member dues, although this is less the case today – and has always been less the case in the United States than in Western Europe or the Antipodes. Programmatic parties take a great deal of time to build, and have a corporate personhood that extends beyond the term of any individual leader or cohort. The canonical examples are the Conservative and Labour parties in Britain and the Democratic and Republican parties in the United States.

Patronage-based parties are looser coalitions of political factions or groups. Leaders – or patrons – gain and retain power by judiciously distributing rewards – or patronage – to their supporters or clients. This patron–client form of politics has a long ancestry, epitomized in the pyramidal feudal system of kings, vassals, and peasants in Medieval Europe. In its modern incarnation political leaders win power by buying votes through a network of allied elites and political brokers. At the level of interaction with voters this form of retail politics is often called clientelism, money politics, or just vote buying. Providing jobs in the public sector was how the legendary Tammany Hall political machine in New York maintained its power, with a third of Democratic voters holding a Tammany job in the 1910s. Similarly, as late as the 1960s, Chicago Mayor Richard J. Daley's Cook County – or *Crook County* – organization traded votes for some 30,000 public sector jobs. In this book, however, we'll be more concerned with the higher-level integration of the leaders of rival but functionally similar political factions. Just as voters are bribed to cast their ballot, individuals who control blocs of votes – brokers – are in turn courted by party leaders. Ministerial appointments, government contracts, and other sine-cures are the currency of patronage party loyalty. Leadership within the pat-ronage party is governed by the strength of rival factions of patrons, brokers, and clients. Factions will come together to gain and keep power, but the association is an instrumental one, borne out of self-interest rather than out of a deep sense of loyalty or shared ideology. As we'll see in Chapters 3 and 4, the distribution of patronage among office-seeking elites was a major occupa-tion of political leaders in the early American republic. In this, Americans were continuing a practice perfected by the famous eighteenth–century British Whig leader and prime minister Sir Robert Walpole. With the demand for patronage always exceeding its supply, Walpole had to judiciously allocate places and pensions to build and keep his majority in the House of Commons – a strategy he executed successfully for some two decades.

Instead of climbing the rungs of the party ladder or forging transactional alliances with supporters, populists gain power by directly mobilizing a mass support base. That is, they communicate directly with voters rather than mobilize them through intermediaries. In populist organizations, memberships and offices are often poorly defined and subject to arbitrary change from above. Preferring to target free-floating or independent voters, some populist parties, such as Geert Wilders' Party for Freedom (PVV), have no membership system at all. Internally, in a direct inversion of the programmatic party structure, individuals matter more than roles. Pure populist parties, moreover, do not have regularized procedures for leadership replacement or succession. In short, a populist leader is unconstrained by rules or by dependence on factional support, which creates a very different relationship between a leader and his political associates than in the case of more deeply institutionalized bureaucratic or patronage-based parties. Even the most established of populist parties are, by definition, the tools of their charismatic leaders.

In practice, some leaders will mix these programmatic, patronage, and populist approaches, and the composition of their strategic portfolio may change over time. For instance, two-time Greek prime minister (1981–89 and 1993–96), Andreas Papandreou, came to power as the charismatic leader of the Panhellenic Socialist Movement (more commonly known as PASOK), but once in power he depended more and more on the distribution of patronage to maintain himself in office. Going in the other direction, the subject of my first book, Indira Gandhi, prime minister of India from the mid- 1960s, shifted from a patronage-based to a populist strategy to retain power after a faction of her party attempted to oust her from power. In places like the United States and the United Kingdom, where two main parties have usually exhausted the political space, successful populists have typically adopted a mixed strategy – for instance, populism to gain control of the party apparatus but then the use of programmatic or patronage-based mobilization to succeed in a general election. However, as noted previously, money and time spent on one strategy cannot be spent on others. There are, in economic terms, opportunity costs to any chosen strategy. Aspiring leaders must therefore trade off a concentration on one approach against another. Populists depend *mostly* on the use of a highly personalist organization that makes direct appeals to voters through whatever the mass communication media of the time happen to be.

Populism in this sense is a matter of degree. Determining whether an individual leader is a "populist" means we need to set a somewhat arbitrary threshold for what "mostly" means. I take a relatively restrictive approach, but there is no reason that a more permissive one couldn't be used. For any given leader, we want to know how much their strategy approximates the populist ideal type just outlined. I've previously suggested several practical questions we can ask of any given leader to help make this judgment. As mentioned, populism has both an internal and external dimension to it. Internally, populists have essentially arbitrary authority within their own personalistic political organization, while externally, they link with voters directly rather than through intermediaries. Along the internal dimension, the critical questions are: Is the movement or party one that the leader formed as a personal electoral vehicle? Is authority within the leader's party or movement arbitrary – completely at the discretion of the leader – or rule based? Does the leader control appointment decisions or is leadership/appointment determined by ballot or some other collective procedure? The main questions to ask with respect to the external dimension are: Does the leader's movement or party rely primarily on mass rallies, mass media, and social media to mobilize electoral support directly, or does it rely primarily on mobilizing voters through its membership, allied unions, churches, or other organizations, or on systematic clientelism? Is the leader himself/herself the primary object of a campaign or is it a party's historical political/group/ethnic linkages to a constituency? Answering these questions, and perhaps others like them, allows us to build up a picture of *how much* a given politician relies on the populist strategy to win and keep power.[13]

Understood in this way, the strategic approach to populism is a good fit for most of the usual suspects: Donald Trump, Geert Wilders, Alexis Tsipras, and Silvio Berlusconi among others would all qualify as highly populist; so would less frequently examined populist leaders such as Charles de Gaulle, Huey Long, or Wendell Willkie. Others, including Andrew Jackson, David Lloyd George, and Jimmy Carter, would also qualify as at least partly populist by these criteria. Consistent with the typical understanding of populism, in my estimation, the criteria would exclude party leaders such as Ronald Reagan, Barack Obama, Margaret Thatcher, or Tony Blair as populists, however personally telegenic or popular they might have been.

It is also the case, however, that other leaders or parties in the contemporary European far right, who are often classified as populist by other scholars, would not count as populist according to the strategic approach. For example, the strategic approach would not classify parties such as the Alternative for Germany (AfD) or the Sweden Democrats as populist; for these parties, the organizational structure is too collective or corporate for them to qualify as populist. Given the tendency to use populism and nativism interchangeably in both academic and popular writing, this omission may bother some readers. However, the problem with the critique that it is "simply impossible to apply [the strategic definition] to European populist parties such as [X, Y, and Z]," is that it begins with the premise that parties X, Y, and Z *are* in fact populist. This has the problem of making and validating concepts backward. We cannot know if parties X, Y, and Z are populist until we have a definition! Scientific concepts need not exactly resemble their folk equivalents. Populism is a term thrown about so casually that to begin from the view that everything ever labeled as populist *is* populist would be very problematic. From here on, then, I treat the objection that "you do/don't include [insert party name here] as populist" as specious.[14]

It is also important to note that if populist parties are "personalist" parties, they are not merely so. Critical to the populist strategy is a reliance on mass communication with supporters that need not be true of personalist parties in general; the latter can primarily exploit kinship networks, patronage, or even more coercive techniques. This strategic approach also differentiates populism from authoritarianism. In the same way that we typically distinguish between democratic and authoritarian government more generally – by whether or not a regime has free and fair elections – we can distinguish between populist and authoritarian leaders. To the extent that coercive tactics – such as censoring the media or arresting opponents – predominate over mobilization through mass communication, a leader is better classified as authoritarian rather than populist. For instance, while Adolf Hitler captured power through an essentially populist strategy, once in power, the Nazi regime became brutally authoritarian. Even if Hitler himself retained much of his mass support, following the passage of the infamous Enabling Act of March 1933, he is better classified as a "popular dictator" than as a populist.

Contrary to other approaches, the strategic understanding of populism makes no assumptions about the content of a leader's appeals or the audience to which they are directed. Decisions about content and audience, we might say, fall into the realm of tactics rather than strategy. The strategic approach is basically consistent with one that classifies populists according to their supposed ideology, but it views discourse – talk – as cheap. Anti-elitism has become so common today as to be totally unexceptional. None except the most politically suicidal leaders would now dare to admonish the masses to leave matters of government to their betters. At the same time, appealing to a virtuous if vaguely defined "people" makes good sense for a politician without strong and stable links to a body of supporters. Sometimes the "people" applies to the lower class, sometimes to the native born, and at other times to the law abiding. In other instances, its application is even less precise. Vague appeals to the people are all too easy to make. There is nothing particularly moral or democratic about them. A "dangerous ambition," Alexander Hamilton wrote, "often lucks behind the specious mask of zeal for the rights of the people." No particular group of political leaders, moreover, has a monopoly on this kind of rhetoric. In the words of an anonymous Columbia County, New York, contemporary of Hamilton: "[I]n a representative government, where every act is the act of the people, to talk of 'an appeal to the people' is nonsense. They are random words, used by superficial politicians and designing men ... in hopes of political advantage." This is a remarkably insightful critique in itself, but what's most notable is that it came not from a paper of Hamilton's *elitist* Federalist Party but from a paper of its democratic Jeffersonian opponents! The anti-elitism typical of populist rhetoric is little more than a politically acceptable, catchall way of demonizing incumbents, while people-centrism is the ideal way of appealing to an ill-defined constituency through the thin but broad approach of mass media. It's a cynical view perhaps, but appealing to the people against the elite is, we might say, just good marketing.[15]

In this sense, more important than what populists say is how they say it. Or to use the adage of Canadian communications theorist Marshall McLuhan, "the medium is the message." The technology of mass communication has varied enormously over history. In Ancient Greece and Rome, populists almost physically connected with crowds of people in the assembly and the forum. Public oratory and lavish parades were the way a man could demonstrate his eminence to the masses. By the time mass democracy reemerged in revolutionary America and France in the late eighteenth century, the diffusion of printing technology and the development of more efficient postal services meant that populists and their entourages could also use pamphlets and newspapers to communicate cheaply with larger numbers of people than ever before. Mass communication took on added sophistication in the interwar period, nowhere more so than in Germany. Hitler's *Mein Kampf* presents a sophisticated if nefarious understanding of the role of mass propaganda in politics. Effective political speech, he argued, must be plain, direct, emotive, and, above all, repetitive. Technological changes served to make direct communication more efficient. In power in the 1930s, the Nazis exploited government control over mass media and the arts to great effect; even the airplane was turned into a symbolic form of communication. Perhaps no brief radio address has so indelibly marked a political career as Charles de Gaulle's *Appel de 18 Juin*, 1940, in which he announced himself as the exiled head of the resistance to the Nazi occupation of France. In the United States, as early as Dwight D. Eisenhower's election campaign of 1952, the television political "spot" – the vacuous thirty-second soundbite still so prevalent in politics today – had become a reality. Not all populists are great orators. Sometimes image speaks louder than words. The politician who didn't look good on the box – think of the febrile Richard Nixon sweating through the first presidential debate with John F. Kennedy in 1960 – paid the price. Even though television – an expensive medium – was co-opted for a time by well-organized and well-financed political parties, eventually outsiders such as Ross Perot and Donald Trump became rich enough to afford to use it for themselves. As political scientist Martin Wattenberg could conclude in the 1990s in the fifth edition of his seminal book on American political parties, "[w]here once candidates for public office had to rely on mustering organizational strength to communicate with voters, it is now increasingly possible for them to establish direct contact through the media." The arrival of social media, especially Twitter, along with other emerging technologies – perhaps most unusually, holography in the case of far–left French presidential candidate Jean-Luc Mélenchon – has allowed populists direct access to our homes and minds like never before.[16]

Maybe discourse doesn't count for much, but might it be that populists target specific groups for support – the "white working class," for instance? Not in any consistent way. A person's level of education is negatively associated with support for populist politicians in some cases but positively in others. Income, too, is a weak predictor of populist support. The urban working class might be a likely base of support in a country without a strong socialist party, but in other places, the suburban middle classes could be a more receptive audience. In turn, a policy message stressing economic inequality or immigration might play better in one state, while a law-and-order appeal could resonate in another. Thus, those who have interpreted populism as a set of socialistic economic policies – common in the understanding of populism in Latin America in the 1990s – or as a set of hard-line law-and-order policies – sometimes called "penal populism" – may be right, but only for special instances. No individual policy is definitive of populism in general. Populists, as power-seeking strategists, tailor their appeals to the context. Racism, nationalism, socialism, chauvinism, and other such persuasions are all vital issues, but we shouldn't muddy the waters by making them synonyms for populism. Populism is a political strategy that relies on mass communication, whatever the technological medium, to win and keep power; nò more, no less. As I'll describe further in the next section, populism in this minimalist strategic sense matters deeply for things we care about, for example, civil rights, economic prosperity, and perhaps even democracy itself. Moreover, if my explanation for why the populist strategy worked for Trump and others holds water, we'll have some potentially actionable ways to reform our political institutions in the decades to come.

TRANSACTION COST POLITICS

Although other scholars have already made a strong case that populism can be best understood as a distinct political strategy, their approach hasn't gained as many followers as it might have. The reason, I think, is that they haven't yet provided a fully satisfying explanation for *why* aspiring political leaders would adopt the populist strategy over others. Each strategy – the programmatic, the patronage, and the populist – comes with its unique set of costs, risks, and potential rewards. *Why populism?* is not a question of ideas but of a hidden strategic calculus.

If votes are the currency of democratic politics, political leaders, like entrepreneurs in a marketplace, want to grow their share at the lowest cost. If this analogy is correct, then there is a lot we can learn from the economics of how and why firms – and their leaders – succeed. Ford Motors, the pioneer of the mass-produced automobile, provides an apt illustration. Ford's Model T was the first vehicle to be made by the assembly of identical and interchangeable parts. Ford sold 16.5 million units of the Model T, making it still one of the best-selling automobiles of all time, and in the early decades of the twentieth century, Ford Motors one of the most profitable firms in the world.

We tend to think that success in the marketplace is driven by offering a superior product – the product differentiation rationale noted earlier. But price is just as important. Ford thrived because it vigorously drove down the costs of production. Compared to the previous practice of crafting vehicles by hand, the reduction in the price of producing an additional car on the line – or its marginal cost – was staggering. In 1929, Ford could turn out a finished automobile every ten seconds; just two decades previously, it had taken fourteen hours. Over that period, the price of a car fell from the equivalent of two years' worth of the typical worker's salary to the amount he could earn in just three months. Ford's vehicles were no better than those of its competitors, such as Daimler, but they were significantly cheaper. Costs matter critically for success in any marketplace – the political one should be no different. The more cheaply a politician can win votes, the more successful he'll be.

For our purposes, Ford's story is illustrative in a second, more subtle, sense too. It demonstrates why some ways of organizing a firm are more cost-effective than others. One of the means that owner-manager Henry Ford used to reduce costs was to bring most elements of the production process in-house, in a process known as vertical integration. Ford Motors famously made almost all of its own parts, assembling them at its massive production facility in Highland Park, Michigan. This allowed Ford to apply his principles of efficiency to lowering the cost of each input. However, the enigmatic Ford still wasn't satisfied. Why was Ford Motors still outsourcing the production of some of its parts? Why, for instance, was it buying tires when it could make them itself? Why buy rubber on the open market when it could grow it too? Ford took the idea of vertical integration – bringing all parts of the supply chain within the firm – to its logical conclusion. Frustrated by what he perceived as the exorbitant price of rubber on world markets, Ford bought up 140,000 hectares of rain forest in Brazil and set up his own rubber plantation. But the endeavor was a miserable failure. Why?

The answer is suggested in a remarkable 1937 paper by economist Ronald Coase. Producing something like an automobile entails two kinds of costs. The first, the direct costs of production, are easy to understand. These are the costs of the parts and labor that go into the end product: the metal; the rubber; the leather; and the wages paid to managers, factory workers, and salesmen. The second, indirect costs, or transaction costs, are somewhat harder to grasp, but they turn out to be very important to understanding the political trade-offs at the heart of this book. In economic terms, transaction costs include the *search costs*, *bargaining costs*, and *enforcement costs* incurred as part of an exchange between buyer and seller. The time spent finding an appropriate supplier, negotiating an acceptable price with them, and then ensuring that the product or service is delivered as ordered all incur costs on a business. What Coase showed was that these transaction costs set optimal limits for the size of the firm.[17]

Coase recognized that in a world without firms, almost any complex economic activity, such as making and selling a car, would necessitate multiple transactions conducted between countless individuals in the marketplace. The transaction costs involved in all of this marketplace activity would be astronomical. In contrast, in a vertically integrated firm like Ford, an employee is contracted to perform a wide range of tasks as demanded by his employer. This reduces the transaction costs involved to a single contract. Costs, in short, are lowered by bringing many processes in house, favoring huge, vertically integrated firms like Ford. However, as Ford's Brazilian misadventure shows, sometimes it is more economical to outsource activities to the marketplace. Rubber could be procured more cheaply on the market than it could in-house. In part in recognition of the comparative advantage possessed by suppliers with specialized knowledge or unique resources, today Ford outsources the production of about 70 percent of the parts, components, and other services that go into its vehicles. Firms grow to the point where they minimize transaction costs, and these costs change over time, sometimes favoring integration, sometimes separation. Not product, not philosophy. The shape and size of the firm are determined by cost.[18]

In the political marketplace, the "buyers" are politicians while the "sellers" are voters. Although other writers have used this terminology before, most existing approaches to political behavior assume what economists would call a *frictionless market*. In this approach, it is only a slight oversimplification to say that the share of votes that various parties receive is assumed to be axiomatically equal to the proportion of the voting population who favor those parties. In this sense, political outcomes can be reduced to a quantitative matching of policy offerings and voter preferences. In reality, however, not only does casting a ballot represent an opportunity cost in terms of time and effort for each individual voter, but every vote won by a party requires the expenditure of human and capital resources to mobilize voters. In Coase's terms, the process of getting votes carries substantial transaction costs. Together, the direct and indirect costs of winning votes are central to understanding the prevalence of populism across time and place.

For the patronage-based party, the monetary cost of winning votes is on crude display. In some cases, candidates and their middlemen – brokers – distribute cash, merchandise, and of course, booze on and before election day. In George Washington's Virginia, "swilling the planters with bumbo" was a near universal practice before an election. Writing to one of his agents on the eve of his first successful election to the House of Burgesses, Washington's concern was less with the propriety of bribing voters than that his agent would fail to spend enough to slake the voters' thirsts. In some cases, a vote has a more explicit monetary value. As a campaign manager in New Deal–era Texas, prior to Election Day a young Lyndon Johnson laid out stacks of five-dollar bills on a big table in a room of the San Antonio Plaza Hotel. Mexican-American men would come into the room, tell Johnson a figure, and Johnson would dole out that number of five-dollar bills. Five dollars was the cost of a Chicano vote in 1930s San Antonio. Somewhat more subtly, political machines like those of Tammany in New York or Mayor Richard Daley in Chicago thrived through to the 1960s by maintaining a lock on jobs in the public sector that they reserved for their supporters. Patronage politics is the classic quid pro quo. A direct cost, the bribe, is exchanged for a vote.[19]

From an economic point of view, however, we can think of patronage politics as incurring a second type of cost: a transaction cost. The great dilemma for the politician engaged in vote buying – ethical quandaries aside – is that voters cannot be trusted to keep to their end of the bargain. As Washington himself knew, there was no guarantee that a feast of rum and sandwiches would necessarily translate into votes. Voters can and do accept gifts from multiple candidates running in the same election. Politicians therefore have to spend additional resources in monitoring the behavior of voters – enforcing the informal contract in other words. This can be done in any number of imaginative ways, but each one incurs a cost. In post–Reconstruction New Orleans, the electoral commissioners under the control of the Old Regular machine could, by law, accompany voters into the polling booth; if a man had promised to sell his vote, the commissioner exited the booth with his pencil behind his ear to signal to a watcher that the voter should receive his bounty. In 1940s Texas, the managers of the feudal political machines of the state's oil barons would often pay voters' poll taxes directly and have a fixer complete the ballots, or they'd also pay off the appropriate officials and count the votes up as they saw fit. Commissioners or brokers had to be paid, and to add a further layer of complexity, these middlemen were hardly any more trustworthy than voters themselves. Brokers too are often happy to work for more than one candidate at once. Whichever candidate gives him the biggest payoff is the one to whom he will deliver his bloc of votes on Election Day. In Gilded Age New York, Joseph Murray, a brawling political fixer in the Democratic Party's Tammany machine, felt inadequately compensated by his erstwhile patron and so surreptitiously directed his gang of enforcers to provide their "services" to the Republican candidate instead; Murray had found better remuneration with his newly elected GOP patron. Voters need to be monitored; monitors need to be monitored. Bring it all up a level, where brokers at each level get aggregated into municipal or regional blocs, where these blocs in turn comprise factions within a national patronage party, and the escalating nature of these transaction costs becomes clear.[20]

Yet, expensive as it may appear, most of the money that fuels the patronage strategy is bilked from public sources rather than private ones. For the political leader, we might say it's a publicly subsidized political strategy. The patronage strategy can provide a low-cost entry into politics, as political hopefuls can promise to deliver the spoils to their supporters *if* they win. The economic approach predicts that patronage should be the modal form of mobilization in new democracies: If political organizations are expensive and time consuming to build, it makes sense to draw on public resources in the short term. Although the evidence is disparate, there is good reason to think this has historically been the case. From the Americas (North and South), to South and Southeast Asia, to sub-Saharan Africa and the Middle East, patronage-based linkages appear to be by far the most common ones used during the early period after democracy is introduced. Even in some states in postwar Western Europe, most notably Italy, Austria, and Greece, a similar pattern of linkage prevailed; go back a little further, and the same was true of England and the Netherlands.

Yet if patronage has a compelling economic logic, especially in the early years after democratization, there are good reasons why it becomes less efficient over time. As I argued in my first book, *Populism and Patronage*, there is a steeply increasing cost involved in managing the patronage racket, one that's hinted at in the often precariously short lifespan of the Mafia Don. Brokers have distinct interests from their patrons, leading to what is called a principal–agent dilemma. Political leaders – the principals – want votes at the lowest unit costs; brokers – the agents – in contrast, aim to maximize the fee they can extract for delivering those votes. Brokers, as we've seen, are disloyal, ever willing to sell their votes to the highest bidder. One historian likens the vote captains of mid-Victorian England to *condottieri* – the military mercenaries of Renaissance Italy. Mercenaries sometimes make effective soldiers, but as Machiavelli noted, they are "disunited, ambitious, and without discipline." Patronage parties thus find themselves engaged not just in a conflict with rival parties but in a perpetual civil war over the spoils. Even if power can be bought with a patronage party, the patron faces the perennial threat of her subordinates' defection. As long as the number of brokers and clients is limited and as long as brokers are tightly constrained from above, patronage is often a cost-effective strategy. However, the costs of maintaining a winning coalition of factions tends to rise over time, as faction leaders exploit their pivotal position for personal gain. The more autonomy, power, and resources that brokers accumulate, the more expensive it becomes to buy them off. Patronage-based costs thus have a kind of ratchet quality, almost always tending upward unless more authoritarian measures are used to cut the brokers down to size.[21]

Direct vote buying sometimes still happens in consolidated democracies like the United States or Australia, but it's unusual now, and when found out, it causes a scandal. As a result, because most of the costs in a typical Western democracy are indirect, transaction costs, it is easy to forget just how expensive it is to seek and keep power. As a result, we typically think about political competition in the West solely in terms of ideological and policy cleavages. In reality, however, the transaction costs facing party leaders in programmatic political systems are qualitatively different but hardly less onerous than those in patronage-based ones. Some transaction costs, such as campaign advertising and staff, are easily measured. In the US in 2016, a staggering $6.4 billion was spent on election campaigning, a third of this total on the presidential campaign alone. In 2020, that total figure more than doubled to $14 billion. Former New York mayor, Michael Bloomberg, reportedly spent over a billion dollars of his own money contesting the 2020 Democratic presidential primary.[22]

By themselves, these are massive sums, but many of the transaction costs in programmatic party systems are hidden and may not even be monetary. They include any cost, whether in terms of cash, effort, or time that goes into affecting a voter's attachment to a given party and her likelihood of turning up at the polling booth. Consider that in late nineteenth–century America, some 5 percent of the entire adult male population was a party worker, each of whom dedicated about ten to fifteen hours to party activity each week. Obama's 2008 campaign made use of the "free" labor of over two million volunteers. Furthermore, many hidden costs are often historic and built into party organizations themselves. In programmatic party systems, voters are wooed, socialized, and deeply embedded into party networks by professional organizations over many years. Building and maintaining the nationwide organization of party branches and officials needed to accomplish this is a time-consuming and expensive activity. Bureaucratic organizations also need constant upkeep, and, even when voters are sympathetic to a particular party or candidate, getting them to make the additional effort to turn up at the ballot box is a colossal – and increasingly expensive – job. Furthermore, even if bureaucratic parties don't explicitly give handouts to voters, they use their organizational resources to occupy government at multiple levels. Parties mediate between people and the state. Without doing anything corrupt, parties help citizens negotiate complex bureaucracies, and advise on matters big and small. This investment of time and organization is not money going directly to voters directly but is another indirect cost of mobilizing their support. At a more abstract level, party brands themselves encapsulate tremendous value. Parties that have presided over a victorious war, an expansion of the suffrage, or even just sustained economic growth enrich their historic brands. This kind of reputation cannot be easily quantified or bought.[23]

For any political hopeful, the laundry list of operations required in building and maintaining such a party bureaucracy is potentially overwhelming. The costs of building and maintaining these kinds of parties is hard to calculate, with much of their capital embedded in intangibles like their brand, historical political loyalties, and their functional experience as actors in government. University of Washington political scientist Margit Tavits' description of the dilemma that faced political leaders in Eastern Europe on the transition to democracy in the early 1990s is revealing; she writes "building a strong organization is costly … because it takes resources and requires long-term and continuous commitment." Aspiring political leaders "would prefer to avoid building such an organization if elections could be won some other way." It is by definition beyond the means of any individual politician. However, because of the great advantage that programmatic parties have in getting out the vote due to their mass memberships, strong brands, and well-oiled local organizations, the power-seeking politician may do well to aim at helping to build or winning control of such a machine. The rub, for the individual politician is that he must sacrifice his autonomy – the programmatic party is inherently corporate in nature. As Napoleon understood, "[t]o govern through a party is sooner or later to make yourself dependent on it." The party politician may aspire to leadership; he may even be the favorite to acquire it; but a programmatic party requires rules and procedures that allow for the removal of any individual. The programmatic strategy entails a costly sacrifice of autonomy that some politicians are unwilling to incur.[24]

By contrast, the populist strategy mitigates the risks and costs of either having to manage rival individuals and interest groups within a complex bureaucratic organization or of having to share the spoils to keep the competing factions in a patronage party satisfied. The modern populist strategy certainly requires some hard cash; direct communication, especially through television and social media advertising, can be costly, and even public rallies require a great deal of staff, incur administrative and regulatory fees, and so on. It is no coincidence that some of the best-known populists – Thailand's Thaksin Shinawatra, Italy's Silvio Berlusconi, and of course, Donald Trump – were already fabulously wealthy when they turned to politics. "Brand awareness" is not bought cheaply, which often limits populism to those with some existing celebrity status. Nor are the costs of mass communication an exclusively modern concern. When, early in his career, Julius Caesar put on lavish public games to win over the Roman crowds, the costs were nearly crippling.

Yet by comparison, when all of the indirect costs of bureaucratic or patronage-based party building are considered, populism is still a minimalist political strategy. Relying on personalist political organizations and direct mass communication, populism, Columbia University political theorist Nadia Urbinati writes, "is an *affordable* politics." Especially for politicians with some preexisting name recognition – successful generals, mayors, or even celebrities – populism provides a uniquely cost-effective route to power. It involves minimal expenditure on organization and avoids the costs of having to monitor agents and brokers. Critically, populists reduce the in-house costs of seeking votes by avoiding the expense of building a national rule-based party infrastructure (programmatic incorporation) or using intermediaries to buy votes on their behalf (patronage incorporation). Populists, like many modern firms, are outsourcers. More akin to today's Ford Motor Company than its 1920s predecessor, populists operate relatively lean and low-cost organizations that seek to do one thing well – the exploitation of unmediated mass communication – thereby lowering the transaction costs involved in getting a vote and ultimately, buying power. As Ecuadorian president, José María Velasco Ibarra, boasted, all he needed to win power was a balcony from which to speak to the people.[25]

WHY POPULISM?

If the programmatic, patronage, and populist strategies each has a distinctive set of costs and benefits, the obvious question is what conditions make the populist strategy more effective than its alternatives? The succinct answer is that populism will be the most efficient strategy when the direct mobilization of a weakly attached plurality of the electorate is sufficient to win and keep power.

The first part of this answer has to do with the preexisting patterns of voter loyalties. Populism is a quick but superficial way of persuading voters. Populists simply throw appeals out on the wind to see what sticks. Based on mass communication, whether public oratory, television advertising, or social media, the populist leader can only really hope to establish weak and transient links with potential supporters. One key condition for populist success is the *availability* of voters who aren't already enmeshed in richer relationships with other parties. As Kurt Weyland, professor of government at the University of Texas-Austin, puts it, populists seek "support from large numbers of mostly *unorganized* followers." This means that populists do not primarily target the already committed union member and frequenter of the local Labour Party pub, or the public employee who owes his job to the local Democratic Party boss. Direct appeals through impersonal mass communication are rarely sufficient to *break* such ties – ties that may be as much social as political. Where voters are relatively unattached, however, populist mobilization can deliver mass support at relatively low cost. This, in turn, raises the question of why voters are available in some countries and at some time periods but not others. No doubt, as previous research has shown, events like economic crises or corruption scandals matter in disrupting party allegiances. Such shocks often provide the impetus for a sudden decline in voter loyalties to established parties. However, such calamities are neither necessary nor sufficient to explain voter availability. The diversity of cases that I cover over the coming chapters reveal a more comprehensive set of sources of voter availability than has previously been described.[26]

The second part of the answer is one that I think is little noted in modern research on populism. Populists, surprisingly perhaps, need not be all that popular. What they rely on, as much as the raw availability of potential supporters, is *a divided opposition*. In a two-horse race, rounding up a little, a successful candidate needs the support of 51 percent of the votes cast; in a three-horse race, if votes are distributed evenly, the winning total can drop as low as 34 percent; in a four-horse race, as low as 26 percent; and so on. Low turnouts mean that the proportion of support from the whole electorate needed to win can be much smaller than the proportion of valid votes that are cast. Additionally, electoral colleges and other rules that make representation disproportionate can reduce these winning percentages even further. Either way, the more divided the opposition, the lower the proportion of the electorate a populist needs to woo. The fewer supporters needed, the lower the cost. Populists very rarely command the backing of a large, or even bare, majority. Populists most often come to power when a *plurality* is sufficient. Silvio Berlusconi first became Italian prime minister in 1994 with little more than a fifth of the vote. French president, Emmanuel Macron, polled just 24 percent in the first round of the French presidential election in 2017; Hungary's Viktor Orbán returned to power in 2010 with a constitutional supermajority thanks to one of the most disproportional electoral systems in the world – with 53 percent of the vote, his Fidesz party took 68 percent of the seats in parliament – and it retained this supermajority in 2014 – this time keeping the same seat share with just 44 percent of the vote.

Trump, of course, lost the popular vote to Clinton in 2016, but more important is the fact that he won the Republican Party nomination with the lowest proportion of the vote since direct primaries became the main means of selecting the GOP's presidential candidate. The Republican Party of 2016 was unusually fragmented. Trump's victory, as we'll see later on, was thus much more contingent than a lot of Monday morning quarterbacking from the political punditry would suggest. Had the support of his opponents cohered behind a single credible rival, it is unlikely that Trump would have become the GOP candidate . Populists in the United States have consistently won or come closest to winning – 1828, 1832, 1896, 1912, 1968, 1976, 1992, 2016 – when the opposition (whether inside or outside a candidate's party) is fragmented.

Populist success thus tends to be greater where the institutional set up allows for direct election to the executive (e.g., presidentialism). In Europe, where proportional representation is the more common form of electoral system, fragmentation works differently. There, when party systems are fragmented, populists often do well enough to gain a share of parliamentary seats, but only rarely have they been able to win sufficient representation to take power themselves or to become the leader of a coalition government. In short, the fragmentation of the group or groups opposing a populist along with the nature of the electoral system will affect the proportion of the vote that needs to be secured, and hence the cost of winning power.

POPULISM: PAST, PRESENT, AND FUTURE

This book explores the economics of populism in the West from its roots in Greek and Roman antiquity through to the Trump era. Within the modern West, I focus particularly on the United States of America, France, and Germany, with briefer reference to Britain, Italy, and other cases. This is an admittedly huge volume of political history to hope to cover in a single book. However, even though I won't have dealt with every case to the satisfaction of specialists, my hope is that the comparative perspective this wide lens allows compensates for its deficiencies. Ultimately, it is only when we look at populism on this longer historical time frame that the value of the supply-side approach becomes apparent. If we focus only on a single point in time, say, post-1990s Western Europe, the factors that affect the big strategic choices between populism, patronage, and programmatic party building are often obscured. In game theory, we'd say that when one strategy is dominant (for instance, programmatic party building), any alternative strategy is going to lead to failure – to the sucker's payoff. It's only at moments of disruption, when the returns to these different strategies potentially change, that we are likely to see them in competition. To capture enough of these moments, I've cast the net as widely as time and space will allow.[27]

For the general audience, I hope this wide-ranging historical account, which begins in the next chapter, will be informative and even entertaining. Although much of this history may be familiar, the interpretation I provide should help readers see it in a new light. For scholars, this is a book that can be understood as an exercise in theory development. There will be no rigorous statistical testing of hypotheses, and although I assess the plausibility of alternative explanations at different points in the book, the main goal is to put forward a novel supply–side framework for understanding populism.

Before we go further, one last question needs answering: Why all this worry about a mere political strategy? Populism is not the same as authoritarianism. It still aims to persuade rather than to coerce. As a superficial mass political appeal not catered to developing enduring loyalties, populism, even if temporarily successful, is almost by design a passing fad. In turns out, however, that the very absence of institutionalization inherent to populism makes it an issue of real concern. Populists, as I'll show in the concluding chapter, face stronger incentives than other types of democratic leaders to erode political and civil liberties. Because they lack a sufficiently large body of organized supporters when they come into power, populists are faced with a great problem in retaining it. They could, as some populists such as Argentina's Juan Perón have done, consolidate support through the distribution of patronage. If this involves the pillaging of natural resources or the nationalization of industrial sectors best left in private hands, the environmental and economic consequences can be quite detrimental. Alternatively, at least in theory, populist leaders could go on to construct more stable programmatic political parties. However, given the necessary sacrifice of autonomy this implies, it has rarely been pursued by populists themselves. Too commonly, populists complement direct mass appeals with the imposition of restrictions on their opponents instead, sometimes in the process crossing the line into dictatorship.

Yet for all this likely erosion of the liberties we associate with democracy, populists often become, well, popular. Even if they come to power with mere pluralities, even if they clamp down on political opponents, even if they do eventually become dictators, they can and often do become more popular over time. Although some political philosophers find solace in the idea that politics is about values, that if better informed and better socialized, people might not turn to the vague, if sometimes illiberal, promises of populist leaders, economics predicts no such thing. Civic education, although probably intrinsically valuable, is not a panacea. The utopian notion that virtue can be inculcated from above should have died along with Maximilien Robespierre – one of the populists we'll meet in Chapter 3. Even if everyone, or the vast majority of people at least, agreed on all the policies and principles of running society, the brutal, if usually now bloodless, contest for power would still go on. Sometimes those objectively closest disagree the most – the narcissism of small differences, as Sigmund Freud put it. Accepting the liberal notion that society is comprised of many groups with legitimately different interests, most mainstream theorists and pundits today advocate adherence to the pluralist rules of the game. But this is an aspiration not a solution. We would do well to heed the advice that Gouverneur Morris, one of the American founders, gave to Marquis de Lafayette, then Commandant General of the revolutionary French National Guard: "[M]en do not go into administration as the direct road to Heaven; that they are prompted by ambition or avarice, and therefore that the only way to secure the most virtuous is by making it their interest to act rightly." Put simply, political actors will agree to the rules when it is in their interest to do so.[28]

The task facing us is to understand why some political strategies are more effective at some times and in some places than in others. Politicians aren't robots and parties aren't algorithms. But just as financial markets adjust quickly to new information – firm valuations and commodity prices moving rapidly in response to economic or political events – the political marketplace also adjusts. As long as populism is cost effective, aspiring political leaders will use it, whatever values or knowledge we might seek to impart to the people. Even good men, as Morris implied, will act badly if we don't provide the right incentives. If we want to live in a rules-based political system that has the benefits of popular participation, simply wishing it were so will not do. What is needed are policies, programs, and inducements designed to influence the cost-benefit calculus of aspiring political leaders. We need, in other words, to create the economic incentives to make free and fair competition between well-organized bodies of people the only game in town.

2

Populists before Parties

Pericles decided to devote himself to the people, espousing the cause of the poor and the many instead of the few and the rich, contrary to his own nature, which was anything but popular. But he feared, as it would seem, to counter a suspicion of aiming at tyranny, and when he saw that Cimon was very aristocratic in his sympathies, and was held in extraordinary affection by the party of the "Good and True," he began to court the favour of the multitude, thereby securing safety for himself, and power to wield against his rival.

Plutarch[1]

And it is our duty,—ours, I say, who are driven about by the winds and waves of this people, to hear the whims of the people with moderation, to strive to win over their affections when alienated from us, to retain them when we have won them, to tranquilize them when in a state of agitation. If we do not think honours of any great consequence, we are not bound to be subservient to the people; if we do strive for them, then we must be unwearied in soliciting them.

Marcus Tullius Cicero[2]

THE MADDENING CROWD

If the way society and its political institutions are organized affects the cost of different types of political mobilization, then Ancient Greece and Rome were places where populism could be a very effective political strategy. The origins of populism, and probably even democracy itself, had little to do with any egalitarian or proto-liberal values. Rather, this chapter shows that direct appeals to the people were part of an intra-elite struggle for power. Why bother to invest one's resources in cultivating a network of self-interested and unreliable elite allies through the distribution of patronage, when one could ride the mob to the top instead? Even though populists were typically unable to retain control for long, the temptation to mobilize the people in competition with other elites was often irresistible. Simply put, populism was cost-effective politics in the ancient world.

Politics in the great cities of Athens and Rome was personal and face-to-face. The open meeting places of the Athenian assembly and the Roman forum were themselves the means of mass communication. Physically gathered, but otherwise unorganized, the crowd in the ancient world was ripe for manipulation and mobilization. A vote by acclamation in an arena or assembly amid the shouting and jostling of the crowd is neither the same as separate individuals quietly filling out a paper ballot in a sealed polling booth nor a calm dialogue among those with differing opinions but set on a common task. A few well-timed and well-executed speeches – or perhaps just one if we are to credit Shakespeare's version of the impact of Mark Antony's funeral oration for Julius Caesar – and the masses could be moved to action. In short, the public assemblies of the ancient world lowered the cost of the direct mobilization of the masses compared to other forms of political leadership. The esteemed Roman orator, Marcus Tullius Cicero, who privately referred to the *plebs* as the "filth and shit" of Rome, nevertheless knew that political success demanded courting the support of the people. At times, the mobilization of the masses was all but necessary to political success in the imperial cities of Athens and Rome.[3]

However, variation in the respective institutional and social setups of Athens and Rome meant that they differed from one another in the frequency, form, and effectiveness of populist mobilization. In Athens, from the time of its democratic reforms in the late fifth century BCE, all free adult male citizens had the right to vote on and even speak in the assembly's proceedings. Populism is an almost constant presence in this period of Athenian politics. In Rome, in contrast, the masses were more indirectly incorporated, with very few citizens actually participating in the political process. Moreover, even though both the Roman forum and the Athenian assembly were public gathering places, their political function was different. While many aspiring leaders in Rome attempted to use the forum to mobilize the masses as had their Greek counterparts in the assembly, this strategy was typically blocked, not just by formal institutional constraints, but by the tighter social and economic networks that bound together Rome's oligarchy. The Roman elite didn't agree on much, but they could at least concur on the need to keep the masses subdued. For most of Rome's early history, politics remained the purview of the elite. Populism hardly featured at all in the Early and Middle Roman Republic. However, when that oligarchic modus vivendi began to fray by the mid–second century BCE, possibly because the spoils of executive office grew along with the extent of the empire itself, the masses were increasingly mobilized in the intra-elite contest for power and prestige. Populism had become part of the strategic arsenal of Rome's elites.

However, unlike Athens, Rome did not at that point adopt a participatory democratic form. As a result, if mass mobilization was legitimately central to the operation of Athenian political institutions, in Rome the crowds were activated only at the edges of legality. The populist strategy in Rome thus often had violent implications. A Roman politician's base among the masses was often a proxy for his armed strength. The most famous, or infamous, populists were as much gang leaders as they were politicians. Gangs in turn gave way to armies. The leading contenders for power could never completely dismiss the Roman people, but from the last years of the republic through to the two decades of civil war that followed, political authority became virtually indistinguishable from military force. Finally, with the new security – or crowd control – apparatus of the empire put in place with Augustus' consolidation of power in the late first century BCE, the cost of the populist strategy rises to the point that it disappears to the margins of political history, until the reemergence of mass democracy in the late eighteenth century.

POPULISM AND THE ORIGINS OF DEMOCRACY

Patrimonialism, rather than bureaucracy or charisma, was the preponderant ordering principle in the ancient pre–democratic world. In the patriarchy of Ancient Athens, an eminent man's political hopes were largely determined by the number of dependents he could bring to the metaphorical, and sometimes literal, battlefield. Family – fathers, brothers, cousins – was the primary basis around which an ambitious man would build his political career. Adoption and marriage were an obvious extension of this principle, allowing powerful families to join forces. Yet, important as this familial base was, it was not usually sufficient to gain power; for that, a would-be leader needed a broader clientele. Elites could widen their networks through horizonal alliances of unrelated peers. In some cases, these may have taken on the form of informal social clubs, or *hetaireiai* – small parties of around ten to twenty upper-class men, who would drink, eat, and talk together. These often-overlapping elite groupings were useful in politics, but the self-serving behavior of their members could never be ruled out. The political elite remained extremely fragmented, each great man constituting a political grouping on his own account. Alliances were fluid and few leaders stayed at the top for long. It is in those intra-elite conflicts that we can find both the origins of democracy as a political system and of populism as a political strategy. Increasingly, from the last third of the fifth century BCE, *hoi polloi* – the common people – were mobilized as part of the intra-elite contest for power.

The origins of Athenian democracy are usually traced to the rule of Solon in the early sixth century BCE. Before Solon's reforms, Athens was governed by nine *archons* annually appointed or elected by the senate-like council of the *Areopagos*. The *archons* – or rulers, the word is the root of our current terms, mon-*archy*, an-*archy*, and so on – were men exclusively of noble birth – the *eupadrids* – as was the *Areopagus*. Amid the factional rivalry endemic to this kind of institutionalized oligarchy, Solon seems to have become ruler-in-chief either as either a kind of consensus-building peacemaker, or simply as the most dominant of the rival contenders for superiority. We lack the contemporary sources to know exactly why Solon pursued the strategy he did, but the most common inference is that his reforms were aimed at addressing a problem familiar to many autocratic regimes – that of a rising economic elite demanding a political status commensurate with its wealth, and we should say, its associated military significance. Like many other Greek city states, Athens of the sixth century BCE depended militarily on the use of the *phalanx*, a formation of *hoplites* armed with shields, spears, and perhaps also shorter stabbing weapons. *Hoplites* were distinguishable as a social class by being able to afford this expensive bronze equipment, thus elevating them above the lowly *thetes* – poor citizens compelled to row in the galleys – but also placing them below the even more elaborately equipped cavalry. A key challenge, in short, was to incorporate this militarily important "middle class." Yet this rationale need not have been exclusive of other private motivations on Solon's part. By extending the rights of political participation to all men of some wealth, not merely those of the hereditary aristocracy, Solon substantially widened his personal support base. Solon may not have been a rabble-rouser as such, but he clearly showed that appealing to the broader, non-elite citizenry was a viable strategy for obtaining and maintaining power.

The Solonian system was not a democracy as we would understand it, but it did transfer significant powers to a new 400-member assembly – the *Boule* – while the elitist *Areopagus* took on the characteristics of an upper house. The new assembly had an important role in choosing and holding to account the city state's magistrates. It was Solon's belief, if we are to credit the later account of Aristotle, that "the people will follow their leaders" if given a little, but not too much, freedom. Solon may have imagined that this new institutional set up would mean rule by the oligarchy as it always had, but it wasn't long before an ally of Solon's, Peisistratos – who dominated Athenian politics between 561 and 527 BCE – demonstrated that it could also lead to rule by the one who could best build a popular following: a *demagogue* – from the words *demos*, or people, and *agogos*, or leader. Peisistratus was, in the words of one historian, "assiduous in cultivating the support of the people." He engaged in public works, put on entertainment, and ensured a measure of sustenance for the masses. However, Peisistratus was so determined to hold on to power that he soon converted his popularity into a dictatorship – he may have been the first but was certainly not the last populist to take this step. Herodotus describes him as a kind of benign dictator, ruling Athens "properly and well." The people thus indulged him his great political power. However, Athenians' fortunes dipped as Peisistratus was succeeded by his son, Hippias, who in 527 BCE installed himself as an autocrat, only this time not of the benevolent sort.[4]

Something more recognizably democratic emerged with the late sixth–century reforms of Cleisthenes. Here the sources are clearer. In 514 BCE, Cleisthenes came to power amid the intra-elite conflicts that followed the denouement of Hippias' dictatorship. Cleisthenes departed more radically from past practice than Solon, overtly putting himself forward as a champion of the people, a real democrat if not also a demagogue. It was no doubt with the likes of Cleisthenes in mind that the philosopher Heraclitus caustically lamented the ease with which the masses were swayed by powerful speakers: "What use are these people's wits, who let themselves be led by speechmakers, in crowds, without considering how many fools and thieves they are among, and how few choose the good." With the support of the masses, and a little help from a Spartan army, Cleisthenes overcame his rivals and began introducing a series of momentous reforms. With Cleisthenes' new constitution, the aristocratic *archonship* lost much of its remaining influence, political power henceforth primarily residing in an assembly – the *Ecclesia* – that included all free adult male citizens. Juries and other magistracies (with the exception of military generals, or *strategoi*) were chosen by lot from those who put their names forward, to conduct the day-to-day business of government. The assembly, as the main institution of government, debated and passed all laws, chose the *strategoi* by ballot, and held the power to ostracize – force into exile – any citizen for a period of ten years. Legislation, which the assembly would debate, was prepared by a council of 500 – the *Boule* – which was chosen by lot. The assembly's remit was broad, extending all the way to matters of life and death, as we will see. Politics remained the preserve of male citizens, and so excluded women, slaves, and foreigners. Nevertheless, Athens had embarked on system of direct democracy on a scale that the world had never before seen.[5]

The assembly created a completely new political dynamic. No longer was power won merely in private gatherings of elites but from the speaker's platform on the Pnyx – the hill overlooking the central *agora* where Athens' citizenry would gather. Politics continued to be a sport of the elite, but the direct mobilization of the people now emerged as a viable strategy. Even though anyone was entitled to speak during the assembly's proceedings, naturally enough, men with the highest social status and greatest oratorical skills predominated. As Socrates put it, Athens' democratic constitution provided "government by the best men along with popular consent." Moreover, among the elite, only the richest of men, Xenophon argued, could throw dinners, provide gymnasia, build parks or temples, fit out ships in war time, and generally play the benefactor sufficiently to earn the reputation, or what Aristotle called "the magnificence," required for leadership. These eminent men built political followings through the distribution of patronage, but of course, nothing like organized political parties were ever created in Athens. As the late Yale University historian, Donald Kagan, one of the foremost experts on the history of fifth-century Athens, wrote: "Athenian politics typically involved shifting groups which came together, often around a man, sometimes around an issue, occasionally with reference to both. There was little or no party discipline in the modern sense and only limited continuity."[6]

Themistocles was the first to exploit the potential of Athens' new democratic institutions, relying on direct mass appeals rather than elite networks to come to power. Themistocles emerges in Herodotus's *The Histories* in the context of rising tensions between Athens and Persia in the early fifth–century BCE. Attempting to deal with the irritant of Greek colonists on the Western edge of its gigantic empire – the coastline of the present-day Anatolian region of Türkiye – the Persians embarked on a military invasion of Greece proper, thereby hoping to secure for itself mastery of the Aegean, perhaps on the way to broader dominance of the whole Mediterranean littoral. A new man, that is, not one of noble birth, Themistocles gained himself a following through his activities as an advocate in the courts and, Plutarch writes, "stirring up the people to all kinds of enterprises" as a speaker in the assembly. Themistocles was elected as chief *archon* in 493 BCE and set about persuading his compatriots of the need to invest in Athens' naval defenses. When Darius, the Persian emperor, ordered an invasion of the Athenian mainland in 490 BCE, Themistocles was one of the ten elected *strategoi* sent to meet them. At the now legendary Battle of Marathon, the Greeks turned back the Persians. When a second Persian invasion was launched in 480–79 BCE, Themistocles was the leading man in Athens, and now his naval strategy would come to the fore. While Athens' Spartan allies marched north to head the Persians off at the narrow Pass of Thermopylae – the place where 300 of them would make their famous last stand – Themistocles persuaded the Athenians to abandon their city and take to the sea to beat back the invaders. Unfortunately, the sources don't tell us what Themistocles said to win over the crowd. What we can infer is that it took a great deal of persuasion, and even the use of all kinds of theatrics. Eventually, the people were convinced, and Themistocles' plan was adopted. At the naval Battle of Salamis, Athenian warships inflicted a crushing defeat on Darius' forces, and within a year, Greek armies had followed up with victory over the Persian military at Plataea, setting Persian designs on mastery of its Western seas back for a generation. Themistocles' prestige was now virtually unassailable. He used his political capital to convince his fellow Athenians to build a new walled port at Piraeus, confirming Athens' newfound status as the preeminent naval power in the Aegean.

Themistocles, who was, according to Plutarch, a new man "who went beyond all men in the passion for distinction," could well lay claim to being the first true populist. We know that he relied primarily on mass support to win supreme power and push through his military strategy. Unfortunately, however, we lack the source material to say much more about him or his political tactics. It is only with the rise of Pericles (c. 495–429 BCE) and the beginning of Thucydides' *History of the Peloponnesian War* that we can start to get a clearer picture of how populist mobilization worked in the ancient world. One of the major powers given to the people's assembly as part of Cleisthenes' reforms was that of ostracism. Recognizing the potential for intra-elite rivalry to boil over into civil discord and even violence, ostracism allowed the assembly to nominate and remove any citizen from the city for a period of ten years. Ostracism could, in theory, be used to punish incompetence or corruption. More often, however, it seems to have been just another weapon the elite deployed against one another, manipulating the crowd in order to eliminate a rival. This, at any rate, is the motivation that Plutarch provides in the case of the ostracism of Themistocles in or around 472 BCE. The assembly banished him "to humble his eminence and authority, as they ordinarily did with all whom they thought too powerful, or, by their greatness, disproportionable to the equality thought requisite in a popular government. For the ostracism was instituted, not so much to punish the offender, as to mitigate and pacify the violence of the envious." The envious in Plutarch's account were not the lowly masses, but Themistocles' elite rivals, not least Cimon who would become Athens' leading citizen for the next decade.[7]

Unlike Themistocles, Cimon was from an esteemed background, the son of Miltiades, a contemporary of Themistocles who led the fighting at the Battle of Marathon. Cimon earned his spurs as a general in his own right in the naval victory over Persians at Salamis in 480 BCE and was a politician very much in the traditional mold. This is not to say that the Cimon was dismissive of popular opinion; he was a prodigious builder of public works and contributor to charity. However, his approach is better described as paternalistic than populist. He was no great orator and led primarily on account of the deference paid to him by regular Athenians for his military accomplishments. This conservatism left him vulnerable to populist outflanking. The radical reforms of Ephialtes in 462/1 BCE, which transferred considerably more power to the poorer strata of Athenian society, were most likely a product of this kind of elite maneuvering. Introduced during a period in which Cimon and his aristocratic allies were absent (on military campaign) from the city, the reforms significantly weakened Cimon's grip on power.

The new institutional environment presented great opportunities to men who could directly mobilize popular support. With Ephialtes being murdered shortly after his reforms, the opportunity to benefit from them passed instead to Pericles. From Thucydides' account, we know Pericles as "the foremost among the Athenians and the most powerful in speech and action." Pericles practiced the art of public speaking, with Socrates describing him as "in all likelihood the greatest rhetorician of all." Pericles certainly cultivated popular support, in line with the new democratic dispensation. As Plutarch notes, his private inclinations may have been far from "popular," but in this political environment, "court[ing] the favour of the multitude" was the most efficient way to secure his preeminence over Cimon, who had a lock on the support of the conservative elite. Cimon was painted as an opponent of democracy, and he would eventually be ostracized. Ultimately, however, Pericles' strategy is best described as a mixed one. Once in power, he became a pioneer of the use of state resources to win popularity; or what today we would call clientelism. Drawing both on the Laurion silver mines and (more controversially) on the defence contributions of the non-Athenian members of the Delian League, Pericles massively increased Athens' public works program, introduced a policy to have the state pay for the admission of the poor to the theatre, and brought in payments for service on juries. Pericles also seems to have cultivated an unmatched level of dominance within the elite itself. Although the Athenians elected ten generals, one for each of the city's tribes, one of the *strategoi* was always more important than the others. Yet, while other leading generals often faced rivals from among their elected colleagues, during Pericles' fifteen-year tenure at the top, there appears to have been little dissention. Thucydides would write that Pericles was so dominant that Athens was "in name a democracy but really a government by the first citizen."[8]

DEMAGOGUES

As towering a figure as Pericles was, even he could not survive unscathed the catastrophe of the Peloponnesian War–time plague in 430 BCE that felled about a quarter of the city's population. Pericles was attacked both from the pacifist left and the war-mongering right, the most notable avatar of the latter being Cleon, one of the few men for whom Thucydides reserves the pejorative moniker, *demagogue*. The assembly removed Pericles from office on charges of corruption; charges, one suspects, which were leveled by Cleon and his clique. Yet with no resolution to the crisisin sight, by spring 429 BCE, Pericles was recalled. As Thucydides caustically writes of the Athenian crowds' capriciousness, "[n]ot much later, as the mob loves to do, they elected him general again and turned everything over to him." In spite of his temporary restoration, however, Pericles would not see out the year, his death most likely caused by the plague that was still ravaging the city.[9]

Pericles' passing ushered in a new era in Athenian politics in which populism would become the predominant political strategy of the elite. Often, clearly too often for Thucydides' tastes, leadership required aggressively courting popular support. Of Pericles' successors, he writes: "And each grasping at supremacy, they ended by committing even the conduct of state affairs to the whim of the multitude." At first, the political advantage fell to the populist Cleon. Cleon had vehemently opposed Pericles' middle-way military approach while the latter was alive, and now in the 420s BCE, he became identifiable as the leader of the war party in Athens. As a result, according to Thucydides, already by 427 BCE, Cleon had become "by far the most persuasive among the people." Although Pericles too had been a commanding speaker, Cleon, we are told, could not have been more different in his style. Cleon seems to have been a powerful orator capable of dispensing poisonous invective. He was, Aristotle wrote, "the first to shout when addressing the people, he used abusive language, and addressed the *ekklesia* with his garments tucked up when it was customary to speak properly dressed." Yet Cleon was no mere panderer. He had choice words for the crowd, likening those persuaded by the "fine speeches" of his pacifistic opponents to "men seated for entertainment by sophists." In spite of, or perhaps because of, his truculent style, Cleon was genuinely popular with

large sections of the crowd. People evidently do sometimes like a bully. When
the Mytilenean revolt on the island of Lesbos was put down in 427 BCE, Cleon
persuaded the assembly to massacre the men and enslave its women and
children. A ship was swiftly dispatched to deliver the awful sentence. Yet just
the next day, the Athenians partially reversed their decision, sending out
another boat to intercept the first with orders to execute only 1,000 of the
ringleaders, chosen largely from the oligarchy. Cleon, though he made a logical,
if cold-blooded, case for his ruthless policy of extermination, was not able to
bring the assembly with him. In Thucydides' view, the episode just confirms the
fickleness of the crowd – with Cleon one moment, against him the next:
"The people were only showing (what he himself had long seen) their incap-
acity for governing, by giving way to a sentimental unbusinesslike compassion:
as for the orators who excited it, they were, likely enough, paid for their
trouble."[10]

With this last remark, Thucydides is looking a bit further ahead in the story.
Following up on this partial victory, Cleon's opponents thought they might
have discovered a way to silence the demagogue more permanently. Long a
pain in the side of the political-military establishment when speaking in the
assembly, Cleon had never himself led a military campaign. He was, his critics
thought, more of a Rush Limbaugh than a General Douglas MacArthur. When
Cleon proposed yet more military offensives, his opponents conceded – on
condition that Cleon himself run for election as general and lead the expedition.
Imagine the irrisory looks among the elite when the galling blowhard was
forced to walk the talk! The great irony, as Thucydides' words quoted earlier
suggest, is that the schemers soon got their comeuppance. Although Cleon had
no military experience when thrust into the role of *strategos*, he proved to be a
bold and brilliant commander. His achievements in the mid-420s helped to
rescue Athens from the abysmal legacy of Pericles's financially draining and
ineffective defensive posture. He was, in other words, no mere gascon. He
pursued a forward military policy that had the support of many, if never all,
of his countrymen.

For our purposes, what Cleon showed was the potential to use populist
appeals to the people to cut through the dominance of the traditional oligarchy.
Cleon had money we know, but direct vote buying in Athens seems to have
played a minor role in assembly decisions, certainly in comparison to republican Rome as we'll see shortly. More importantly, as a merchant rather than a
member of the nobility, Cleon was ridiculed by the traditional noble elite.
Excluded from the circles of power, he was in no position to build up a network
of elite allies and their associates in order to assume political leadership by
degrees and thence push through his favored policies. As Plutarch tells us, he
effectively renounced this strategy, turning directly to the masses in the intra-
elite struggle for power: "[B]eing rough and harsh to the better classes he in
turn subjected himself to the multitude in order to win its favour." The
moderate Periclean path was not possible for him, even had he sought it.

The elite shunned him as much as he shunned it. Direct communication with the masses, along with all of the rabble-rousing techniques that entailed, was the one way in which an outsider like him could break into the halls of power. Great orators could do without the alliances traditional to Greek politics; as Xenophon writes, "the man who can persuade needs no [accomplices]." So disgusted by the turn toward rule by common merchants like Cleon was the playwright, Aristophanes, that he has an oracle in the play *Knights* say that: "Leading the people is not the work of an educated man of good character, but demands an ignoramus, a jerk." Cleon would not be the last populist to bear such an epithet. What his then novel strategy demonstrated was that the old, slow path requiring land ownership, a choice marriage, and years of public service, often in the military, was no longer necessary to rise to the top. The populist strategy, writes classicist W. H. Connor, provided "a rapid way to power for the inexperienced." Cleon had found a shortcut. He had reduced the *cost* of winning power, and as we will see, others quickly learned.[11]

As the satirical work of Aristophanes suggests, popular as Cleon was among the masses, he was not universally adored. Adherents of Pericles' moderate policy, including Nicias, still retained half or more of the ten generalships into 426 BCE. With Cleon's death in battle in 424 BCE along with that of the equally belligerent and equally gifted Spartan general Brasidas, the Athenian peace faction got its opening. Named for its leading politician, Nicias, Athens and Sparta signed a new peace accord that, nominally at least, restored most of the status quo ante bellum. Yet, even though Pericles had begun the war largely to keep intact what Athens already held, the Peace of Nicias was not a beneficial one to Athens. Many of the territories formally returned to Athens' imperial sphere of control by the peace agreement remained effectively independent. Athens would have to fight if it wanted to restore de facto control over its erstwhile subordinates and make good any debts owed to it. At the same time, Sparta sued for peace, not because it accepted Athenian supremacy in the Aegean, but because it needed time to rebuild its fleet. Obvious in retrospect, but even likely apparent to many contemporaries, this was a truce rather than a permanent peace. Our chief guide to these events, Thucydides, wrote, albeit with the benefit of hindsight, "it cannot, it will be found, be rationally considered a state of peace, as neither side gave or got back all that they had agreed." Indeed, the agreement had hardly been formalized when Nicias' Athenian rivals saw an opportunity to rise to prominence by opposing the peace.[12]

ALCIBIADES AND THE CRISIS OF ATHENIAN DEMOCRACY

The man to take the populist war–mongering approach to its logical fulfilment was Alcibiades. Few characters in Ancient Greek history evoke as much fascination. The toing and froing of his career makes the plot of *Game of Thrones* seem prosaic by comparison. Scion of not one, but two of the most powerful families in

Athens, married to the daughter of Athens' wealthiest man, adopted ward of none other than Pericles, Alcibiades was intelligent, rich, and so we're told by all who care to mention him, immeasurably handsome. Plato has one of his characters say to Socrates, long suspected of having an amorous relationship with Alcibiades, "[f]or surely you cannot have found anyone more beautiful, at least not in this city." Alcibiades had a speech impediment, mispronouncing his *r*'s as *l*'s, but it seems that this affectation only further charmed his listeners. He spent lavishly on entertainment, cultivating considerable fame as the first Greek to field seven chariots in the Olympic Games of 416 BCE, in the process taking home first, second, and fourth prizes. He even supposedly invented a new shoe style, and either because he didn't play the flute very well, or as he claimed, because he disliked how playing it made his face look, contrived to have the instrument removed from the preparatory curriculum of well-bred boys in the city.[13]

So much for trivialities. More relevant from our perspective is Alcibiades' noted ambition for power and the means he deployed in attaining it. A member of Socrates' circle of followers, as were many young Athenian aristocrats, Alcibiades' lust for glory earned him a reproach from the master philosopher:

What is the hope that fills you? I will tell you. You think that if one day you address the people—and you intend to do so very soon—Athenians will immediately be persuaded that you merit even more respect than Pericles or anyone before him, and you will say to yourself that henceforth you will be the most powerful man in this city. And if you are the most powerful man among us, you will be the same among all Greeks; no, not just among Greeks, but among the barbarians who inhabit this continent.

Alcibiades would indeed appeal to the people to become the most famous leader in Athens, Greece, and beyond. At the same time, Alcibiades' indifference toward democracy was evident to those who knew him, even in his youth. In an argument with his adoptive father, Pericles, he objected to the idea that laws were just, simply on account that they had been passed by a majority in the assembly. Alcibiades didn't think much of the mob but he would use it just the same.[14]

In 416, when a conflict among rival Greek colonists on the island of Sicily broke out, Alcibiades rose to political prominence as an advocate of an ambitious new naval expedition. Nominally, the armada was a response to a request for aid from Athens' Sicilian ally, Egesta, and arguably the intervention didn't violate the terms of the Peace of Nicias. It certainly seems, however, that Alcibiades had grander things in mind than assisting Athens' friends – a military takeover of the whole island of Sicily, perhaps even, of the whole Mediterranean – developments that certainly would have thrown the whole Graeco-Persian world into open war. Notoriously ambitious, as Socrates saw, Alcibiades gave voice to a new, expanded vision of Athens' dominion, a Greek empire on the scale of the Roman one that would follow in the centuries to come. Even if Alcibiades kept his militaristic agenda somewhat hidden, he was not shy about his personal ambitions. In the debate on the Sicilian expedition, he openly expressed his hubris: "Nor is it unfair that he who prides himself on his position should refuse to be upon an equality with the rest. He who is badly off has his misfortunes all to himself." In other words, I'm better than you, so be grateful for my leadership![15]

Athens' latest saber-rattler was as strenuously opposed by Nicias, author of the now teetering peace agreement, as was Cleon before his death. So disruptive had the conflict become between Nicias and Alcibiades that in 415 BCE, Hyperbolos, described in the sources as a radical democrat, a rascal, and even a demagogue in his own right, proposed ostracizing Alcibiades. Plutarch offers several slightly different versions of the events that followed, but the most commonly accepted account is that Alcibiades, ever the charmer, managed to persuade Nicias to join forces against Hyperbolos. Rather than have their supporters vote against one another, they should all vote to ostracize Hyperbolos. The poll was nearly unanimous, but having achieved its object of ostracizing the troublemaker, the temporary alliance between Athens' two leading men quickly expired. When it came to the final debate on the Sicilian expedition, Nicias offered all kinds of reasons why the assembly should vote against it. His final argument was that the proposed invasion force was so small, it was sure to fail. Yet rather than see this as a reason to abandon the Sicilian expedition, the assembly instead increased its scale from twenty to one hundred ships – in fact, even more when those of its allies were included. Alcibiades had gotten even more than he asked for.[16]

From here, however, things soon turned south for Alcibiades. Just as the ships were preparing to launch, a scandal engulfed Athens. Many of the *hermai* – columnar stone statues, typically carved with the head of a god and male genitals – throughout the city were violated – more precisely, their penises were removed. The mob was outraged by this seemingly coordinated act of sacrilege. A commission of investigation was launched into the emasculation of the *hermai* and other alleged profanities. Denunciations and counter-denunciations ran rampant through the city and it wasn't long before allegations of impiety touched Alcibiades. Although popular with the masses, Alcibiades had plenty of enemies among the elite, as his near ostracism illustrated. According to Thucydides, the ones doing the persecuting were "those most jealous of Alcibiades as an impediment to their own positions of leadership of the *demos*, who thought that if they got rid of him they would be first." Alcibiades asked that a trial be conducted immediately in order that he could be cleared of what he was sure he could prove were trumped up charges. His accusers artfully delayed, forcing Alcibiades and his men to leave for Sicily. They then almost immediately summoned Alcibiades to face trial, which he would have to do without the backing of his armed retinue.[17]

The first result of Alcibiades' recall was that the Sicilian mission lost all cohesion. Now led by Nicias, the man who had done most to oppose it, the expedition's failure was almost a foregone conclusion, although the extent of the annihilation – Nicias himself would be among the dead – was nevertheless a shock. The second result was that Alcibiades was forced into exile. With most of his supporters in the military *hoplite* class unknowingly on the way to their deaths in Sicily, he knew he had little chance of a fair trial back in Athens. Slipping the net of those sent to escort him back to Athens, he fled. And where did this enemy of the state go? Remarkably, to Athens' chief military rival, Sparta. It was a spectacular defection that has earned Alcibiades much scorn through the years. By providing the kind of military intel that allowed Sparta to gain the upper hand over Athens, Alcibiades was brought close to the circles of power in his new home. Yet this very proximity was ultimately his undoing. The beguiling Alcibiades soon found his way into the bed of the wife of one Sparta's joint rulers, fathering her a child. King Agis was none too pleased, and Alcibiades again found himself on the run, taking up exile this time with the Persians in Asia Minor. Extraordinary as this series of events was, they couldn't compare with what was to follow.

Despite the famed history of the early fifth–century Graeco-Persian conflict, both Athens and Sparta actively sought the support of their imperial neighbor in their internecine rivalry. In fact, one of Alcibiades' roles in Sparta before his excommunication was precisely to obtain Persian financial backing. Abandoned by Sparta, Alcibiades, now with the ear of the fantastically rich Persian satraps in Anatolia, offered Persian support as a reward to Athens for recalling him from exile. In 412–411 BCE, Alcibiades made his approach to the Athenian force on the island of Samos, close to the Anatolian coastline. However, presumably still not trusting the crowd that had banished him, he is reported to have said he would only return if Athens installed an oligarchy. When the oligarchic revolution in Athens came in 411 BCE, however, Alcibiades still wasn't sure it was safe to return. He was probably right. A democratic restoration followed in 410 BCE, but the one to benefit in the short term was another demagogue, and an opponent of Alcibiades, Cleophon.

Amid this welter, Alcibiades still didn't give up hope of a heroic return. Although still effectively unable to enter Athens, Alcibiades provided the de facto leadership of a string of Athenian naval victories in the years that followed. When, eventually, in 407 BCE, Alcibiades made his triumphal homecoming, Athens seemed closer to victory over Sparta than at any time in the whole Peloponnesian War. On few occasions was there ever such unadulterated hero worship in the city. After his landing, the people "ran in throngs to Alcibiades with shouts of welcome, escorting him on his way, and putting wreaths on his head as they could get to him." He was elected, for the only time we know of in Athenian history, commander in chief.[18]

Yet the Athenian assembly remained prone to wild swings in direction, a caprice that is illustrated in a revealing episode, not long after the defeat of Athenian forces under the command of one of Alcibiades' subordinates at the battle of Notium in 406 BCE. Along the Anatolian coast, at Arginusae, Athens had again found itself engaged with Spartan forces. Although by this time much depleted and relying on relatively inexperienced draftees, the Athenians nevertheless obliterated the Spartan navy. The success was spoiled, however, by a storm that followed, preventing the Athenian ships from recovering their dead. Thus, in spite of Athens' overall victory, some 2,000 *hoplites* and many more *thetes* and *metics* may have died. Although it is unlikely that the eight generals in charge of the fleet could have done anything to avert the disaster, the assembly put them on trial. The judicial proceedings were full of errors. Euryptolemos made an impassioned speech to try the generals according to the law, allowing them to make a proper defence. Socrates, in attendance, also objected, saying that he would "do nothing that was contrary to the law." In the end, however, as Xenophon writes, "the mob again shouted so furiously that those men were forced to withdraw their summonses." The people should rule, uninhibited: "the multitude shout out that it was a terrible thing if someone prevented the people from doing whatever they wished." The six of the eight generals who were present were executed immediately. Alcibiades was again forced into exile, probably at the urging of Cleophon, this time to Thrace.[19]

Alcibiades appears one last time in the history books before his death, offering advice to an Athenian fleet stationed near his residence in exile. His astute words went unheeded and the Athenian forces were crushed by the Spartans at Aegospotami. In 404 BCE he met his ignominious end, being assassinated in Phyrgia where he had been living with a high-class prostitute named Timandra. Oligarchs exploited Athens' defeat to overthrow democracy once more, instituting the infamous, and vicious, rule of the Thirty Tyrants. Alcibiades was in some respects an anomaly. At a time when power was increasingly being wielded by new men – those such as Cleon – Alcibiades was a throwback to earlier times. He was as aristocratic as they came. For this reason, he is sometimes contrasted both with Cleon, who preceded him, and a series of other leaders, Cleophon the most notable, who followed him. These leaders from the merchant class – hemp traders, sheep dealers, and sausage sellers, as the satirist Aristophanes caricatured them in *Knights* – are described as the real demagogues. True enough, Alcibiades seems to have been ambivalent about democracy. Yet to infer that he was engaged in a battle of ideologies between oligarchic and democratic forces is to seriously misconstrue events. As the celebrated French classical scholar Jacqueline de Romilly put it, "Athenian politicians cared little about policies and general principles." The ambitious on both sides drew from the same strategic well.[20]

Alcibiades no doubt had a greater network of influential allies than his commoner rivals. In the end, however, the quest for power and prestige required of him that he win the crowd. Very often, it seems, he could do this. The ambitious Sicilian expedition is only the clearest example. P. J. Rhodes, one of Alcibiades' biographers, writes that he "was an aristocrat who was beating the upstart demagogues at their own game." Alcibiades rose and fell with the support of the Athenian *demos*. Viewed with deep suspicion, and perhaps jealousy, by his elite peers, Alcibiades went directly to the masses. What his rollercoasting career reveals is both the potential for the populist strategy to provide a fast route to power but also the inherent limitations in such a disorganized political movement. The crowd could turn on a dime. Without parties or mass political organizations of any sort, either a populist like Alcibiades would have to secure his power in the form of a popular dictatorship in the way that Peisistratus did, or he risked being outflanked by the next panderer to win the mob's temporary affection. Cleophon, an even more notorious warmonger, followed Alcibiades, and after him, Aristotle writes, "there was an unbroken series of demagogues whose main aim was to be outrageous and please the people with no thought for anything but the present." Populism, in other words, had become all but endemic.[21]

When democracy was restored after the ousting of the Spartan-backed rule of the Thirty Tyrants in 403 BCE, some procedural adjustments were made in order to tame these violent swings of opinion. Something like a process of judicial review was introduced so that shotgun trials and executions like that of the generals after Arginusae wouldn't happen again. Yet the changes, such as they were, were tragically inadequate to save Socrates from the prejudice of the crowd. In 399 BCE he was charged with impiety and corruption of the city's youth. With adherents of his philosophical school including Alcibiades, and worse, some of the oligarchic coup plotters responsible for the tyranny, the trial of Socrates was as much a trial of anyone who had, or who would dare to, stymie the freedom of the people to do just what they wished. Once Pericles had introduced the idea of paying citizens for their participation in the city's political institutions, any curtailment of this privilege was going to be hotly contested. Athens could not make a direct transition from a direct participatory democracy to a mediated or representative one. Populism thus remained a feature of Athenian democracy down to its denouement in the late fourth century BCE.

Athens was much chastened by its defeat in the Peloponnesian War. Sparta dominated Greek affairs until 371 BCE followed by Thebes until 362 – periods known respectively as the Spartan and Theban hegemonies. However, as Athens recovered its autonomy in the international sphere, the ramifications of populist persuasion in the assembly were again felt across the Greek world and beyond. Demosthenes, many of whose speeches survive, was only the most famous of the city's demagogues in the revivified democracy. Longinus, a first–century Roman literary critic, writes that a great orator, the "master of our emotions, is often, as it were, red-hot and ablaze with passion." Demosthenes, he continues, "is vehement, rapid, vigorous, terrible; he burns and sweeps away all before him; and hence we may liken him to a whirlwind or a thunderbolt." Cicero idolized Demosthenes, while Quintilian said he was the "greatest" of the orators: "Such is the force and compactness of his language, so muscular his style, so free from tameness and so self-controlled, that you will find nothing in him that is either too much or too little."[22]

Demosthenes had made a living by writing speeches for the law courts, but before long he sought a greater station. With the art of persuasion still counting for more than anything else in the assembly, Demosthenes dedicated himself to developing his delivery. Like Alcibiades, Demosthenes suffered from a speech defect: lisping and struggling with both *r* and *l* sounds. Nonetheless, he did not let this hold him back, honing his oratorical skills in front of the waves crashing against the rocky shore, and allegedly practicing speaking with stones in his mouth. In the assembly, Demosthenes flouted the convention that gave elders the right to speak first, seeking to directly set the agenda himself. As other Athenian populists like Cleon and Alcibiades before him had done, he styled himself as the rabble-rousing war hawk in opposition to the then dominant peace faction, first led by Eubulus and then Aeschines. Describing Athens' precarious security situation in the face of Philip II's then rising kingdom of Macedonia, in classic antiestablishment style, he said: "Look at the politicians who are responsible for these things. Some of them were beggars and are now rich; others obscure and are now prominent ... The more our city has declined, the more these men have flourished." His anti-Philip orations – giving rise to the term *philippic* for a bitter verbal attack – were not immediately successful in changing Athens' pacific political course, but eventually he persuaded his compatriots. Led by Demosthenes' firebrand rhetoric, Athens braced for all-out war with Macedonia. Whether Demosthenes' strategy of resistance was wrong or just poorly executed, Athens ultimately fell to army of Phillip II at the Battle of Chaeronea in 338 BCE, an event that provided Alexander the Great, Phillip's son and heir, the secure base from which he would conquer one of history's vastest empires. The crowd, duly mobilized, could make and break both men and empires. The crowd, via the technology of the assembly, was the weapon of choice of Athens' populists. Populism was dangerous and unpredictable, but above all, it was cost-effective in a polity that had mass participation but not political organization.[23]

POPULUS ROMANUS

Roman democracy was always of a much more limited and indirect nature than that of Athens, and this difference greatly affected the frequency and success of the populist strategy there. Even more so than in Athens, politics in Rome was the preserve of the elite. Democracy in Rome was neither direct, nor even very representative – especially as the city state's territorial frontiers expanded. The role of the people was to provide affirmation of elite decisions rather than to debate them or propose measures of their own. As a proportion of the population, far fewer Roman citizens were involved in selecting its office holders than in Athens. By aggregating votes according to thirty-five geographical "tribes" – just four of which represented the densely populated city of Rome – the electoral system was heavily weighted to rural areas. Moreover, with all balloting conducted within the city, elections not only excluded those far away but also the poorest citizens who could least afford to take the time off needed to hear speeches and vote in person. As a result, some experts reject the idea that Rome was democratic at all.

However, even if Rome fails to meet contemporary standards of democracy in terms of participation, the important fact for our purposes is that the masses could be – and in the Late Republic (c. 145–44 BCE) arguably had to be – mobilized to win and keep high office. Roman elites like Julius Caesar sought honor above all else. In crossing the Rubicon in 49 BCE to launch the civil war that effectively ended the republic, Caesar's main motivation was the affront to his "*dignitas*" – the best translation being something like prestige – posed by his rival Pompey and his backers in the Senate. As Caesar himself put it, his standing was "more important than his life." Or as his rival Cicero caustically wrote, his "cause lacks nothing but a cause." Caesar was far from unique. Some aristocrats undoubtedly saw senatorial humdrum and military service as burdens. For instance, it seems that a declining proportion of the old elite were willing to leave their massive estates to go on long military expeditions abroad. However, for the ambitious among them, the ladder of offices known as the *cursus honorum* – the race for honor – was an all or nothing affair. Normative commitments meant little if they stood in the way of power.[24]

Aristocratic birth alone was no guarantee of success. All holders of executive office had to win elections that could be highly competitive and to secure popular ratification of their policies. Roman elites – or *optimates* – had to cultivate a reputation for honor and dignity, to reward their supporters, and to campaign for office. Although Cicero was privately contemptuous of the mob, he acknowledged the need to canvas for office and publicly sought to portray himself as a true representative of the people's interests – a *popularis*. In his defense speech at the trial of his client and friend, Cnaeus Plancius, on charges of electoral fraud in 54 BCE, Cicero hints at the power of the crowd and the need to tend to its whims:

And it is our duty,—ours, I say, who are driven about by the winds and waves of this people, to hear the whims of the people with moderation, to strive to win over their affections when alienated from us, to retain them when we have won them, to tranquilize them when in a state of agitation. If we do not think honours of any great consequence, we are not bound to be subservient to the people; if we do strive for them, then we must be unwearied in soliciting them.

Public opinion mattered. When the noted stoic Cato, Caesar's longtime nemesis, ran for the highest office of *consul*, he perversely sought to distinguish himself from what he saw as the typical, greedy, pandering Roman politician by explicitly promising absolutely nothing to the people. He lost. Political competition was very real, and this competition was won, at least in part, by directly cultivating popular support. Moreover, the mob of late republican Rome exerted a political influence beyond its institutional limits, with the threat of withholding approval, and ultimately of violence and disorder, ever present, especially given the absence of a police force and the well-justified reluctance of the patrician class to deploy the army within the boundaries of the Eternal City. The people were part of the governance structure of Rome, even if not in the modern democratic sense.[25]

Like Athens, Rome had its beginnings as a monarchy. Putting aside the mythical Romulus, son of Rhea Silvia and the god Mars, the historical regal period lasted from 753 BCE to the expulsion of Tarquin the Proud in 509. Just as Cleisthenes was about to introduce his democratic reforms in Athens to stave off a return to tyrannical rule of the sort Hippias had exercised, the Roman elite instituted an equally novel but distinct form of government to contain and manage its intra-elite rivalry: a *republic*. A *Senate* was constituted of the city state's nobility, with two members of that class being chosen as magistrates – later named *consuls* – to jointly execute the oligarchy's will for a period of a year. Given the relatively small number of elite families, this essentially amounted to rule by turn. Gradually, as the tasks of government grew more complex, further magistracies were added, including – in ascending order of responsibility – *quaestors*, *aediles*, and *praetors*. Would-be leaders had to climb the *cursus honorum*, with election to each level being more challenging than the last and eligibility limited by experience and increasing age limits. While there might be as many as twenty quaestors, there were no more than eight praetors and two consuls. Candidature for these magistracies was restricted to a small, elite segment of society, but among that social group, the contests were highly competitive.

Although the august senatorial class provided all of the state's leading men, as a republic, in Rome it was theoretically the people who were sovereign – only the people in a properly constituted assembly could pass legislation, make treaties, declare war, or elect magistrates to run the government. Late Republican Rome had several voting assemblies in which regular people participated, the most important of which were the *comitia centuriata*, which was responsible for electing senior magistrates, and the *comitia tributa*, which was responsible for electing lower magistrates and tribunes. True, the people's role in these institutions was not participatory in the same way as that of the populace of Athens. Yet Rome's republican form of government meant that however much the elite ruled in practice, they were impelled to present themselves as representatives of the whole people's will. When the elite failed to make good on their end of the deal, popular discontent could follow. This gave rise to a dynamic of intra-elite competition in which the people were often competitively mobilized.[26]

Without splits within the elite, as the famous orator, Marcus Antonius – also the grandfather of Mark Antony of later fame – argued, "neither could kings have been expelled from this city, nor tribunes of the people have been created." As early as 494 BCE, the lower classes, the *plebians*, went on strike, refusing to work the fields or man the legions. A new office, the *tribune* of the plebs, was introduced by the elite to provide an institutional safeguard for the interests of the masses. For Cicero, the office of the tribune was only there to give the mere "appearance of liberty" rather than to provide a serious check on elite control. But that didn't mean that tribunes, and occasionally other elites, didn't use their offices to appeal directly to the people, and sometimes, even if inadvertently, to advance the latter's interests. As the historical sociologist E. P. Thompson famously noted in his study of penal policy in eighteenth-century England, despite the interests of the dominant classes, the law can "acquire a distinct identity, which may, on occasion, inhibit power and afford some protection to the powerless ... For 'the law', as a logic of equity, must always seek to transcend the inequalities of class power which, instrumentally, it is harnessed to serve." Grain doles, land redistributions, and other subsidies resulted from elites outbidding each other for popular support. The suffering of the Roman people when even this pseudo-democracy was replaced by naked military rule during the two decades of civil war from 49 BCE suggests it was not completely worthless.[27]

OPTIMATES AND POPULARES

It is, however, sometimes taken as a signal of the undemocratic nature of Roman politics that many of the most prominent *populares* who attempted to improve the lives of the masses – tribunes including the Gracchi brothers (133, 121 BCE), Saturninus (100 BCE), Drusus (91 BCE), and Clodius (52 BCE) – were murdered, most likely by their fellow elites. Indeed, the last century of the Republic, roughly from 145 BCE to 49 BCE, is often interpreted in terms of an escalating ideological conflict between oligarchic (*optimates*) and democratic (*populares*) factions, but, unlike in Athens, with the wealthy few consistently winning out over the masses. The Roman republic was certainly extraordinarily unequal in material terms, a situation that the introduction of the tribunes did little to alter. Indeed, it seems probable that as Rome expanded its control across the Mediterranean during the Middle Republic period (c. 264–146 BCE), the divergence between haves and have nots widened. The final sacking of Rome's great Mediterranean rival, the North African city of Carthage, in 146 BCE produced yet more spoils for the elite to divide among themselves. While the rich were waited on hand and foot, peasants and proles barely eked out a living. Given this economic and political inequality, it is tempting to interpret the rise to prominence of Tiberius Gracchus, perhaps the most famous tribune of the plebs, as a consequence of discontent from below. His actions in office – most notably the redistribution of land – certainly give the impression of a man elevated by, and motivated by, reformist sentiment. Yet such a class-based interpretation would be to misunderstand the nature of Roman politics. Tiberius Gracchus appealed to the crowd because it was the most cost-effective strategy available to him.[28]

Although the tribunes technically had to be plebians themselves, in practice they too were elites, even if typically more part of the *nouveau riche* than the traditional nobility. Indeed, on rare occasion, as in the case of Publius Clodius

Pulcher in 59 BCE, a *patrician* could renounce his status in a special ceremony in order to stand for election as a tribune of the plebs. Tiberius Gracchus came from a patrician family of the highest order. He was the son of Cornelia, and through her, grandson of the legendary Roman general, Scipio Africanus. After serving as military tribute in Africa under Scipio Amelianus – the son of Scipio Africanus – and as quaestor in Spain, he returned to Rome in 133 BCE to contest the election for tribune of the plebs. Although not part of the *cursus honorum* that led ultimately to the consulship, the office of tribune was well known as a means for a politician to increase his name recognition and status among the people, advantages to be used later in the cutthroat elections for higher office that would inevitably follow. Indeed, many elites sought the office of tribune when the more direct route to praetorian or consular office was cut off to them by their rivals. When Sulla restricted the powers of the tribune during his dictatorship (82–79 BCE), he was less concerned with suppressing the masses per se than with the demagogues who sought to use them to come to power outside the established elite channels.

Tiberius' turn to the tribunate was propelled, at least in part, by the Senate's rejection of what its aristocratic members deemed a humiliating surrender to Numantian forces that Tiberius negotiated in 136 BCE. Tiberius may have been justified in accepting onerous terms in order to save his centurions' lives, but for the senators this was no excuse. Although Tiberius was not without friends in the Senate, henceforth he did not have a wide enough network of supporters among the elite for a purely insider strategy to make it to the upper reaches of power. As a result, he had little left to lose by posing as a champion of the plebs – a *popularis*. On winning office as tribune, Tiberius proposed sweeping land reforms that would redistribute the *ager publica* – state lands nominally acquired by Rome following a military conquest, but which in practice had long since come under the effective dominion of the aristocracy. According to Plutarch, writing in the first century CE, Tiberius was appalled at the parlous state of the peasantry as he traveled through Etruria, observing that "they have not a single clod of earth that is their own." Whether the *Lex Sempronia Agraria* was motivated out of intrinsic sympathy for the plight of the poor, or perhaps more likely, as the second–century Greek historian Appian suggests, out of concern for the declining capacity of the Roman military, which depended on a robust free rural population for the majority of its recruitment, it was clear that the legislation would win Tiberius Gracchus tremendous credit with the masses. Indeed, Plutarch himself also tells us that a major motivation in taking up the issue of land reform was Tiberius's desire to outdo "in fame and influence" his political rivals.[29]

Whatever the motivation, such a de facto redistribution of wealth could hardly fail to alienate the landholding elite. Most likely anticipating some resistance, Tiberius had eschewed tradition by refusing to consult with the Senate on his bill, putting the legislation directly to the people for a vote instead. The Senate enlisted one of Tiberius' fellow tribunes, Marcus Octavius, possibly with the inducement of a bribe or the promise of future electoral support, to veto the legislation. Tiberius then proposed an even more redistributive version of the law, which Octavius again vetoed. This obstructionism was, of course, within the purview of Octavius' office, but Tiberius countered that the plebian veto should be used only when it truly reflected the interests of the plebs themselves. Tiberius was in effect claiming that the people's will stood above the law, and, just as critically, that he had the exclusive right to say what the "people's will" was. He took the unprecedented step of putting forth legislation that would remove Octavius from office. Octavius refused to back down, but the people supported both of the Gracchan measures, first removing Octavius and then passing the land reform bill. However, implementation of the reforms was a different matter. Fearing that his successors might undermine his legacy before it had a chance to take effect, Tiberius again violated tradition by running for the office of tribune for a successive year. The intra-elite contest for prestige and fame now became a battle of the streets. Tiberius and his supporters took over the temple on the Capitoline Hill, where voting was due to take place, while the Senate gathered its forces. Led by Cornelius Scipio Nasica, the *pontifex maximus*, Rome's highest priest, who shouted "[l]et those who would save our country follow me," an armed mob marched on the Capitol, scattered Tiberius' followers, slayed the famous tribune, and dumped his mangled body in the Tiber River.[30]

The experience of Gaius Gracchus, elected tribune of the plebs in 123 and 122 BCE, is almost an exact replica of that of his older brother; after a short but high-profile political career, the younger man met an equally grisly end with his slave slitting his throat as the armed retinue of the elite trailed him in hot pursuit. We need not delay too long on the details other than to note that Gaius' crime, in the view of his elite opponents, was to take up the *popularis* mantle of his brother, extending the land reform program and proposing an "unprecedented" grain dole for the urban poor. What is relevant about both Tiberius and Gaius Gracchus for our purposes is the way that each sought to mobilize the populace directly, using the mass communication technology of the time, the public oration, to gain prestige and power. Gaius in particular was renowned as having an "incomparable power in oratory," making other speakers in the city "appear to be no better than children." Although their rivals at the time described them as tyrants in the making, both of the Gracchi were, I would argue, simply making full use of the tools available to them within Rome's institutional set up. Populism, for them, was the economically rational strategy.[31]

Roman politics was a compact in which the elite sought dominance and status over one another. This applied equally well to those aligned with the *optimates* or senatorial faction as it did to those who supposedly appealed directly to the masses, the *populares* faction. In her classic book on the Late Republic, *Party Politics in the Age of Caesar*, Lily Ross Taylor writes that "the *optimates* were working for the maintenance of an oligarchy while the great figures who adopted popular methods were usually attempting to establish personal supremacy." In other words, even if the *populares* might seem the more democratic, as the representatives of the many against the few, such an appearance is misleading. Examples of *optimates* like Cato expanding the grain dole along with supposed *populares* like Caesar reducing it, illustrate the challenge of any policy-based classification. Not even the best-known *populares* such as Tiberius proposed the kind of radical constitutional reform that would give more power to the people. That the oligarchic Senate supported Marcus Livius Drusus as an alternative to Gaius Gracchus, even though Drusus proposed an even more ambitious colonial land distribution program, is evidence of the slippery nature of any group classification.[32]

Ultimately, the factional conflict within the elite was less a clash of values than one of tactics. What distinguished the *populares* was that they set themselves up to use the people as a weapon in the contest for intra-elite dominance. Classical historian Robert Morstein-Marx concludes that "there was, in fact, no *overt*, fundamental clash of political ideology" between so-called *optimates* and *populares*, but a contest between elites over the claim to embody the interests of "the people." In a recent reexamination of the sources, Henrik Mouritsen concludes that while we can speak of a *ratio popularis* – a populist strategy – it is fairly meaningless to speak of the *populares* as a well-identified political group. As historian Christian Meier wrote, the *populares* "had no common cause," except to "oil the popular apparatus in order to make use of it." Roman historian and ally of Julius Caesar, Sallust, probably had it about right when he wrote that whether an aspiring leader claimed to be "defending the rights of the people" or to be upholding "the prestige of the Senate," he was "in reality ... working for his own advancement." As in Athens, political conflict was not a matter of policy but of individual and familial rivalry. Historian Richard Alston argues that it's more productive to interpret Roman society in terms of networks of power and influence, centered around rival elites, rather than through the artificially modern lens of class, or even more anachronously, political parties. Moreover, although there were intricate and widespread networks of family, marriage, and patronage binding members of the elite class to one another, self-interest was always the primary consideration. In fact, an often-overlooked consequence of the breakout of peace with the fall of Carthage in 146 BCE was that the Roman elite, characteristically united in a time of war, could henceforth turn their competitive spirits inward.[33]

Winning high office in this context demanded a combination of elite coalition building, the distribution of patronage, and popularity with the crowd. Given the even greater concentration of wealth and smaller electorates in Rome than in Athens, high office could, at a stretch, be bought. In 54 BCE, two of the candidates for the consulship offered ten million *sesterces* for the vote of the *prerogativa*, the influential first vote publicly cast in the *comitia centuriata*, the assembly that voted for the military offices of consul and praetor. Indeed, there even existed a semi-formal structure for this kind of electoral bribery, with agents known as *divisores*, who organized the distribution of cash or goods to voters in tribes and centuries. *Sequestres* had a similar function, but as the Latin root of our work sequester suggests, they would typically hold on to the "gift" until the outcome of the election or trial in question was known. Elections were often highly competitive and the people could have a decisive say. The large sums spent on winning the votes of the masses, whether directly through cash or indirectly through games, feasts, or other club goods is indicative of just how much their votes mattered. Yet prevalent as bribery and patronage were in Rome, money alone was usually insufficient for predominance. The once dominant view that the Roman masses were tied to their betters in dense patron-client networks has now been largely discarded. Patronage alone was not a source of enduring partisan loyalties as Crassus, Rome's richest man, and the third of the famous ruling triumvirate that also included Pompey and Caesar, discovered. Crassus could buy tremendous influence among the elite, on several occasions bankrolling the ambitious Caesar, but he was unable to turn this into political preeminence. More broadly, large scale land redistribution and grain doles of the sort proposed by the Gracchi could buy the temporary affections of the masses, but neither man was able to make the transition toward building a more loyal mass base. Caesar, and even more so Augustus, would learn from these failings.[34]

As a result of the challenges of patronage-based party building, some direct popular appeal was typically necessary for any member of the elite looking to rise to the top. Even Cicero was not above pandering to the "wretched starveling rabble that comes to meetings and sucks the treasury dry" when it suited his needs. Cicero, the upwardly mobile *novus homo*, assiduously cultivated his popularity with the crowd on his way up the ladder, only to turn against it with the viciousness of a reverse snob in his later years. Cicero earned himself a reputation as a "deserter" for his tendency to sometimes side with the people and sometimes with the elite. We have no reason to think the Gracchi, far more blue-blooded than Cicero, would have done otherwise had they lived longer. Appealing to the people was especially important for elites who lacked a sufficient winning coalition of support within the ruling elite. *Populares* like the Gracchi were those elites who lacked sufficient *amici* – friends in high places. The Gracchi came from within the elite but were not those with the densest network of political connections. What they sought was advancement. Gaius Gracchus himself, the supposed champion of the people, articulated this realpolitik logic more clearly than most. Democrats may not be what they seem. "Citizens," said Gaius, "if you wish to employ your wisdom and courage, you will find, even if you search, that none of us comes forward here without his price. All of us, who make speeches, are looking for something, nor does anyone come before you unless he may take something away." In Gaius' case, what he was looking for was "a good reputation and achievement." Behind those popular appeals, moreover, as Gaius' acknowledged, came an implied threat to take something from the people if their demands were not met. We thus need not assume that the Gracchi, or any of the other rabble-rousing tribunes who followed them, were bent on social revolution. None proposed a radical redistribution of power. Similarly, as we'll see, Caesar, though he claimed descent from the gods themselves, was born into a patrician line down on its fortunes. Patronage and populism were then, as now, strategic substitutes.[35]

Popular support was an important legitimating tool over which elites fought. The elite Senate often sought to coordinate in order to prevent the undue rise to prominence of one of their own, but patrician networks being as fragmented as they were, loyalties and alliances among them were fragile and fleeting. This fragmentation of the elite left a perpetual opening for aspiring politicians willing and able to exploit it. As historian Erich Gruen concludes in *The Last Generation of the Roman Republic*, "ambitious politicians could capitalize on discontents to promote their own careers and to shake the establishment." This didn't necessarily mean, as Gruen argued, that populists had to win away the disaffected plebian clients of the elite. Rather, most potential supporters were already *available* with few of those in the lower and even middle social rungs having any attachment to the senatorial class. Henrik Mouritsen estimates that the "popular" followings of the Gracchi and other populists may have been no more than a few thousand men. Populist mobilization could buy influence on the cheap. *Popularis* politics was a "technique," a "method" more than a motive.[36]

CROWD CONTROL IN THE ROMAN REPUBLIC

Even if we now have some idea of why members of an essentially closed Roman elite might be tempted to appeal to the masses, we haven't yet looked at how they did this. In a world without mass communications technology like radio and television and in a world of minimal literacy, what means did populists employ? Looking at the final years of the Roman Republic, we'll see two tactics that stand out. Roman politics was fundamentally based on face-to-face communication, and on the dissemination of reputation by rumor and gossip, within the public space of the forum. Although late Republican Rome was closer in form to a nation-state dominated by its capital than a simple city-state, its political system remained calcified in its earlier form. The first technique of mass mobilization was, as in Athens, the public oration. Roman assemblies did not work in the same way as Greek ones. The people did not listen to, or participate in, a debate between rival elites and then proceed to cast their votes. The process of voting was deliberately separated from the submission of legislation. New laws had to be publicly displayed for several weeks prior to a vote to dissipate the possibility that legislation would be passed by rousing up the crowd. Yet the lead up to a legislative vote was accompanied by regular public argument. A tribune proposing a new law, would in the *contio*, or public gathering in the forum, present his case to the assembled masses. Sometimes, an opponent of the law, perhaps a *praetor*, *aedile*, or even an ex-officio leader, would be given a chance to put his case, but more often, these were one-sided presentations. Yet even if the people were not formally entitled to speak, this did not mean that the people were mere passive observers. They could cheer. They could heckle. Even more cruelly, sometimes they could be silent altogether. Increasingly in the late Republic, politicians sought to control the composition of the audience, turning the *contio* into something resembling a political rally. In this sense, the *contiones* presented a way for speakers to demonstrate their popularity – the focus being on mobilizing partisans rather than persuading neutrals. Yet the point remains that politicians could and did communicate directly with the non-elite population to advance their careers.[37]

Popular tribunes like Clodius were masters of the *contio*. His case, however, also illustrates the limits of public oratory in Roman politics. In spite of the reputation of Clodius as an inveterate demagogue that has come down to us through his nemesis, Cicero, his early political career was completely in line with the dictates of traditional patrician decorum, the *mos maiorum*. Clodius, however, was badly tainted by the Bona Dea scandal of 62 BCE, a part religious, part sexual affair in which Clodius was alleged to have dressed up as a woman to gain access to this mysterious, all-female rite. Clodius was acquitted, in part through bribery of the jury, but his prospects for an *optimate* route to power through the backing of the Senate's elite henceforth looked dim. Cicero, never one to miss an opportunity to gain publicity at another's expense, continued to heap scorn on the young patrician. In part to escape Rome, Clodius sought and won election to the quaestorship for the year 60 BCE, but perhaps sensing that this was as high as his senatorial revivals would let him climb up the *cursus honorum*, he then sought to renounce his noble status. This act, engineered by the triumvirate of Caesar, Pompey, and Crassus – in part to strike a blow at their rival, Cicero – opened up the office of tribune of the plebs for Clodius, which he took in the year 59 BCE.

Clodius may have owed his ascent to triumvirate machinations, but he also recognized that he could potentially gain power in his own right by remaking himself as the people's champion. His legislative program, which included a provision for the distribution of grain, won him enormous popularity. A dedicated band of followers, the *Clodiani*, gathered around the tribune. As an example of the kind of politicized *collegia* – social or occupational groups – that proliferated in the Late Republic, the *Clodiani* were motivated not just by ties of patronage but also by the popular, raucous, and social nature of the movement itself, and were often willing to deploy violence on his behalf. Cicero's continued opposition pushed Clodius further in a demagogic direction. If Cicero had the support of the *optimates*, Clodius had no choice but to gravitate toward the *populares* triumvirate and its mass support base. With their backing, in 58 BCE, Clodius successfully pushed Cicero into exile for the latter's role in executing the chief conspirators of the infamous Catiline coup. Clodius, buoyed by his success in banishing the famous Cicero, then turned against his one-time backers, Pompey and Caesar. In the years that followed, the gloves decidedly came off, with competition between rival factions often playing out in pitched street fights. Clodius eventually fell at the hands of a rival's gang in 52 BCE. With legitimate forms of popular participation limited, appealing so directly to the mob in Rome remained a deeply fraught approach.

If talk was cheap, and mobilization on the street risky, there was another other more acceptable if expensive set of populist tactics available. In the movie *Gladiator*, albeit set in the early empire rather than in the Republic, one senator is observed remarking to another that Emperor Commodus "knows what Rome is. Rome is the mob. Conjure magic for them and they'll be distracted. Take away their freedom and still they'll roar. The beating heart of Rome is not the marble of the Senate. It's the sand of the Colosseum. He'll bring them death. And they will love him for it." The real-life Commodus – emperor from 161 to 192 CE – threw some of the most lavish games in history, and in a first for a politician of such stature, participated himself. Along with the grain dole, public entertainment would become one of the twin pillars of popular support for the empire in Rome, the Roman people wanting "bread and circuses" above all in the poet Juvenal's famous phrase. Of course, for Republican-era politicians like Caesar, the same kind of overt cultivation of a personality cult as pursued by Commodus was not possible. But putting on spectacular events still contributed to a man's public esteem. As Cicero put it, public events where the crowds gathered could be barometers of "[t]he popular feeling." Reputations could be won in the arenas, and politicians were not above manipulating the crowd. Cicero noted that some ambitious politicians would hire a kind of professional cheering squad to try to start chants and abuse political opponents. Acclaim from the crowd could be "worthless and corrupt," but authenticity hardly mattered. Exploiting the interactive nature of group psychology, popularity could be contagious.[38]

Games, parades, and festivals were not inexpensive. Most of the costs, however, were borne from the public rather than the private purse – or rather from the fruits of military victories abroad. Pompey's Triumph – the festival accorded to a general who achieved a noted military victory – in 61 BCE was so splendid and magnificent, according to Plutarch, that it took two days. Wild beasts, chests of gold, and of course prisoners awaiting public execution, were all part of the ceremony. Pompey further used the spoils of his victorious war against the Pontic King Mithridates to construct Rome's first permanent theatre, which naturally, was eponymous. On occasion, a politician could risk his whole private wealth on such an endeavor. In 65 BCE, still early in his political career, Seutonius tells us that as *aedile* Julius Caesar "made for the amusement of the people," entertaining "them with the hunting of wild beasts, and with games." Caesar assumed the entire expense himself, such that even though the events were nominally run with his co-aedile, Marcus Bibilus, Caesar got all the credit – Caesar would outshine his rival so much that when he shared the consulship with Bibilus, wags quipped that they were in "the consulship of Julius and Caesar" instead of "Bibilus and Caesar." True enough, in putting on the games, Caesar exceeded his budget and went into some debt, but subsequently given a military command abroad, he soon earned the money back; for the populist, lavish spending on public entertainment, in other words, was a calculated investment. Caesar's gambit continued to pay off. In 63 BCE, he spent unrestrainedly to win election to the important ceremonial position of *Pontifex Maximus* – head of the state religious order. Had he failed to secure this prestigious position, Caesar feared he would have to go into exile to escape his creditors. Populism was a risky strategy in Rome, and hardly one without its costs, but for those elites marginalized by the Senate, it was perhaps the best option to achieve their ambitions.[39]

POPULISM AND ORGANIZATION

Caesar is undoubtedly the best known of the so-called *populares*. He was a gifted orator, like Cicero, developing his early reputation in the law courts. Yet he equally well understood propaganda by deed. Aside from throwing lavish games, Caesar sought popularity with the Roman masses in other ways. Barred from the popular office of tribune of the plebs himself as a patrician, he supported a slate of *populares* for the office, most notably Clodius. In this way he connected himself with the popular policy issues of subsidized grain distribution as well as the allocation of land to urban colonists. Caesar also exploited better than anyone else the propaganda effect of military success. In a strategy presaging that of Napoleon Bonaparte in the 1790s, Caesar sent back glowing – if not always factual – reports from the front in Gaul. Written in the third person, the accounts, sometimes by Caesar and sometimes by a ghost author, are a testament to his very modern understanding of the value of political image. Caesar also minted commemorative coins with his family's likenesses. Seemingly never shy of telling audiences of his descent from the gods through his mother, Caesar sought to be more than a man. He studiously cultivated his charisma.[40]

However, much as Caesar's early rise was in line with the populist strategy of other *populares*, exploiting the weapon of a directly mobilized crowd, the last years of his rise to power mark a modification of approach. That is, Caesar appears to have intuited the limitations of a pure populist strategy of relying only on the plebs. His elite rivals in the Senate had demonstrated an eagerness to dispose of political upstarts by violent means; Caesar would have been a fool not to have learned from the demise of fellow patricians such as the Gracchi, Drusus, Sulpicius, and Clodius. Had Caesar followed the Senate's instructions and returned to Rome from his proconsulship in Gaul in 50 BCE without the protection from prosecution provided by a new consular mandate, it is not difficult to imagine that he would have met a similar fate. Caesar thus embarked on a historically novel, mixed strategy, intuiting that he had to draw on the institutional foundations provided by the Roman state to build a more stable base of support, one that could protect him from the vicissitudes of intra-elite conflict. But how to do it?

Elite politics were too factionalized to build an enduring mass party around the distribution of patronage alone. Most of the patrician elite was so wealthy that they could remain aloof from such commitments, while the *equitores* – members of the mercantile class who were dependent on patronage in the form of state contracts – were not politically influential enough to overcome senatorial resistance. At the same time, Caesar could not form a modern, bureaucratic party either. One thing that the present-day analyst must appreciate when probing Rome, Athens, or most any other classical civilization for political lessons, is that private corporate entities in the way we know them had not yet come to exist. Although not much noted today, a key feature of an organization like a political party is its corporate personhood. While we sometimes tend to think of parties as a representation of underlying "interests," they are first and foremost *organizations*. A true political party is an organization that exists separately of its members and that has its own legal rights, especially that of ownership.

The Romans could and did conceive of the idea of corporate personhood. However, the elite energetically restricted the formation of such organizations. If the *collegia* were at one time state-sanctioned occupational associations – akin to guilds – by the Late Republic, many collegia, like the *Clodiani*, operated on (or over) the edge of legality as the quasi-gangs of influential patrons. That is, to the extent that there were political "organizations" in the late Republic, they were fundamentally personalistic rather than bureaucratic. There was no legal corporate model for a political organization based on blood, marriage, and patronage to utilize. The analogous commercial corporation had not been created, not because it could not be imagined but because it was not needed. Power and wealth were personal. Institutional forms, such as the corporation sole, are created when they are required by people with the appropriate sources of power. The elite in Athens and Rome had little need for long-lived organizations (economic, political, or otherwise). As long as assets – including the privilege accorded to aristocratic birth – could be passed from one generation to the next, there was no need to make alterations to the existing framework of property rights. In the commerial realm, partnerships and family ownership were the preffered ownership structures, and political associations took an analagous form.[41]

The corporation as an organizational form developed only with the institutionalization of the church. As the Roman Catholic Church's wealth grew in the centuries after the Emperor Constantine's conversion in the fourth century CE, the problem of how to keep this property within the church, rather than in the persons of its vicars, necessitated the corporate form. Autonomous corporate entities were just not needed in the ancient world and so the legal institutional framework to construct a party in the modern sense didn't exist. Indeed, by creating the opportunity for a separate class of professional politicians –

distinct from amateur aristocrats – institutions of this sort would have threatened the very structural power of the elite.

Without the option of creating a bureaucratic political party, Caesar instead built on two other sources of institutional authority. In part, once he had won the civil war that raged from the crossing of the Rubicon in 49 until 45 BCE, he began to draw legitimacy from the main model of rule in the ancient world – monarchy. Already by 44 BCE he had begun to think seriously about succession, and had he not been assassinated, one might suppose that he would have made the accession to power of his grandnephew and heir, Octavian, less bloody and traumatic than it turned out to be. But the adoption of the monarchical form was very much incomplete by 44 BCE. Caesar, after all, felt compelled to turn down the diadem publicly offered to him by Mark Antony shortly before his murder that year. Caesar's main institutional turn was not toward a Tarquinian-style monarchy but toward an historically novel military dictatorship.

Caesar's main political innovation was not just to combine popularity with force – this Marius had already done in the 90s – but to build an institutional basis for his rule. What Caesar did, in short, was to demonstrate the power of a personal political organization. Caesar grounded his authority in the Roman Army, the latter's importance deriving not just from its coercive role over the populace of Rome, which was minimal, but from the fact that soldiers and veterans, along with their dependents, accounted for a sizeable proportion of the Roman populace itself. It was not just a question of muscle power in other words. His legions were not simply, or even, a private army as has often been proposed. Caesar patronized the Army. Even as he rationalized the budget by reducing eligibility for the subsidized grain dole, he lavished resources on the Army. Caesar's legions, and eventually the Roman Army at large, had become a constituency that would support Caesar as he made the transition from populist to popular dictator.

That Caesar could ground his support in the Army in this way was the result of a long process of militarization. Many other ancient kingdoms and city-states had large armies, but never before were these simultaneously professional and citizen armies. Already by 200 BCE, Livy notes that for some men, service in the Roman Army was in effect a career; but overall, the Army at this stage was still far from being a fully professionalized institution. From the turn of the first century BCE, however, two processes pushed Rome strongly in this direction. First, the empire's accelerating geographical expansion – both east toward Asia Minor and west into Spain and Gaul increased the financial resources available to successful generals and provincial governors. It was the perennially successful general and many-time *plebian* consul, Gaius Marius, who began explicitly distributing the spoils of war – especially land – to his soldiers, with the result that with him, the soldiery began to develop partisan ties with their commanders. Second, some years later, the outbreak of the Social War (91–87 BCE) – in effect a civil war initiated by non-Roman Italians demanding equality of status within the Empire – increased both the demand and supply of (non-Roman Italian) manpower for the Army. In short, through these processes, the Roman army increased massively in size and became increasingly professionalized. There thus developed a separate and large organized interest group that materially benefited from continued military expansion, and that in turn, supported the bellicose politician-generals who would deliver it.[42]

Sulla was the first to take advantage of the developments pioneered by his rival Marius, marching his legions on Rome; the purpose being to prevent his legions being stripped of the opportunity for booty that had been their promised reward for taking part in Sulla's proposed campaign in the east. Sulla, though he established a temporary dictatorship, which executed or exiled Marius' supporters, did not seek to have a popular one. Sulla was rather *primus inter pares* among the senatorial, oligarchic elite. He emasculated the tribunes and demobilized the plebs. Caesar's status was clearly different. If by the 50s, both Pompey and Caesar were able to richly reward those who served under them, both in cash and land, each had a quite different relationship to the rest of the senatorial elite. Although Pompey flirted with the masses, as an awkward speaker, he never established a genuine rapport with the mob. Caesar, in contrast, because he *could* and *did* appeal to the masses, was viewed as an unacceptable threat by the senatorial elite. Caesar's relationship with his legions was thus of necessity of a different and higher order of importance. Unlike Sulla or Pompey, he needed the legions more than they needed him. The point here, as I noted, is not that Caesar sought to build a up private army geared toward an assault on power but as a political base. Although critics have sometimes accused Caesar of seeking early on to emulate Sulla's coup d'état, there is little in the historical record to suggest this was actually the case. Rather, Caesar was using the resources gained by imperial expansion to buffet his *political* network. Soldiers and veterans were studiously cultivated as a significant political constituency. When Cato led the *optimate* objection to Caesar's proposed distribution of land to Pompey's veterans in 59 BCE, the Senate could only seem reactionary to the grunts who made up the bulk of the legions. What Caesar did was to establish a large-scale and enduring patronage network around the Army for the first time. By the time Caesar crossed the Rubicon in 49 BCE, the Army was by far the largest political organization in Rome. The result of this was that military dictatorship, not democracy, would become the prevailing political order. With Caesar's assassination in 46 BCE, power devolved to those who could marshal military power. The era of warlordism only came to an end with Octavian's victory over Mark Antony in 29 BCE. Octavian – Augustus from 27 BCE – reinstituted what was a monarchy in all but name. After decades of war and deprivation, Romans were content to exchange order for liberty.[43]

The cases I've examined in this chapter can seem pretty far removed from modern concerns. Of course, Athens and Rome are intrinsically fascinating.

But I think we can in fact also learn something more general from these cases. The founders of the American and French Republics, some of whom we'll encounter in Chapter 3, were not shy in drawing lessons from them, and we shoudn't be either. What is most interesting to me is how intrinsic populism was to these early examples of democracy. Populism and democracy, to an extent, went hand in hand. The politically ambitious everywhere seek power at the lowest cost. In an era before democracy this was done by assembling networks of elite partners and their armed dependents until a large enough force to outdo all rival alliances could be mustered. The most successful institutionalized their rule as divinely ordained kings, but staying at the top of this pyramidal system was a delicate balancing act. Unless rival elites were appeased, they could upset the system, styling themselves as champions of the people – as democratic revolutionaries.

Even with full or partial democratization, support among the elite mattered, and continued to be a path to power. The noble and wealthy controlled substantial clienteles. Power could still be bought through these networks. However, for those without such connections, or who lacked the resources to do so, support had to be sought in a different way. Populism was always a latent possibility. The very institutions of classical democracy created just the right conditions for populism to flourish. By assembling masses of people together in a single place, whether the assembly or the forum, the ancient democracies and republics made direct appeals to the people cost effective. Going around the intermediary structures of clan and patronage, populism was an economically efficient strategy for elites excluded from the insider path to power.

3

After the Revolution

Every party is then criminal, because it is a form of isolation from the people and the popular societies, a form of independence from the government. Every faction is then criminal, because it tends to divide the citizens; every faction is criminal because it neutralizes the power of public virtue ... The sovereignty of the people demands that the people be unified; it is therefore opposed to factions, and all faction is a criminal attack on sovereignty.

Louis Antoine Saint-Just[1]

Solicitations for office are the most painful incidents to which an executive magistrate is exposed. The ordinary affairs of a nation offer little difficulty to a person of any experience, but the gift of office is the dreadful burthen which oppresses him.

Thomas Jefferson[2]

POLITICAL SHOCKS

On April 5, 1794, Georges-Jacques Danton, perhaps the greatest orator of the French Revolution, breathed his last; the Revolution, like Saturn – as Pierre Victurnien Vergniaud declared shortly before he too was sent to the guillotine with his Girondin allies – devouring its young. Danton's rise and fall epitomized the vacuum of political authority created by the Revolution. The overthrow of the Bourbon monarchy violently disrupted the costs of different types of political strategy. Unmoored from the repressive political networks of the *Ancien Régime*, the masses were open for direct mobilization – they were *available*. Within a few years of the famous July 14, 1789, storming of the Bastille, Danton, a mere provincial lawyer, had exploited the power of the mob in the radical Parisian *arrondissements* around the Cordeliers section to make himself France's leading politician. Staying at the top, however, proved to be an insurmountable challenge.[3]

For the elite, mass mobilization is always a double-edged sword. As we saw in the ancient world, the masses – the mob – can be a potent weapon against one's elite enemies. But the crowd can be fickle. The French revolutionary leadership lacked an enduring model of mass incorporation. Their deep suspicions of independent executive power, which too closely resembled monarchy itself, led them to create a weak and incoherent collective form of rule. The resources of the state were not used to build the kinds of parties that might have monopolized executive power. The result was recurrent populism from the margins, until the coup of 18 Brumaire, 1799, when Napoleon Bonaparte realized a Caesarean path to power that combined mass popularity with the armed imposition of order.

Consider now the other great democratic revolution of the late eighteenth century. In the American case, the first elevation of even a quasi-populist to national power – Andrew Jackson – took half a century from the Declaration of Independence in 1776. With the patronage-based Jacksonian party system taking root in the 1830s, no other populist or quasi-populist even came close to power until William Jennings Bryan won the joint presidential nomination of the Democratic Party and the People's Party in 1896. Bryan in turn went down in a resounding defeat, with the Republican Party hold on the presidency broken only once between then and the election of FDR in 1932. Not even the massively popular former president, Theodore Roosevelt, who ran as a third-party candidate in 1912, could crack the entrenched party duopoly. Although the French and American revolutions occurred almost contemporaneously, and even though political events on both sides of the Atlantic were deeply intertwined, the two upheavals turned out very differently with respect to populism. Why?

One possibility is ideology. By this logic, the democracy produced by the French Revolution was more radical but less liberal than its American counterpart. For sure, revolutionaries like Danton and Robespierre were unapologetic radicals. The pamphleteer and journalist, Jean-Paul Marat, perennially avowed his enthusiasm for "the cutting off of heads." Robespierre thought of his opponents as "monsters." However, such examples notwithstanding, most French revolutionaries were moderates rather than extremists. Moreover, there is little evidence that American political thought was obviously more conservative than French philosophizing of the time. The English-born, radical republican pamphleteer Thomas Paine would be lauded and imprisoned in France in turn, but his initial fame was won in America. Similarly, at the level of ideas and at least his early writing, Thomas Jefferson could be every inch the utopian that was Robespierre. Even as heads started to roll in the streets of Paris, Jefferson wrote to a Virginia friend, "[m]y own affections have been deeply wounded by some of the martyrs to this cause, but rather than it should have failed, I would have seen half the earth desolated. Were there but an Adam and an Eve left in every country, and left free, it would be better than as it now is." Jefferson viewed a violent anti-tax revolt by farmers in Massachusetts in 1786 known as Shays' Rebellion with equal equanimity, writing to his friend and protégé, James Madison, that "a little rebellion now and then is a good thing," and to another confidant that "[t]he tree of liberty must be refreshed from time to time with the blood of patriots and tyrants. It is its natural manure." Jefferson, acolyte of the Enlightenment that he was, saw his opponents as monocrats, as tyrants, as illegitimate. "Liberty or death" was a cry of American and French patriots alike.[4]

Setting ideas aside, this chapter asks whether the conditions affecting the relative cost of populist and non-populist political strategies in each case might instead explain the differing outcomes. Although the corporate form had long since come to exist in the commercial world, in neither the French nor the American case was there anything like a programmatic party in existence at the time that their respective revolutions broke out. However, there was a critical difference between the two cases. Parties of a sort had existed in Britain at least since the Glorious Revolution in 1688. Although the Tory and Whig parties of that era did not have anything like fixed corporate personhoods, being associations or affiliations rather than organizations as such, these parliamentary entities formed the basis of the broader factional groupings that would eventually become patronage-based political parties on both sides of the Atlantic.

To be clear, prior to the American Revolution, mass parties were not yet in existence. What did exist were groups of elites with ample experience of contesting elections, forming legislative coalitions, and distributing patronage. Americans had in place the basis for a patronage-based party structure. Such proto-democratic parties did not exist in France prior to its Revolution. Because America and France began their democratic revolutions with very different prior conditions, patronage became a cost-effective strategy for forging factions into parties in the former, but not the latter, where populism would instead predominate.

THE *VOLONTÉ GÉNÉRALE*

Any explanation for why populism – the direct mobilization of the people – came to be a successful strategy in revolutionary France must take account of both context and contingency. The French Revolution has become notorious for its bloodletting, but its early steps were moderate enough. Like the American Revolution that preceded it, underlying much of its radical rhetoric was the opposition to pullulating royal taxes. The Estates General, called into being in 1789 after an absence of more than 170 years to address the government's budget crisis, entailed millions of Frenchmen voting and competing in what were probably the most broad-based democratic elections in history to that time. Liberal nobles and commoners alike were agreed on the goal of a constitutional monarchy, even if the representatives of the three estates – clergy, nobles, and commoners – disagreed on how power should be distributed among them. Fearing its marginalization, the Third Estate – that of the commoners – proclaimed itself a National Constituent Assembly, and before long, the clergy and – more reluctantly – the nobles joined it. Urged on by a populace increasingly restive in the face of food shortages, inflation, and widespread brigandage, the Assembly constituted itself as a provisional government, and in a spasm of self-sacrifice on August 4 that many aristocrats soon came to regret, swept away the old feudal system from top to bottom. However, forfeiting this early momentum and relative harmony, the Assembly took more than two further years to produce the Constitution it had tasked itself with creating. In this state of institutional suspended animation, political organization remained ephemeral; petty, personalistic factions competed among themselves for power.

Unlike in America, as we'll see, these factions were never united into coherent proto-party blocs. *Ancien Régime* France, in spite of its relative wealth and political sophistication, did not provide fertile territory for the formation of patronage-based political parties. Prior to the Revolution, neither the aristocracy nor ordinary people had much of a say in the absolutist French political system. The Estates General, France's feudal system of representation in which the three orders were consulted on fiscal and foreign policy, had not met since 1614.

The thirteen provincial *parlements* – most notably that of Paris, which covered half the country – had more independent authority. Their membership was drawn almost exclusively from the aristocracy and the *parlements* were often a source of resistance to the absolutist pretentions of the crown. However, having their origins in Germanic (Gaulish) moot courts, the primary function of the *parlements* was as appellate courts, not as legislative assemblies. The Parlement de Paris was required to register (i.e., approve) royal laws and edicts, but its members were typically more interested in using this leverage to limit their tax exposure than to promote the welfare of the common man. Much as some *parlementaires* sought to characterize themselves as champions of liberty against royal absolutism, this claim rang hollow in the face of their rigid defence of their own privileges. The *parlements*' refusal to countenance the imposition of taxes on their elite memberships proposed by Louis XV and Louis XVI signaled their near total autonomy from below, and as it proved, contributed to the revolutionary upheaval that followed. The *parlements* – despite the name – were thus in no sense proto-democratic institutions on which conservative political factions or parties might build.

The Assembly of Notables, convened by Louis XVI in 1787 for the first time since 1626 as an alternative to the ineffective *parlements* on the one hand, and to the more dramatic step of calling the Estates General on the other, proved no more up to the task forging coherent political blocs. As an ominous sign of what was to come, the notables on the Assembly found their leverage enhanced the more radical their rhetoric. However, not only did this alienate them from the monarch as a possible conservative medium of co-opting the masses in the fashion of the English aristocracy, but when the nobility found that it couldn't reconcile its position as both mobilizer of the masses and as defender of its own privileges, they found themselves cast off by the people too.

Even outside of these institutional forums, the aristocracy showed little inclination to develop mass political networks. By the late eighteenth century, there was no equivalent of the English or American parliamentary landed elite that had begun to incorporate the masses – even that thin sliver of the masses among whom we would count the petit bourgeois or the independent yeoman – as clients against each other or against an overbearing monarch. As mostly venal officeholders who bought their places from the crown, unlike their English contemporaries, members of the French provincial *parlements* didn't even have to cultivate – or even buy – the support of a small number of electors in their boroughs to win their place.

This is not to say that patrimonial links were unknown under the *Ancien Régime*; for instance, Maximilien Robespierre's education was sponsored by a local noble. Having a lawyer or another professional as a client was personally useful to a wealthy aristocrat, but a small number of ad hoc ties such as these did not constitute a political base. Moreover, as of 1789, the French aristocracy was, if anything, becoming increasingly detached from its rural roots. French rural society remained feudal in some respects, but it was becoming increasingly commercialized. Formal serfdom had long been abandoned, and unlike in Eastern Europe, there was a sizeable property-owning peasantry. But French nobles spent far more time earning the King's favor at court than in shoring up the loyalty of their rural clients. The richest nobles had migrated to Paris and Versailles and the lesser ones to regional cities. In short, as the eighteenth century drew to a close, the social ties that had once bound peasants to their *seigneurs* – ties of proximity if nothing else – had attenuated.[5]

Patronage-based mobilization or incorporation of the masses was further stifled by the radical course of France's revolution. A catastrophic sequence of harvests in the late 1780s, relentless tax impositions, and botched market liberalization, especially in the textiles sector, drove people to make frantic collective appeals for relief. The price of bread doubled in the year before the Revolution alone. Although Marie Antoinette likely never actually said the words, "let them eat cake," the perception that the *Autrichienne* (the Austrian bitch) and her aristocratic clique, if not the King himself, were to blame for the poor's plight was very real. The gains in dignity, but not yet wealth, that the Revolution brought to those at the bottom of the social hierarchy, meant that the masses very quickly outstripped the leadership in their radicalism. The people began to see economic restitution, social revolution – especially the removal of aristocratic and clerical privileges – and political reform as part of a package deal. Vicious, if low intensity, internecine conflicts roiled across much of the country from the Day of Tiles, a riot in Grenoble on June 7, 1788, more than a year before the better-known raid on the Bastille armory.

Even as agrarian conditions improved after a good autumn harvest in 1789 itself, the relief was only temporary. With the people ever vigilant to capitalize on the reduction of dues, tithes, and other burdens that they believed they had earned by their participation in the Revolution, the specter of domestic violence could never be far from the minds of France's political leaders. Through the media of newspapers and pamphlets, the masses were made ever alert to any sign of elite backsliding. The almost continuous publication of extremist polemics, like Jean-Paul Marat's newspaper *L'Ami du People*, kept the population at fever pitch. The alleged speculation and hoarding of merchants only heightened the sense of outrage. Just weeks after the passage through the Assembly of the famous August 26, 1789, Declaration of the Rights of Man, angry mobs still threatened to burn down the houses of waverers if they continued to seek to impose institutional checks on the *volonté genérale* – the people's will. The expropriation of church properties – the *biens nationaux* – might have furnished the means to tie men to a party of government, but the result was instead a disorganized feeding frenzy in which each man looked only to satisfy his own appetites.

Nevertheless, as the Assembly got down to work, it seemed as if liberal democracy might actually take root. The de facto government had not yet established control over France's varied and traditionally autonomous local administrations, but by the time of the Revolution's first anniversary, politically at least, the national leadership looked to have struck a moderate balance. Men of means, the bourgeoisie, dominated the Revolution's early trajectory; a mere 14,000 of Paris's 600,000 residents could vote in elections for the city's de facto government – the *Commune*. The city's elite sought to impose order, acclaiming the Marquis de Lafayette as commander of the city's militia – subsequently christened the National Guard. Lafayette's fame as a hero of the American Revolution, and thus a champion of liberty, was unsurpassed. If anyone could reimpose order, it would surely have been him. Yet even Lafayette found himself carried on by events. If he deserves credit for the limited bloodshed that accompanied the transfer of the King from Versailles to Paris in October 1789, that it occurred at all was an indication of the limited ability he had to lead the crowd. The Constitution adopted in 1791 was in the end a moderate one that sanctified property rights, limited the franchise, and retained the monarchy, even endowing the King with stronger veto powers than his British counterpart. Elections to national office were indirect, which tended to mitigate the importance of appeals to the masses. Paris remained a tinderbox, but Danton himself, in spite of his undoubted fame and popularity among Parisian radicals, could not even get elected to the National Assembly that first sat in 1792.

However, as a body without a head, the Assembly was a de facto government that was almost impossible to control. The exceptional case of the *ci-devant* noble, Honoré Gabriel Riqueti, comte de Mirabeau, one of the few aristocrats to root his power in his mass popularity, reinforces the point.

Mirabeau – a philanderer, adventurer, and all-round *enfant terrible* – was spurned by the nobility – including his father who had him imprisoned – before he became the most popular man in France in the early days of the Revolution. Mirabeau drew both on his oratorical skills within the Assembly and his general celebrity to dominate the early direction of revolutionary politics. Yet Mirabeau knew that popular appeals alone could not provide for governmental stability. He sought a constitutional monarchy with an independent executive – a system in which, without doubt, he saw himself as the King's first minister. Having established his reputation as a leader in the Assembly, he convinced Louis XVI that he was the King's best bet for retaining a modicum of control. With Louis' financial support, Mirabeau quietly restyled himself as a dispenser of royal patronage. At the height of his influence, he was reputed to have bought off up to a third of the Assembly. Yet because affiliation with the royalist faction could imply a death sentence depending on one's location, in a period in which ballots were still cast in the open, none of this could occur as overt patronage-party organization. The allegiances he bought were highly transactional and fragile. Mirabeau would not be able to replicate the strategy of British Whig leader, Robert Walpole. With Mirabeau's death and the King's execution, any prospect, however remote, of a "court party" being established was equally moribund. As politics radicalized over the early 1790s, regular electoral politics and party building had become all but impossible. The taming of the Assembly's earlier radicalism by the moderate Feuillant majority and the continued potential for an elitist counterrevolution by *émigrés* nobles who had fled the country only galvanized fanatics. Politics quite literally became "a blood sport."[6]

FRIENDS OF THE PEOPLE

For men of bourgeois or professional backgrounds, especially lawyers and other members of the intelligentsia, the discordance of the Revolution presented a tremendous opportunity. In economic terms, with no established political parties or patronage networks to compete against, the direct mobilization of the masses was a potentially cost-effect strategy for anyone who could build a public reputation through writing, speech, or action. There was a veritable explosion in the number of newspapers with the lifting of censorship in the wake of the Revolution. The *Moniteur* quickly established itself as the paper of record, but inflammatory tabloids like Marat's *L'Ami du Peuple* and Jacques Hébert's profanity-laden *Le Père Duchesne* were major sellers. The production of newspapers was also heavily biased toward the major cities, and Paris well above all others, giving articulate political leaders based in the city, or elected to the first National Assembly, a cost advantage in building a national reputation. Many leading politicians, Robespierre and his longtime friend, Camille Desmoulins, included, were accomplished writers, and in time gained national reputations as their work was dispersed through the emerging network of political clubs across the country. Some seventeen Parisian journalists would gain election to the National Convention in 1792. Yet it is easy to overstate the role of the press as a medium of political communication early in this period. Literacy was highly uneven, almost universal among aristocrats and white-collar professionals, quite uncommon among laborers and sharecroppers, and somewhere in between for better off peasants and artisans. Thus, newspapers appealed directly only to a largely urban, and, we might say, working middle class – whether white or blue collar – constituency. Other forms of mass communication, especially public speaking, therefore remained significant in reaching the masses.[7]

In this context, it was Danton who sparkled brightest of the Revolution's charismatic leaders. Danton was no ideologue. He did not develop an original or consistent political theory and has left very little by way of a written record. Unlike Robespierre, he did not transcribe his speeches for dissemination (or posterity), and as a result, his influence is often downplayed in the historical record. Resident in the middle-class Cordelier section of Paris, for the bourgeois Danton, the Revolution was both a threat and an opportunity. Through his public speaking skills, Danton developed a reputation as an effective barrister, and on the eve of the Revolution, had bought himself a position as King's counsel, and joined a local lodge of the Masons. Yet Danton's sonorous voice, if not also his distinctively scarred face and bull-like physique, was tailor made for the crowd, not the court. He quickly established himself as a popular performer in the open-air meetings at the Palais Royal, the venue opened for such public speaking by Louis Philippe II, the Duc D'Orléans – cousin of the King, later to adopt the (excessively) republican moniker of Philippe Égalité. Consistently advocating for "the people," Danton built up an enthusiastic following.[8]

Danton joined meetings in the Cordelier Club, named for the convent refectory the group used, and his speaking gained him instant notoriety. The Cordeliers were an eclectic bunch, but the club's low membership fee, just two *sous*, gave it a more radically democratic hue compared to other debating clubs that were to develop around the same time, not least the Jacobin Club. Already before the attack on the Bastille, Danton was the Cordeliers' acknowledged frontman. However, despite his prominence in Paris, he seems to have had no role in that famous event – at least the one that occurred on July 14. Camille Desmoulins, his close friend and fellow Cordelier, was the one responsible for whipping up the crowd's enthusiasm that day. Danton had great respect for the power of propaganda by deed though, so he staged his own assault on the fortress the following day, arresting the then *pro*-revolutionary governor, M. Soulès, who had been assigned by the leadership of the Paris Commune to replace the royalist governor who had been summarily executed the day before. Danton demanded a late-night audience with the city's chief of police, Lafayette. Somewhat embarrassed, with Lafayette's approval, the Hôtel de Ville quietly reinstated the new governor and let Danton on his way. Farcical as Danton's behavior might seem, as novelist Hilary Mantel suggests in *A Place of Greater Safety*, the episode served its purpose: Lafayette and the Commune could not ignore the rough-hewn Danton.

Even though Danton's position was growing as the de facto leader of the city's most radical *arrondissements*, especially the working-class Faubourg St. Marceau section, this fact made him anathema to the bourgeois leadership of the Constituent Assembly and the Paris Commune. Relations became so frayed between him and the political leadership on account of his continued radicalism that an arrest warrant was issued for him in March 1790. Danton's supporters rose in opposition and, for fear of a riot or worse, the Assembly chose to quietly drop the proceedings. Danton continued to stoke the outrage of the masses all summer, and with elections due for the Paris Commune, he sought to legitimize his mastery of the city. Although Danton won a landslide majority in the popular vote, forty-two of the city's forty-eight sections blocked him from taking up his seat. Danton's power remained confined to the streets. In August 1790, Danton took up the memory of a group of soldiers who had been executed for mutiny, forcing the resignation of the ministers responsible. It was only after this "sacking" of Louis' ministry that he was finally elected to an official position on the governing council of the Department of Paris. Danton was at last in respectable company, joining fellow department administrator Mirabeau in pledging loyalty to the King.

The peace was momentary and with it went any possibility of Danton building a more formal political party from his governmental base. The King's reputation was badly damaged by the botched attempted escape to royalist forces at Varennes on the Franco-Belgian border in June 1971. Most of the Assembly sided with the Feuillants faction led by Antoine Barnave and remained loyal to the King. However, a minority, among them Danton and the Cordeliers, called unequivocally for the formation of a republic. When on July 17, 1791, crowds in the capital protested the continued support of the moderate Feuillants for the King, dozens of Parisians were shot by Lafayette's Guards on the Champs de Mars and many more were arrested there and across the city. The King had been saved temporarily, but the carnage badly dented the reputations of the moderate leadership. Lafayette's popularity among the Parisian masses imploded. Robespierre was among those ready to profit from Lafayette's fall from grace; "[s]trike down Lafayette and the nation is saved," he declared. Danton too raged against the head of the National Guard, claiming that Lafayette's use of force was a premeditated massacre. Lafayette left Paris, and though he was soon put at the head of one of three new 50,000 strong national armies, the time was not yet ripe for the emergence of a Napoleon-style general-cum-populist. If a populist leader was to triumph in the short term, it would not be Lafayette.[9]

In spite of, or perhaps because of, Danton's reputation as champion of the people, election to the new Legislative Assembly (1791–92) eluded him. Marat's touting of Danton as the dictator needed to save the Revolution hardly helped his case with the city's bourgeois voters. Excluded from the highest ranks of power, Danton remained compelled to rely on a direct relationship with the masses cultivated through his public oratory. On June 20, 1792, *sans-culottes* invaded the Tuileries Palace, terrifying the royal family and humiliating the King – having him don a red, republican, bonnet. Lafayette returned to Paris in late June 1792 to protest the mob's accosting of the King, but all this did was to confirm his increasingly anachronistic moderation. Events were leading men. On the night of August 9, 1792, Parisian radicals pronounced the creation of an insurrectionary Commune to replace the capital's existing government and to take control of the city's National Guard contingent. If the coup thus far had been relatively peaceful, through August 10, it would reach its bloody climax. An angry crowd stormed the royal residence at the Tuileries, this time butchering some 900 of the palace guards. Power had firmly passed to the mob with Danton at its head. Although the Republic was not declared for some weeks, Danton had in effect abolished the monarchy. Even the relatively moderate Marquis de Condorcet said "[w]e need a man who has the confidence of the people whose agitators have overturned the throne. I choose Danton, and I do not apologise." Danton's reward for toppling the King was to be named minister of justice – but in effect first minister – in the provisional government.[10]

The Revolution, meanwhile, remained threated from abroad and at home. There could be no letup in the agitation of the masses. Enemies had to be fought, traitors rooted out. It was in this context that on September 2, 1792, Danton delivered his most famous speech: "*Il nous faut de l'audace! Encore de l'audace! Toujours de l'audace! Et la France est sauvée!*" he cried – "Daring! More daring! Always daring! And France is saved!" Danton's searing rhetoric stiffened the resolve of volunteers headed to the front, but it also inflamed, and perhaps even terrified those who remained at home. On the same day as Danton's famous speech, *sans-culottes* stormed the capital's prisons – where alleged enemies of the Revolution were rumored to be held – massacring over 1,200 detainees. From then on, Danton's great struggle was to douse the flames he had thus far fanned. "It's the people, the populace that has brought us to power," said Danton to a group of his friends, "[d]on't think you can stop the Revolution at the hour you set your watches." To repurpose the expression of his contemporary, Thomas Jefferson, Danton had the wolf by the ears; he could neither hold him, nor safely let him go. Danton's role in this prison massacres would taint him in the years to come. It seemed his ministry was giving way to mob rule, even if the French victory over allied forces at Valmy on September 20 bought the government, and Danton, some breathing space.[11]

Basking in the glow of victory, the new republican assembly, the National Convention, first assembled the following day, September 21, 1792. Notably, it was with the Convention that Danton won election to national elective office for the first time. He received the most votes of any of Paris' deputies and more than twice as many as Robespierre. Danton was surely the most popular political leader in the capital, if not the country at large. Indeed, the old rumours that he would seek to impose a popular dictatorship resurfaced. In reality, however, there was a power vacuum at the heart of the state. With the king now dead, the absence of an executive around which groupings could formally organize meant that neither Danton nor any of the other popular leaders lasted long at the top. Like its predecessor, the Convention did not put in place a workable model of government. The division of responsibility over the legislative and executive functions of government and between national and local levels of administration remained confused and contested. The abolition of the monarchy gave further weight to those who could mobilize the populace directly, especially in the streets of Paris. With the adoption of the republic complete, all that remained in doubt was whether Louis XVI should also die for his alleged crimes. Extremists like the young Louis Antoine Saint-Just argued that there was no choice but execution. "One cannot reign innocently," as he later put it. Danton, though not morally opposed to the monarchy – having once had its favor – saw which way the wind was blowing and put himself at the vanguard of the *regicidaires*, declaring, "I vote for the death of the tyrant." Louis Capet was beheaded on January 21, 1793.[12]

The King's death was followed by a violent peasant insurrection in the Vendée, with Catholic and royalist forces quickly occupying towns across the region. As civil war raged in the countryside, Danton attempted to use his stature to institutionalize power, to control the violence. In April 1793 he created and assumed control of the Committee of Public Safety, a de facto executive, whose status and membership was ratified on a monthly basis by the broader Convention. Danton proclaimed that "the laws must now be terrible" in punishing criminals and traitors. Danton, however, soon sought to limit the Terror's excesses, which gave his more radical opponents the opportunity to outflank him. After just four months in executive office, Danton and his allies were accused of moderation by Robespierre and his Montagnard faction. Against Danton's wishes, the comparatively moderate Girondins were persecuted for their alleged treachery, and before long, Danton and his allies were voted off the committee. The Terror was now in full swing, with thousands of alleged traitors being executed in shotgun trials. In April 1794, Danton himself was condemned to death by the very Revolutionary Tribunal that he had created.[13]

VIRTUE TRIUMPHANT

Robespierre was the next to seek the crown, but his ascendency in the helter-skelter of civil war France lasted less than a year, as he too was undone by a coalition of his rivals. As Danton was dragged off to the guillotine, he uttered his prophetic last public words: "I leave it all in a frightful confusion," he said, "not a man of them has an idea of government. Robespierre will follow me; he is dragged down by me." His prediction that Robespierre would be dead within six weeks was not far off. With ten days to the week in the revolutionary calendar, Robespierre was dead in seven. Like Danton, Robespierre was another of the "obscure provincial advocates" derided by British conservative, Edmund Burke, in his *Reflections on the Revolution in France*. He had the motivation to engage in politics, but, under the conditions of the aristocratic-dominated *Ancien Régime*, not the means. More the scholarly Jefferson to Danton's bombastic Patrick Henry, Robespierre won his battles in court through preparation and rational persuasion rather than coruscating oratory. He would frequently take the cases of poor peasants and artisans against their masters, but at least through the 1780s he was no radical leveler. Yet when the Revolution came, he had no compunctions about exploiting lower class hysteria in competition with his rivals. Seeking his place as a representative of Arras in the Estates General of 1789, Robespierre developed into a vigorous campaigner; to his critics, of course, he was the crudest of rabble-rousers, flattering and "winding up" a "credulous" mob, "whom he had until then distained and whom he barely knew." Whether or not his newfound affinity for the people was disingenuous, what was genuine was his popularity. As one of his contemporary critics observed, "[i]t is hard to describe the intoxication with which he is received ... The people are so convinced of Robespierre's virtue, so predisposed in his favour, that they could watch him picking their neighbour's pocket without believing it."[14]

Robespierre's rise to the leadership was, however, a slow burn. Through his general demeanour, he cultivated a public image that was the embodiment of *virtù*. Few doubted his sincerity – Mirabeau quipped that Robespierre would go far because "he believes everything he says." Whether or not his ascetism was that of a poseur or a fanatic, Robespierre's persona, as much as his speechmaking, won him widespread respect. Yet with his monkish personality, he was not seemingly equipped for a direct assault on power. Robespierre was widely regarded as an "eloquent" though not very captivating orator. He lacked the natural speaking ability of Mirabeau or Danton, his voice being high-pitched and often inaudible in large spaces. His speeches were also often irritatingly self-referential and peppered with rhetorical questions. He spoke frequently in the Assembly, indeed, on hundreds of occasions between 1789 and 1791. He was lauded for his learning and his steadfastness, but the vast majority of his legislative proposals – universal suffrage, opposition to the royal veto, etc. – were unsuccessful. Robespierre's political ascent owed more to his writing – or at least the written versions of his speeches – than to rabble rousing per se.[15]

Robespierre's ultimate political triumph is thus inexplicable except in terms of the concomitant rise of the Jacobin Club. It was through the club that Robespierre gradually cultivated his populist strategy, turning his eventual prominence in that often venerated and sometimes vilified group into a fame that could be more widely exploited for his political ends. The Jacobin Club – the Society of the Friends of the Constitution – was, despite appearances to the contrary from our present perspective, *not* a political party. Rather, it was primarily a meeting place and correspondence network that *rival* revolutionary leaders used in their competition for attention and influence. It was, in other words, more a means of communication, if not a venue for dispute, than an organization with a distinct corporate persona.

The Jacobin Club was to be constantly riven by personal and regional factionalism through its short existence as rivals sought to dominate it as a publicity vehicle. The club's early membership in the city was comprised mostly of members of the Assembly itself. Almost functioning as an assembly in its own right, or at least as a caucus or clearinghouse, the Jacobins debated policies and principles at the club before bringing them before the broader representative Assembly. Surrounded by allies at the club, Robespierre's turgid, academic prose gained a more respectful ear there than it often did at the Assembly. Publishing and distributing the speeches from its Parisian base across the country, its membership grew quickly, although unlike the Cordeliers, the Jacobin Club had a high membership fee, deliberately restricting it to professionals and the more established of merchants and artisans. It was a venue for bourgeois intellectuals. Because of its esteemed membership and the sophistication of its debates, sister clubs emerged across the country seeking affiliation with the Paris headquarters. Ultimately, there may have been several thousand such affiliates – we do not know the exact number. Provincial clubs functioned as conduits for political discussion, disseminating many of the new pamphlets and newspapers to emerge in the early years of the Revolution. Robespierre instantly saw the potential to grow his influence through this network. Beginning in early 1790, when there were still few such affiliates, he was already sending printed copies of his speeches to provincial clubs.[16]

In spite of its growing national presence, and even though it had a constitution and a formal membership, the Jacobin Club lacked the key requisites of a political party, for it had neither an electoral machinery nor permanent officers such as a whip to enforce any kind of party discipline on the voting of members once inside the Assembly itself. Even though its membership was drawn from a similar social base, the Jacobin Club was an internally heterogenous group. Moreover, being a venue for debate, it did not have a coherent program, and being extra-governmental, it lacked any means to attach supporters to it other than providing a channel for prominent personalities to make their appeals to the public. Although local members of the club sometimes intervened in elections, quietly proposing electoral slates in some sections, as a body, it did so only irregularly and with limited effect. For instance, despite its best efforts, the Jacobins only obtained an estimated 136 seats in the Legislative Assembly (1791–92), compared with 264 for the moderate Feuillants – a splinter political club from the original Jacobins – and 350 who remained neutral.

At this time, Robespierre, despite his growing influence within the Jacobins, remained on the political fringes, not least because of the passage of his proposal that he and other members of the Constituent would be barred from taking seats in the new Assembly. It was time for a modification of his strategy. Although in his speeches and journalism Robespierre shied away from the gratuitous bloodlust of Marat's writings, he was not averse to calling for the utmost dedication and sacrifice in pursuing the revolution. By turns, Robespierre became more socially radical, calling for the kind of economic intervention that was anathema to much of the predominantly bourgeois membership of the Jacobins. This meant also a realignment toward Paris, placing the city and its *sans-culottes* at the vanguard of the Revolution. The location of the weakly protected government in the capital, by default if not design, gave Parisians enormous influence over the course of events. Robespierre learned to exploit this leverage; a few thousand men and women on the streets could accomplish more efficiently what years of political organization and parliamentary debate seemingly could not. Robespierre forged an alliance between his Montagnard faction and the Parisian *sans-culottes* who dominated the Commune. Robespierre defended both the assault on the Tuileries Palace in August 1792 that resulted in the arrest of the King and the slaughter of his guard, and the prison massacre that followed shortly thereafter. Robespierre returned to office with the National Convention that began sitting in September. But siding firmly with the Parisian street, like Danton he became one the most outspoken of the *regicidaires*. The self-styled purist, Robespierre would have denied any role for personal ambition in his actions. Yet, given the antipathy to Robespierre both among the majority of the still moderate Assembly and in the court, his power and influence would be limited as long as the King remained. With the King dead, Robespierre could turn against his former allies.

By now, so influential was Robespierre in the Jacobin Club that he could henceforth expel those with whom he disagreed over principle or whom he saw as rivals. The club was, by degrees, becoming more and more a personalist vehicle for Robespierre. Against the wishes of his chief rival, Danton, in May 1793, Robespierre exploited *sans-culottes* disaffection to have Jacques-Pierre Brissot and other leading members of the rival Girondins faction arrested and executed. The mastery of Robespierre's Montagnard faction was not yet complete, however. The even more radical *Hébertistes* on the one hand and Danton's *Indulgents* on the other would have to go before that happened. Recurrent food shortages and price hikes had provided an opening to fire eaters like Jacques Hébert and Jacques Roux who gave a voice to the *enragés* – the "enraged ones." In a one-two strike, Robespierre first eliminated the threat of Hébert on his left and then of Danton on his right.

Only then, in April 1794, with most of his enemies purged did Robespierre emerge as the unequivocal front man of the Revolution. Although the Committee of Public Safety technically remained a collective form of rule, Robespierre was its most prominent member, not least as he remained in Paris while most other members spent considerable time away on deputation. Still, lacking a clear institutional hierarchy within the committee, Robespierre's predominance was always under threat. Taking on what he perceived to be the excessively radical secularization of some of his committee and Convention colleagues, Robespierre embarked on a bizarre scheme, whose true meaning and motivation remains unclear today. With the old sources of authority – monarchy and church – banished, the deist Robespierre felt it necessary to inculcate new icons. The Cult of Reason of 1793, followed by the Cult of the Supreme Being in 1794, were massive ceremonies that aimed to bind people ideologically and emotionally to the new secular state that the Revolution had created. Contrived as they sound in retrospect, recent historical research suggests that they were genuinely popular events, with some 500,000 people showing up to the latter event at which Robespierre performed as the new "pope." If Robespierre himself seems to have experienced the event as transcendent, his enemies didn't take long to disabuse him of his megalomania.

Much as Robespierre was at the height of his public celebrity in early 1794, he found himself in a bind. Although he was in effect first among equals on the committee, his power was contingent on the implicit threat that he and his allies in the Commune and the National Guard posed to his fellow governors. Saint-Just's quixotic attempts to have Robespierre given de jure dictatorial powers to manage the emergency confirmed the suspicions of Robespierre's committee rivals that he promised to be another Caesar or Cromwell. It was then that Robespierre took an unexplained six-week hiatus from the activities of the committee, even as he continued to diligently attend the nightly meetings of the Jacobin Club. Robespierre appeared to be distancing himself from government and shoring up his popular base in advance of another purge of the nation's, or at least his, enemies. In what proved to be his final speech in the Convention, Robespierre flung accusations of corruption and treason against unnamed conspirators in the government. With the Sword of Damocles hanging over them, Robespierre's rivals, who came as much from the even more radical left as from the moderate center, preempted him. Robespierre, and his closest followers – Saint-Just, Georges Couthon, and Augustin Robespierre (Maximilien's younger brother) – were arrested and imprisoned across the capital in a coup known for its date: the Thermidorian reaction (occurring on 9 Thermidor, Year II of the revolutionary calendar, or July 27, 1794). Then, in what amounted to a self-fulfilling prophecy, a band of Robespierre's supporters in the Paris Commune launched an armed assault on the Convention and sprung him from captivity. Robespierre and his fellow outlaws held up at the Hôtel de Ville. Yet much of the Parisian populace remained indifferent, if not loyal to the Convention, and government forces under the sure-footed command of Paul Barras, quickly regained control. With his enemies closing in, sometime after midnight, Robespierre shot himself in the jaw in a botched suicide attempt. The executioner finished the job later that day. In the end, all of Robespierre's appeals to the people could not save him. Populism was a strategy for winning power in revolutionary France, not exercising it.[17]

DOUSING THE FLAMES

Robespierre, Saint-Just, and other radicals may have believed in what they said. But there is not much evidence that the same was true of the masses. For sure, populists flattered the people. More so, though, they sought to lead public opinion. Certainly, revolutionary – liberal and republican, if not socialist – rhetoric thoroughly permeated French culture from the late 1780s. But, as George Rudé writes in his famous study, *The Crowd in the French Revolution*, "the inescapable conclusion remains that the primary and most constant motive impelling revolutionary crowds during this period was the concern for the provision of cheap and plentiful food." For the people who became the mass support base of populists like Danton and Robespierre, political radicalism was a means to an end: the satisfaction of basic wants, namely, food and safety. Ultimately, the once adoring crowds shed few tears when those who failed to make good on their material promises lost their heads.[18]

Really, what was needed were institutional mechanisms through which to incorporate the people and channel their demands into the policymaking process. However, as Saint-Just put it, the organizations most likely to fulfill this role, political parties, were not accepted as legitimate tools for governing but were instead "criminal." If the suppression of the radical left with Robespierre's overthrow on Thermidor might have provided an opportunity to develop mass political parties, it was a road not taken. Seeking to reimpose some order after the excesses of the previous five years, the new constitution – the Constitution of Year III (1795) – traded the universal franchise for a limited, property-based qualification for the right to vote. The masses would be contained rather than incorporated. A bicameral legislature (the *Corps Législatif*) replaced the previous single-chambered parliament, with the Council of Five Hundred and the Council of Ancients becoming the lower and upper houses of the legislature, respectively. Seeking to more effectively separate executive and legislative arms of government, the Directory – a rotating five-man governing council, none of whose five members could come from the elected councils – replaced the Committee of Public Safety as the executive branch.

Patronage-based mobilization of this much more restricted electorate is conceivable in retrospect, and this is essentially the approach that took hold during the Second Empire (1852–70) and persisted into the Third Republic (1871–1940). However, the revolutionary leadership again failed to exploit the opportunity it had to build stable political organizations, whether of a programmatic or patronage sort. Still seeing parties as pernicious, if not "criminal" factions, the Directory's approach was instead to clamp down on any form of political organization. The headquarters of the Jacobin Club was itself shuttered by the degree of 21–22 Brumaire (November 11–12) and the society as a whole was prorogued the following year. The two councils of the Directory period also proved to be highly unstable. Its members, effectively prohibited from forming parties, were much more sharply divided than those of the United States Congress, with monarchist, Jacobin, and liberal Republican – or *Ideologue* – factions locked in a state of mutual suspicion, if not a phony civil war. Aiming to steer a middle course, the Directory soon found itself with enemies on both the left and right. On the one hand, a movement led by leftist radical, François-Noël Babeuf, advocated the radical redistribution of wealth, while on the other, rumors abounded of a right-wing putsch to restore the Bourbon monarchy to the throne.

The directors attempts to bring about political demobilization rather than political incorporation were understandable, and arguably, sensible. Undoubtedly, the limited franchise of the Directory had for a time stayed the wild impulses of the revolution. But competition for power among the revolutionary leadership continued and the temptation to appeal to the masses remained in place. The patronage-based strategy might have been used to consolidate political power, but with the aristocratic elite decimated by the social upheaval of the revolution and the people determined to escape the vestigial bonds of feudal and ecclesiastical domination, building a stable coalition of elite-dominated patron–client networks out of this inheritance was beyond the talents of any French leader of the day. Conservatives proved completely incapable of forming a stable political organization in spite of growing public sympathy for the restoration of order. Antoine d'André's effort to create a royalist network, The Philanthropic Institute, was a complete failure. One disappointed supporter wrote, "I had reason to believe that a party had been formed ... How surprised I was to discover that all this only existed on paper ... Nothing had been done! Even in Paris there was no party, no organisation." Even as the neo-Jacobins recovered their energy after 1798, rather than build a party of its own, the Directory focused on demobilizing the radicals, forbidding meetings of *any* political societies. After losing its legislative majority to royalists in the elections of 1797, the unpopular Directory survived only by throwing out the results (the *Fructidor* coup); it repeated the act in 1798 when the revived Jacobins were the ones purged (the *Floréal* coup). With this, any prospect that the Jacobin *Cercles Constitutionnels* might have developed into an organized political party went with it. With the people politically agitated; no enduring liberal constitutional framework in place; and no political parties, populism – the direct mobilization of the masses – remained a viable path to power for those who cared to use it. Indeed, as long as a return to monarchy remained off the cards, it is difficult to see how any other strategy could have competed with it. Enter Napoleon Bonaparte.[19]

THE POPULIST EMPEROR

Napoleon remains, rightly, one of the most studied characters in modern history. The boldness that brought unprecedented military success, and the hubris that brought his empire crashing down, are the stuff of legend. From our perspective, the puzzle is how and why France's democratic revolution went full circle, ending as it began – with a monarch sitting on the throne, albeit the later one earning, rather than inheriting, his crown. Only twenty years old when the Revolution began in 1789, the green artillery officer Napoleon was propelled up the military ladder by the radical clear out of the aristocratic old guard. After masterminding the recapture of the Mediterranean city of Toulon from an English expeditionary force in 1793 and putting down a counter-revolutionary insurrection in Paris on 13 *Vendémiere*, Year IV (1795) – after which he supposedly commented that he dispersed the rabble with a "whiff of grapeshot" – Napoleon's star rose yet further on the back of military exploits in Europe and the Levant. For admirers, his status approached godlike propor-tions, marking him out as the very definition of a charismatic leader.[20]

As early as 1796, Napoleon's successive conquests had made him indispens-able to the political leadership. His Army of Italy was largely financing the regime through its looting of defeated kingdoms on the peninsula. The Directory instructed Napoleon to leave nothing of value in Italy that might be carried off, not least Italy's vast trove of artworks. Napoleon took to his task with gusto, systematically pillaging the territories he "liberated." In the pro-cess, though, Napoleon took pains to portray himself not just as a victorious general but as a patron of the arts. Paintings and other rare objects were of particular interest to Napoleon, with hundreds being taken off to French galleries. Aside from the financial benefit, the Directory basked in the reflected glory of his continuous victories. Yet Napoleon's growing personal popularity was a cause of concern. Even as Napoleon was presiding over the sanctioned pillaging of Italy, the Directory tried to subordinate him to another general more to its liking. However, when Napoleon then threatened to resign, the directors had to ignominiously back down, giving the general even more latitude than before. Indeed, as historian Michael Broers argues, Napoleon established in Italy what was in effect a modern, autocratic regime, fully under his personal control; it was an exact blueprint for the kind of regime he would go on to establish in France itself. One confidant reported Napoleon as saying, "[d]o you believe that I triumph in Italy for the Carnots, Barras, etc. [the directors]? ... I wish to undermine the Republican party, but only for my own profit and not that of the former dynasty." But if Napoleon's end goal was a popular dictatorship, to an even greater extent than Caesar, he exploited a populist strategy to get there. Napoleon was no demagogue. He rarely spoke in public, except to men under arms. Nevertheless, he cultivated popular support with great acuity, through the propaganda of deed more than word. Publicly, indeed, like his near contemporary, George Washington, Napoleon gave the appearance of shunning personal ambition for power. French society remained, after all, wary of despotism. In 1797, after his victorious campaigns in Italy, on hearing that he was to be feted in an elaborate ceremony in Paris, he is said to have requested that the festivities be canceled. In October he wrote to the Directory promising, like Washington had, to retire from public life and "take up the plough of Cincinnatus." Napoleon's self-calculating modesty only earned him further plaudits.[21]

The directors sought to put Napoleon out of reach of the capital's adoring crowds. An invasion of Britain was floated but soon abandoned in favor of an alternative campaign to capture territory from the then waning Ottoman Empire. The directors' hopes of keeping Napoleon out of the public eye failed. Even though the French occupations of Egypt and the Levant never really took, this did not prevent Napoleon from exploiting the invasion for all the propaganda value it was worth. For sure, the technology of mass communication was nothing like it would be even half a century later. However, printing was cheap, and the market for what today we call "infotainment" was abundant. As the leader of France's armies in Europe, Napoleon had issued regular dispatches – called bulletins. These reports from the front often contained details that would be suppressed in registered outlets, such as the *Moniteur*, and so were popular with the people. In 1797, riding high from his victories in Italy, Napoleon created two newspapers of his own. Although this was something other generals did at the time, the articles in Napoleon's papers, many of which were syndicated in other widely read outlets, went much further in criticizing the republican government for its corruption and ineptitude, dismissing the royalist alternative, and portraying Napoleon as a providential leader above faction. Although Napoleon had in effect been forced to return to France with his tail between his legs after the destruction of the French fleet at Aboukir Bay off the delta of the river Nile, he managed to portray himself as a virtual Alexander, reconquering a barbarian East in the name of Western civilization.[22]

With his foray to the east faltering, Napoleon sensed that the time was approaching when he would have to strike at home. As he told one of his generals before returning to France in 1799, "I shall arrive in Paris, I shall drive out that pile of lawyers who care nothing for us and who are incapable of governing the Republic, and I shall put myself at the head of the government." Massive crowds greeted his procession as he marched north toward Paris from his landing point at Saint-Raphael on the Côte D'Azur. One contemporary wrote that Napoleon had become so popular that he could see "no other end for him but the throne or the scaffold." Napoleon knew what he was doing. Even though he privately scorned the mob, writing to his brother after witnessing the storming of Tuileries Palace in Paris by an angry mob on August 10, 1792 that "the people are hardly worth the trouble we take to win their favour," he nevertheless knew that the masses, even more so than the Army, provided his route to power. The people just needed leadership. Napoleon could not understand the King's passivity. "If only Louis XVI had climbed up on a horse," Napoleon wrote to his brother of the events of August 10, "victory would have been his." Louis had not the constitution to remake himself a Caesar, but Napoleon was more than willing. Napoleon vowed to one intimate: "I have tasted command and I would not be able to give it up. I have made up my mind: if I cannot be master, I will leave France." It was by then clear, however, that if there was eventually to be a dictatorship, it would have to be a popular one. When, in late 1797, in the brief period between his Italian and Egyptian campaigns, he was sounded out by other military leaders to partici- pate in a coup, he warned his fellow generals: "Military government will never catch on in France." The supreme tactician, Napoleon would wait for the "pear [to be] ripe."[23]

By late 1799, facing the prospect of further radicalism at the hands of the newly resurgent Jacobin and royalist factions on the Council of Five Hundred, it was apparent to moderates among the directors – and to the political elite more broadly – that the regime was teetering and that a putsch – from one direction or other – was likely. Members of the Directory had, after all, perpetrated two coups of their own in defence of the regime already (against the right in 1797 and the left in 1798). The directors moved to take preemptive action again, but even at this late stage, Napoleon's ascent was far from assured. In spite of Napoleon's role in propping up the Thermidorian regime, not least in 1795 when he helped put down the *Vendémiere* insurgency in Paris, the general was not the automatic choice of the moderate Directory, but with Generals Lazare Hoche and Barthélemy Joubert both dead, there were few alternatives who could match Napoleon's extraordinary name recognition – never mind his popularity – across almost every stratum of French society. Barras, though an ally of Napoleon since at least the retaking of Toulon in 1793, pushed forward General Hédouville, but the latter's role in putting down the conservative insurgency in the Vendée made him a divisive choice. General Moreau's renown came closest to Bonaparte's, but he had little appetite for a political role, telling the conspirators on the news of Napoleon's return from Egypt: "There's your man." By degrees Napoleon had become the only realistic military front for a more throughgoing revision of the constitution. The coup, however, soon became his, not that of his backers, the most prominent of whom was, Emmanuel Joseph Sieyès.[24]

The abbé Sieyès, author of the famous pamphlet, *What Is the Third Estate?*, was one of the great survivors of the Revolution. Staying aloof from factional squabbles, he had managed to ride out a turbulent decade with his neck, if not his reputation, intact. For his part, Sieyès envisaged a coup d'état and a new constitution with Napoleon the war hero as its figurehead. Napoleon, as Sieyès saw it, would just be a convenient "sword," no more. Although Sieyès recog- nized Napoleon's political acumen as well as his military talents, at least part of the attraction for Sieyès was Napoleon's ideological flexibility. Although Napoleon was an admirer of Robespierre's, he had long since been deplored by the all too frequent mob violence in Paris from whatever ideological source it sprung. At least since his Italian campaign, Napoleon had been cultivating the backing of the moderate *Ideologue* faction, mostly comprised of artists, lawyers, scientists, and philosophers associated with the Institut de France learned society, something that could not have escaped the notice of Sieyès.

Yet Napoleon was no reactionary either; he continually averred his republican credentials – at the time, the coup that followed was interpreted as anti-Royalist. Confirming his preference for victory over ideals, Napoleon threw his lot in with the faction he believed would be most congenial in elevating him to power; in 1799, this meant the moderate group concentrated in the Council of Elders affiliated with Sieyès. Napoleon's choice of allying with Sieyès, as biographer Philip Dwyer remarks, was "politically opportunistic."[25]

The chaotic toppling of the Directory on 18 Brumaire, Year VIII – or November 9, 1799 – brought Napoleon to power, but it very nearly might not have. The first day went according to plan. A majority of the five directors – including Sieyès – resigned and the remaining two were placed under arrest, effectively abolishing the government. Meanwhile, under the pretence of a Jacobin insurgency, the members of the councils were persuaded by Napoleon's brother, Lucien, president of the Council of 500, to relocate to the suburban Château de Saint-Cloud, where events could be better controlled. The following day, the deputies were put under pressure to pronounce Napoleon as head of government to meet the supposed emergency. The deputies resisted, and when Napoleon entered the chamber, he was shouted down and, as legend has it, nearly stabbed. Lucien effectively saved the day for the putschists, dramatically pointing his sword at his brother's chest to persuade the grenadiers outside the chamber that he would kill Napoleon himself if he believed that his brother's intention was to betray the republic. The guardsmen proceeded to empty the chamber and faced with a quiescent rump in the legislature, Lucien effectively had the councils vote themselves out of existence.

Sieyès had by then been working on his post-coup constitutional scheme, in which Napoleon would take the role of a Grand Elector. The Grand Elector, as per Sieyès' plan, would have the power of appointment and removal of two consuls who would in turn form the real executive (in foreign and domestic realms, respectively). Napoleon, however, had other ideas. "Have I heard you correctly?" he said on hearing in Sieyès' schema, "[a]re you proposing for me a position where I will name those who are given something to do, while I myself am to be involved in nothing?" Napoleon compared the whole notion to a fattened pig. Once Napoleon got his hands on it, under the new constitution of Year VIII (1999), the mooted position of Grand Elector was transformed into that of a First Consul, who would govern as a member of an executive triumvirate. Nominally just one of three, Napoleon quickly marginalized the other two consuls, Jacques Régis de Cambacérès and Charles-François Lebrun, and then proceeded to emasculate the new regime's nominally autonomous lawmaking institutions, the Senate, tribunate, and the *Corps Législatif* (legislature). Positions in the well-remunerated Senate were essentially sinecures for Napoleon's supporters, and this body's power over the composition of the tribunate very quickly ensured the latter would also be in sympathy with Napoleon's wishes. In any case, it was the Council of State, a body of experts directly appointed by Napoleon, which effectively both wrote and implemented the law.[26]

Napoleon's ascension to the consulship was in part the result of elite machinations. Even if ratified by a national plebiscite, there was no open, competitive national campaign for the office. Had Napoleon been continually stymied in gaining a seat at the high table – he was ineligible for the directorate in 1799 because he was under forty years of age – he could arguably have attempted a purely military coup d'état. Yet given the still fragmented nature of the French army, such a strategy could well very have resulted in a bloody civil war. Napoleon, in fact, flatly rejected such an idea. His distinct advantage, both over political and military rivals, was his enormous popular base. Even if he believed in the necessity of singular national leadership, he knew this had to rest on popular support. As he put it, "confidence comes from below, power from on high." It was this factor that made Napoleon's elevation to sole power so ineluctable. As with the notorious case of Adolf Hitler in the 1930s – the subject of Chapter 5 – his popularity was critical to his invitation into the circles of power and the subsequent consolidation of his personal authority. The Coup of 18 Brumaire certainly expedited matters, but it is not hard to imagine a similar outcome by different means. Should there have been an open electoral competition for an office like the American presidency, it is difficult to see anyone coming close to Napoleon. With his absolute control over the institutions of state assured, Napoleon appealed directly to the people, getting himself confirmed as First Consul for Life via a national referendum in 1802. His popular support was overwhelming: 3,568,885 votes in favor to 8,374 against. Significantly, the turnout on this occasion was 60 percent, compared to the 25 percent, at most, that had approved the 1799 Constitution. An equally large majority voted to confirm him as emperor in another plebiscite in 1804.[27]

Without the legitimacy conferred on his personal rule by tradition, in power, Napoleon continually courted popular support. Napoleon was a pioneering and astute user of visual propaganda, if not "fake news." Casualty figures in his reports often bore a tenuous relationship to reality, and many of the paintings he later commissioned to celebrate famous victories were indeed works of "art." The arts in general, and painting in particular, were directed toward shaping, not merely reflecting, popular opinion. His visage decorated canvases, sculptures, engravings, and medals that made their way all over Europe. French historian Jean Tulard has written that Napoleon "forged his own legend. His genius was to have understood very early the importance of propaganda." In his 1950s classic, *Napoleonic Propaganda*, historian Robert Holtman wrote that in power Napoleon was the "first sovereign to talk to his subjects directly and frequently, partly through mediums such as the bulletins ... which he was the first to exploit." To the end, Napoleon insisted on the bond between him and the people. To the liberal politician and writer Benjamin Constant, he later wrote: "The people, or if you wish the masses, want only me ... I am not only, as has been said, the emperor of the soldiers, I am the emperor of the peasants, the plebians of France ... That is why despite the past, you can see the people gather to me. There is a bond between us." Even as he consolidated his power as First Consul, he declared that if he lost the satisfaction of the people, he would happily give it all up. In 1802, disavowing any personal ambition, he declared "[i]n three years, I shall retire from public affairs. I will have an income of fifty thousand livres, and with my tastes that is more than I need." Napoleon of course didn't give up power willingly.[28]

Napoleon sought and received his legitimacy directly from the people. He had no interest at all in forming a political party to institutionalize his rule. It was not that Napoleon was ignorant of the potential for a party to work as an instrument of government. However, as he put it, "to govern through a party is sooner or later to make yourself dependent on it." Napoleon instead attempted to remain above the fray. When the day of his coup d'état came, he declared: "I refused to be the man of any faction," grandiosely vowing that he instead belonged to the faction of the nation. Yet without a deeply institutionalized base, Napoleon remained dependent on the cultivation of popular support, and in turn on the need for repeated military successes. Napoleon himself wrote, "[m]y power depends on my glory and my glory on the victories I have won." Presciently, he continued, "[m]y power would fall if I did not give it as its foundation further glory and new victories." Continued military adventurism was baked into Napoleon's sense of his own legitimacy.[29]

However, just as Napoleon rose to power on the fame won by his military victories, illustrating the lack of institution building often entailed in populist mobilization, he was quickly undone by military defeats. The French military became badly bogged down amid a guerrilla war in Spain that began in 1808 and dragged on until its unsuccessful resolution in 1814. The Russian Campaign of 1812 was a greater disaster, with only 112,000 of the 612,00 strong French army making it home from Russian territory. No amount of censorship or propaganda could hide such casualty figures. The alliance of European armies invaded France and took the capital in spring 1814. Napoleon was forced to abdicate and was exiled to the island of Elba in the Tyrrhenian Sea. Although, after three weeks on the island, in a remarkable last hurrah, Napoleon escaped his exile and was shortly restored to the throne; his second reign lasted for only one hundred days. After a further devastating military defeat at Waterloo in June, Napoleon was given up to the British and exiled to the tiny volcanic island of St. Helena in the South Atlantic where he died six years later.

Even at its height, to a greater degree than Napoleon himself realized, his popularity rested more on the restoration of order and a modicum of prosperity at home after years of civil war than it did on military success abroad. Of course, victories in battle against Europe's mightiest kingdoms were certainly popular; all Frenchmen could bask in that reflected glory. However, military victories were important not just for their own sake but because they ultimately promised an end to war, a return to peace. Efforts, albeit incomplete, to clamp down on the widespread brigandage that plagued the French countryside were most welcome. Napoleon's legal and administrative reforms were highly effect-ive. Napoleon also introduced some sensible and popular economic reforms, even if economic policy remained subordinate to foreign policy. Ultimately, however, Napoleon invested too little in sources of popularity other than military glory. When France's enemies caught up tactically after several years on the back foot, the weight of force eventually told. Napoleon then had little on which to fall back. The people didn't clamor for his removal, but neither did they fight to save him. Napoleon's ouster saw not the return of democracy but a restoration of the Bourbon monarchy. Charles X would in turn be overthrown by his cousin, Louis Philippe, Duke of Orléans in 1830, resulting in the promulgation of yet another constitution. Democracy, and populism as a political strategy, would be put on hold until another revolution in 1848, when another Bonaparte would take up the opportunity to be a populist leader, whose support was grounded in order and prosperity.

THE AMERICAN REPUBLIC

In spite of Europe's legacy as the home of the first direct democratic govern-ments in Ancient Greece, of republicanism in Rome, of the traditional parlia-ments of the Germanic world, and of the bourgeois and dynastic assemblies of the late Medieval and Early Modern eras, *democracy* as such – that is, govern-ment based on something like a near full franchise – was first reintroduced, not in the old world, but in the new. In expanding the franchise to a majority of adult males, the American Revolution promised a radically different conception of republican government to anything that had existed in the recent past, including, it should be said, in Britain itself. Politics under Britain's unreformed parliament entailed regular elections, to be sure, but direct appeals to the voting public were of minor importance. The American revolution thus introduced something qualitatively new: large-scale, representative democracy.

The prominent role played by regular Americans in enforcing the embargoes and in fighting the war for independence meant a significant erosion of the old patterns of deference. The state constitutions adopted from 1776 were much more democratic than the colonial regimes that preceded them. Within a decade of the Declaration of Independence, all states had abolished the aristocratic legal relics of primogeniture and entail. Pennsylvania's was probably the most democratic constitution ever enacted up to that point in history. Middling folk were even beginning to make their presence felt inside government. The common men who filled the revolutionary committees and militias were not content to return to their farms and workshops. The encroachment of "blustering ignorant men" into state offices, abhorred by one Massachusetts conservative, was widespread. This political revolution was matched with demands for socioeconomic leveling during the years on either side of inde-pendence. State governments passed a spate of tax and debt relief measures in the late 1770s and early 1780s, the result of which was to greatly dismay the wealthier classes. In places like Rhode Island, the proliferation of paper money promised a substantial de facto transfer of wealth from creditors to debtors. As William Plumber of New Hampshire put it, "our rights & property are now the sport of ignorant unprincipled State legislators." Shays' Rebellion in western Massachusetts, an anti-tax revolt by a cash-strapped yeomanry that lasted from 1786 through 1787, provided a vivid illustration to the elite of how the popular classes left to their own devices might burst forth into outright insurrection. The less violent and now less well-known agitation for debt relief by farmers in Greenbrier, Virginia, in mid-1787, was no less troubling. Judging by these trends, America should have been fertile territory for populist strategists in the wake of the Revolution.[30]

However, even as the Revolution unleashed its "unruly" elements – poor farmers, artisans, "mechanics" or blue-collar workers, and even slaves – there were swift and effective countervailing efforts to contain them. As it transpired, in matters economic, the Revolution ended up as a deeply conformist event, preserving, or rather advancing, the liberties of the wealthy, mostly landed and often slaveholding elite, who temporarily buried their sectional and familial differences to oppose the grabbing hand of an assertive, and increasingly foreign, monarchy. If, to use the words of Mao Zedong, "[a] revolution is an insurrection, an act of violence by which one class overthrows another," the American Revolution was hardly a revolution at all. Landless laborers, workers, and eventually the descendants of slaves would eventually make substantive gains under democracy, but it would be anachronous to read these developments into the political dynamics of the founding decades. The immediate result of independence, as we'll see, was that patrimonialism, not populism, would be the prevailing form of political mobilization in the early United States of America. The core tension in the early decades after the Revolution was less one of the poor masses versus the privileged elite but of rival elite factional conflicts over control of the new state apparatus.[31]

Whatever their later affiliations, Federalist or Republican, most of the Revolution's leaders were by no means democrats. Prior to 1776, the men who would lead America to independence – most conspicuously Benjamin Franklin – primarily spoke in favor of royal government and against the tyranny of the British Parliament. The Revolution was as much about preserving the privileges of the elite as it was extending those of the masses. The ever-ornery John Adams, president of the United States from 1797 to 1800, spoke for many when he fretted that democracy would mean that "every man who has not a farthing will demand an equal voice with any other." The more urbane, if more blue-blooded, Gouverneur Morris, a signatory to the Constitution, voiced a different concern. He worried about the susceptibility of regular people to manipulation by the elite. The "rich," he said "will take advantage of their passions and make these the instruments for oppressing them." Arch-Federalist Alexander Hamilton was of course a well-known skeptic, in one of his final writings calling democracy a "disease" and a "poison." He and other nationalists sought a powerful chief executive who could oppose the "excess of democracy" evident at the state level, which the revolutionary state constitutions of the late 1770s and the weak Articles of Confederation had allowed to flourish.[32]

It is important to stress that these views were not merely held by a small group of closet monarchists or reactionaries. Thomas Jefferson was probably the exception to the rule among the founders in his opposition to any form of monarchy, but even the most illustrious opponent of the Federalists and the first Republican president (1801–08), was somewhat of a snob who preferred the people in theory rather than in practice. As early as 1776 he argued against the direct popular election of senators in his native Virginia, writing "I have ever observed that a choice by the people themselves is not known for its wisdom." He continued that he would prefer almost "any thing than a mere creation by and dependence on the people." In fact, he was even prepared to have lifetime appointment for the Senate, rather than have it be subject to popular election. Nor did Jefferson have much patience with parliament. In 1785, after several years' of working in the Virginia House of Delegates (1776–79) and then with the state's legislative body as Virginia's governor (1779–81), Jefferson bewailed that "[a]n elective despotism was not the government we fought for," and that "173 despots would surely be as oppressive as one." Like the Greek and Roman philosophers, whom he so greatly admired, Jefferson worried that unfettered democracy could lead to tyranny. Madison, Jefferson's key Anti-Federalist partner, believed it was dangerous to go "disturbing the public tranquillity by interesting too strongly the public passions." His great concern in drafting the Constitution was not the domination of a majority by a minority but precisely the opposite: the domination of a minority by "the major number of the constituents." As he wrote in 1786 to fellow Virginian, James Monroe, another future president, "it would be the interest of the majority in every community to despoil and enslave the minority of individuals." Like others of his social standing, he was worried that democracy would let the poor soak the rich.[33]

The first institutional rollback of the political intrusion of the lower classes occurred at the state level. Even if some states, most notably Pennsylvania and the newly established Vermont, virtually eliminated property requirements from the franchise in their constitutions, the majority of states, not least Virginia, moved in the other direction in their revised constitutions, retaining or even stiffening economic restrictions on voting, especially for national office. In fact, in Virginia – the seedbed of Jeffersonian democracy – the old patterns of political deference to the landed elite lasted longest, with restrictions on the franchise, even in the free white population, persisting until the 1850s. As historian Richard Beeman writes, in Virginia the Revolution "only strengthened the power of Virginia's provincial ruling class." Even this institutional stemming of the democratic tide, however, was felt by some of the elite to be insufficient. The Rhode Island government, subject to annual elections, continued to cater to popular demands with loose monetary policy. Property holders – whatever the type of property – were dismayed. They could almost all agree that a more powerful national check on the impulses of state-level democracy was needed. The United States Constitution, drafted in 1787 and ratified a year later, reflected this moderating impulse.[34]

The setup of the federal government was designed in large part to provide a check on the alleged excesses of state-level democracy, while at the same time ensuring that there would be no populist path to executive leadership at the national level either. Indeed, Harvard professor of law, Michael Klarman, has gone as far as to characterize the Constitution as an elite "coup" against popular democratizing sentiments. Even if a growing proportion of adult males could technically vote as a result of the revolutionary constitutions adopted in the states, the de facto role of the populace in selecting the federal government would be heavily mediated. The Senate was to be selected indirectly, with state legislatures or governors determining who would represent the state in the Senate – direct elections for the Senate were not introduced until the twentieth century. Similarly, none of the framers could envision, and indeed they would have abhorred, the idea that the president would be chosen by a popular vote. They designed the system so that the choice of president would reflect the consensus views of the elite – those who had traditionally dominated colonial politics. The Electoral College was a manifestation of this approach, whereby the president was to be elected indirectly by a conclave of state representatives, not a direct popular ballot. As of 1796, in seven states presidential electors were chosen by state legislatures, while popular elections were allowed in eight (with Tennessee a hybrid). For the elections of 1800, only five states retained the popular choice of electors, with four states reverting to the indirect method (offset by the state of Rhode Island going in the other direction). It wasn't until 1832 that almost all states (still barring South Carolina) adopted the direct method for choosing presidential electors. Moreover, the Electoral College system still meant that the presidential race would continue to be a series of state-level contests rather than a mass popularity contest. This remains the case today, where the outcome of presidential elections often comes down to a small number of "swing" states. Executive authority in the early republic, moreover, would be balanced by a separately elected two-house legislature and an appointed and independent judiciary – "Ambition," as Madison put it, "to counteract ambition." The whole institutional setup of the new regime thus weighed very heavily against the strategy of seeking power by directly appealing to the people.[35]

In any case, in the closed system of the new republic, not only would directly seeking public approval have been of limited use, but to have even sought it would, paradoxically enough, likely have been disqualifying. The extensive experience of limited, patrimonial democracy under British tutelage fostered a strong normative bias against overtly seeking office. Here George Washington's experience is illustrative. Washington was born in February 1732 to a Virginian family of comfortable means. Never quite a full-fledged member of the rarefied class of rural grandees, Washington nevertheless scrupulously aped the manners of the Whig elite. This first meant ostensibly shunning any ambition for personal power. Of course, Washington did desire power and the respect it conferred. He sought out a military career for the personal fame and status this would bring. On retirement to civilian life, he wasn't above plying voters with drink to secure his first elected position to the House of Burgesses in Frederick County, Virginia in 1758. Nevertheless, appearances mattered. Public office was a solemn duty. This meant that neither Washington nor any other aspiring leader could engage in the kind of demagoguery that became common a century later. Aaron Burr was one of the few to openly electioneer for national office in this period, and his reputation suffered for it. As late as 1860, when Lincoln's nemesis, Stephen Douglas, actively campaigned for the presidency on his own account, he was roundly derided. Washington's retirement might be seen as having created an opening for new mass appeals – no tradition of succession having been established – but even as the franchise expanded and the national press proliferated, the presidential elections from 1796 through at least 1824 were not mass popularity contests. Rather, it remained far more economical for an aspiring leader to purchase the loyalty of key state brokers – those who controlled the Electoral College votes – than to appeal to the people directly.

PARTIES AND PATRONAGE

The framers of the United States Constitution were ostensibly just as opposed to what we would term parties, or as they often termed their precursors, "factions," as they were to designing demagogues. Washington himself famously inveighed against the "baneful effects" of the "spirit of party" in his farewell address in 1797. Jefferson even declared that "[i]f I could not go to heaven but with a party, I would not go there at all." Most of the founding fathers adhered to a republican philosophy in which parties were viewed as the instruments of narrow sections or interest groups. "Factions," an even more pernicious label, were associated with personal cliques, motivated only by their own gain. Even while Madison could, in Federalist No. 10, see some virtue in parties as vehicles to prevent the dominance of one economic interest group to the exclusion of others, factions were malignant and deserving of no such approbation. Building on the British experience of the eighteenth century, in the still developing republican theory of government, society was idealized as unitary, and parties characterized as tools of division. Most notoriously, with the passage of the Alien and Sedition Acts in 1798 by the John Adams government, political opposition itself was virtually cast as treasonous.

Arguing against an inappropriate reading back of modern notions of parties and party systems, many historians have thus been at pains to qualify the use of the term "party" for this period. Certainly, neither Federalists nor Republicans had parties in the modern, bureaucratic sense. Even if partisanship at the national level was conspicuous by the mid-1790s at the latest, the penetration of party organizations down to the state level was very uneven. In Virginia, even though the sentiment of the political and social elite leaned strongly against the Federalists, there was hardly an Anti-Federalist party organization to speak of. Elections to the Virginia House of Delegates were largely determined by the personal prestige and patronage networks of individual candidates. Often, in fact, candidates' political views on critical issues were unknown until they took their seats. In other cases, such as Pennsylvania, because the balance between competing factions was more finely balanced, party organization was somewhat more advanced. Yet even then parties lacked institutionalized roots in civil society organizations, whether through craft associations, social clubs, or establishment churches. The Democratic-Republican societies or clubs that opposed Adams and Hamilton (especially after the Jay Treaty of 1794, which aligned the United States with Britain, rather than France as Jefferson would have preferred) proliferated in the mid-1790s, but they proved ephemeral, disappearing mostly by 1795 and entirely with Jefferson's election in 1800. In the early republic, as Princeton historian Sean Wilentz writes, the notion of a "permanent electoral machinery" that would link political leaders to voters was "alien" to both Federalist and Anti-Federalist (Republican) alike. According to the late Joel Silbey, a prominent historian of the nineteenth century, early political "[o]rganizational development was both primitive and erratic." There was simply no organized system for selecting candidates, raising money, or running campaigns. "The essential characteristic of the era," Silbey wrote, "was individualistic in political temperament, volatile in voting and result."[36]

In spite of this anti-party sentiment and the challenges of formal party organization, the incentives to coalesce in some way for the purposes of winning power were ineluctable. The evidence is overwhelming that by the mid-1790s a First Party System with Federalists on the one side and Anti-Federalists on the other was taking shape, with these groups being divided along reasonably clear sectional lines. Federalists were dominant in New England, Republicans in the South, while the mid-Atlantic was contested. This sectional consciousness was hardly new – it had animated key debates throughout the Continental Congress and the Constitutional Convention. Slavery was the most obvious basis of the North–South cleavage, but it is worth noting that many of the most substantial slaveholding Southerners, especially those in South Carolina, saw in the Federalist Party the surest protection against any leveling impulses. At the same time, opposition to the Federalists was often found in indebted rural areas in the North and mid-Atlantic, including the western parts of Pennsylvania and Massachusetts – where rebellions like that of Shays occurred in the 1780s and 90s. In any case, the sectional divide went beyond slavery per se, given broader fears of Southern economic domination by a dynamic, mercantile North. Virginia's most popular politician after George Washington, Patrick Henry, feared the "subserviency of Southern to Northern Interests." Fellow Virginian, Richard Henry Lee, went as far as to countenance disunion rather "than to live under the rule of an ... insolent northern majority." In a private letter to Madison in 1795 from his temporary retirement at Monticello, Jefferson also inadvertently revealed his sectional consciousness, writing that his "sole object" was to prevent the success of the Adams-Hamilton Federalists, something he believed would be "fatal to the Southern Republican interest" – the chauvinist label of "Southern" tellingly being crossed out in Jefferson's papers for the more idealistic sounding "Republican." Statistical research has confirmed that relatively coherent and consistent voting blocs had begun to emerge at the Federal level by the mid-1790s and that these blocs had a strong – though not exclusively – sectional flavor. Something very much like partisanship, if not parties, had come to exist.[37]

Focusing either on the role of ideology or of supposedly objective class or sectional interests, historians have had great difficulty in squaring the circle of a clearly stated opposition to parties and the dearth of formal party organization at the state level in the face of very clear partisan political behavior at the national level. The frequently stated antipathy to "party" expressed in much public writing and speaking of the time needs, I believe, to be interpreted with some skepticism. The same is true of the supposed Republican equation of patronage with "corruption" and monarchism. No politician with leadership ambitions could openly advocate the use of government patronage to build political support. This was what the British monarchy had long done both in the colonies through its appointed governors and at home in cultivating the support of the "court" party. However, at the level of practice, if not rhetoric, things were different. Actions, we might say, speak louder than words. Both main political groups, Federalist and Anti-Federalist, would use patronage to build effective political machines.

What much of the historiography on the early republic has neglected is the fact that the first party system was a patronage-based party system. The logic of patrimonial party building is different from that of programmatic party building. Precisely what we would expect in the former case is a situation with weak national "party" penetration to the local level but the intense use of inducements and persuasion at higher levels to create winning political coalitions out of the available set of competing elected local notables. From a distance, in other words, the appearance may be one of a coherent national party system, but up close, the picture is much grainier. Factional rivalries within the American states were grounded more in personal ambition than in ideological conflict, and these interpersonal rivalries were transmuted into party competition. Unlike in France, Americans proved adept at building governing coalitions through patronage. The Federalist and Republican networks that consolidated from the mid-1790s were built on well-established patrimonial foundations. Although they might not have been bureaucratic parties, with set offices, rules, and delineated memberships, they were formidable organizational structures that stood in the way of a direct populist strategy.

The American spoils system so indelibly associated with Andrew Jackson's Democratic Party of the 1830s – on which more in Chapter 4 – had a very long history on the continent. Indeed, by the mid-eighteenth century, America's colonial governors – allied to the crown – had seemed poised to follow a patronage-based strategy to entrench their dominance as had Walpole and successive English prime ministers following him. However, lacking the same control over colony budgets (except in the case of New Hampshire), as the British prime minister had at Westminster, colonial governors were generally unable to manage political factions to the same degree. Instead, control over the patronage fell to the colonial gentry elite itself. Colonial legislatures typically made nominations of men for sheriff, justice of the peace, and other positions of status, which imperial governors were obliged to accept, although the situation subtly varied from colony to colony. It was especially evident in the likes of New York, Virginia, and South Carolina, which were politically dominated by landed grandees, slaveholding or not. Massachusetts and Pennsylvania were more socioeconomically egalitarian than aristocratic New York and Virginia, not to mention South Carolina – both had a larger proportion of independent yeoman and urban artisans – but political factions held together by patronage were present there too.[38]

For the most part, throughout the Revolutionary era, local elites remained in control of their relative sections. Across the solid Northern and Southern sections, and even in most of the mid-Atlantic, the political order generally endured. The state assemblies that convened during the war were dominated by the landholding gentry, lawyers, and other elites, and this situation would largely resume in the 1790s. The only real instance of spontaneous mobilization occurred in the mid-Atlantic, where neither section predominated, the elite was particularly divided, and there was thus already a tradition of political party organization. As the Revolution progressed in Pennsylvania, the Quaker electoral oligarchy was out-mobilized by a group of several hundred well-organized radicals, most of whom were from distinctly "middling" backgrounds. But as historian Eric Foner points out, Pennsylvania was "the only state in which there was virtually no continuity between pre-independence and post-independence political leadership."[39]

Across the rest of the country, even as partisanship became entrenched at the national level in the 1790s, locally prominent men were the ones elected to Congress. In part these men, men like Virginia's Henry, were elected on the back of their oratorical skills or renown as political leaders. Writers have referred to the *deference* of people for such political leaders. Yet more mundane issues were often involved. There was, certainly, some direct vote buying, as Washington's experience illustrates. Perhaps more common but difficult to see in the historical record, was the effect of local socioeconomic standing. In the commercial North, where wealthy merchants had jobs to dispense, such deference had clear economic undertones. In the agrarian South, where elites relied almost exclusively on slave labor, the ties of dependence linking the free white yeoman or laborer with the planter were more diffuse – the sharing of distribution networks, mills, and other small favors. All of this meant that political factions or parties at the national level were bound together not just by ideology or by "objective" interests such as slaveholding but by ties of family (including marriage), friendship, and, very often, patronage.[40]

As much as prominent colonial elites publicly decried the political use of patronage as a tool of royal control, with independence, they too became skillful exponents of the art. Although Hamilton openly abhorred the notion of parties as much as any of the other framers, he studiously cultivated elite support for his program, especially in his adopted state of New York, through the distribution of patronage. Nationally, Hamiltonian Federalists had a substantial advantage over their Republican opponents. As historian Noble Cunningham writes, Hamilton's party "controlled the federal patronage, and they were not disinclined to use this power to entrench themselves in office." Hamilton made the Treasury into the largest branch of government, distributed lucrative jobs in customs, and whenever the Army was needed, recruited the officer class with great attention to its likely political effect. Post Office department jobs were plum patronage positions in the hands of the government and could often be used as supplemental income to buy the support of influential newspaper editors. Hamilton's Treasury may have had some 800 such positions to distribute. Beyond placements, legal rulings over land disputes – not least in contested Indian territory; military provisioning contracts; contracts to print official publications; and public works projects such as roads and port facilities were all grist for the patronage mill. Taxation and commercial policy, though less precisely allotted to specific individuals, could similarly be deployed to buy regional or sectoral loyalty. Even parts of the Southern slaveholding elite, especially that in South Carolina, which was tied to New England mercantile interests through Caribbean and British trade, could be bought over as enthusiastic supporters of Hamilton's commercial system.

Republicans publicly deplored Hamilton as another Walpole. Yet principled as this "country" Whig opposition sounds, it had a very obvious strategic logic. Hamilton had more patronage to distribute, so they had to do all they could to discredit the strategy. Whatever they said, however, for Republicans as well as Federalists, because of the political structure created by the Constitution, the most efficient path to the presidency in the Early Republic was through putting together a winning coalition of patrician elites and their state and local factions, not in directly mobilizing public opinion. After Jefferson's failure to take the presidency in 1796, he and Madison recognized that winning the election in 1800 would require stacking up the support of state-level factions of elites, most of whom maintained their own positions through traditional patronage. Yet without access to Federal resources, Republicans at the national level were constrained in their ability to buy the support of already elected politicians.

Little wonder they railed against Hamilton's "monarchical" looking use of Federal patronage to buttress his legislative majority.

The challenge for Jefferson was how to overcome Hamilton's patronage network. Notwithstanding all of Jefferson's "professions of democracy" as Chief Justice John Marshall put it, the populist strategy was never a contender. There was simply no way to feasibly connect directly with voters over the heads of the local patronage-based political units that existed all across the country. Jefferson would instead seek to beat Hamilton at his own game. Yet without access to government resources – outside of states like Virginia – he instead had to appeal to outsider factions in the states. If they could take power in the states and deliver Jefferson the Electoral College votes he needed, they would be well rewarded. Moreover, Jefferson would in reality only have to shift a handful of states into his column in order to win. Most states in both 1796 and 1800 lined up as their sectional allegiances and economic interests would predict – New England for Adams, the South for Jefferson. The contested terrain was the mid-Atlantic. Sitting between relatively coherent Southern and New England blocs, New York almost alone decided the outcome of America's earliest contested presidential elections. This is where Jefferson and Madison would focus their attentions.[41]

In spite of the notorious subsequent fallout of the two men, by far the most important bargain that Jefferson struck in his bid to win the presidency was the one with Aaron Burr in New York. The outcome of this deal was ultimately to elevate Burr to the vice presidency in 1800 in return for the support of New York's Clinton, Livingston, and Burr factions against Adams. It was Burr's masterminding of the Democratic-Republican victory in the New York state legislative elections of 1800 that gave all thirteen of the state's Electoral College votes to Jefferson. Disputes over the allocation of patronage at the state level allowed Burr to put together an incongruous but winning coalition. Burr is often credited as one of the first modern party organizers for his activities in 1800. He engaged in a tremendous level of electioneering, managing a network of ward committees across New York City. Yet in building up his rival Democratic-Republican political base in New York, Burr employed just the same patronage tactics as Hamilton, using the proceeds from the Manhattan Company bank charter to pay off legislators from across the state's factions on the one hand and to win wider support by opening shareholding and cheap credit to the city's artisans and petty merchants on the other. In 1799, the entire Federalist slate had been successful in the state legislative elections. The crux of Burr's strategy for 1800 was to run a highly distinguished slate of notables – men like former governor George Clinton and Revolutionary War officers Horatio Gates and Brockholst Livingston. Burr's allies in New York were duly rewarded with the positions of district attorney, US marshal, and collector of customs. None of this might have mattered, however, had the Federalists remained cohesive. Burr was successful, in part, because of the split between Adams and Hamiltonian factions of the Federalist coalition. Adams would remark of his Hamiltonian opponents in the wake of his defeat to Jefferson in 1800, "they killed themselves and ... indicted me for the murder." Illustrating the cutthroat nature of these political transactions, however, Jefferson, having won the presidency, switched his patronage to Burr's New York rival, DeWitt Clinton. In part due to concerns that Burr's popularity threatened Jefferson's planned succession to fellow Virginian James Madison, and in part in payback for Burr's supposed scheming to take the presidency from Jefferson in 1800, Jefferson kicked him off the Republican vice presidential ticket in 1804 in favor of DeWitt's uncle, George Clinton, and refused to even endorse him for the governorship of New York. [42]

The distribution of Adams' and Jefferson's support in Pennsylvania in 1800 was similarly the result of factional rivalry within the state. There too the candidates had run extremely close in 1796, so Jefferson needed to pull only a few factions to his side to take the state's Electoral College votes. Promises of patronage also seem to have been made by Republican senator Charles Pickeney in South Carolina to ensure Jefferson's victory in that state – Pickeney's friends received appointments and he himself was made minister to Spain. Jefferson may have put himself forward as the people's tribune against an oppressive, Anglophile, monied aristocracy, but his path to power rested on such intra-elite bargains. Indeed, the Democratic-Republicans were not above switching the choice of presidential electors back from popular vote to nomination by the legislature if that better suited their purposes. One of Jefferson's main tasks on taking office in 1801 was the distribution of patronage. As he lamented some years later, "[s]olicitations for office are the most painful incidents to which an executive magistrate is exposed. The ordinary affairs of a nation offer little difficulty to a person of any experience, but the gift of office is the dreadful burthen which oppresses him." In his study of party building in New Jersey, Carl Prince finds that in the years of Jefferson and Madison's presidencies (1801–16), some two-thirds of Republican party workers held a patronage position; the proportion of those with federal appointments increased over the years, as Federalists were ousted in favor of Republicans. Patronage was the key to party building in the early republic. [43]

This is not to say that popular mobilization played no part in Republican strategy. Indeed, because it lacked access to federal patronage to buy the supported of already elected politicians, the Republican leadership was heavily constrained by what it could offer to state and county bosses. Burr's unusual status as a minor but highly effective politico in New York who was excluded from the highest state offices, made him more willing to make a risky bet. Elsewhere, Jefferson and Madison were compelled to intervene at an earlier stage to ensure that those already loyal to the Republican Party would be elected. This meant mobilizing new voters. On the one hand, Republican elites were minded to preserve their own wealth and status against the poorer and middling classes. However, as Jefferson recognized, their best chance of gaining power was to mobilize exactly those forces against what he called a (Northern) monied aristocracy. Learning from the minority Federalists in their own state of Virginia, who conducted the first mass political appeal in the state at a meeting in Richmond in 1793, Republicans would have to appeal, at least somewhat, to the common man. The goal was never a political or social revolution in which real power or wealth would pass over to the masses – white or black. Rather, a greater degree of popular mobilization would allow one elite – a Southern, agrarian, and slaveholding one – to displace another – a Northern, mercantile, free labor one. In the South, although mass mobilization ostensibly ran against the interests of Virginia's planter elite, they retained a studied control over local politics that prevented the process from running amok. Not only were property qualifications on the franchise retained, but the allocation of representatives in the state was heavily weighted in favor of the Eastern tobacco planting class. The Tidewater elite's experience gave it a reasonable expectation that it could control "democratic" politics after the Revolution, much as it had in the past. Virginia was among about a third of signatory states that hardened franchise requirements in the years that followed. Democratization – patronage-based democratization – posed a low, and hence acceptable risk, for Southern elites.

The Republican mobilization of new voters among the common classes would instead be concentrated in the New England bastion of Federalism and in the battlegrounds of the mid-Atlantic. It was in New England, where the Federalists offered the stiffest opposition, that the Republican machine was best developed. There, mass mobilization threatened precisely the opposing elites – merchants and financiers – who controlled the Federalist Party. For Northern elites, in contrast, who lacked the planters' paternalistic control over the region's comparatively much larger free white population, the implied cost of incorporating the masses was greater. The same would be true in South Carolina, which would remain in the Federalist camp. Even though a slave state, South Carolina was dominated by especially wealthy commercially oriented slaveholders, who feared the leveling effects of mass participation more than they did any Union government attacks on slavery. In the South as in the North, the early Federalist strategy remained to bring locally prominent politicians into the party through federal patronage, not to mobilize voters directly. Federalism's opponents rightly intuited that such a strategy would be more likely to succeed the smaller the electorate, the more restrictions that could be placed on opposition activity, and the more funds that were available to the state for use as patronage.

De facto as well as de jure democratization could only help the Republican outsiders and harm Federalist insiders, especially in the North, as the limited patronage they controlled would have to be dispersed more widely. Gordon Wood, one of the preeminent historians of Revolutionary America, writes of the increase in political activity: "This expansion of popular politics originated not because the mass of people pressed upwards from below with new demands, but because competing gentry, for their own parochial and tactical purposes, courted the people and bid for their support by invoking popular whig rhetoric." For the most part, this mobilization was done not through direct mass communication but through the piecewise incorporation of local political factions. There just wasn't an end run to the people around the state level brokers. Building on a long colonial tradition of patrimonial governance, patronage party building was cost-effective politics in the early Republic. Nevertheless, by mobilizing at least some new voters, Jefferson's Republican Party contributed to the rise of democracy, and in the process sowed the seeds for the success of a populist strategy in the future.[44]

LOOKING BACKWARD, LOOKING FORWARD

The material conditions of preindustrial France and America are closer in some respects to the ancient world than to today; it's easy to dismiss them as historical curiosities. Yet these cases reveal something important about the economics of populism. The viability of populism in new democracies depends, in large part, on the way democracy is introduced and on the kind of regime that went before it. Where democracy has been introduced unexpectedly with little or no proto-democratic forbearer, populism may be the quickest and cheapest way to gain power. To the extent that it is successful once, this can create a powerful demonstration effect; a kind of recurrent populism in which one demagogue is outbid by the next. In contrast, in places where that transition has been more gradual, and where some kinds of pre-democratic patrimonial links persist, patronage-based mobilization is a powerful obstacle to the populist strategy. The upshot is that political shocks, like economic ones, have different effects in different places.

The development of rival political factions and then parties in the early American republic can be taken to demonstrate that patronage was a more effective strategy for winning and keeping power in its institutional context than was populism. That the Federalist Party would itself rent along the lines of Adams and Hamilton blocs in spite of considerable shared economic interests and political philosophies is indicative of the persistent role of personal allegiances and factional rivalries in the early republic. Contrary to the idealized view of Jefferson and Madison as *philosophes* above the fray of regular politics, the Republican Party they built was every bit as dependent on the distribution of patronage as that of its Federalist rival.

As Madison and Hamilton outlined in the Federalist Papers, American democracy was to be well fettered by indirect elections, divided government, and Federalism, all of which placed severe limitations on populism as a political strategy. There was no simple, cost-effective way of mobilizing Electoral College votes through a direct appeal to the masses. To try to gain the presidency in this way would have meant a gigantic multistate election campaign to influence the results in state assemblies, which would, in turn, have determined the outcome of the Electoral College. Some of this might theoretically have been achieved by the distribution of newspapers and pamphlets. However, without a national network of loyal local brokers, including especially local postal officers responsible for distributing political mail, it is difficult to see how even this could have been accomplished without great cost. Even then, the state legislators elected in this way may not have proven to be reliable allies. It is hard to see how populism could work as a strategy under such circumstances.

The French experience paints a stark contrast. With a social revolution that swept away existing patrimonial ties and centralized an administration that failed to reestablish a means of bringing together the new political factions that emerged, populism was a dangerously efficient political strategy. Moderates, and there were many in post-1789 France, were not effectively bound to the administration. They put up weak resistance to their demagogic opponents; Danton, Robespierre, and Hébert among them. The inability, or unwillingness, of even the more constrained Directory regime to build governing coalitions through the distribution of patronage left it politically vulnerable to challenge from left and right. With essentially no attachments to political parties, the people were ripe for the celebrity appeal of Napoleon. Literally the man on horseback, Napoleon could credibly promise to bring about the longed-for return to order. Patronage may seem a calculating, unseemly basis on which to build a democracy. But in the short term, as Hamilton and even Jefferson recognized, it is instrumental, even if, as Chapter 4 shows, the institutionalization of a democracy based on the distribution of patronage may not be a long-term prophylactic against the menace of populism.

4

Democracy's Children

"Well, in our country," said Alice, still panting a little, "you'd generally get to get somewhere else—if you ran very fast for a long time, as we've been doing." "A slow sort of country!" said the Queen. "Now, here, you see, it takes all the running you can do, to keep in the same place. If you want to get somewhere else, you must run at least twice as fast as that!"

Lewis Carroll, *Alice's Adventures in Wonderland*, 1865

To the victor belong the spoils

William L. Marcy, speech to the United States Senate, 25 January 1832

PRINCIPALS, AGENTS, AND POPULISTS

As the case of postrevolutionary America illustrates, patronage-based bargains can be more efficient than populist mobilization, especially when political participation is itself constrained by practices such as the indirect selection of presidential electors. Yet every institutional set up generates losers as well as winners. Those excluded from their share of the spoils in a patronage-based setup have every incentive to try and change it. In a context where the percentage turnout is only in the single digits, most voters have at best weak attachments to political parties. The mobilization of just a few thousand additional voters could be sufficient to swing the results of national elections and populism provides an effective means of doing so. Critically, by drawing in new voters, by increasing political participation, populists drive up the costs faced by patronage-based political leaders. Picking up the historical narrative of both the American and French cases in the early nineteenth century, we'll see that the more open democratic competition becomes – fairer elections, greater participation, a freer press, etc. – the higher the cost of maintaining power through the distribution of patronage. Eventually this complex and expensive network of transactions becomes uneconomical. As this chapter will show, Andrew Jackson's populist turn in the 1820s was precisely a response to these dynamics; so too was the reemergence of populism in France and America at the end of the nineteenth century. Patronage is economical initially but eventually becomes unsustainable.

Why, over the longer term, do patronage based political systems seem to sow the seeds of their own destruction? The answer can be found in another insight from microeconomics, known as the principal agent dilemma. The principal agent dilemma describes a conflict of interest between one party (a principal) and another party (an agent) who is contracted by them to them to perform a particular task. The classic example in the economics literature refers to the differing interests of owners (principals) and managers (agents) of a firm. The owners of a firm are primarily, if not solely, concerned with the value of their investment – in other words, they like the share price of the firm to be high. Managers, however, need not have the same motivations. A manger might want to raise his own salary, take on pet projects, hire cronies, or do other things that make himself richer and happier even if this could reduce the value of the firm. Managers' salaries can be easily monitored, but because they – as agents – have access to information about the firm's operations that shareholders – or principals – do not, much of their other behavior is hidden from view. For this reason, modern managers are often partially compensated in shares – to turn them into owners – but even this may not be sufficient. Agents adapt, soon finding ways around and through the monitoring schemes that principals put in place to discipline them. Like Lewis Carroll's Red Queen, principals find themselves running faster and faster just to keep pace, adding in ever more complex and expensive mechanisms of control.

To understand the implications of this principal agent problem for the rise of populism, let's consider the economics of patronage in more detail. As I suggested in the introduction, the costs involved in the patronage-based mobilization of popular support are perhaps the most transparent of political costs – people are often literally paid in cash for their votes. These direct costs make clientelism an expensive business, as the number of electors (voters) runs into the thousands, or even millions, depending on the size of the constituency. However, as I also noted, the direct costs of clientelism likely pale in comparison to the indirect ones, the transaction costs. The major problem with relying on patronage to buy votes is that politicians today just can't be sure that voters hold up their end of the bargain. Although it is usually possible to find out *if* people have voted, it's not easy to tell *how* they've voted. Whole electoral wards can be punished by a candidate if his winning vote share isn't sufficiently high. However, for a losing candidate, punishing an electorate for failing to support him might feel good, but this blunt approach would be costly and wouldn't change the result. Scale this up to the national level, where aspiring leaders don't purchase votes directly but acquire support indirectly through a vast franchising operation of intermediaries, or brokers, and the difficulties are compounded. Voters sell their support to village heads and ward bosses, these local brokers to councilors, councilors to governors, and governors to presidents. The more freedom that each intermediary has to sell his block of votes to those above him in this vast pyramid scheme, the more costly patronage becomes as way to maintain power. Where brokers – agents – can't be disciplined from above by political leaders – principals – they are free to sell the support of their clients to the highest bidder. They're also free to lie and cheat, accepting payment from multiple masters at once, skimming from the bribes intended for voters, or otherwise increasing the costly need to monitor their behavior. Only in more centralized and closed – if also less democratic – patronage-based systems, might a disobedient broker, like a mayor, find himself removed from office, thereby restraining costs.

As the world's first modern exponents of mass democracy, it is perhaps unsurprising that America and France should remain the locus of populist mobilization as the nineteenth century progressed. Yet once the opening era of revolution had come to a close with Napoleon's defeat exile in 1815, the relative roles would be reversed. If the construction of a democratic political system based on the distribution of patronage rendered populism an ineffective strategy in the early American republic, this was not a permanent situation. Indeed, the maturation of a patronage-based form of authority actually created the conditions for successive populist challenges. Populists, as we'll see, are ever ready to take advantage of any weakening of the defences, and none was more prepared to exploit the breach than General Andrew Jackson. In turn, even as Jackson institutionalized his rule, he laid the conditions for a new cycle – a second spoils system and a renewed populist challenge – to begin.

As we saw, the early decades of American politics were dominated by the Southern, indeed, Virginian oligarchy. So dominant was it that by the 1820s, America had become a one-party state. Andrew Jackson, president from 1829 to 1836, and Martin Van Buren, Jackson's most important backer and presidential successor, were the beneficiaries of changed social, economic, and political conditions that made a breakup of that old system increasingly likely. Over the early 1800s, the accretion of ever greater patronage powers in the office of the presidency made it an office increasingly worth fighting over. Those excluded from power – those outside of the Virginia oligarchy – wanted a share. The very absence of interparty competition in the early 1920s freed personalistic factions to compete among themselves. This process compelled rivals into increased political mobilization, and ultimately, increased democratization. The masses, as we've seen on several occasions already, were recruited by populists like Jackson in the intra-elite contest for power.

However, once in power, Jackson, contrary to the characterizations of his Whig detractors – who liked to style him King Andrew – instituted not a form of plebiscitary dictatorship but a mass patronage-based democracy. Much as Jackson attempted to appeal directly to the people, he found himself frequently frustrated in dealing with his own nominal allies in Congress. The spoils system was not new to the 1830s, but it is in this period that it begins to flourish. The crisis of the Second Party System in the 1850s saw another general-president, Zachary Taylor, seek to rise above party and appeal directly to the people. However, mid-century populism died a death along with Taylor, and a new party system based on section – the free labor North and the slaveholding South – was constructed on the foundations of the old. Once the dust of the Civil War settled, Republicans and Democrats proved adept at converting the vastly expanded resources of the Reconstruction state into grist for the patronage mill. It was in the Gilded Age of the latter part of the century that money politics reached its perverse apogee; rent by competing factions more concerned with dividing the spoils of government patronage, the major parties were susceptible to populist appeals to the growing number of their increasingly dissatisfied clients.

In France, the overthrow of Napoleon and the restoration of the Bourbon monarchy was no step forward for democracy. Louis XVIII sought nothing less than a return to the prerevolutionary absolute monarchy of 1788, if not 1715. With the legitimacy, and coercive strength, of the crown much diminished, however, Louis had to settle for a constitutional monarchy, albeit one in which the franchise was restricted to less than one hundredth of the population, and in which the bicameral chambers of parliament would have only a consultative role. Any effective constraints on the crown these institutions provided were emasculated with the accession of Charles X in 1824. As with his cousin in 1789, however, Charles was in turn undone by the failure to address France's economic stagnation. In the late 1820s, the peasantry again faced severe economic hardships, and the bourgeois elite pushed for a new round of liberal reforms. In 1830, liberals, led by Adolph Thiers, escalated their pressure on the ailing monarch. As the King attempted to reassert control, the Parisian crowd took the side of the liberals. Louis Philippe, of the Orléanist line, was put on the throne, with the hope for a bourgeois-dominated constitutional monarchy – that failed aspiration of Mirabeau in 1789 finally looking bright. Whereas elites in America – and even Britain – acknowledged, however begrudgingly, the emergence of a mass middle class – rather than merely a narrow bourgeois elite – the French ruling class remained deeply fearful of democracy and obdurately resisted the incorporation of the masses in any form. With its political inclusion choked off, it was only a matter of time before the laboring classes took matters into their own hands, overthrowing the monarchy in the revolution of 1848. Democracy again had its chance, yet, still without any effective mass political parties, it would be a democracy in which the populist strategy was the most efficient. Exploiting his family name, Louis Napoleon was elected France's first president in 1848. With his regime, by turns democratic and authoritarian but always populist, we'll see the emergence of a political form that looks decidedly modern. Populism would continue to rear its head in the French Third Republic that followed Napoleon III's overthrow in

1871. Only the personal incompetence of General Georges Boulanger prevented him from taking power in the Bonapartist – populist tradition as he rose in popularity in the 1880s. The consolidation of patronage-based parties in the last decade of the century, however, would make the populist strategy ineffective for some time.

MASS DEMOCRACY

Andrew Jackson was sworn in as the seventh president of the United States of America in Washington, DC, on March 4, 1828. An estimated 20,000 flocked to the capital to catch a glimpse of Old Hickory, the Hero of New Orleans – the last battle with British forces on American soil. Jackson's speech was brief and few in attendance could actually hear it. With the formalities concluded, Jackson retired to the White House to receive well-wishers. Crowds descended on the president's official residence and it wasn't long before Jackson himself was nearly crushed in the melee. Ushered out under the protection of some of the gentlemen in attendance, Jackson slipped off to the nearby Gadsby Hotel where he was still staying. The mob grew wilder, destroying furniture, smashing windows, and drinking everything in sight. "I never saw such a mixture. The reign of king mob seemed triumphant" remarked one distressed Supreme Court justice.[1]

Jackson's election was, if not a turning point, certainly a critical milestone in American political history. Well into the 1820s, American politics was dominated by the Southern – espcially Virginian – oligarchy. Washington, Jefferson, Madison, and Monroe were all at least moderately wealthy land – and slave – owners. Only John Adams broke that trend among the first presidents, and he, although more well-educated than well-born, was no rabble-rousing outsider to the political elite. In the years since Jefferson had left office, the prospects of radical change to this conservative system seemed only to become more remote. With the virtual dissolution of the Federalist Party after 1815, there was essentially only one political party left standing. More than ever, the presidency was to be determined within the elite of the Republican Party caucus. There was every indication that Monroe's successor would be chosen in the same way, even if some felt that a party caucus selection of the president was not what the founders, or the people, had ever intended. Even still, into the 1820s, it remained both unseemly and impractical to make a direct bid for the presidency. Winning the presidency required elite, not popular, backing. In less than a decade, Jackson would disturb this apparent consensus. Exploiting the rapid growth of the electorate, Jackson made the first tentative steps at popularizing the election of the president. Yet institutional, social, economic, and technological constraints still limited the effectiveness of a pure populist strategy. Jackson failed to secure the presidency in 1824 and was successful in 1828 only because he exploited a more mixed strategy that would inaugurate a new period of mass patronage politics.

In the early decades of the nineteenth century, national government was still a minor presence in most Americans' lives with the result that even presidential elections did not occupy the attention that they do now. Although turnouts for local elections gradually rose under Jefferson's presidency (1801–08), reaching as high as 70 or 80 percent, they remained at about half of this level for presidential elections. Moreover, turnout actually fell from the time Jefferson left office through to the mid-1820s. In numerical terms, the people appear to have had no greater a role in determining the choice of its chief executive than when the revolution began nearly half a century before. Jefferson was succeeded by his nominated fellow Democratic-Republican, James Madison in 1808, and he by another Virginian, James Monroe in 1816. So demobilized had the American populace become that Monroe's reelection in 1820 was virtually unopposed and frankly underwhelming – only 87,343 voters, just 10 percent of the electorate, bothering to vote. In his native Virginia, where there was essentially no contest, the turnout was only 3 percent.

Monroe may have been effectively made president by acclamation, but he was hardly universally popular. With no such thing as a primary election, the public had almost no say in choosing the man who would occupy the White House. Rather it was all decided by just 119 Democratic-Republican congressmen; that is, not even the full 182 members of Congress. Monroe only won the Republican Party caucus' nomination over former Secretary of War and then Secretary of the Treasury, William H. Crawford of Georgia, by the narrow margin of 65 to 54. The transaction costs entailed in winning those sixty-plus votes in the Republican caucus needed to take the nomination would have been dwarfed by the cost of trying to determine the makeup of the caucus itself. In this world, if national power is what was sought, appealing directly to the people would have been a massive waste of time and money. Given the indirect nature of the selection process, through to the mid-1820s, patronage rather than populism remained the most efficient political strategy to win and keep power in America.

In short, even as there was an ineluctable opening of participation at the base of society in the early decades of the nineteenth century, the occupancy of the presidency itself remained very much a decision made in proverbial smoke-filled rooms by small caucuses of elites, who were, at least temporarily, united in an "Era of Good Feelings" around the issue of national development. By the end of the War of 1812, there had emerged a substantial National Republican elite consensus around the twin needs for expansion and developmentalism, the main components of which were Indian removal, southwestern expansionism, the reconstitution of a national bank (even bigger than the Hamiltonian one Republicans had so opposed), a system of protective tariffs, and to a more contested degree, infrastructural improvements. Even if Southerners were in general resistant to the National-Republican agenda, the rapid economic recovery after the War of 1812 helped to paper over the party's divisions. Whether the people were themselves as enthused about this expansive tax and spend program is very doubtful. Patronage in theory trickles down, but the evidence suggests that the richest flows were stanched well before they got to the bottom. Monroe, in any case, retained his old Jeffersonian scruples against federal overreach, so was never the most enthusiastic promotor of grand infrastructural schemes. As a result, even as Monroe explicitly sought sectional harmony through the distribution of patronage – every important region gaining some kind of position in his cabinet – factional discontent simmered under the surface.[2]

An opening of the political order – democratization – typically occurs when the elite itself splits, as rivals mobilize more and more of the masses in order to best their opponents. The status quo, by definition, serves the incumbent well, so any injection of new issues or cleavages is unlikely to come from this quarter. As we've seen, opposition to Hamilton's northern, elite, commercially oriented faction drove Jeffersonian outsiders to appeal to small farmers and urban artisans. In turn, however, the outsiders then became insiders. The Republican-Democrats, who had such an overwhelming majority by the end of Jefferson's tenure, had no need to further agitate the masses. As new, southern, slaveholding states joined the union, the Virginian-Republican party elite's monopoly over the presidency seemed secure. In this context, we might expect efforts to mobilize the masses to have come from the northern Federalist opposition, but with the National Republicans adopting an ultra-Hamiltonian agenda of its own, it was unclear what issues were left for the rump group of Federalists to exploit. In any event, with the debacle of the Hartford Convention of 1816, in which the New England states contemplated secession amid a simmering schism over the war with Britain, the taint of treason had effectively eliminated the Federalist Party.

In politics, of course, all consensus is temporary. For outsider elites in search of power, the challenge is finding the right button to push. By the 1820s, the revivified sectional conflict over slavery raised by western expansion suggested a new wedge that could see northern elites win power within the union. John Quincy Adams himself recognized that antislavery might be "the basis for a new organization of parties," one that could unseat the Virginia dynasty. However, with the Missouri Compromise of 1820, the issue again receded, and the formation of a two-party system along sectional lines was delayed until the 1850s. Both southern and northern elites could maintain their place with Monrovian developmentalism providing just enough of a benefit for both sections to form a workable political consensus. The uptick in mobilization of the 1820s came not from northern abolitionists seeking to challenge southern political supremacy but from a growing population excited primarily by the issues of Indian removal, the expansion of the frontier, immigration, infrastructure, and tariffs – issues that cut unevenly across sectional lines in the old North and South.[3]

The outsider who emerged to take advantage of this western expansion was Andrew Jackson. Much more so than any of his presidential predecessors, Jackson's early circumstances were inauspicious. On account of the death of his father prior to his birth in South Carolina in 1767, Jackson was raised in a mixed extended family by his mother and uncle. He fought briefly as a boy in the Revolution, but his youth was characterized more by frivolity, if not debauchery, than by political activity. The self-taught Jackson took up the law, moved east into the Tennessee region, and attached himself to the influential politician and land speculator, William Blount. In 1789, North Carolina ceded to the United States the area that became the Southwest Territory, with Blount becoming its inaugural territorial governor. Appointed, rather than elected, the governor had enormous power, with virtually every patronage position in the territory under his remit. Jackson was no scholar, but with a reputation as an effective lawyer and public prosecutor, he had no difficulty in drawing Blount's attention or approbation. Jackson was made attorney general of Mero District on the frontier and given a commission in the militia. In 1796, Jackson won election as a delegate to the state constitutional convention that preceded the territory's admission to the Union as the state of Tennessee. He was subsequently tapped to be the state's only representative in Congress; he kept a low profile in Philadelphia but by most accounts was diligent and competent. His most notable success was to secure federal reimbursement for Tennessee militia expenses incurred in operations against Cherokee Indians. Less auspiciously, he asserted his Republican credentials by refusing to support a letter of approbation for George Washington upon his retirement as president. When in 1797 his patron, Blount, was impeached and expelled from the United States Senate for conspiring to begin an unauthorized war in Spanish-held Louisiana, Jackson won the election in the Tennessee legislature to take up his seat.[4]

Jackson, however, resigned from the Senate after less than six months in office. The reasons for his sudden resignation remain unclear. His most prominent biographer, Robert Remini, speculates that Jackson lacked the temperament or the learning to feel at home in the august Senate. Jackson was no shrinking violet, however, so it seems a stretch to imply that his resignation was motivated by personal feelings of inadequacy. Others have suggested that financial concerns brought him back to Tennessee, where he could better attend to his various land speculation schemes. We will never know. In any case, even while Jackson did recover his finances during this period, he kept one foot in politics as a justice on the Tennessee Supreme Court. Jackson developed a reputation as an effective, if unlearned, judge in the Tennessee backcountry. Constant travel around the western part of the state and the careful cultivation of men of influence in political and economic circles meant that Jackson was never short of invitations to return to electoral politics.

Jackson, however, made his early mark not in electoral politics but as a commander of the Tennessee militia. When war was declared against Britain in 1812, although initially denied his opportunity to win fame in battle against the British, Jackson nevertheless earned the admiration of his men: the Old Hickory moniker dating from the early days of this campaign. Eager for action, Jackson turned his attention against the Native American tribes to the South, defeating the Red Stick faction of the Creek tribe at the Battle of Horseshoe Bend in 1813. He pursued the survivors south into Alabama and Mississippi, eventually extorting a cession of some 23 million acres of Indian territory – approximately a third of the area of the present-day states of Alabama and Georgia. Jackson's exploits won him appointment as a major general in the United States Army, a position that would further burnish his reputation with the famous victory he led over British regulars at the Battle of New Orleans in 1815. Although a favorable peace had in fact already been signed two weeks before the battle, Jackson's victory seemed a fitting revenge for the British torching of the White House the previous year, and may well have influenced the British ratification of the treaty that was still to follow. Jackson would forever be known as the "Hero of New Orleans" – his Scots-Irish roots and this humiliation of the English would later make him especially popular among non-Anglo voters.

With his military services no longer required, and debts still mounting at home, Jackson returned to the Hermitage, his estate in Nashville, Tennessee, to reassume the life of a planter. In spite of his modest beginnings, by the time Jackson became president, he had become one of the richest men in the state, accumulating some 150 slaves. Although his growing wealth was a welcome development, Jackson never gave up on the idea of returning to the national political stage and the military route provided his surest means to do so. Appointed commander of the Southern Division in May 1815, Jackson refocused his attention on Indian troubles along the frontier. In 1818, he won another bloody war against the Seminole tribes in Florida, controversially crossing into Spanish territory without congressional authorization. Jackson's disregard for such constitutional proprieties led critics like Speaker of the House, Henry Clay, to compare him to Caesar, Cromwell, and Napoleon. Jackson, however, received the tacit backing of President Monroe, and was later cleared of wrongdoing by a congressional investigation, while a condemnatory Senate report was permanently tabled. Monroe named him governor of the newly acquired Florida Territory in 1821. Jackson's tenure as governor was short-lived, but it is nevertheless instructive. Jackson supposedly was unenthusiastic about relocating there, but "one motive for accepting the governorship," as his nephew Andrew Jackson Donelson would later write, "was the promotion and assistance of his friends." In other words, he took the position on the assumption that it would afford him a platform to distribute political patronage in the form of administrative positions and land deals. Jackson would often distain such activity by his opponents, and denied doing it himself, but it is clear that he was already adept at the politics of patronage well before the famed Jacksonian Democratic system came into being in the 1930s.[5]

It was in 1822 that Jackson returned to the national political spotlight, possibly less on his own initiative than at the behest of his friends in the Willie Blount-John Overton faction that remained so influential in Tennessee politics and finance. Losing the governorship to the rival Erwin faction's candidate, William Carroll, in 1821, Overton and his allies – otherwise known as the Nashville Junto – at first put forward the idea of Jackson competing directly for the governor's office in 1823. Carroll, also a veteran of the Battle of New Orleans, had exploited popular anti-bank sentiment to win the governorship (and keep it for some fourteen years). Jackson thus seemed to be the perfect tool for the wealthy Junto to not only tap popular resentments but also to prevent any further erosion of its financial interests in the state. Jackson, however, was uninterested in the governorship, so Overton instead began to manoeuvre Jackson's entry into the 1824 presidential race, which would serve the Junto's purposes just as well. More machinations followed. To prevent Erwinite control of the state legislature – and in turn to control Tennessee's delegates to the Electoral College – Jackson's backers had to first run him for a seat in the United States Senate. Jackson had little enthusiasm for a return to the upper house, reluctant as he was to encumber himself by having to publicly stake out positions on controversial issues. Jackson won, and in the end, beyond raising awkward questions about his position on the tariff, his brief stint back in national office did him no harm. In Washington, he remained on his best behavior, allaying northern fears that he was an intemperate, tomahawk wielding chieftain.[6]

Jackson failed in an extraordinarily close presidential race in 1824, but the reality is that he never would have gotten so close had William H. Crawford, secretary of war, the Republican Party caucus' preferred candidate – the other main contender for the Southwest's anti-improvement vote – not had a massive and debilitating stroke in 1823. Although Crawford stayed in the race, barely able to speak or stand, he was effectively ruled out as a serious candidate. Jackson was further aided by the fragmentation of party support among his other rivals: John C. Calhoun, John Quincy Adams, and Henry Clay. Calhoun, secretary of the Treasury and then a hardcore developmental National Republican, was the youngest of the bunch. Although he shared much of the policy program of Adams and Clay, as a South Carolinian, he had the added draw of being potentially acceptable to the slaveholding south. Yet he remained behind favored sons almost everywhere. Once his support in Pennsylvania drifted away to Jackson, he pulled out to become the party's only vice presidential candidate. Clay, Speaker of the House, though born in Virginia, was the western candidate, associated especially with national infrastructural development (and the tariffs needed to pay for them). Adams, the New Englander, son of the former president, and then Secretary of State, had perhaps the most impressive credentials, if the least personal appeal.

In contrast to his opponents, Jackson had not yet staked out a distinctive set of policies, whether on internal improvements or the tariff – something his astute backers saw as an asset rather than a liability. Jackson supporters could see in him whatever they wanted. What they mostly saw was that he was not part of the Washington establishment. In that paradoxical style that has become so familiar to American politics, Jackson would run as the nonpolitical politician of the bunch. In spite of his own substantial wealth in land and slaves, he was identified as a common man who might stand opposed to the elite interests that had for so long dominated American politics.[7]

In the five-way, and then four-way race that followed, Jackson won a plurality of the popular vote and had a substantial lead in electors over Adams in the Electoral College. Although Jackson, befitting the custom of the time, outwardly abjured the appearance of seeking the presidency, privately, he was undoubtedly excited by the prospect. Once his nomination was made public, he campaigned "as hard as decency allowed." Jackson's folk nativism, viscerally demonstrated in his Indian fighting record, was massively popular in the Deep South and the Southwest. He also did surprisingly well in Pennsylvania, where long-simmering factional rivalries had already split the Republican Party. Jackson's victory there was as much the result of an internal revolt against the elite "Family" backed candidacy of Calhoun. In this context, the more charismatic elements of his campaign, not least his backing in the widely read *Observer*, generated genuine bottom-up enthusiasm, especially among non-Anglo voters. Yet whatever mass support Jackson and his surrogates managed to directly mobilize, this was still not enough to win the presidency in 1824.[8]

With no candidate gaining a majority in the Electoral College, the Constitution determined that a selection from among the top three candidates would be made by the House of Representatives, with each state's delegation of congressmen getting one collective vote – thirteen was the magic number of states needed to win. Clay had been confident that if the contest went that far, as Speaker of the House, he would easily prevail. In retrospect, this impression may have been misplaced, but coming in fourth place, it would never be tested as he was forced to pull out. Although the House vote couldn't be determined by Clay alone, he nevertheless held significant leverage to swing the vote, especially of the western states that had gone for him, one way or another. He encouraged his supporters from Kentucky and elsewhere to fold in behind Adams, keeping Jackson out of the presidency.

The notoriously hot-headed Jackson was indignant, believing that his command of a plurality of the popular vote entitled him to the presidency. Jackson, so he claimed, believed in the simplicity of majority rule: "the first principle of our system—that the majority is to govern." He himself claimed to have eschewed any political maneuvering, declaring to a friend: "I intermix with none of those who are engaged with intrigues of caucus, or president makers, nor do I intend ... I have but one feeling and that is, that the people make a good choice." Ever one to assume that he was the victim of a grand conspiracy, for Jackson, Adams victory had the stain of a "corrupt bargain." Although Clay was resolved to support Adams over Jackson long before the election results were known, in a move that did neither man any good, Adams offered, and Clay accepted the position of Secretary of State – then seen as the stepping-stone to the presidency – in the new administration.[9]

The interpretation of Jackson as the "people's choice" denied by elite machinations was repeated by Jackson supporters incessantly over the next four years. Admirers of Jackson have since endorsed it with little criticism. There are, however, several problems with this reading of events that are relevant for our purposes. First, Adams was the only candidate who shared Clay's policy agenda of internal improvements and an opposition to the spread of slavery, if not its abolition. Even if Jackson came second to Clay in Kentucky, this does not imply that Clay voters would not in fact have chosen Adams over Jackson in a two-horse race. Second, it has to be recalled that Jackson won only 27 percent of the popular vote, far from a commanding majority. Third, if all states had in fact held popular votes to choose their electors – many state legislatures, including New York, still made the selection indirectly – Adams would probably have had the most votes by some distance. Fourth, Jackson's Electoral College vote was inflated by the three-fifths rule that overweighted southern slaveholding constituencies. Last, Adams' vote was much more regionally balanced than that of any of the other candidates, including Jackson. Adams, in short, most likely *was* the popular choice. All of this suggests, in other words, that it was not simply a "corrupt bargain" that kept the popular – and populist – Jackson from the presidency in 1824. At that point in American political development, the populist strategy alone was simply unlikely to be sufficient in mobilizing enough votes to win the presidency.[10]

For Jackson and his partisans, the result confirmed their affirmation that the swamp needed to be drained. Adams had hardly been inaugurated when Jackson and his supporters began a four-year long campaign for "vindication." In 1828, Jackson relied to a great deal on direct empathy with voters, especially new voters, to come to power. As several modern historians have argued, 1828 was in many respects the first modern political campaign. Although campaign biographies, public rallies, and so on were not technically new to 1828, they were henceforth of an unprecedented scale. Yet at the same time as this populist strategy was executed, the failure of Jackson's backers in the political dark arts in 1824 had taught him a bitter lesson in Electoral College math. In 1828, Jackson supplemented his genuine populist appeal in the West and rural parts of the mid-Atlantic with an alliance with the Calhoun clique in the South and the patronage machines of Isaac Hill's Concord Regency in New Hampshire and Martin van Buren's Albany Regency in New York. As Van Buren put it, winning the presidency in 1828 would require combining Jackson's "personal popularity with the portion of old party feeling yet remaining."[11]

New York, which controlled the largest number of electoral college votes of any state, had been the key swing state in the House vote in 1824; turning it around was instrumental to Jackson's success in 1828. Events there give a sense of how important patronage would be as a complement to Jackson's populist strategy. An affable and effective political operator, Van Buren had been developing his party machine as a member of the New York Senate and state attorney general since at least the mid-1810s, but his initial progress had been checked by the powerful "old money" DeWitt Clinton faction. A pioneer in the use of the caucus, Van Buren imposed rigid discipline on his Bucktail faction – a name derived from the emblem of the Tammany Society in New York City with which it was associated – eventually leading it to gain a majority in the state legislature. In 1821, with United States senators still chosen indirectly by the state legislature, Van Buren was himself then selected for national office. Before leaving for Washington, however, Van Buren took up the task of revising New York's state constitution, something that had been on the cards at least since the War of 1812. With a majority of the delegates behind him, Van Buren engineered a modest set of reforms, one of the most critical of which was to give the Bucktail-dominated Senate a much more powerful role than in the past. The following year, Van Buren's faction, henceforth known as the Albany Regency for its near total control over state and federal patronage in New York, was successful in wresting control away from Clinton and installing its own man as governor. The Regency became the model of a new patronage-based party, one that would eventually be emulated by Jacksonian Democrats at the national level. As Jabez Hammond, a contemporary New York politician and later historian commented, "no portion of the Union [was] so much influenced by the distribution of Patronage" as his state. Not that all was smooth sailing for Van Buren. When the Regency removed Clinton as president of the Erie Canal Commission in 1824 – Clinton had been largely responsible for securing construction of the canal – the popular backlash was swift, and Clinton was reelected governor as a People's Party candidate. Van Buren's Albany Regency also in turn lost control of the state nominating process in the contested 1824 presidential election, with Adams narrowly edging out Van Buren's man, Crawford.[12]

Van Buren was determined to win back control of his state and to secure all the federal patronage he could in the process. Thus, as much as he had his reservations about Jackson, Van Buren knew a winning ticket when he saw one, and so in 1828 he threw the Regency's support to the Tennessean. Clinton's death in 1828 greatly simplified matters, as he too was a rival to be Jackson's man in the state. Nathaniel Pitcher, a Van Buren ally, succeeded Clinton in the governor's office. Van Buren had disagreed with Jackson over the latter's more expansive nationalism, but whenever Van Buren had to choose, "politics took precedence over ideology." Jackson was clearly the lesser of two evils. Adams' program of federally funded improvements was anathema to Van Buren. With New York having already paid for the Erie Canal itself without any federal support, Van Buren in turn opposed using "our money to build internal improvements in other states."[13]

The machinations of Van Buren and his machine are instructive of the role that patronage played in Jackson's second shot at the presidency. It should be noted, moreover, that the New York machine was not the only one to back Jackson. The era's three other most developed party machines, those of Isaac

Hill in New Hampshire, Thomas Ritchie in Virginia, and most critically for Jackson, John Overton in Tennessee, all threw their support behind Old Hickory in 1828. For these men "the goal was personal and party political advancement more than ideology." Thus, much as Jackson portrayed himself as an opponent of the old corruption – patronage politics – his team's more successful intrigues at the second time of asking were critical to placing him in the White House.[14]

This lengthy caveat aside, it is still worthwhile to speak of Jackson as a partial or quasi-populist. Although Jackson, like his predecessors, never personally campaigned for office, delivering stump speeches or the like, his direct appeal to regular voters was critical to his success. He was the first celebrity president since Washington and his team wasn't slow to draw comparisons with the nation's first general-president. Yet if Washington became president by acclamation, Jackson, or rather his backers, needed to campaign. Throughout 1827 and 1828, the masses were mobilized directly by Jackson surrogates through a growing suite of Jackson-aligned newspapers. Picnics and parades – usually heavily alcohol fueled – were another occasion for getting out Jackson's name. In a theme that has become familiar to all populists, Jackson was portrayed as the outsider, the victim of the mythical "corrupt bargain," the anti-politician who would clean up a dirty system. Mass appeal mattered more to Jackson than any American president to that date. Indeed, it was Jackson's "personal popularity" that persuaded faction leaders like Van Buren to back him. Van Buren knew well the machine politician's guiding principle, later so acidly stated by Chicago Ward Committeeman, Bernard Neistein: "Don't back no losers."[15]

What changed from the early decades of the nineteenth century to allow Jackson to pursue this more direct quasi-populist strategy? As with any populist or quasi-populist leader, Jackson's personal qualities – not least his stubbornness and his ambition – mattered. First and foremost, he was a war hero, one who had defeated not only the hated British and Spanish, but who also ruthlessly pursued the expulsion, if not extermination, of Native Americans. Jackson thus had an enviable degree of celebrity or name recognition. Moreover, although wealthy, he was also, and this was still then a relative novelty in elite politics in the United States, a man of common background; neither an Old School (i.e., Virginian or South Carolinian) planter nor a Yankee gentleman, the two types of elite who had hitherto dominated American politics. Unlike his predecessors, but like most of his countrymen, Jackson was not well educated. Jackson could thus put himself forward as a man of the people in a way that his rivals could not.

However, as historian Wilentz summarizes, "[t]he kind of political charisma (and, for many, scariness) he [Jackson] emanated could not have been produced by his military glory and personal fortitude alone. For more than half a century, Americans of all persuasions had been preparing the way for Jackson, or some democratic leader like him." In other words, contextual – socioeconomic and demographic – factors, not just Jackson's personality, were responsible for the success of his charismatic leadership style. Over the course of the previous three decades, some major societal changes had been occurring that upset cost–benefit calculus underlying the patronage–based political status quo. The first and most important of these was the general democratization of society. The restricted franchises of the 1790s had been decidedly opened up, even if turnouts themselves remained low through to 1820. With the exception of women and people of color, essentially every adult had the right to vote. And the process of incorporation was only accelerating. The total turnout nearly quadrupled from just over 300,000 in 1824 to more than 1.1 million in 1828. This was a staggering increase in political participation that aided the politician who could connect directly with voters. The modest levels of patronage resources then available were too small to instantly incorporate all of these new electors. Moreover, not only had the absolute size of the American electorate grown, but its center of gravity had also shifted. Although the American government had, like the British colonial government, sought to limit westward expansion, in practice there was little it could do to halt migration over the Appalachians. The temptation of first and second generation immigrants from Europe to secure land of their own was too great to resist. With land in the West plentiful, farming families could eke out a comfortable, if modest life on as little as twenty acres. Largely detached from the market, they lived a life of subsistence, cherishing the preservation of their autonomy over the accumulation of wealth. Populations in the lightly populated West mushroomed, especially as the threat of attack from Native American tribes receded. Jackson had himself contributed greatly to this state of affairs, winning a string of bloody victories against indigenous American inhabitants up and down the western frontier and into Florida. Kentucky (1792), Tennessee (1796), Ohio (1803), Louisiana (1812), Indiana (1816), Mississippi (1817), Illinois (1818), and Alabama (1819) were all newly admitted as states of the Union by the 1820s. It should thus hardly be surprising that Jackson's base of support came to be concentrated in the newer territories of the West and Deep South; this is where the voters were available. Still largely unincorporated into the haphazard elite political networks of the Era of Good Feelings, America's growing population played a major role in Jackson's rise to power. The political factions in these new states were yet to be fully embedded into existing party networks before the election of 1824 arrived; the mid-1820s saw a patronage-based political establishment that was fragmented not just by section or faction but virtually by state. Not even the master of compromise, Henry Clay, could pull these disparate groups together.[16]

On a second-order level, important procedural changes also facilitated Jackson's candidacy in 1828. While in 1800, eleven out of sixteen state legislatures had indirectly selected the Electoral College delegates who would choose between Jefferson and Adams, in 1824, voters in three quarters of the states selected electoral college delegates directly. Between 1824 and 1828 alone, four states – New York, Vermont, Georgia, and Louisiana – switched to the direct popular vote for presidential electors. By 1828, only two out of twenty-four states retained the indirect method. Prior to the 1820s, in other words, the president was indirectly chosen by other political elites. There simply was no populist route to power, when the people had little say over the process. As a consequence of the greater procedural role for the masses, ironically a result of factional competition within the states, the people understandably became more involved in politics. The turnout rate almost doubled between Jackson's first two campaigns in 1824 and 1828, rising to 56.3 percent (where it roughly stayed until 1840 before rising dramatically again). More and more ordinary people could now vote and they, like Jackson, valued their autonomy and they saw in him someone who could protect it.

Last, complementary to these trends, the 1820s saw a tremendous increase in newspaper circulation, lowering the cost of a mass communications strategy to mobilize the growing electorate. Jackson's backers acquired newspapers across target states and, of course, in Washington, DC. The media at this time was unabashedly partisan. Politicians and their supporters would anonymously pen vicious attacks on their opponents and probably, like today, focus on exciting their base rather than persuading swing voters. This mediatization of politics was in turn facilitated by two underlying developments. The first was the subsidization of newspaper distribution through the postal network. In effect, this meant that once popular votes had started to matter in the mid-1820s, regular mail users were used to subsidize the distribution of political propaganda. The second was an accelerating transport revolution. The early decades of the nineteenth century saw a massive expansion in the United States' turnpike network, allowing for considerably faster interstate communication. Mimicking the syndication of news programs today, partisans could publish a hit piece in their local paper and then have it rapidly reprinted across the country. Collectively, these demographic, institutional, and technological changes altered the cost of direct, popular appeals to voters. Jackson cut his bargains with the necessary patricians. But he never would have been in place to do so, nor have been so successful, had he not been able to trade directly on his heroic name in an increasingly national, news–obsessed society. He was America's first populist, or at least, quasi-populist president. Economics more than ideals had made this possible. Jackson had shown that in a rapidly developing society – with all of the demographic upheaval this entailed – populism was becoming an effective strategy on a national scale. Others would be quick to learn.

THE REVENANT

Louis Napoleon, or Napoleon III, is today perhaps best known as the target of one of Karl Marx's most stinging barbs. In his famous essay, "The Eighteenth Brumaire of Louis Napoleon," first published in 1852, Marx offered the following comparison of France's second emperor to his famous uncle:

Hegel remarks somewhere that all great world-historic facts and personages appear, so to speak, twice. He forgot to add: the first time as tragedy, the second time as farce. Caussidière for Danton, Louis Blanc for Robespierre, the Montagne of 1848 to 1851 for the Montagne of 1793 to 1795, the nephew for the uncle. And the same caricature occurs in the circumstances of the second edition of the Eighteenth Brumaire.

Indeed, there was much about Louis Napoleon's bid for power that was farcical. His first coup attempt, a one-man assault on the French garrison at Strasbourg, saw him get berated and slapped by the mother-in-law and wife of the commanding officer, Théophile Voirol, before being exiled to the United States. His second attempt in 1840 fared even worse, as his expeditionary force (made up mostly of his personal staff), was thrust back on its landing at Bourgone, only for Louis Napoleon himself to panic and shoot an unarmed grenadier in the face. This time he didn't get off so lightly, being sentenced to confinement in the prison fortress of Ham in Picardy "in perpetuity."

We should, however, be wary of taking Marx's polemical assessment of Louis Napoleon as a "grotesque mediocrity" too literally. After all, Napoleon III was nothing if not devoted to order and progress in the name of the bourgeoisie, hardly a platform to endear him to the coauthor of *The Communist Manifesto*. More importantly for our purposes, Louis Napoleon's ascent to power was not as haphazard as the post-1871 caricatures of him would suggest. As early as 1832 he seems to have resolved to restore the empire with himself at its head. In 1839 he published his progressive if somewhat authoritarian political manifesto, *Des idées Napoléoniennes*, to significant popular acclaim. Like his uncle he basically envisioned a monarchy legitimized by mass support. On his arrest for the attempted coup in 1836, he had justified his actions saying, "I wanted to establish a new government, one elected by a full popular vote." Through 1839 and 1840 he sought to build a popular base of support, subsidising newspapers critical of the Orléanist regime and backing a number of Bonapartist political clubs. At the same time, it was clear in his mind that to the extent that there was to be a democracy, it would be one where the people would vote how they were told. In 1840 he wrote, "[t]he fundamental vice (which is eating away at France today) . . . is the exaggerated interpretation of the rights of the individual, of his scorn for authority." Like his uncle, Louis Napoleon sought power unencumbered by a political party or a complex of elite alliances. He was willing to put whatever fortune he had toward gaining power, but whatever he spent, it was a pittance in comparison with the prize at stake. With such celebrity, he wouldn't need to advertise or campaign much for political leadership, never mind having to build a national party with officers and branches. Louis Napoleon has a good case to be recognized as the first unequivocal modern populist.[17]

Although beset by challengers on the right as well as the left by the mid-1840s, the collapse of the July Monarchy only appears as an inevitability in hindsight. The Orléanist line, installed by a coup of its own in 1830 to replace the unpopular restored Bourbons, brought a measure of political and economic stability to France. King Louis Philippe was himself no reactionary. However, his regime never endeared itself to the French public. Ultimately, like the *Ancien Régime* before it, the July Monarchy was in large part undone by its unwillingness to gradually incorporate the middle classes as a way to stave off a more revolutionary challenge from below. Across the Channel, the 1832 Reform Act gave the vote to one in every twenty-five Britons; in France, the number was still just one in 170. Although nominally a constitutional monarchy, given its tiny franchise, there was little incentive for aspiring power brokers to develop mass political organizations. In most constituencies, there were fewer than 1,000 electors and most of them could be easily bought or coerced. Political meetings were in any case banned in 1834, making any kind of political association more or less impossible. The presence of arch-conservative, François Guizot, in the prime minister's office hardly helped. Had he not stuck to his adamant refusal to relax the 200 franc tax-paying qualification on the franchise, instead telling the lower middle classes that they should "get rich" if they so badly wanted to vote, Parisians may not have been so quick to man the barricades that went up around the city at the end of February, 1848.

When rampant food inflation brought disaffected crowds onto the streets of Paris on February 22, 1848, the July Monarchy disappeared with barely a whimper. After forty-eight hours of rioting, Louis Philippe abdicated, and a provisional government was declared at Paris' Hôtel de Ville on February 24. So unexpected was this "revolution" that there was no coherent program for what would follow. In addition to emerging working-class discontent with the monarchy, by the mid-1840s at the latest, there was a significant body of support for a Bonapartist restoration. The first Emperor's legacy had only been burnished with time. His disinterment from the island of St. Helena and re-entombment to great fanfare in the Invalides in Paris in 1840 was the most visceral symbol of this refurbishment. However, at this stage, a subset of radical republicans turned out to be the best organized alternative to the monarchy, and led by poet-politician Alphonse de Lamartine, the provisional government quickly moved to reintroduce universal manhood suffrage. At the stroke of a pen, the electorate increased from just 250,000 to more than 10 million. In turn, the government lifted restrictions on the press and instituted a system of national workshops – the *Ateliers Nationaux* – to address the unemployment crisis. In Paris, some 54 percent of the population was out of work. Problematically, however, funding for the provisional government's plan to put the city's jobless back to work came largely from the already financially stressed peasantry, which as the contemporary observer Alexis de Tocqueville noted, pitted city against countryside not for the first (or last) time in French history. As a result, the majority of seats in the Constituent Assembly, elected in April 1848, went not to the progressive left but to the reactionary right, whose support in rural France remained strongest. A remarkable 84 percent of the newly enfranchised male population turned out to vote in April 1848, but to the disappointment of

radicals like Alexandre Ledru-Rollin who had championed mass enfranchisement, the outcome was essentially conservative. About two thirds of the
Assembly could be classified as moderate, if not reactionary, while at most only
70 to 80 of the 880-member Assembly had overtly radical sympathies.[18]

The Moderate Republicans, led by General Louis-Eugène Cavaignac, held
a solid majority in the Assembly. However, this was hardly an organized
political party in the modern sense. It had no party list, no offices, and no
organizational structure to speak of. Even the more ideologically coherent
Party of Order, which nominally held 200 seats in the Assembly, was no more
than an alignment of members *in the Assembly*, not an organization with a
national presence in the electorate. Universal suffrage had been achieved, but
politics continued to be a sport of the elite – the *notables*. To Marx's dismay,
ultimately, the "revolution" of 1848 had little effect on the distribution of
local wealth and power, with the result that local notables able to distribute
patronage ruled the day. As historian Roger Price, an expert on the period
puts it, "[i]n the absence of organised parties the choice of candidates in most
areas, and especially in rural constituencies, remained dependent on the
activities of small groups of politically experienced notables." At the same
time, this was not a well-organized conservative political machine, the likes of
which soon developed in Britain. Even if the propertied classes were in power,
the reality was that the right "remained dangerously fragmented." This was a
situation – mass enfranchisement and weak political organization – ripe for
the emergence of a populist.[19]

It was in this context that Louis Napoleon reentered the political fray. His
imprisonment at Ham, although not under the most austere of conditions,
had begun to affect his physical if not mental state. He resolved to escape. In
disguise, he absconded to London in May 1846, where he recovered his health
and his determination to make another attempt at capturing power. The
democratic opening of 1848 provided the occasion for him to plot his
revanche. As he put it to his cousin "I'm going to Paris, the Republic has
been proclaimed. I must be its master." Louis- Napoleon entered France on
February 27 and headed straight for Paris. However, with the Bonaparte
family still officially banned, he was quickly asked to leave. Back in exile, he
later jumped on the opportunity to win a seat in the Assembly as an independent candidate in June by-elections. Unable to campaign in person, his candidature was entirely based on name recognition. Yet before he could engineer
his homecoming from London, Paris erupted in an orgy of violence. In part a
spontaneous response to the closure of the government sponsored workshops,
and perhaps more broadly to the conservative hue of the Constituent
Assembly, the June Days saw thousands of workers take to the streets.
Afraid of a repeat of the prolonged chaos of 1789–94, the repression, directed
by Cavaignac, was swift and brutal, one contemporary writing that "the earth
[was] red with blood." Modern estimates are of more than 12,000 insurgents
killed or imprisoned.[20]

Although peace was restored, the insecurity felt by conservatives and moderates remained palpable. The constitution they promulgated in November reflected these fears, introducing for the first time a directly elected executive office – the presidency. Louis Napoleon swiftly announced his candidacy for the new office. His main rival was Cavaignac, who though he commanded a majority in the legislature, won just 1.5 million votes in comparison to Louis Napoleon's 5.5 million – three-quarters of the total. Although Cavaignac was by no means a radical, rural elites and their clients – those with Bourbon sympathies – could hardly flock to his banner. He was still a republican after all. In any case, just how willing the peasantry was to go along with the rural notables who continued to dominate politics after so many postrevolutionary decades of disappointment, is doubtful. Indeed, much of Louis Napoleon's support ultimately came from the French peasantry, although his popularity in the cities – not least Paris, where he won 58 percent of the vote – was hardly negligible. Marx may have wished to dismiss Louis Napoleon as the "[c]hief of the *lumpenproletariat* [the scum of society]," but his support genuinely cut across regions and classes, including the working class who hadn't forgotten the promise of his political economic tract, *The Extinction of Poverty*, published in 1844.

Having taken possession of the keys to the Elysée Palace, Louis Napoleon continued his charm offensive, taking a grand – publicly funded – tour of the countryside. He found his initial, largely monarchist ministry, tolerable at best. When it pretended to be responsible to parliament rather than to the president, it rapidly lost his confidence. He dismissed his ministers and pushed the Constituent Assembly to dissolve itself and hold long overdue elections for the new National Assembly. The monarchist and conservative Party of Order won 500 seats in the May 1849 general election compared to 200 seats for the Democratic Socialists or Montagnard movement, which was perhaps France's first serious attempted mass political party. For reactionaries, in spite of this considerable majority, the continued presence of leftists in the Assembly was too much to bear. The Electoral Law of May 31, 1850, cut the franchise in half, and even though it robbed Louis Napoleon of the bulk of his base, he nevertheless signed it into law, privately justifying this apparent act of political suicide as providing cover for the coup to come: "One day this will encourage the Assembly to overstep themselves ... and when they do, I shall strike." Louis Napoleon sought to hit back at The Party of Order, both by reversing the Electoral Law and by seeking a constitutional amendment that would extend his term in office from four to ten years. His gambit was narrowly defeated in the Assembly by 353 to 347 votes, but the conflict between the president and the Assembly was soon to come to a head.[21]

With the growing threat of disorder from the left and the continued obstinance of the right to any substantive reform, the large moderate middle increasingly turned to Louis Napoleon to resolve the impasse. Putting the ham-fisted coup attempts of the past behind him, Louis Napoleon, in part guided by his half brother, Charles Auguste de Morny, was this time more meticulous. At midnight on December 1, 1851, Operation Rubicon was launched. Early in the morning of December 2, dozens of likely opponents – including fourteen members of the Assembly – were peremptorily locked up, and on December 4, more than a hundred rebellious workers and bourgeois in Paris' infamous faubourg Saint-Antoine were shot dead. In the weeks that followed, at least 26,000 insurgents were arrested, many of whom were deported to penal colonies from Algeria to French Guiana. The coup had been swift, brutal, and successful. A plebiscite on December 20, 1851, endorsed the *autogolpe*, 7.5 million votes to 600,000, with 1.5 million abstaining. Another referendum followed on November 21/22, and Louis Napoleon's transition from populist to popular dictator would be confirmed with his coronation as Napoleon III.

Much as the Second Empire was a government of order – a major source of its legitimacy being its ability to keep the "Red menace" at bay – it nevertheless retained the essentially full franchise electoral system that had been brought in with the Revolution of 1848. The Second Empire was a popular, elective monarchy, not a tyranny. Napoleon III kept control – albeit imperfectly – over the legislature by promulgating a list of official candidates, essentially proscribing the opposition. The people could vote, but they voted for approved candidates. This does not mean that Napoleon III had it entirely his own way. Local notables and the *haute bourgeoisie* could mobilize sufficient resources of their own to represent a challenge for any "official" candidate that might oppose them. In such cases, Louis Napoleon's strategy was to incorporate these notables, although this gave his regime a somewhat incongruous character. The very elites who backed his regime were opposed to many of the expansionist and developmentalist programs to which Napoleon III was committed. Their desire to avoid taxes was almost as strong as their fear of the poor. Sitting above these factional squabbles, Louis Napoleon himself remained popular throughout most of the Second Empire. Even though Napoleon III's popularity had waned in the wake of diplomatic reverses from 1866, he was still in a commanding position as late as early 1870; it was only catastrophic defeat, invasion, and his own capture by Prussian hands later that year that brought him down. The surprisingly enduring popularity of Louis Napoleon's self-coup had poignant implications for European politics in the decades that followed. Resting on an alliance between an urban bourgeoisie and a reactionary peasantry as a counterweight to socialism, the Second Empire suggested the lines of a political coalition that would reemerge across much of Western Europe in the crisis years of the 1930s – most troublingly in Nazi Germany.

THE PARTY PERIOD

It is not without irony that even though Andrew Jackson relied partly on a populist approach to prevail in the election of 1828, it was the other element of his strategy that would predominate in the decades that followed. Nursed by

Martin Van Buren, Jackson's rise to power birthed the modern mass clientelist party. Jackson's quasi-populist strategy could be successful because of a substantial sudden de facto democratization in the mid-1820s. He could appeal to the millions of new voters without party affiliations that had joined the rolls in the bourgeoning southwest. Once in office, though, Jackson's party effectively cut off that populist route to others. Those who had voted for Jackson in the 1820s were forged into partisans. As Van Buren saw, party loyalties, once established could last for a generation or more. More than any of his contemporaries, Van Buren believed that transactional party politics was a positive good, allowing the country to quietly get on with its development and expansion while submerging divisive issues such as slavery. As we saw, a significant change in Jackson's strategy in 1828 as compared to 1824 was the incorporation of Van Buren's Albany Regency machine into his coalition in order to win New York's Electoral College votes. Jackson, unlike John Quincy Adams, who maintained the founders' ideal that the president should be above party, distributed government jobs on the basis of political loyalty – this too is no small irony given Jackson's professed indignation at the supposed "corrupt bargain" that saw Adams appoint Clay as his Secretary of State in 1824 in return for his support in congressional ballot. On taking power, Jackson adopted the policy of "rotation" to pay back his supporters, removing Adams' men, and installing his own. While Adams, like George Washington, removed just 9 officeholders, Jackson removed some 919 (about 10 percent of the total).[22]

As Chapter 3 showed, patronage was not an invention of the Jacksonian era. Van Buren's New York patronage–based model had been in operation at the state level for several decades at least, and even Jefferson had relied on it to consolidate his Republican Party's national coalition in the early 1800s. What was new about the Jacksonian era was the way in which patronage was used to build a *mass* national party. The Jacksonian system would long outlive the man himself, with patronage forming the backbone of the party system that prevailed until the eve of the Civil War. The Democratic Party used the spoils system to build a network of allied political brokers, who used the full range of mobilization tactics to get increasing numbers of voters to the polls. Jobs were the reward for a victorious faction, as was so acidly stated in 1832 by New York senator and ally of President Andrew Jackson, William L. Marcy, when he coined the phrase "to the victor belong the spoils" in defence of Jackson's distribution of public sector sinecures to his supporters. Former Federalists and others who found themselves marginalized in this system gradually organized themselves. The Whig Party was a heterogenous coalition, mostly bound by its opposition to "King Andrew," whom they accused of corruption and executive overreach. After successive defeats in 1832 and 1836, the Whig Party soon reproduced the organizational approach of the Democratic Party. So well had the Whigs learned from the Democratic example that after General Henry Harrison stormed to victory over Van Buren in 1840 on the back of a highly organized campaign that saw a record 80 percent turnout, one Democratic newspaper griped that "[w]e have taught them how to conquer us!"[23]

The collapse of the Second Party System in the 1850s is typically explained as the result of growing sectional conflict over slavery – the ideological issue that Van Buren had long sought to keep buried. By the mid-1850s, a North–South Republican–Democratic cleavage replaced the Whig–Democratic one that had cut across geographic lines. Without doubt, conflict over the fate of slavery increased with the acquisition of new western territories in the 1840s. However, Whig and Democratic parties had long been able to manage the differing views on slavery of their northern and southern supporters. In effect, Whigs and Democrats each said one thing in the North and another thing in the South. As Van Buren had envisaged, political elites remained more concerned with patronage than with ideological purity. Policy differences over banks and other issues were hardly absent from this system. In part, they were a means to stake out a distinctive brand from the opposing party, but as with views over slavery, these policies could differ from one state Whig or Democratic party to another. Just as importantly, "policy" matters such as the incorporation of banks or infrastructure spending were also grist for the patronage mill. Ironically, as historian Michael Holt argues, it was the disappearance of many of these local differences over economic policy between Whig and Democratic parties in the early 1850s that presaged their end. Take the issue of internal improvements, which had perennially divided the parties across the states. With the new revenues that railroad expansion promised, Democrats soon embraced it as enthusiastically as the Whigs – the parties, or rather candidates, rivaling each other only in how avidly they boosted new rail lines that favored their particular constituencies. The parties thus differed little over policy. At the same time, dissatisfaction over the distribution of the spoils led many states to revise their constitutions, converting many positions in the administration and the judiciary from political appointments into directly elected roles. State leaders were thus deprived of old sources of patronage at the very time they needed it to maintain the flagging allegiance of their clienteles. The combined result, Holt agues, was that voters had little reason to bother with one party over the other, turnouts thereby falling through to the mid-1850s.[24]

One of the first political leaders to appreciate the looming party system crisis was Zachary Taylor. Whigs, recognizing that their party had become increasingly identified with opposition to the expansion of slavery into the Mexican Cession, promoted the candidacy of the unaligned war hero, General Taylor, as a candidate acceptable to both sections. Much as Taylor was a political outsider – supposedly never having even voted – his was not a populist campaign. Even though Taylor would have preferred to run without a party nomination, he eventually conceded that one was necessary. Taylor would never have won the presidency, nor the nomination, without insider backing from party elites, especially Whig party kingmaker, Thurlow Weed. For Weed and other party elites, Taylor would be the vehicle through which the Whigs could push through their agenda in Congress. Even Abraham Lincoln abandoned his beau ideal of a political leader, Henry Clay, for Taylor because he thought "Old Rough and Ready" had a better chance of winning.

Once in power, however, Taylor escaped the clutches of his handlers, pushing his "no party" image, even styling himself a Republican *avant la lettre*, rather than a Whig. With a view toward elections in 1852, his personal supporters sought to form a new set of national party alignments around the general himself, mooting the idea of a "Taylor Republican" party. To the extent that Taylor sought to develop a party, however, it would not be of the patronage-based Whig or Democratic type. He despised the patronage side of politics. In spreading the patronage widely, and thereby denying it to the Old Whig followers of Clay, Daniel Webster, and New York governor, William Seward, Taylor succeeded in fracturing the Whigs but not in creating a national personal party of his own. However, with Taylor's death halfway through his term in 1850, the prospect of a political realignment around the figure of a singular populist leader faded too. Seeking to revive the fading Whig party, his successor, Millard Fillmore, reversed Taylor's nonaligned patronage strategy and tied himself much more clearly to Seward, Webster, and other party regulars. However, by supporting the 1850 Compromise, which conceded too much to pro-slavery forces for the tastes of the northern leadership of the party, Fillmore lost his chance at nomination for reelection in his own right. Seeking a rerun of 1848, the Whigs instead nominated another war hero, General Winfield Scott, for the presidency in 1852. Scott's shellacking at the hands of Franklin Pierce fractured what was left of the Whig party. While this rupture might have marked an opening for a potential populist campaign, ultimately, there were too many well-organized groups – the Free Soil Party, the American Party, and eventually the Republican Party – which were ready to fill the gap instead.

Although the absence of populism per se amid the collapsing national party system of the mid-nineteenth century is a topic that has received relatively little attention – not surprising given how large the Civil War looms over the period – the economic approach to political organization suggests a partial answer. Even as the national parties, Democratic and Whig, bled electoral support in the north and south, respectively, in the early 1850s, they retained considerable local organizational capacity elsewhere. Moreover, defecting partisans quickly took their well-honed political party skills with them when they created or joined new organizations. In short, even as national parties broke apart, local political machines, both at the state and municipal level, either remained intact or quickly reformed under new guises. The millions of new immigrants, largely Irish and German, added to the voter rolls in the 1840s, were rapidly incorporated into these local political party networks. For the new parties emerging at the time that lacked access to the spoils of government normally used to buy votes, new institutionalized and mediated linkages with voters were established. This was the era in which large bureaucratic civil society groups such as the Order of the Star Spangled Banner were formed, creating in the process the potential for the bureaucratic political strategy to enter American politics. The Order, for one, became the basis of the anti-immigrant American Party, or "Know Nothing" Party (as its members were instructed to disavow all knowledge of the nativist secret society). The Farmers' Alliance would similarly provide the organizational basis of the People's Party later in the century.

Although in other periods, party system fragmentation has facilitated populist appeals from above, in the 1850s local political organization functioned as a significant roadblock to the populist strategy. The absence of suitable technology to communicate directly with voters over the heads of local political bosses at low cost meant that party building remained the most effective strategy. Newspapers remained mostly locally owned and distributed while the national rail network was only in its infancy. As a result, direct popular appeals without the cooperation of locally based networks of brokers and backers was still almost logistically impossible. Recall that Jackson's strategy of the 1820s was only partially populist, given that he allied with local political machines, who distributed propaganda on his behalf. Moreover, even this partially populist strategy was viable only because so few voters were at the time systematically incorporated into existing party networks. That is, there were many floating voters, who needed only light persuasion to support Jackson. Jackson was thus able to win by mobilizing only small pluralities of the total electorate. However, with turnouts approaching nine out ten voters by the mid-1840s, the easy votes were no longer there. Most voters were already embedded in local political networks. A populist strategy could only have had a very marginal impact. As a consequence of the party institutionalization that Jackson's system wrought, winning the presidency demanded building an organization to tie together a coalition of disparate, but internally closely knit political groups, all of which were at least partly motivated by winning a share of the spoils. This in turn continued to favor the patronage–based political party strategy, not the populist one.[25]

During the high-water mark of what is often known as the "party period" in the second half of the nineteenth century, patronage-based parties provided the main link between people and the state. Even the Republican Party became an astute exponent of the patronage strategy. These decades were in many ways the height of legislative and political party supremacy. This was the era, indeed, in which many of the famous urban political machines – such as New York's Tammany – were born. Although the Civil War itself had greatly strengthened the executive branch, state and city leaders, the bosses, were quick to reassert their political predominance. The president was often a tool of these subnational elites. Of presidents between Abraham Lincoln (1960–65) and William McKinley (1897–1901), only Ulysses S. Grant managed to win reelection. As the vanguard of the victorious North, the Republican Party emerged as the predominant political force during Reconstruction. Andrew Johnson, essentially an unreconstructed Democrat who assumed the presidency after Lincoln's assassination in April 1965, faced a Republican opposition with supermajorities in both houses of Congress. Yet even when Grant – effectively a Republican by the mid-1960s given his successful prosecution of the war – was easily elected president, it was the GOP leadership of Congress that remained in control. Like Washington and Jackson before him, Grant was incredibly popular, in his case in the Republican Party's northern and western base. Party elites were thus well aware of his long coattails, and they had no hesitation in confirming his renomination in 1772. But none of this meant that Grant would be able to simply impose his will on Congress. Instead, Grant found himself in a constant struggle with the congressional leadership. He was eager to enforce Reconstruction and pacify the West, but the burgeoning GOP machine was determined to hold onto the reigns of patronage. The first shot across Grant's bow was fired when his nominee for Secretary of the Treasury, retailer Alexander Stewart, was rejected by the Senate at the behest of New York's political boss, Senator Roscoe Conkling. As the 1870s progressed, the party's local political machines entrenched their control, developing close alliances to the rapidly expanding business community, especially, but not only in the intricately tied fields of railroads and finance.[26]

On the electoral side, with the Democrats still reeling from the war, the GOP machine used its access to the state to dole out jobs and services to their supporters; the latter provided votes in return. In short, patronage remained king, especially in the rapidly expanding ethnic urban enclaves of the Northeast and the Midwest, although Republicans also attempted to build a base in the South through economic development. The consensus view of Grant was that he himself was credulous rather than venal, but his administration (1869–76) was nevertheless blighted by a series of corruption scandals. He remained personally committed to fighting back again southern obstructionism of civil rights and of the erosion of Indian rights in the West. Ultimately, though, his success was limited by the same lack of interest of his northern base in paying the economic and social costs for moderation elsewhere. The compromise over the contentious election of 1876 saw Republican Rutherford Hayes, a less renowned but more pliant former Union general, become president in return for walking back the enforcement of Reconstruction. As a consequence, through unrelenting violence and intimidation, Southern Blacks were kept disenfranchised and subordinated, ushering in a century of Democratic control south of the Mason-Dixon. As Reconstruction ended the Gilded Age began, with the emerging industrial "robber barons" like John D. Rockefeller and Jay Gould feeding corrupt urban machines in return for enormous government subsidies and concessions, not least in the burgeoning West.

THE POPULISTS

The inequality that so defined the Gilded Age began to surge with the industrialization of the mid-nineteenth century. Small farms in the West, Midwest, and Upper South, especially those on environmentally unsustainable lands, ran into trouble, while monopolies and "trusts" reaped enormous profits. The "panic" or economic crisis of 1873 set off an era of deflation that would persist for the next two decades. Tolerable to the creditors of the Northeast, deflation, aided and abetted by protectionism, brought misery to farmers in the Plains and the South and gave rise to the Farmers Alliance, a rural pressure group that initially endorsed the candidates of existing parties. In the South especially, where white farmers were loath to risk throwing power to the Republicans and their "negro" supporters, the Alliance sought to capture the Democratic Party from within. However, with little change accruing in the platforms of the two major parties, which remained aligned with the economic policies of the Gilded Age coastal elites, agrarian radicals felt they had little choice but to give a third party one last firm push. Built on the organizational back of the Alliance, the new People's Party (or Populist Party as it was often known) was indelibly focused on the interests of small farmers, whatever efforts it made to ally with urban workers and discontented radicals.

In part thanks to tactical alliances with other parties, the Populists picked up nearly forty seats in the House in 1890. Then, in 1892 the People's Party put forward its own candidate for president, James Weaver. Weaver, a former Union Army general, had an eclectic background, making his political debut as a Republican, switching to the Greenback-Labor Party, which emerged after the panic of 1873 to push for the loosening of monetary policy, before later accepting the nomination of the People's Party in 1892. In the presidential election of 1880, Weaver, then as a Greenback candidate, had departed from the still prevailing norm that presidential candidates shouldn't stump for themselves. He concentrated his public speaking in the South and West, where his inflationary soft-money and anti-monopoly program would have the most appeal. However, the dominant Republican and Democratic machines restricted his vote share to just 3 percent. In 1892 Weaver increased his vote share to 9 percent, capturing four western states, thanks largely to the organizational work of the Alliance, which had grown substantially in the interim. However, Weaver, although an outsider, was no small-p populist. Even if the Populist Party remained organizationally diffuse, at least through the height of its popularity in the latter nineteenth century, it was by no means a personalist party, whether under the leadership of Weaver, Alliance president L. L. Polk, Georgian firebrand Tom Watson, or anyone else.[27]

Despite its rapid growth up to 1892, Weaver's failed campaign would be the People's Party's high-water mark. One reason is that despite its substantial organizational underpinnings and clarity of ideological purpose, it lacked an effective national hierarchy. It remained an alliance of alliances, in which western populists differed in their interests and organization from Southern populists; white populists from black populists; rural populists from urban ones; and so on. More importantly, though, the Populist Party failed because it could not crack the organizational dominance of the Republican and Democratic parties. There was just too little space for it to grow into. Unlike the Republican Party, which emerged to fill the gap left by the moribund Whig Party as the second and then the first party from the late 1850s, the People's Party faced two well dug-in opponents. Not only did those parties benefit from their control of national and state patronage, but at least in the post-Reconstruction South where the Populist's agrarian appeal was especially strong, the Democrats could also wield many of the coercive tools of an authoritarian regime: slander, coerced voting, multiple voting, even the throwing out of valid returns. The South, indeed, became more a one-party state than a two-party state. With the Populists' defeat of 1892, the Alliance and its main industrial counterpart, the Knights of Labor, both went into decline. Any prospect of the Populist Party breaking the old duopoly had passed.[28]

The decline of the Populist Party did not, however, preclude the use of a populist strategy if it was aimed instead at capturing one of the two major parties. In 1896, the Democratic Party made the surprise decision to nominate thirty-six-year-old William Jennings Bryan as its presidential candidate. Bryan, a two-term congressman, had been building a reputation as a staunch advocate of the free coinage of silver, this inflationary measure being especially popular with indebted farmers – the beating heart of the Populists. His later fame notwithstanding, Bryan was a dark horse as the 1896 Democratic National Convention in Chicago approached. Like many Nebraska Democrats, Bryan had been squeezed out of his seat in Congress by Republicans on one side and Populists on the other. Bryan was, however, a brilliant orator, and in an age before electronic amplifiers, this skill still mattered: like a modern sports stadium, the site of the convention, the Chicago Colosseum, could fit some 20,000 bodies. Delegates could be swayed by the passion of the moment, something that Bryan was banking upon. As he told his wife after one speaking engagement as far back as 1888, "[l]ast night I found that I had power over the audience. I could move them as I chose. I have more than usual power as a speaker." Bryan's speaking skills certainly mattered, but he also benefited from the fact that the Democratic Party was horribly divided coming into the convention. Bryan deserves some credit for this, as prior to the convention, he encouraged state nominating conventions to send uncommitted silver delegates to Chicago. At the same time, even though the unpopular incumbent Democratic president, Grover Cleveland, wasn't being considered for renomination, he still had many supporters at the convention. Bryan was a wild card, but these divisions meant that party regulars were unable to secure the nomination of a more reliable silver candidate through the usual convention horse trading. Bryan was fortunate that speeches would be made on the party platform before the nomination of the presidential candidate. It was in this context that his oratory carried the day as he famously articulated the Populists' soft money policy in emotive terms that remain well-known today: "[Y]ou shall not crucify mankind upon a cross of gold." Bryan won the nomination on the fifth ballot. He boasted afterward that he had spent a mere sixty dollars in expenses at the convention, an amount that was "probably as small as anyone has spent in securing a presidential nomination." Even adding the $2,000 he paid toward securing an editorial column in the *Omaha World-Herald* to disseminate his views, his presidential candidacy was obtained for a paltry sum.[29]

After an intra–People's Party battle, Bryan was also nominated as that party's presidential candidate. As a sop to those "mid-roaders" who opposed fusion with the other parties, the People's Party convention also selected one of its own, Tom Watson, as its vice presidential candidate. Watson was by then easily the best-known Populist. He had entered Congress in 1890 for Georgia's 10th congressional district as an Alliance-backed Democrat but left the caucus to become the South's foremost Populist. That the popular Watson lost his reelection bid to an uninspiring Democratic candidate provides ample demonstration of the predominance of patronage – and in the South, coercion – to a successful political strategy at that time. The Democratic Party refused to nominate Watson as its vice presidential candidate, sticking incongruously with wealthy industrialist, Arthur Sewall. It is true that for a time Bryan appeared set to cause an upset, suggesting the potential viability of the populist strategy, at least within the limited context of a badly factionalized party with an open convention. His rallies were packed, and he acquired a remarkable celebrity status, many supporters worshiping him as a hero or messiah. In the general election, however, the Bryan-Watston-Sewall tickets failed abysmally. In the end, no matter how aloof Bryan might have stood from the Democratic Party Cleveland regulars, there was probably nothing he could have done to shake off voters' distrust of a party that had presided over four years of economic depression. Bryan also faced in a Republican Party machine organized by Mark Hanna an unprecedently slick and well-financed political operation. Hanna raised a massive campaign war chest from the wealthy, "frying the fat" out of the corporations as he put it. Indeed, the nexus between party fundraising and political power that would characterize much of the twentieth century began – or at least was greatly intensified – here. The GOP raised some $3.5 to $4 million, most of which went toward the distribution of millions of pamphlets and an avalanche of newspaper advertising. The 1896 William McKinley campaign even produced a short movie to be displayed in theatres. Bryan won the nomination on a shoestring, but the imbalance of resources against McKinley was so stark that it is unlikely anything he did would have avoided defeat in the general election itself.

In the wake of Bryan's defeat, the monied interests and the bosses who served the parties seemed more secure than ever. The Populist Party resumed its status as a minor third party with a presence in those southern and western states where its original agrarian program had a residual appeal. However, so marginalized was it after the failure of its 1896 fusionist campaign that Watson declared that "[o]ur party ... does not exist any more." Watson disappeared from frontline political competition for the next eight years but maintained his public profile through a steady output of popular writing. When he reentered the political battlefield, the Populist Party organization was moribund.

Henceforth, it would be a personalist party, organized entirely around the charismatic figure of Watson and his proprietary media operation. As a candidate for the 1904 and 1908 presidential contests, Watson's vote share never rose above 1 percent. Watson retained considerable influence in Georgian, if not national, politics, but more as a commentator than a contender. It was only in 1920 that he again won office, but this he managed only by returning to the Democratic fold.[30]

Populism as an outsider mass communication political strategy was basically unsuccessful during this period, but it would have one last appearance that is worth noting. Theodore Roosevelt began his rise to political prominence first as a New York state assemblyman with an independent streak, before winning greater fame as commander of his "Rough Rider" regiment in Cuba during the Spanish-American War of 1898, and then as governor of New York. In spite of his loathing for machine politics, Roosevelt was in practice a loyal Republican, always stumping for the party's eventual presidential candidate. Yet as a machine regular, Hanna never trusted the reformist Roosevelt. When McKinley agreed to Roosevelt as the vice presidential nominee, Hanna fretted that the decision left only one life between a "madman" and the presidency. However, the desire of the Republican machine in New York – led by boss of bosses, Senator Thomas Platt – to be rid of the reformist governor prevailed over Hanna's hypothetical concerns.

When McKinley was assassinated in 1901 by a jilted spoilsman, Hanna's worst fears were realized. Roosevelt was a progressive president, even if in practice his actions were always tempered by the reality of having to work with a much more conservative and machine-dominated Congress. His modest reforms, however, were still too much for the party's conservative bosses. In 1904, it seemed that Hanna – the master of the purse strings – was himself poised to take the Republican Party nomination from the president. Hanna's surprise death gave Roosevelt a reprieve. Come the Republican National Convention, the party needed Roosevelt far "more than he needed the party" and he easily won reelection as a Republican in November. Even if Roosevelt was less the radical than his conservative enemies made him out to be, his second term was marked by significant change in the style and substance of the presidency itself. Roosevelt became the first president with truly global celebrity, and with some justification saw himself as bigger than the Republican Party. His view of the presidency was that anything not expressly prohibited to the office by the Constitution was fair game. Roosevelt assiduously courted the press, seeking to communicate directly with voters. As he described his strategy while New York governor, he "adopted the plan of going over the heads of the men holding public office and of the men in control of the [Republican Party] organization, and appeal[ed] directly to the people behind them."[31]

Having had almost a full term already as McKinley's replacement in addition to his own term, he put himself out of the running in 1908. Roosevelt gave the nod to his Secretary of War and protégé, William Howard Taft. Roosevelt's popularity at this time was extraordinary. If he sought to give Taft some breathing space by disappearing on an extended safari to Africa, his absence only seemed to make his star shine brighter (and Taft's wane ever dimmer). Returning to America in June 1910, via a well-publicized segue through Europe, Roosevelt was probably the most famous man in the world. Piqued that Taft seemed to be squandering what Roosevelt saw as his progressive legacy, not least in returning to a more limited conception of the presidency, Roosevelt challenged him for the Republican nomination in 1912. In his years out of office, Roosevelt had in some respects become more radical in his views, propounding an expansive program of government regulation and intervention in the economy, and, most controversially, rolling back the autonomy of the judiciary. Yet Roosevelt also straddled in important ways, suggesting that Taft was the more radical in seeking to break up large corporations through anti-trust suits, rather than merely regulate them, a strategy that put those like finance magnate, J. P. Morgan, in the firing line.

Privately, and sometimes not so privately, Roosevelt expressed his equanimity toward unfettered popular participation in politics; as he put it, "only certain people are fit for democracy." The "voice of the people" was as liable to be the "voice of a fool" as it was the "voice of god." However, in spite of his moderation on the issue of trusts, Roosevelt's notion of popular control of the judiciary was deeply disturbing to the propertied classes, who in the form of the Stalwart faction of the Republicans, were firmly set against him. Once it became impossible for him to win the backing of the RNC by traditional means, Roosevelt came around to supporting a much more participatory form of democracy, including the introduction of direct presidential primaries. "Let the people rule" became the rallying cry of his campaign. Roosevelt won a majority of the open primaries, in which he faced stiff competition, not only from President Taft but also from firebrand Wisconsin senator and former governor, Robert La Follette. Roosevelt's triumph in the president's home state of Ohio was a remarkable demonstration of his popularity. Fully convinced of his own importance, Roosevelt said on the eve of the Republican national convention "I have absolutely no affiliation with any political party." Yet no matter how popular Roosevelt might have been, the party machinery was firmly in control. With the powers of presidential patronage, Taft essentially had a lock on the party caucuses and state conventions, especially those of the South. In practice, both sides engaged in malfeasance, likely bribing and coercing delegates to their side. Ultimately, Taft controlled the Convention Committee, and his men sided with the president in every instance where Roosevelt contested delegates' legitimacy. The president won on the first ballot. Crying "theft," Roosevelt went it alone with his newly formed Progressive Party. Roosevelt's stamina on the stump was remarkable, even pushing himself to deliver a campaign speech with an assassin's bullet still in his chest. In spite of putting in the best ever performance of a third-party candidate, capturing 27.4 percent of the popular vote, the main result was to split the Republican ticket, allowing Democrat Woodrow Wilson to sneak into the White House on a plurality vote. For all its ideological fervor, the Progressive Party, so dependent on Roosevelt's charisma, quickly imploded. Roosevelt had neither the patience nor the inclination to build it into a full-fledged bureaucratic party.[32]

Roosevelt in 1912 came about as close as anyone who followed a pure populist strategy. Although he lost, Roosevelt's championing of the primary, would have momentous consequences in the years to come. However, even though a number of twentieth-century politicians with solid state machines behind them, most notably Huey Long of Louisiana and George Wallace of Alabama, whom we'll encounter in the chapters that follow, made significant dents in the support of the establishment, they never seriously threatened to beat a system that was well and truly stacked against them. Parties, for all their faults, even after the death of "King Caucus" in 1912, remained the surest means to power in the United States. Although patronage could be a precarious means of building a national party, the constrained role of party primaries in determining presidential candidates through to 1972 made a populist end run around the party bosses almost impossible. In 1828, Andrew Jackson exploited a temporary window where there was no effective national clearinghouse for the patronage – in a world with only one party, there were, in effect, no parties. However, with coherent patronage-based parties emerging in the 1830s, it would be a century and half before another populist would successfully repeat Jackson's success.

POPULISM, PATRONAGE, AND DEMOCRACY

The bloodletting of the years of social revolution around the turn of the nineteenth century, both in Europe and in the Americas (including the Caribbean), cast a pall over democracy's prospects for generations to come. Yet, as much as the Americas' oligarchies and Europe's monarchists sought to constrain the masses, by the latter half of the nineteenth century, truly mass politics now became possible, if not inescapable. Increasingly urbanized populations found the will and, just as importantly, the organizational capacity to demand political inclusion. One corollary of this was that programmatic party building became increasingly feasible. Indeed, by the end of the century, it had become virtually necessary for any serious political aspirant. In short, just as the transaction costs of patronage-based mobilization were rising, those of bureaucratic incorporation were falling.

Clientelism is an expensive business especially when the number of voters begins to grow. Few cases illustrate this dynamic better than Britain. It was the relatively small size of the British electorate that rendered its patronage-based political system so stable throughout the eighteenth century. So entrenched was the ruling elite that the long eighteenth century has been termed the Age of Oligarchy. Certainly, there were some fiercely contested electoral races. However, those few urban constituencies with several thousand voters were the exception not the rule. So-called rotten boroughs had few voters, all of whom cast their ballot by a show of hands. About four in ten constituencies had fewer than a hundred voters. Many had just handfuls, while one technically had no voters at all on account of having fallen into the sea because of coastal erosion! Not only were the direct costs (any benefits provided to voters) low in this kind of closed patronage–based system, but so were the indirect transaction costs; it costs little to employ an agent to monitor the behavior of a hundred voters, and if they must declare their intentions openly, punishing noncompliance is also straightforward. Outside competitors couldn't impose costs on voters for not choosing them and lacked the information to identify the right individuals to bribe for their support; entrenched, local patrons could do this much more efficiently.

Throughout the eighteenth century, vote buying was the main path to office, although by its end, there were inklings of change. John Wilkes, who later gained fame on both sides of the Atlantic as the father of civil liberties, vowed in his first electoral contest "I will never take a bribe, so I will never offer one." The 400 or so Aylesbury voters were less than impressed by Wilkes' probity. They expected their payoff – up to five pounds or more. In his next attempt, Wilkes learned to play the game, writing to a friend of his opponent, "[d]epend upon it, I will sink Willes by the weight of metal." If Willes gave five pounds a vote, Wilkes would give six; if his opponent gave six, he would give seven. Wilkes, however, sought, or was compelled, to go beyond the clientelist strategy. Possessed of a sharp intelligence and caustic wit, Wilkes was a popular and controversial journalist. When his patron William Pitt the Elder fell from power, Wilkes turned his pen on the government. Whatever the accuracy of his accusations, the subjective nature of British libel law left Wilkes open to prosecution. Excluded from parliament as an outlaw, Wilkes continued to stir up the public through his writing. Even though he couldn't take up his seat, he was so popular that he nevertheless kept winning elections. Wilkes showed that the populist strategy had potential, at least in a setting like that of his Middlesex constituency, which had a large, urban electorate. Still excluded from the House of Commons, Wilkes won election as Lord Mayor of London in 1774. However, when Wilkes later proposed the introduction of a near universal franchise for the Commons, which would have brought all other constituencies more in line with that of Middlesex, the ruling elite prevailed. They were not about to voluntarily increase the cost of controlling parliament. The crowd would be kept out of the halls of government, at least for some time yet. Wilkes, for all his bluster, was but a minor irritant. Right through the Revolutionary era, to form a government, a prime minister like Lord North (1770–82) mostly just had to keep the other grandees happy; favorable legislation, plumb appointments, and monopoly licenses were the inducements on offer. In the vast majority of constituencies, there were still few enough clients to make it all affordable.[33]

In the years that followed the French Revolution there was agitation in Britain for more rapid democratization from outside the halls of power. As the world's leading industrial nation and as its most urbanized, Britain was one of the first places where the ruling classes became susceptible to mass political pressure from below. The Great Reform Act of 1832 was a significant break-through for these popular forces, but the pace of reform remained glacial, giving rise to further agitation. At its height, the radical Chartist movement that took off in the 1830s had some three million supporters. However, by the time that the Corn Laws – popular with the landed elite but not with the consuming masses – were repealed in 1846, a more modern form of patronage – clientelism – had reasserted itself as the predominant form of political incorpor-ation. Votes increasingly had to be bought, and this suited many sellers rather well. Not just the middle class but the upper end of the working class, was doing rather well. If radicalism seemed to have gone into abeyance by 1860, a new generation of politicians recognized that the growing urban working class could be mobilized as clients in the intra-elite contest for power. However, with votes then running at about forty pounds a head, as the number of electors increased with the franchise-extending reforms of 1832 and 1867, the cost of winning elections through patronage had become enormous by the latter quarter of the century. The Corrupt Practices Act of 1883 was promulgated in large part because of candidates' growing complaints that they were being fleeced by greedy agents come election time. With the practice of localized clientelism being curbed, political organization became increasingly profession-alized. Paid party workers took the place of mercenary brokers. Out of eco-nomic necessity, the bureaucratic strategy was born.

All of this organizational work cost, of course. Both Liberals and Conservatives found themselves leaning on businessmen for "contributions." With this in mind, it may seem less surprising that it was the Conservative Party – not a party of the left – that was the first to adopt a more programmatic approach to recruiting support under the conditions of mass democracy. Whatever its policy preferences, the party recognized that power would result from establishing its organizational roots among a broad cross section of society. Popular associations, most notably the Primrose League, became essential tools in organizing the Conservative vote, especially among the so-called Tory working class. The Liberals never quite made the fraught transition from the Victorian to the Modern Age of organized politics. Although party leader William Ewart Gladstone was a renowned orator who avowed a determination to "back the masses against the classes," Gladstone's Liberals were ill-equipped for the new era of mass politics. Gladstone could draw a crowd but he actually lost at the hustings on a number of occasions. The Liberal party was never a personalist vehicle and at the same time remained organization-ally thin, eventually being eclipsed by the political vehicle of the trade unions – the Labour Party.[34]

Even though the 1884 extension and regularization of the franchise made possible a greater role for direct mass mobilization, Britain's parliamentary system rendered the newly emerged bureaucratic party nearly impregnable. Although the fracturing of both Liberal and Conservative parties over Home

Rule threw political alignments into a state of flux, no politician could become leader without a substantial parliamentary plurality – if not majority. Thus, much as appeals "out of doors" mattered, this was never as critical as the high politics of internal party management. Even though Lord Randolph Churchill was a wildly popular stump speaker who burnished the Tories' image, especially among the lower classes, the Tory elite viewed him with suspicion. Intuiting that Churchill was more comfortable as a gadfly than an administrator, then prime minister, Lord Salisbury, made him Chancellor of the Exchequer and Leader of the Conservative Party in the House of Commons. Salisbury knew his quarry. It wasn't long before Churchill took the rope he was given and tied a noose for his own neck. Attempting to leverage his popularity in a bid to oust Salisbury, Churchill tendered his resignation to the prime minister. To Churchill's chagrin, Salisbury accepted and within a fortnight, he had found a replacement for Churchill in the Commons. Churchill's one-time supporters in parliament towed the party line; "the rats desert the sinking ship" observed Churchill as he watched his rebellion peter out. Churchill proposed forming a new "National Party" in alliance with another man too independent to tolerate party discipline, Liberal notable, Joseph Chamberlain. The plans got nowhere, and Churchill saw out the remainder of his career in relative obscurity. Charisma was not without value, but it couldn't buy the premiership by itself.[35]

Populism did appear again in Western Europe in the second half of the nineteenth century, but it was limited to those few places where democratic or pseudo-democratic openings were maintained, and it was never fully successful. The French case, as ever, is illuminating. After defeat in the Franco-Prussian War, Napoleon III was forced from power. The revolutionary Paris Commune of 1871 jolted the French elite sufficiently that it finally settled on institutionalizing a broader democratic franchise, albeit one tempered by patronage-based incorporation of the masses. This time around, democracy proved more enduring. Providing further support for the idea that the way in which old regime legacies matter for the outcome of a democratic transition, the structure of the Second Empire provided a much more promising context for a stable, if moderate, regime change than either the First Empire or the *Ancien Régime* had. The two decades from Louis Napoleon's coup in 1851 were ones of sustained economic growth and modernization. France's railway network expanded enormously, providing not just market integration but social and political integration. Just as in Reconstruction America, the state-backed construction of the rail network provided a great deal of patronage for the consolidation of local political fiefdoms. Democracy henceforward was dominated by a well-greased coalition of moderate professional politicians and their clients. On the right, bankers and industrialists joined the ranks of the landed elite among France's better-off. The first preference of the conservative National Assembly elected in 1871 was for the restoration of monarchy, but the two-thirds of the Assembly who felt this way couldn't agree on the right candidate. As Adolf Thiers put it, "[t]here is only one throne, and three men can't sit on it." Yet, even though they remained divided as a group – not forming a mass party of empire and order in the way that Britain's Conservative Party had done – French elites were better prepared as a social class for the transition to democracy than they had been in either 1789 or 1848. Napoleon III had retained a parliament elected every six years based on a universal franchise; the polls were not exactly free and fair, but participation remained high. The result was that bourgeois elites who dominated the imperial parliament gained experience operating in a patronage-based mass democracy, even if it was one in which they were unlikely to be unseated.

Much more so than America, Third Republic France persisted in its fear of concentrated executive power, refusing to create a strong presidency. The intention – as after 1789 – was to make it more difficult for a single charismatic leader like either of the Napoleons to do without the political class. Under the new Constitutional Laws of 1875, the existence of a president indirectly elected by an indirectly elected upper house promised a check on popular radicalism, but the result was much less effective than its designers intended. When voters gave Republicans – those vehemently opposed to a restoration – a majority in 1876, the conservative president, Patrice de MacMahon, was impotent to prevent it. He dismissed the Republican government, but fresh elections resulted in another Republican majority. MacMahon acknowledged that using his prerogative to dissolve the legislature again would have been pointless; henceforth, the president was reduced to a mere figurehead. Parliamentary supremacy was confirmed, but the result was not the formation of well-organized bureaucratic parties. Rather, French parties, including the Republicans led by Léon Gambetta, remained very much fragmented, with personalistic cliques retaining their autonomy in a way not even possible in the United States.[36]

The failure to develop programmatic parties in this case was not due to the absence of class or regional conflicts, or of differing political ideas (e.g., socialism, royalism, liberalism) more broadly, but of a strong political incentive to organize. The French political elite could have power without parties, so they felt little pressure to create them. Deputies could simultaneously hold local and national office, giving mayors and other officials considerable tools with which to build enduring personal power bases. A typical deputy, in the words of historian David Hanley, "spent most of his time neither debating nor even in committees, but in dealing with requests for job references, decorations, exemptions from military service, job postings in the public or private sector, or for a word in the ear of those who, in the public or private sector, could offer life chances of various sorts." Unlike British prime ministers, French leaders had few carrots or sticks with which to control their potential supporters, while regular politicians for their part simply didn't need, or want, to be subordinate to a leader. Political alliances remained transactional and contingent. As another historian describes the situation, "deputies were expected to do their utmost to cultivate ministers and obtain favours for their constituents." Parties, such as they were, remained loose groupings comprised of local notables who retained their positions by cultivating clienteles through patronage. By the 1880s, according to historian William Irvine, "an effective republican patronage network was being established," but this was a far cry from the disciplined political machines of Britain or America. Parliamentary groupings did come into existence over the course of the Third Republic, and by the turn of the century at the latest, these groups displayed some internal discipline – electing their leaders and so on. Yet, as far as mobilization or incorporation was concerned, these parties or proto-parties remained highly fragmented into their constituent units – individual deputies.[37]

Given this fragmentation, populism retained its residual potential as a low-cost strategy, but its utility was constrained by the continued weakness of the executive branch. In the Third Republic, the French elite had institutionalized a system that allowed them to rule locally as individuals but which prevented any one of them from establishing his permanent preeminence at the national level. The executive simply had no separate power to control the legislative process. Even if a populist did get elected, he couldn't govern. Of course, this didn't stop those on the right from seeking a charismatic frontman to test the waters. In the wake of the humiliating signing of the 1871 Treaty of Versailles, General Georges Boulanger gained popularity as the voice of anti-Prussian revanchism. Much more poorly organized than their progressive opponents, for a time, both Royalists and Bonapartists saw in Boulanger an antidote to the radicalism of the Parisian mob. Boulanger did especially well in areas of Royalist support, winning election in multiple constituencies, including in Paris, in the 1880s. Yet as the radical threat dissipated, his conservative backers lost interest. Boulangism was singularly dependent on the charisma of the general himself. A new prohibition against running simultaneously in multiple constituencies – something Boulanger had repeatedly done – killed off the organizationally bereft Boulangist surge. Exactly as we'd expect, Boulangism failed where a network of well-entrenched notables with its own political aims was strong enough to keep him out. The easy votes were not available. Despite the looseness of French parties through the Third Republic, the absence of a strong central executive office to grab meant that patronage was still a more cost-effective strategy than populism. Whatever the social or economic pressures, whatever results an election might throw up, there were enough spoils to make possible an ever-shifting kaleidoscope of elite coalitions that would keep populism at the margins.[38]

THE LOOMING CRISIS

In spite of its halting start, the bureaucratic strategy was eventually to become the dominant one in twentieth-century Europe. However, like any political order, it could be vulnerable in times of stress. Few political contexts have been more disruptive than the total world war of the first half of the twentieth century, which effectively proceeded in two active stages, the first from 1914 to 1919 and the second from 1939 to 1945. Chapter 5 takes up the German case in the wake of the punitive Versailles Treaty of 1919, where Hitler's capture of power demonstrates the role that an extreme and prolonged crisis can play in making populism an effective strategy. But the signs that populism might emerge as a viable political strategy from the wreckage of the First World War were evident even before it had ended. However, the first polity to succumb to the crisis was not authoritarian Germany but democratic Britain.

Britain entered the war in 1914 under the leadership of H. H. Asquith's Liberal Party. Although divided over the thorny question of Home Rule for Ireland, the Liberal Party had retained its unity though a transformative period of progressive legislative activity. However, after more than a year of bloody and inconclusive fighting along the Franco-Belgian border and with his party fractured over conscription, Asquith was forced to take the Conservative Party and the Labour Party into a "national" cabinet. If the give and take of coalition government has its merits in peacetime, it utterly failed to provide the decisive command structure needed to successfully prosecute a war. Such circumstances present opportunities.

In 1916, David Lloyd George emerged as a very unlikely kind of British prime minister – a prime minister without a party. A Liberal MP since 1890 and a member of the cabinet since 1905, Lloyd George was no political outsider. Yet unlike most of his contemporaries in Westminster, Lloyd George was from a working-, or at least, lower middle-class background. As a firebrand orator and champion of welfare reforms against the resistance of the aristocratic House of Lords, it would be fair to say that by the time the war broke out, he was the nation's best known and most popular politician. For that very reason, he was viewed with deep suspicion by much of the old elite. Lloyd George was rightly perceived to be fiercely independent, ambitious, and egotistical. If he deferred to anyone – and that is an open question – it was to the press lords – Rothermere and Beaverbrook (a.k.a., Max Aitkin). In acknowledgment of Lloyd George's popularity with the masses, Asquith, like his predecessor, Henry Campbell-Bannerman, had little choice but to keep him in the cabinet rather than on the backbenches, where he might be even more of a loose cannon. With Asquith as prime minster, Lloyd George as chancellor of the Exchequer, and a young Winston Churchill as president of the Board of Trade, the government saw through landmark social legislation prior to the outbreak of the war.

Lloyd George's path from there to the premiership was convoluted, reflective of the extreme exigency of a wartime governmental crisis. Desperate for a more direct role in the prosecution of the war effort, in May 1915, Lloyd George surrendered the Treasury to become Minister of Munitions. There, he successfully increased the output of British armaments, but in advocating conscription to overcome the shortage of recruits, began his inexorable alienation from the majority of the Liberal Party. Subsequently installed as Secretary of War on the death of Lord Kitchener in mid-1916, Lloyd George chafed at his lack of authority over the military brass. If Lloyd George had any qualms about perpetrating what was effectively a coup at a time of war, he didn't dwell on them. He sought to replace the large coalition cabinet with a narrower war council that could govern peremptorily on behalf of a national government. Lloyd George's scheme was never likely to work; while he proposed that Asquith would remain in place as prime minister, it would be Lloyd George, as chair of the war council who would hold all the power. Unsurprisingly Asquith demurred, but as the hecatomb of the Somme dragged on through the second half of 1916, by year-end, the majority of Conservatives had completely lost faith in the prime minister. With a general election still deemed out of the question because of the ongoing conflict, Tory leader Bonar Law found that he could only keep the confidence of his caucus if he withdrew the party's support for Asquith. Even though the King offered Law the prime ministership, he acknowledged that "Lloyd George was marked out in the public mind as the alternative to Asquith." It was Lloyd George's turn in the hot seat.[39]

Although Lloyd George was viewed with equanimity by both Liberals and Tories – to say nothing of Labourites – he was just about the only man for the job. Most would say he knew it. Described by one historian as "the nearest thing to a popular dictator since Cromwell," Lloyd George brought the concentration of power implied in his war council proposal to the extreme, taking many key decisions almost singlehandedly. For all of Lloyd George's unpopularity at Westminster, he was still the people's champion. If that meant something like a popular dictatorship for the duration of the war, much of the elite was willing to go along. Arthur Balfour, Tory potentate, summed it up: "If he wants to be dictator, let him be. If he thinks that he can win the war, I'm all for his having a try."[40]

Lloyd George may be the best known British politician to have exploited the crisis for a chance at power, but he was not the only one. With a name, and a career, like that of a Dickensian villain, Horatio Bottomley had a notorious, if short-lived, impact on British politics in the first decades of the twentieth century. Orphaned at just five, Bottomley combined resourcefulness and ruthlessness in equal measure. Largely self-taught, Bottomley worked his way through various odd jobs until falling into the publishing industry. He established his own company and was invited to run as a Liberal Party candidate in 1887. Bottomley was unsuccessful and rededicated himself to his entrepreneurial activities, most of which seem to have skirted legality. Despite his growing reputation as a swindler, he continued to run for office, and was eventually successful in the 1906 Liberal landslide. He launched a weekly tabloid magazine, *John Bull*, which became wildly popular. Yet his roguish past soon caught up with him and losing a suit in 1912, he had to withdraw from Parliament in disgrace. But the breakout of war in 1914 would offer another reprieve. *John Bull* adopted a hyper-nationalist position, railing against Germans and peaceniks alike. Bottomley declared himself the voice of the man in the street and Lloyd George even sought to exploit his popularity to maintain support for the government's war program. Bottomley delivered hundreds of patriotic speeches over the course of the war, but he was never satisfied in his hopes of being rewarded with a formal position in the government. If Bottomley had his eyes on Number 10, Lloyd George was not about to cut him a set of keys. There was only room for one people's champion.

When the war ended with Britain victorious, Lloyd George was unquestionably the most popular politician in the country. Yet Asquith remained leader of the Liberal Party. The result was that Lloyd George adopted a populist strategy. Eschewing party labels, Lloyd George ran on a "coupon" ticket with the backing of defectors from the Liberals and a Conservative Party still led by Law. While many Tories questioned the need for the continued political alliance, the growing militancy and electoral strength of the Labour movement made a Conservative–Liberal coalition the safest response. The Lloyd George–fronted coalition won in a landslide, but with the unusual situation that the prime minister led the smaller of the parties of government. Without a solid base in parliament, or even in the cabinet, Lloyd George continued the personalist style of government he had honed during the war. Always aware of his dependence on his press backers, Lloyd George built up a massive personal political fund from the sale of honors, which he used in part to effectively purchase his own national newspaper, the *Daily Chronicle*.

With the Conservative–Liberal coalition sitting on an unsustainably large majority, parliament, if not the nation at large, was calling out for a reorganization of the parties. Coincidentally, after finally discharging his bankruptcy, Bottomley at this time returned to parliament as an independent, winning four in five of the votes in his constituency: "I am now preparing to proceed to Westminster to run the show," he declared. However, Bottomley's attempt to construct a personalist party on the right through his media organs utterly failed. That side of the political spectrum was simply too well covered by the Conservatives. Lloyd George and Churchill floated the idea of a new center party based on his faction of the Liberals along with Conservative defectors. However, this effort also ran aground; neither organization was willing to sign its own death warrant on the premise that they needed Lloyd George's charisma to keep the socialists at bay. A further electoral realignment was inevitable, but the ones to benefit would be the best organized, Labour on the one side, the Conservatives on the other. Although with just fifty-seven seats in 1918, Labour was only the fourth largest party behind the Irish nationalist party – Sinn Féin – it received nearly 21 percent of the popular vote, a massive upswing of 14.5 percent from 1910. Its time would come soon. In the short term, as elections approached in 1922, the Conservatives were determined to capture power for themselves, withdrawing their support from Lloyd George. No politician from outside of Labour or the Conservative Party would be prime minister again. Under anything like normal circumstances, populism would remain on the margins where organized bureaucratic parties were entrenched.[41]

5

Crisis and Charisma

No gentlemen. The Führer is the Party and the Party is the Führer.

Adolf Hitler[1]

Never let a good crisis go to waste.

Winston S. Churchill[2]

DISASTER STRATEGISTS

Short sellers have never been particularly popular. Most of the time, stock market speculators look to identify firms they believe will increase in worth in the future. So-called value investors, the most famous being American billionaire Warren Buffet, go "long" on stocks, betting on firms – if not the economy in general – prospering. When firms do well, stock prices rise, and investors realize a capital gain. But because a firm's employees and customers also tend to be happy during good times, in a sense, everybody wins. "Short" sellers, in contrast, gamble, not on a firm or a stock market index or currency rising in value but on it *falling*. They profit from disaster. In 2007, as Michael Lewis describes in his best-selling book *The Big Short*, a small number of canny investors bet against the American real estate–backed financial derivatives that were being engineered by leading investment banks such as Morgan Stanley and insured by the likes of AIG. Financial investors are not the only ones who seek to profit from catastrophe. For sure, long-term patterns of economic and social development influence the general pattern of political incorporation. Bureaucratic politics, as we saw at the end of Chapter 4, became viable with the industrial takeoff of the late nineteenth century. However, this chapter shows that demographic, security, and socioeconomic crises have the potential to profoundly disrupt existing patterns of political incorporation, in the process making populism a cost-effective strategy.

As the first decade of the twentieth century drew to a close there was every reason to expect that Germany, as one of the wealthiest countries in the world, would continue its gradual processes of democratization and the bureaucratic political incorporation of its growing population. By 1914, Germany had become Europe's most dynamic economy. Productivity gains in agriculture and industry brought increases in per capita wealth even as its population grew by over two thirds between 1871 and 1914. Germany was the world leader in the chemical and electrical engineering sectors of the so-called second industrial revolution, its only rival being the much larger United States. It had the largest, most literate, and highly skilled population in Europe. It led the way in scientific research, producing fifteen Nobel Prize winners between 1901 and 1914 (compared to five for Britain). Industrialization also led to a massive expansion of the urban working class. The industrial wage labor force had grown to 30.6 percent as early as 1901 while the number of Germans living in cities grew to 35 percent by 1914. Even though the executive branch remained staunchly conservative, union-backed political parties had peacefully assumed prominent places in national and state legislatures, while Germany had implemented one of the most generous, if paternalist, welfare states in the world. It possessed a highly professionalized civil service with the result that corruption was notably low. Why then did Germany not follow Britain or other countries in northwest Europe in becoming a consolidated, liberal democracy, dominated by bureaucratic parties? Why did Adolf Hitler's Nazi Party become the most popular political organization in Germany in 1932 with the result that democracy itself was prorogued a year later?

In his still widely read 1960s classic of comparative history, *The Social Origins of Dictatorship and Democracy*, Harvard sociologist Barrington Moore gave an impressively succinct answer to this question: "No bourgeois, no democracy." The essence of Moore's argument is that liberal – or pluralist – democracy only emerges and survives when the transition to industrial modernity is driven by the middle class rather than through a revolution of a backward peasantry. In contrast to the English experience where a property-owning middle class was gradually created out of the privatizations of church lands during the Reformation and the Enclosure Acts – legislation that excluded peasants from using common lands for grazing or foraging – which followed from 1604 to 1914, the landed elite in Germany, especially the Prussian *Junkers*, continued as feudal lords in all but name. When industrialization took off in the late nineteenth century, German landlords allied with big business to supress the political incorporation of the peasantry and the working class – the coalition of "iron and rye." The blockage of the kind of gradual democratic reforms that occurred in England, and with them the pressure for the formation of liberal or bourgeois political parties, led to the emergence of more radical Communist and Fascist reactionaries instead.[3]

Moore's argument is breathtaking in its scope, but as with most *longue durée* accounts, it is silent when it comes to specifics: Why Hitler? And why in 1933? Thus far, we have seen that the degree to which it is possible to mobilize a sufficiently large proportion of the people to win power through mass communication is a good predictor of when and where we'll see populists be most active. The worlds of classical Greece and Rome and of revolutionary America and Europe were ones in which mass political parties hadn't yet come to exist. In these cases, the major determinants of populist success were the extent to which a large mass support base, rather than just the connivance of the elite, was needed to come to power. The extent of the franchise; the kinds of formal political institutions that conditioned how popular preferences were controlled, such as the use of indirect elections in the early American Republic; and demographic growth all played a part in determining whether populism, patronage, or something else prevailed.

Across interwar Europe, in contrast, mass political parties were already a reality. On the eve of the First World War, the Social Democratic Party of Germany (SPD) had half a million members and was the largest party in the Reichstag (in spite of an electoral system that favored more conservative rural areas). In the prototypical style of a bureaucratic party, the SPD built its base of support through cultural organizations, pubs, bars, sporting clubs, and, of course, labor unions. In the first postwar elections in 1919, the SPD increased its vote share to 38 percent from 35 percent in 1912. Two other large and well-organized parties, the Catholic Centre Party and the liberal German Democratic Party (DDP), won nearly a fifth of the vote each in 1919. The conservative German National People's Party (DNVP) secured a further 10 percent of the vote in 1919, a share that doubled in 1924. How then did a radical populist party like the Nazi Party make the breakthrough to power in the early 1930s?

As of the mid-1920s, the incorporation of the masses into the German party system was uneven. The right of the political spectrum was much less well organized than the left. Even as the SPD had incorporated much of the urban vote, especially in "Red Berlin," rural and middle-class voters had far weaker allegiances. Political scientists have shown that Germany differed from England well before the First World War in at least two critical dimensions. In *Liberalism, Fascism, or Social Democracy*, Gregory Luebbert demonstrated that Germany lacked a single national liberal party that could bring together the votes of the working and professional classes. More recently, Daniel Ziblatt has argued in *Conservative Parties and the Birth of Democracy* that it was the absence of a national conservative party that could have brought together small- and large-scale landowners, which best explains the failure of democracy in Germany. Conservatives were not entirely without organizational roots in civil society in late nineteenth-century Germany, but they remained concentrated in a multitude of veterans' associations and agrarian leagues, which themselves had an ambiguous view of liberal democracy to say the least.

Moreover, these organizations looked nothing like the multi-million-member, cross-class Primrose League, which was allied to the British Conservative Party.[4]

Although these historical legacies are surely important, they are not determinative. No bookmaker would give me, along with my descendants, very good odds on the wager that even American democracy won't last a thousand years. "In the long run," as British economist, John Maynard Keynes, quipped, "we're all dead." For at least two decades before 1914 both peasants and artisans had been prone to demagogic appeals, but these never matured into a movement of sufficient strength to cause the Kaiser much worry. The question of "why 1933?" requires that we consider more contingent events. More than any other case we'll consider in this book, Germany was afflicted by a series of wrenching social and economic crises that destroyed the budding organizational links between liberal and conservative parties and their voters. First, defeat in the Great War massively delegitimized the German ruling class in a way that was not true in victorious Britain. Second, the compromise peace signed at Versailles in June 1919 seriously eroded support for the constitutional parties, especially the SPD, which had emerged at the forefront of German politics at the end of the war. Critically, moreover, the war and the series of economic crises that followed through to 1924 devastated the middle class and severed its links with existing liberal and conservative parties. Contra Moore, it was not that a classical liberal bourgeoisie, which might have supported gradual democratization along British lines, did not exist in Germany. Rather, both the educated, white-collar professional class – the *Bildungsbürgertum* – and the petit bourgeoisie or lower middle class of shopkeepers, clerks, and other small-time property owners – the *Mittelstand* – saw their modest wealth wiped out by a vicious cycle of inflation, deflation, and mass unemployment. There was an economic equalization in postwar Germany, but it was achieved by pushing the middle downward, not pulling those at the bottom up. Because of these developments, there was a large body of voters, especially in rural areas but also among the downwardly mobile middle classes, available for mobilization in Germany after the First World War in a way that was not true of Britain or any of the other victorious allies.[5]

Important as these events of the 1920s were, even they do not fully capture the role of exigency in the Nazi surge. The Nazi vote was still only 2.6 percent as late as 1928, and Weimer democracy, although troubled, survived until 1933. Hitler's success would have been extremely unlikely – I would argue, impossible – without the unprecedented social and economic crisis of 1929–31. None of the great powers particularly thrived during the interwar period, but in most countries, the 1920s saw a resumption of the upward trends in trade, industrialization, and growth that had prevailed before the war. Germany was the exception; hyperinflation and the loss of the industrial heartland of the Rhur, compounding its economic and social difficulties. Even though the currency stabilization of 1923 aided a tentative recovery in the second half of the decade, economic – and hence political – tranquillity had been bought at the cost of enormous exposure to international capital markets. When the American stock market bubble burst in 1929, international liquidity dried up. The German economy went into free fall, and when banks began to fail in 1931, whatever chance the constitutional parties might have had to build up their bureaucratic organizations was cut off at the knees.

As with historical legacies, however, a crisis is not a sufficient cause of populist success. Populism is a strategy; it will be a much more economically efficient response to a crisis if a political leader already has the mass communication machinery in place to exploit it than if he has to build this up from scratch. To paraphrase an old joke about making good comedy, the secret of populist success is – wait for it – timing. In Germany, voters might have been available for populist mobilization in the early 1920s, but no political leader was poised to take advantage. Right through the hyperinflation crisis of 1921–23, Hitler's Nazi Party was weakly committed to electoral politics. In the early 1920s, the far right – including the Nazis – was then more interested in putsches than elections. It was only after Hitler fully reoriented the Nazi Party toward a mass communications strategy – a populist strategy – to mobilize voters by democratic means after 1925, that it would be ready to pounce on the next disaster. Just as short-sellers are primed to make fortunes when economic bubbles burst, the Nazis bet on being prepared to sweep up votes in the wake of an economic crisis. Hitler was a gambler, a short-seller waiting for the right time to call the strike. Although the rise of the Nazis can seem inevitable in retrospect, we have to keep in mind just how contingent this outcome really was. The economic disaster of the late 1920s took some time to arrive; so long in fact, that some of Hitler's followers were ready to give up on him and his populist strategy as a lost cause. Reluctant to invoke unforeseen events in contrast to long-term trends, comparative historians have neglected the role of crisis in allowing Hitler, like other Fascists, to gain support and even power. However, what the interwar period shows, is that unexpected events can upset what appear to be ineluctable long-term trends – at least, they can when someone is prepared to take advantage. What is a crisis for some is an opportunity for others.

THE DARK POWER OF CHARISMA

It is Friday, February 27, 1925: the Bürgerbräukeller in Munich is packed to capacity; 3,000 people are jammed into the grand hall, while 2,000 more have been turned away. Adolf Hitler has just been released from Landsberg prison, where he had been detained after a failed putsch that was launched at the very same venue in November 1923. Tonight's gathering not only celebrates Hitler's release but is an event to mark the "reestablishment" of the Nazi Party. The headline speaker is, as usual, late. Hitler knows from experience that crowds are more receptive as the evening wears on, in part as a consequence of the steins of beer that continue to flow in his absence. He appears on the dais at around eight o'clock. The speech begins calmly, Hitler detailing the historical trajectory of the Nazi Party to date. However, the fevered attacks on Germany's enemies – Communists, Jews, bourgeois collaborators – soon begin to pour forth. Anyone in the audience showing the slightest sign of disapproval is removed by one of Hitler's henchmen. Only the fanatics remain and the content of what is to come is familiar to everyone left in the hall. What they have come for is not new information, but for Hitler himself. As the two-hour speech draws to a close, Hitler makes it clear that the new Nazi party would represent the whole of the *völkisch* movement and be a party for all of Germany. The splits and the localism of recent years would not be repeated. All nationalists must bury their differences and unite against the common enemy. Hitler feeds off the crowd, working himself up to a frenzied crescendo, like a fire and brimstone revivalist minister, spitting, sweating, throwing his arms up to the sky. This is Hitler's movement. "Gentlemen," he says, "let the representation of the interests of the movement from now on be *my* concern!" Only his unconditional leadership would be tolerated. "I am not prepared to allow conditions [on my leadership] as long as I carry personally the responsibility ... And I now carry again the complete responsibility for everything that takes place in this movement." The enraptured crowed chant "Heil!" and then deliver a boisterous rendition of *Deutschland über alles*. Writing in the *Völkische Freiheit*, Joseph Goebbels wrote of Hitler's comeback, "[t]here, rolling in the distance, dull, accusing, clearer—a drumbeat! The outcry of the masses! They call to you from the depths! Drummer, drum for German freedom! They call for salvation!"[6]

As a public speaker, Hitler was peerless. As he described the experience of one of his first speeches in *Mein Kampf*, the autobiographical manifesto he'd written while imprisoned at Landsberg, "what before I had simply felt within me, without in anyway knowing it, was now proved by reality: I could speak!" Hitler learned that there was something particular about the mass meeting. The man in the audience was no longer an individual with critical faculties but an indistinguishable part of a heaving mass, whose resistance was easily swept away. Hitler was described by his audience as "a born popular speaker." One follower, Kurt Lüdecke, declared on witnessing Hitler for the first time in August 1922, [m]y critical faculty was swept away ... He was holding the masses, and me with them, under a hypnotic spell by the sheer force of his conviction ... His appeal to German manhood was like a call to arms, the gospel he preached a sacred truth. He seemed another Luther ... I experienced an exaltation that could be likened only to religious conversion ... I had found myself, my leader, and my cause." In the words of Joseph Goebbels, "[a]s a speaker he achieves a wonderful coordination of gesture, action, and word. A born demagogue! You could conquer the world with that man." One of Hitler's Austrian opponents even commented on feeling the "extraordinary magnetism of his eyes," and that no matter how repulsed by his worldview, there was "something that I could only call attractive and compelling."[7]

Although Hitler's charisma was indispensable to the Nazi's success, it would not have been sufficient if the social and political conditions that made possible the rise of a demagogue had not been present. As I've stressed to this point, populism should be successful only when the cost of a mass communication strategy is less than the alternatives of bureaucratic party building or patronage. By the late 1920s, Hitler had gathered around him a following that was sufficient to exploit a gap in the market once it came along. In the German case, as Oxford historian Ian Kershaw writes, "the impact of his power has largely to be seen not in any specific attributes of 'personality', but in his *role* as *Führer* – a role facilitated by the collaboration, underestimation, mistakes, and weaknesses of others." Most of all, perhaps, Hitler was an opportunist, who took advantage of circumstance. In the face of a near existential crisis for Germany, he offered simple solutions to complex problems. As Hitler put it himself, "[o]ur problems seemed complicated. The people did not know what to do about them … I, on the other hand, have simplified the problem and reduced them to the simplest formula. The masses recognized this and followed me." Charismatic authority, as we've seen, is in the eye of the beholder. To explain his power, therefore, we must look in the first instance to others, not to Hitler himself. Who then were the men, and occasionally women, who became his early disciples? Who made up the throngs showing up at the Bürgerbräukeller in 1925, or at the "Rally of Victory" at Nuremberg in 1933?[8]

To answer these questions, we have to begin by looking at the pattern of political affiliations that existed in Germany as Hitler began his political career in the early 1920s. On the one hand, as Ziblatt has argued, the party structure of the 1920s had deep historical roots. In many ways, Germany's economic modernization brought about exactly the kind of political transition that we would expect. Being a world leader in modern industry, especially chemical and electoral products, German cities gave birth to one of the largest and most effective labor movements of the nineteenth century. As in other parts of the continent, the assertiveness of the working class was first met with resistance. Although as early as 1849 the Prussian Diet authorized factory workers to form mutual welfare funds, it proscribed them from forming full-fledged unions, whose political machinations they feared. The first autonomous working-class movement, the General German Workers' Association (ADAV), wasn't established until 1863. Locked out of the political process by Prussia's Iron Chancellor, Otto von Bismarck, and the conservative elite, the ADAV moved in a more explicitly socialist direction. It advocated for worker rights although it remained an intellectual rather than mass movement until its merger with the Social Democratic Workers' Party of Germany (SDAP) in 1875 to form the Socialist Workers' Party of Germany (SAPD). The SAPD won some 9 percent of the vote in the Reichstag elections of 1977. Its steady growth bred concern on the right and the SAPD was proscribed under the Anti-Socialist Law of 1878. Despite being forced underground, however, the process of political and social organization on the left continued. When the ban on socialist parties was lifted in 1890, it reconstituted itself as the SPD. Its membership rose to 100,000 while its vote share increased to 19.7 percent. In 1912, the last federal election before the First World War, it won 34.8 percent of the vote, compared to just 16.4 percent for its closest rival, the Center Party.[9]

Yet prior to the war, in spite of holding a collective majority in the Reichstag, the socialist and Catholic opposition parties could not agree on a common program, leaving the conservative elite patronized by the Kaiser in control of the government. The aristocracy retained its traditional opposition to the political incorporation of the lower orders, and it was joined by powerful industrialists, who were resistant to the creeping development of the welfare state. For their part, however, despite their common opposition to the SPD, liberal and conservative parties were not nearly as cohesive as the parties of the left. On the liberal side were the National Liberals and the Progressives; on the conservative side stood the German Conservative Party (DkP) and the Catholic Center Party. While the latter had begun to incorporate the lower and middle masses through churches and various cultural organizations, the former remained a party of notables. The DkP was not only dependent on electoral fraud and clientelism for its vote but it was internally weak and unprofessional.[10]

Overcoming internal division through more assertive foreign policy has always been a temptation for unpopular governments. Although following German unification and the resounding victory in the Franco-Prussian War of 1871, Germany appeared relatively acceptant of the territorial status quo on the continent, further afield, its irredentism accelerated. In search of its own "place in the sun," Germany brutally established colonies in Africa, Asia, and the Pacific, executing or starving to death thousands of Herrero tribesmen in German Southwest Africa (now Namibia). In North Africa too, it continually looked to expand its colonial possessions and access to natural resources posing a substantial threat to British and French dominance, revealed not least by the narrowly averted conflicts over Morocco in 1905 and 1911. Yet given the mutual benefit that was to be had by further trade and financial integration, a war of the scale that eventuated from 1914 to 1919 was by no means inevitable. As Norman Angel argued in *The Great Illusion*, published in 1909, Europe's leading states were so interdependent and the likely cost of war between them so great that war between them was almost inconceivable. Churchill thought claims of an inevitable conflict between a predominant Britain and a rising Germany "nonsense." Recently, economists have speculated that the war itself was the result of class conflict within Germany and the other great powers. Most historians, however, take the view that Europe "sleepwalked" into war. Much as we like to identify big causes for big events, miscalculations and misapprehensions played a major role in the outbreak of hostilities that followed.[11]

The Great War, as it became known, was unlike anything that Europe had seen before. Gone were the wars of position and manoeuvre. This was human slaughter on an industrial scale. The strategy of German Chief of Staff General

Erich von Falkenhayn was simply to "bleed France white" – killing or disabling its young men until there were literally no more left to fight. Until the full development of combined mobile artillery, tank, and aerial tactics, defence had the upper hand over attack, resulting in prolonged strategic stalemates on all fronts. Despite its victory over the Russians in the wake of the Bolshevik Revolution of October 1917, after a shockingly bloody but futile last attempt to achieve a military breakthrough on its Western front in the Spring of 1918, Germany's defeat became only a matter of time. By mid-1914, German units had fallen back to the Siegfried Line, almost exactly where they began the war five years prior. Military units began to mutiny in November 1919, most infamously at the Kiel naval station. Seeing the writing on the wall, General Erich Ludendorff advised accepting the armistice terms. Germany's capitulation was complete.

Although the fatherland avoided occupation during the war itself, the social and economic devastation wrought by the conflict is hard to overstate. About 85 percent of eligible German males had been mobilized to fight at one point or another. An estimated two million of those men were killed; that is, about 15 percent of the 13 million who served. At least four million more were wounded, amounting to 9–14 percent of Germany's prewar population. Another 750,000 noncombatants died prematurely from disease and deprivation during the war. The continuation of the Allied blockade of German ports persisted for an agonizing eight months after the Armistice, perhaps taking another 100,000 lives, as the victors attempted to starve the Germans into a chastening peace. A further half a million Germans died from the Spanish flu epidemic that ripped across the world as the conflict wound down in 1919. Germany, in four years, had gone from being the world's preeminent industrial power to near destitution. Loaded on top of this came a dose of humiliation. With the Treaty of Versailles that brought hostilities to a formal close, Germany was assigned total responsibility for the war. All of its colonies were surrendered to become mandates of the newly created League of Nations; Alsace-Lorraine, captured from France in 1871, was returned; smaller territories were ceded to Belgium, Lithuania, Czechoslovakia, and Poland; the Rhineland was to become a demilitarized buffer zone between Germany and France; a Polish Corridor henceforth separated East Prussia from the rest of Germany; German arms were strictly circumscribed; and an obligation to repay massive financial indemnities for the damages and losses caused by the war – reparations – were imposed (with the exact figure to be determined later).

On January 19, 1919, 30 million German men and women, 83 percent of the adult population, elected a Constituent Assembly. The SPD emerged as the dominant party in the Assembly, winning 38 percent of the vote amid widespread dissatisfaction with the conservative forces that had brought the country to military and economic disaster. In August, the people ratified the Constitution of the German Reich, agreed on by the German National Assembly in the town of Weimar. The Constitution called for elections to a new unicameral national parliament, or Reichstag, in June 1920. Amid the social and economic chaos of the first half of 1920, the SPD's support quickly retreated back to its working-class core, with its vote share dropping to 22 percent – nearly half the level it reached just six months before. Unfairly perhaps, stepping into the hot seat meant that the SPD was saddled with the blame for atrocious postwar privations and a shameful peace settlement, even though it bore limited responsibility for either. Although there were bastions of left-wing radicalism that flourished during the hardships of the early postwar period, the so-called Spartacist government that took control in Munich lasted only two weeks in April 1919 before being brutally suppressed by the *Reichswehr* and the *Freikorps* (right-wing militia). The SPD government's role in the repression of the radical left, and the extrajudicial execution of its leaders, Karl Liebknecht and Rosa Luxemburg, meant that there would be no grand coalition of the hard and soft left. Opposed by the Communists, the SPD was instead thrust into alliance with Catholic centrists and moderate liberals.

The Center Party, because of its strong links with the Catholic Church, was one of the only nonsocialist parties to have anything like a well–integrated mass base of support. In spite of the massive expansion of the franchise that Weimar brought about, conservative forces for their part had hardly modernized at all. The German National People's Party (DNVP) was founded in 1918, representing a sizeable but disorganized body of conservative, nationalist sentiment. The party's share of the vote grew from 15.1 percent in 1920 to 20.5 percent in December 1924, and it had a potentially large base of support in rural Germany that it could have tapped to grow further. Although, the DNVP recruited nearly a million members at its height in 1923, it never incorporated its supporters into anything like a coherent organizational structure. Rather, it relied heavily on the resources of local land and county associations. At the same time, while the DNVP obtained the votes of many members of the radical anti-Semitic German-Racial Defence and Defiance League, which had some 200,000 members nationally, the party never became the exclusive political front of the radical right. Rather, through the democratic "golden era" of 1924–28, the DNVP leadership kept such extremists to the margins. The party's weak organization among the mainstream conservative electorate left it susceptible to take over from within or defeat from without by a party that chose to aggressively target and incorporate these voters. To use a poker metaphor, the DNVP left many potential supporters on the table, failing to incorporate them when it had the chance. As a result, into the late 1920s, there was a large and *available* body of non-Catholic conservative and nationalist voters who were weakly incorporated into mainstream parties on the right.[12]

Through this opening strode Adolf Hitler. Hitler's life to that date had been unremarkable; he was, as biographer Peter Longerich puts it, "a nobody." Hitler was born in modest circumstances, his Austrian father, Alois, planning for young Adolf to emulate him in pursuing a career in the civil service.

However, losing both his father and mother before his twentieth year had begun, Hitler's life began a downward spiral. He failed in his ambition to be an artist and refused to do the menial work for which he was qualified. Although he was left with a modest inheritance, he frittered it away and soon learned what it was like to sleep rough and to go hungry, eking out a bohemian and directionless life in multicultural Vienna. For Hitler, as he later wrote, the outbreak of war in 1914 was "a release from the painful feelings of my youth." As Heinrich Hoffman's now famous photograph of Hitler among the throngs celebrating Germany's declaration of war at Munich's Odeonsplatz on August 2, 1914, illustrates, Hitler experienced how it felt to be swept up in the crowd, to be part of something bigger than himself, his eyes "upraised and fixed . . . [his] hair . . . uncut and unkempt . . . a man transported." Hitler served honorably as a soldier for the German army in the First World War (despite being an Austrian). Although he won the Iron Cross, first and second class, he only ever received one promotion, possibly early evidence of a difficulty in getting along with others. He remained in the army after the war, assigned to political duties, first under the short-lived socialist government, and then with greater distinction under the right wing one that replaced it. Captain Karl Mayr, who directed a propaganda department in postwar Munich, recruited Hitler to his team and saw to it that the lance corporal attended training courses in German history and economic theory. These courses would be Hitler's only formal advanced education. Hitler was assigned to "educate" soldiers who had been tempted by socialism. A contemporary described Hitler as he held his fellow soldiers enrapt: "I saw a pale, drawn face underneath a decidedly unmilitary shock of hair, with a trimmed moustache and remarkably large, light blue, fanatically cold, gleaming eyes." His lectures, Hitler claimed, brought "many hundreds, indeed thousands" of his comrades back to the fatherland.[13]

It wasn't long before Mayr had assigned Hitler to a new task, to infiltrate one of the many extremist nationalist groups that had emerged in Berlin in the months since the armistice. As the story goes, Hitler was dispatched to a meeting of the German Workers' Party (DAP) in Munich's Sternkelerbräu. The main lecture of the September 12, 1919 meeting, delivered by Gottfried Feder, a self-trained economist and one of the founders of the DAP, was unremarkable. What piqued Hitler's ire were the remarks of another one of the attendees, Professor Baumann, who spoke in favor of Bavarian separatism. Hitler launched into a withering tirade, leading Baumann to depart the hall "like a wet poodle" as Hitler put it. "Goodness, he's got a gob," Anton Drexler, then chairman of the DAP is alleged to have said, "we could use him." Hitler was invited to join the small party, and although he hesitated – still then contemplating establishing his own party – he ultimately consented, becoming member number 555 – actually, he was more like member 55, as the inflated numbering system began at 501.[14]

The party was a relative rabble – just one among many organizations amid a burgeoning right–wing milieu – but this was in many ways to Hitler's liking. He could make a name with it and indeed he quickly became the party's star attraction. In February 1920 Hitler delivered a speech to 2,000 people at the first mass rally of the freshly renamed National Socialist German Workers' Party (NSDAP or Nazi Party) at the Hofbräuhaus, announcing the "25 points," which were to become the party's unalterable credo. In March, right around the time of the failed right–wing Kapp Putsch in Berlin, his role in the Army came to an end and he became a full-time political agitator. By the end of the year, Hitler had addressed more than thirty mass meetings, with audiences of between 800 and 2,500. In early February 1921, he spoke to 6,000 supporters at the Circus Krone. Already to the Munich public, "Hitler was the NSDAP." His indispensability to the party was soon reflected in fact. In April 1921, he threatened to resign, and in July demanded, and was given "the post of chairman with dictatorial powers" over the party.[15]

The occasion for Hitler's manoeuvre at this time was a sharp division over the strategic direction of the NSDAP. For some time, Hitler had envisioned the Nazi Party as the spearhead of the emerging Pan-German nationalist movement. Back in December 1919, Hitler forced out Karl Harrer, one of the founders of the DAP, because of Harrer's willingness to operate under the broad right–wing banner of the conservative DNVP. Hitler had no interest in playing such a subsidiary role. This time around, Hitler objected to talks of a possible merger with its sister party, the German Socialist Party (DSP). Although the DSP was almost indistinguishable from the DAP in terms of program and membership profile, the former's preferred strategy was to build a wide network of party branches and to pursue a parliamentary strategy. Drawing inspiration both from the Catholic church and the Marxist left, Hitler instead wanted the NSDAP to concentrate on propaganda to build a mass following. In Hitler's words, "[t]he best organisation is not that which inserts the greatest, but that which inserts the smallest intermediary apparatus between the leadership of a movement and its individual adherents." He would mobilize support directly.[16]

Remarkable as Hitler's rapid ascent to dominance within the NSDAP was, the path from curiosity of Munich's radical right speaking circuit to the chancellor's office was hardly obvious. In fact, although it has become common with the benefit of hindsight to write of the collapse of Weimar democracy as a matter of *when* rather than *if*, the system's resilience during the 1920s was quite remarkable. After the war, the German economy was hobbled by a miserly economic settlement, one that British economist John Maynard Keynes famously predicted in *The Economic Consequences of the Peace*, would eventually lead to economic catastrophe and renewed conflict. Just as important as immediate French demands for reparations was the deflationary push by the United States and Britain to return prices to their prewar levels. Although Germany's industrial infrastructure remained hardly damaged by the war, the drop in worldwide demand precluded a resumption of Germany's prewar export–led growth strategy. The only way Germany could fulfill its financial obligations was to print money. From around 90 marks to the dollar in early 1921, it took 320 to buy one a year later. By the end of 1922, inflation had begun to spiral out of control, requiring 7,400 marks to purchase a dollar. Germany could no longer make its repayments and its default triggered the French occupation of the Rhur valley – Germany's coal-producing industrial heartland. Political humiliation was lumped on top of economic despair and the Rhineland descended into a state of undeclared war. The government backed its citizens' refusal to work in the occupied territories, but it could only finance this economic shutdown by printing yet more money. By late 1923 the mark had hit a staggering 4.2 trillion to the dollar. Inflation had for a time sustained an economic recovery of sorts. Propped up by a bloated public sector, unemployment in 1921 and 1922 was in the low single digits. By mid-1923, however, the fiction of a paper-based recovery couldn't be sustained. In Prussia, unemployment rose from 2.7 percent in January 1923 to 24 percent in October. In Hessen, it rose from 0.7 percent to 37.4 percent. In Dresden it shot up to 60 percent and in Hamburg to a staggering 64.8 percent. When the commodity-backed *Rentenmark* was introduced in late November to halt the inflationary juggernaut, its value was set at one trillionth of the prevailing value of the paper mark. Those who had loaned the government the money to pay for its war saw their investments cut to naught. Savings big and small were wiped out.[17]

Yet in spite of the economic and social chaos, not only did democracy survive but populism remained on the margins. The SPD, the DNVP, and Center Party remained the largest parties through the 1920s. Economic conditions alone, however desperate, are not sufficient to explain populist success. A populist strategy may be cheaper than long-term party building, but it is not free, and someone has to be willing to bet on such a strategy for it to be successful. In the disorder of 1923, for Hitler and the Nazis, an armed route seemed the quicker and more economical option. Eying the example of Italy, Hitler saw himself as Germany's Mussolini; or in his wilder fantasies, as the Messiah himself: "I must enter Berlin like Christ in the Temple of Jerusalem and scourge out the moneylenders." With the federal and state governments in crisis, Communists in Saxony, Thuringia, and Hamberg were all on the verge of launching coups of their own. Even as that threat receded, armed groups on the right continued to pose a threat to state governments, if not the national government. It was in this context that in Bavaria, the right-wing triumvirate government of Gustav Ritter von Kahr, state commissioner of Bavaria; Otto von Lossow, head of Bavarian police; and Reichswehr General Hans Ritter von Seisser resolved to take preemptive action against the Nazi Party. With the Nazi's Stormtroopers baying for blood, Hitler and Ludendorff, the former general and leader of German forces at the end of the First World War, resolved to act. Marching on a meeting of the triumvirate and its supporters at Munich's Bürgerbräukeller, about 350 Nazis seized hold of Kahr, Lossow, and Seisser. Behind closed doors, pistol in hand, Hitler strongarmed the three into declaring their support for the putsch. However, when Hitler left them in the custody of Ludendorff, the latter foolishly set them free. It didn't take long for them to betray Ludendorff and have him, along with Hitler, arrested. However, a poorly prosecuted trial allowed Hitler to present himself as a patriot rather than a seditionist. For his treason he was sentenced to a mere five-year period of imprisonment at Landsberg. With good behavior, Hitler was released in December 1924, and in February 1925, the ban on the Nazi Party was lifted.[18]

In Hitler's absence, the NSDAP had become rife with factionalism. Though he could have intervened, Hitler remained focused on his writing instead. Even if this meant that the party lost much of its lustre, Hitler's apparent neglect was the result of an astute calculation. With each faction at war with another, no one could challenge Hitler's total dominance within the party. The failure of his rivals to coordinate their actions left Hitler effectively unopposed on his release. Out of prison, Hitler set off on a new legal path to power. It might seem fatuous to suggest that the Nazis, of all movements, were indifferent to whether they came to power by armed struggle or the ballot box. Yes, Nazi ideologues like Goebbels later pontificated about the purity of muscle power and spoke contemptuously of democracy. Political virtue was, in part, measured by one's willingness to shed blood – whether one's own or someone else's. But power for its own sake stood above all that. After his release from prison, Hitler never wavered in his commitment to a democratic, that is, electoral, route to power, seemingly much to the chagrin of Goebbels and other true believers. At Landsberg, Hitler came to another realization. No longer would he be content to be the "drummer" for Ludendorff or anyone else. Hitler now had a grander destiny. As his speech at the Bürgerbräukeller in late February made clear, henceforth Hitler would be unimpeachable in all respects within the party. "Brilliant in style and content" said Goebbels of Hitler's reassertion of dictatorial party control. After reading *Mein Kampf*, Goebbels confessed to his diary "[w]ho is this man? Half-plebian, half-god! Is this really Christ or just John the Baptist?" "This man has all it takes to become king. A born people's tribune. The coming dictator."[19]

We might add here that style mattered at least as much as, if not more than, content. Popular culture, if not much of academia, sees Hitler and other Nazis as manic ideologues. With his unique anti-Semitic brand of Fascism, Hitler in the 1920s and 1930s supposedly articulated a set of ideas that fit with Germans' latent desires. Fascism's ideological combination of nationalism, holism, statism, corporatism, idealism, voluntarism, romanticism, mysticism, militarism, imperialism, and in the German case, anti-Semitism, supposedly appealed to those who wanted to submit to an identarian form of political order above all else. But several elements of this idea-driven approach are problematic.

First, simply, for most voters, even for most Nazis, ideology was of limited importance. Nazi Party–expert Michael Kater writes, "[t]o the regular party worker, what mattered was not so much the content of the ideology as the method of disseminating it. The manner of presentation was the message, and

emotional appeal was superior to dialectic." Or as Robert Paxton, a historian
of fascism at Columbia University, put it, in the German case as much as in any
other, fascism is "better studied as political behavior than as creed." Second, in
the German case specifically, although Nazi Party members were distinct in
their virulent anti-Semitism, most research suggests that this was a minor factor
for the preponderance of Nazi voters. In fact, Hitler's earlier – pre-1923
putsch – rhetoric was more heavily imbued with anti-Semitism than was the
Nazi election propaganda of the late 1920s and early 1930s when the party
finally gained a mass following. Similarly, the idea that all, or even most, Nazi
supporters were imbued with some kind of irredentist blood lust is hard to
sustain. Ironically, indeed, one part of the Hitler myth that appealed to most
Germans was that he would secure *peace*. Even in the late 1930s, in spite of the
reverence in which he was held by a majority of Germans, Hitler could not
convert this into enthusiasm for war, although the latter was very much his own
aim. Third, in part influenced by the popularity of Freudian psychoanalysis,
other scholars writing after the Second World War argued that individual
support for Hitler and other Fascists was driven by underlying authoritarian
personality traits. That is, those with submissive personalities should have been
more likely to support Fascist leaders like Hitler. Although subsequent studies
have found modest support for the authoritarian personality thesis at the
individual level, and although personality traits differ modestly across countries, personality also does a poor job of explaining the timing of the Nazi
surge. If personality traits are relatively constant over time, as most psycho-
logical research demonstrates, they do not provide a very useful explanation for
the spectacular jump in the Nazi share of the vote from 2.6 percent in 1928 to
18.3 percent in 1930 and 37.3 in 1932. Social ties are instead likely to have
been more important to this remarkable, we might say nonlinear, jump in Nazi
support. For instance, we're told that the patrons of one particular pub acted as
a unit, collectively switching overnight their allegiance from the Communists to
the Nazis. This was not a matter of individuals voting according to their
conscience. Fourth, much less even than in the case of Communism, Fascism
was never coeval with a single, coherent set of ideas. Neither Hitler nor
Mussolini were at all consistent in the ideas they espoused. Hitler, for instance,
incongruously demonized Jews both as factious trade unionists and as exploit-
ative finance capitalists. What's more, even though the twenty-five points were
set in stone as Nazi doctrine, their application was notoriously flexible. Even if
both Nazi Germany and Fascist Italy eventually settled on a kind of state-
managed capitalism, corporatism was in reality a pragmatic discovery, not an
ideological first principle. Both Hitler and Mussolini swerved from socialist to
reactionary positions on the economy prior to settling on the corporatist model.
The Nazi Party was never the darling of conservative or industrialist interests.
Ideas were weapons in Hitler's strategic arsenal. Hitler biographer, Ian
Kershaw, succinctly notes that "ideas held no interest for Hitler as abstractions.
They were important to him only as tools of mobilization."[20]

Simply put, the success of Hitler was based much less on his ideas than on the form in which they were delivered. And that form was primarily one of mass communication through public rallies. As Kershaw concludes, "the great popularity of Hitler before the war had for the most part little to do with fanatical belief in the central tenets of the Hitlerian racial-imperialist 'world-view', and even less to do with belief in the Party, whose leader he was." It was instead based on Hitler's charismatic appeal as leader. Take the case of Nazism's truest devotee, Joseph Goebbels, who confessed to his diary in October 1923, "[i]t doesn't matter what we believe in, as long as we believe." Goebbels was true to his own aphorism. Although he had long been committed to socialistic principles of public ownership and redistribution, when Hitler expunged these ideas from the Nazi program, Goebbels first confessed his disappointment to his diary, "I'm sick at heart ... Probably one of the greatest disappointments of my life. I no longer believe fully in Hitler." Yet in a remarkable *volte face*, Goebbels quickly accommodated himself to the party's switch in economic platform. Within a matter of weeks, Goebbels was writing "brilliant," "I love him," "[s]uch a sparkling mind can be my leader. I bow to the greater one. The political genius." Hitler's followers portrayed him as the heroic leader born to return Germany to glory, well before he even came to see himself in this way. In the words of Hermann Göring, later commander of the Luftwaffe, "[t]here is something mystical, inexpressible, almost incomprehensible about this one man ... We love Adolf Hitler because we believe deeply, steadfastly, that he was sent to us by God to save Germany ... For us the Führer is simply infallible in all matters political and all other issues concerning the national and social interest of the people." Nor were Nazi luminaries like Goebbels and Göring the only ones to place the leader above the platform. Hitler's appeal was that of the quintessential charismatic. Ernst Hanfstaengl, another early devotee, wrote "[f]ar beyond his electrifying rhetoric, this man seemed to possess the uncanny gift of coupling the gnostic yearning of the era for a strong leader-figure with his own missionary claim and to suggest in this merging that every conceivable hope and expectation was capable of fulfillment – an astonishing spectacle of suggestive influence of the mass psyche."[21]

In the mid-1920s, Hitler continued to make good on his assertion of total supremacy within the Nazi Party, picking off his rivals one by one. After the failure of the Munich putsch, resolving on a democratic strategy, Hitler first looked to tame the party's paramilitary force, the *Sturmabteilung* (SA), often known in English as the Brownshirts for their color of their uniform. In spite of the failure of the 1923 putsch, Ernst Röhm, leader of the SA, saw himself as an equal of Hitler and viewed the fractious organization as a genuine military force. Hitler instead envisioned the SA as a tool of the party to be used primarily for propaganda purposes. Röhm was pushed aside, and although many right-wing armed gangs and organizations persisted, the SA ceased to be a rival to Hitler under the weak leadership of Franz von Pfeffer. Hitler dealt with Ludendorff, perhaps the most credible rival to his leadership of the radical right of German politics, by having him run for the Reich presidency in 1925. When the general won a humiliating 1.1 percent of the votes cast, Hitler told Hermann Esser, "[t]hat's alright ... now we've finished him." The remaining leaders within the Nazi Party fold declared their obedience to Hitler at the Bamberg Conference in February 1926. Gregor Strasser, a key northern regional party leader, or *Gauleiter*, and perhaps then Hitler's only real rival within the party, was compelled to fully withdraw his pretentions as the party's intellectual leader. Strasser, like Röhm, would pay with his life for his challenge to Hitler's authority in the Night of the Long Knives in 1934. But the end of July 1926 had already marked the establishment of Hitler's "supreme mastery over the party" in fact as well as theory. The movement henceforth would be based on the *Führerprinzip* – the leader principle. Hitler's bets had been placed.[22]

THE LOOMING CRISIS

Although the Führer cult was already taking shape on the extreme Nazi fringe by the mid-1920s, the party was unable to achieve a broader breakthrough. As late as the federal election of May 20, 1928, the Nazis won only 12 of 491 seats in the Reichstag. Goebbels, never an enthusiast of the electoral strategy, was despondent. Contrary to the idea that the Weimar system was perpetually on the brink of collapse, the mid-1920s was not fertile ground for the Nazis. After the monetary stabilization of late 1923, and the adoption of the Dawes Plan in 1924, which restructured reparations payments, a gradual economic recovery took hold. Fueled in large part by renewed investment from the United States – mostly, unfortunately it would turn out, in the form of short-term private capital inflows, or "hot money" – Germany experienced a mini economic boom from 1924 to 1929, with exports doubling over the period. However, even as the Nazi Party ran out of money, Hitler kept faith with the democratic approach, believing that, eventually, opportunity would come knocking. What Hitler needed, he recognized, was a crisis.

The slowdown in Germany began in 1927, as a stock market boom on Wall Street drew speculative American investment away from European assets. The beginnings of an agrarian crisis in 1927 weakened support for moderate conservatives in the rural electorates that were key to the DNVP. With that party's vote share dropping to 14.5 percent in 1928 (from 20.5 percent in 1924), industrialist and nationalist Alfred Hugenberg conducted a well-orchestrated takeover of the DNVP, pushing the party toward the ideological extreme. Support for the moderates, especially on the right, was ebbing, but the Nazis still remained a minor party on the political fringe. When the tightening spigot of foreign capital was shut off entirely with the Wall Street crash of September 1929, Germany's economic recovery was stopped dead in its tracks. Unemployment shot up from 1.4 million to over 2 million. As welfare expenditures increased and tax revenues declined, the government was forced into harsh austerity measures, which only exacerbated the economic crisis. The sense that these travails were the result of outside influence did nothing to help the government parties' popularity. Drafted by an international committee in mid-1929 to replace the Dawes Plan on reparations, the Young Plan proposed a further de facto reduction in Germany's liabilities, but the economic slowdown made *any* repayment scheme, whatever its objective merits, politically untenable. In fact, it was the politically toxic Young Plan that gave Hitler and the Nazis their big break.

Unsurprisingly, nationalist parties, principally in the form of Hugenberg's DNVP, led the opposition to the American Plan. For the DNVP and their fellow travelers on the far right, any form of reparations was an admission of liability and was thus *verboten*. Hugenberg founded the Reich Committee for the German People's Petition against the Young Plan and the War-Guilt Lie. When the petition was put to a referendum on December 22, although 95 percent of those voting supported it, turnout was far below the 50 percent threshold needed for it to be binding – just 15 percent of eligible voters participated. The Young Plan was adopted, but even still, the failed plebiscite had been a massive publicity coup for Hitler. Invited into the committee by Hugenberg for his ability to mobilize the mob, Hitler soon took total ownership of the anti-Versailles and antifinance issue space. Lacking the charisma to bring new voters over to his nationalist movement, Hugenberg gave Hitler access to his media empire, making him a household name well beyond the narrow circles of the extreme right. Hitler now had powerful, and wealthy, friends. When the SPD–led Grand Coalition government of Hermann Müller collapsed on March 27, 1930, Reich president, Otto von Hindenburg, called on Center Party leader Heinrich Brüning to form a minority government. Brüning turned to austerity to restore the country's finances, but he was opposed by an "unholy alliance" of the SPD, the Communists, the DNVP, and the Nazis. Hindenberg pushed Brüning's austerity measures through by presidential decree but at the cost of having to dissolve the Reichstag. New elections would be needed. Hitler, the short-seller, was poised to strike.[23]

It was the financial crisis of the early 1930s that finally allowed Hitler to connect the dots between Germany's international weakness, economy misery, and the spectre of Jewish-Bolshevik domination. The overriding theme of the 1930 Reichstag elections was the breakup of German political life into a "heap of special interests." People were genuinely dismayed. There was a general mood of protest, resentment, and above all alienation from the parties, especially in rural areas. Many voters were ready to abandon the Weimar parties in large numbers. "There was nothing worse than a political party"; such was the view of locals in Gandersheim near Hanover. Although the Nazis originally saw urban workers as their natural constituency, the SPD and the Communists more or less had a lock on these groups. The Nazis evolved instead into what Thomas Childers, one of the most respected analysts of Nazi voting, described as a "catch all party of protest." Seeking cheaper, more available voters, it turned in particular to peasants who were resentful of their neglect at the hands of liberal and conservative parties. 1930 and 1931 saw the florescence of a genuine *Landvolk* or rural people's movement. Peasants no longer saw working through agrarian interest groups oriented toward the conservative parties as being worthwhile. As historian Peter Fritzsche puts it, "Nazis did not take over innocent townspeople in some sort of audacious invasion; they gave sharp political definition to imprecisely held affinities and frustrated expectations." In this sense, there was a *zeitgeist* that was captured and given direction by the Nazis, rather than simply being created by it. What Nazi propaganda did was to give this resentment a face. The message that Hitler, and only Hitler, could effectively stand up to the nefarious forces facing regular Germans was central to the Nazi campaign. Indeed, the ballot card in the 1930 elections referred not to the NSDAP or the Nazi Party, but to the *Hitlerbewegung* – the "Hitler movement." This was no regular political party.[24]

When the ballots were counted, the Nazi's vote share had shot up to 18.3 percent, making it the second largest party in the Reichstag, and finally giving Hitler real political leverage. Nazi votes came mostly at the expense of the DVP, the DNVP, and the Landbund, establishing the NSDAP as the main party of the right. Brüning remained chancellor but following the collapse of one of Germany's big four banks, Danatbank, in July 1931, and a subsequent run on other major banks including Dresdner Bank, the economy went into free fall. Whatever chance Brüning had of holding on in normal times, it was clear that his government would not see out a financial crisis whose scale is hard to overstate. Already by January 1930, unemployment had risen to over 3 million, or nearly 15 percent of the "working age" population; taking into account underemployment, some have put the true figure at 4.5 million. Between 1929 and 1932, industrial production fell by half. Real Gross Domestic Product (GDP) – an inflation adjusted measure of total economic output – shrank by 25 percent, and real GDP per capita by 17 percent. Suicides in Germany in 1932 were double the rate in the United States and four times that of Britain. The Nazis continued to rail against the system. In state elections in late 1931, the NSDAP won 26.2 percent of votes in Hamburg and then Hessen, 37.1 percent. In early 1932, it won 36.3 percent in Prussia, 32.5 in Bavaria, 26.4 percent in Württemberg, 31.2 percent in Hamburg, and in Anhalt 40.9 percent. In Oldenburg at the end of May and Mecklenburg-Schwerin on June 5, the party won 48.4 and 49 percent of the vote, respectively. In Hessen in June, it increased its vote to 44 percent.[25]

New Reichstag elections were scheduled for July 1932 and again the Nazis were primed to take advantage of the chaos. The party's propaganda machine went into overdrive. This kind of campaigning, of course, didn't come cheap. Even if the German masses, or rather, subsections of them, had become alienated from other parties, the Nazis still had to reach them, and to do so on a limited budget. Hitler had acquired some wealthy backers – most notably, Fritz Thyssen – but the Nazi Party was never the instrument of the economic elite.

The Nazis still needed to keep to a budget. The core of the Nazi propaganda machine was the mass meeting or the mass rally. The Nazi Party planned as many as 34,000 meetings across Germany in the last month of the campaign alone. In a political first, Hitler used an airplane to travel from city to city, sometimes delivering speeches at multiple rallies per day. At the crescendo of the *"Hitler über Deutschland"* campaign, he delivered twenty speeches to massive audiences of up to 30,000 in the last six weeks of the campaign. On April 23, 1932, Hitler addressed 120,000 at the speedway track at Lokstedt in Hamburg. Throughout the campaign, Goebbels, then director of Nazi propaganda, also commissioned the production of a great deal of visual propaganda including posters, banners, and flags that were plastered all over Germany. Loudspeakers were mounted on trucks to broadcast Nazi songs and sound-bites. Public marches, in which Nazis paraded in military formation through cities and towns, were another means of propaganda. Goebbels utilized more novel technologies as well, circulating 50,000 copies of a gramophone record that featured Hitler in action. The Nazi campaign was based not on specifics of policy or the provision of information but on the evocation of emotion. Propaganda, both Hitler and Goebbels appreciated, must be simple to be effective. Hitler himself wrote in *Mein Kampf*,

[a]ll propaganda must be popular and its intellectual level must be adjusted to the most limited intelligence among those it is addressed to ... The receptivity of the great masses is very limited, their intelligence is small, but their power of forgetting is enormous. In consequence of these facts, all effective propaganda must be limited to a very few points and must harp on these slogans until the last member of the public understands what you want him to understand by your slogan.

The Nazi Party also by then had an army of volunteers, drawing in this respect on the bureaucratic or programmatic strategic approach. Yet their role was less to incorporate or socialize voters into the party in the way that the SPD or the Center Party would have done than it was to be instruments of propaganda themselves. Nazi uniforms and Nazi collective rituals, performed by party members, were similarly part and parcel of the party's mass communication strategy.[26]

The 1932 election saw the Nazis increase their vote share to 37.4 percent. With 230 seats they were the largest party in the Reichstag. The rest of this story has been well told elsewhere and so I will not dwell on it here. Commanding such a large share of the popular vote, Hitler now knew that Hindenburg and the other conservatives in charge, for whom any alliance with the SPD was unthinkable, could no longer ignore him. Hitler, however, ever the brinkman, refused to join any cabinet except in the position of chancellor. Eventually, then chancellor, Franz von Papen, convinced Hindenburg to relent. Hitler was leader of Germany.

As I argued already, we need not speculate on people's attachment to Nazi ideology or resort to psychoanalysis at a distance to explain Hitler's ascent to power. Rather, we can instead identify the parts of the populace most likely to be susceptible to direct appeals through the party's propaganda machine. As we know, the Catholic and socialist vote remained largely impenetrable, leaving Hitler to gain support on the center right in those areas where traditional conservatism collapsed. What the most sophisticated recent analyses of the 1930 and 1932 elections show is that the Nazis did best in those areas most severely affected by the economic crisis that were not already in the Center Party and SPD camps. Even in 1921, Hitler acknowledged "the difficulty of winning over to us workers, who, in some cases, have been members of organizations for decades." For most voters, Nazism was appealing as much for what it was not, as for what it was; the Nazi Party was an antiestablishment party of protest. German historian Martin Broszat writes that Nazism was "broad-based, not deeply rooted" and Childers that support for the Nazis was "a mile wide" but "at critical points an inch deep." There was no *en masse* conversion to Nazism. Rather, knowing a limited amount about Hitler or the Nazis, unattached voters, especially young people, were willing to give him a chance. This doesn't mean that the Germans were all socially alienated from one another, or individuated, as Hannah Arendt argued in *The Origins of Totalitarianism*. Rather, the Nazis were able to "penetrate the network of clubs and associations (*Vereine*) that were the social framework of so many provincial communities. Where local leaders, enjoying respectability and influence, were won over, further converts often rapidly followed." At a time of deep economic and social crisis, support on the resentful right was easily, and relatively cheaply, won.[27]

Hitler seems to have appreciated the contingent nature of his backing better than his contemporaries and even many subsequent historians. It depended, he knew, on making good the charismatic bond he had established with voters. The horrendous repression of the later Nazi years should not blind us to the fact that Hitler was extraordinarily popular prior to the Second World War. During the war itself, the Nazi government crushed any hint of dissent, but before this, Hitler knew how much his goals of racial purification and territorial expansion depended on his continued popularity. Charismatic leaders may actually depend on popular support to a greater degree than other types of leaders who can draw on tradition and the law to legitimate their rule. As Max Weber put it, the "genuinely charismatic ruler" is "responsible to the ruled – responsible, that is, to prove that he himself is indeed the master willed by God ... If the people withdraw their recognition, the master becomes a mere private person." Charismatic leadership "rests on the faith of the ruled."[28]

In fact, the authority of the purely charismatic leader derives from popular adoration alone in contrast to other merely personalist rulers, who might, for example, rely on the military and secret police to repress any public dissent. True enough, as the Nazi regime depended more and on coercion, it became less populist and more overtly authoritarian. What made Hitler and the Nazis exceptional was less their ability to drive public opinion than to divine and channel it. Hitler's chief propagandist, Joseph Goebbels, insisted that party functionaries go out to "the bakeries, butchers' shops, grocery stores, and taverns" to learn what people were saying. In fact, so dependent on the caprice of popular opinion is charismatic authority that it tends to be limited in duration. Ecstatic as the crowds at Hitler's rallies were in the mid-1930s, this enthusiasm soon ebbed away in the wake of military catastrophes like the Battle of Stalingrad. As with Napoleon before him, Hitler's popularity could not outlast his defeats.[29]

POPULISM IN HARD TIMES

Esoteric as the German case is, we can learn a great deal from it. For one, even in a movement so supposedly ideologically driven as Nazism, we can see that its ascent to power was driven more by contingency, opportunity, and the force of personality than by ideas. Populists like Hitler rely on mass communication to directly connect with voters. The success of these appeals is conditioned, in large part, by the degree to which people are already socially embedded in other political networks. What makes the interwar German case so interesting is that, unlike in the classical Mediterranean or in revolutionary America or France, political parties did exist. Yet for a variety of historical reasons, only parts of the German populace were captured bybureaucratic-style political organizations – Catholics by the Center party and urban workers by the SPD. Other sections of the voting public remained potentially available. Looking forward from late 1919, if we were to guess as to the part of the populace where a populist might gain a mass following, it would be among the non-Catholic rural middle class and peasantry. That, as we've seen, is exactly what happened.

The German case is informative for yet another reason. Even if voters on the center right, especially those in rural areas, were *available* for Nazi mobilization, their first inclination was to turn toward more regular conservative and liberal bureaucratic parties. The repeated socioeconomic crises of the 1920s and early 1930s, however, made it almost impossible for new centrist bureaucratic parties to establish enduring links with these voters. Such parties made a relatively poor bet for politicians aspiring to power on the right. History is important, but it's not destiny. The interwar socioeconomic crisis made party building extraordinarily difficult. The resources that would have had to be poured into the cultivation of a bureaucratic political organization to incorporate the economically stressed petty bourgeois and rural smallholder were not there. Mass communication, through rallies, marches, and later other accoutrements was a more economical proposition.

To revisit the idea with which I began this chapter, an opportunity is only realized if someone takes advantage of it. As British Prime Minister Winston Churchill said during the Second World War, one should "never let a good crisis go to waste." Objectively speaking, Germany was probably hit hardest by the economic slump of the late 1920s and early 1930s. Coming on the back of the partial dismemberment of the country after the First World War, the punishing imposition of reparations, the destruction of the currency, and the erosion of the private savings of much of the middle class, Germany was already in a highly vulnerable place when economic conditions soured again in 1929. But wartime depredations and economic crisis were hardly limited to Germany.

In spite of the frequent comparisons – and interrelationships – between the movements of Mussolini and Hitler, in fact they proceeded in almost opposite directions. Mussolini, seeing his electoral strategy fail, turned to a putsch; Hitler, as we've seen, after the dismal failure of his own attempted coup, gained power through the ballot box. Incomplete as was party development in Germany by the end of the First World War, it was still incomparably superior to the state of affairs in Italy. The prewar system, though nominally a democracy, was in effect an assembly of landed notables who ruled their corners through a combination of carrots, and just as frequently, sticks. Belatedly throwing its lot in with the Entente Allies, Italy – to its people's dismay – was largely excluded from the spoils dished out at Versailles. Italy's debts were enormous and there was social chaos. The Socialists and the Popolari together held about half of the seats in the 1919 legislature, but neither party was in any position to put together a stable coalition government.

Himself a journalist and veteran of the war, Mussolini became the voice of a bitterly disaffected Italian nationalism. Although he was initially inclined toward a variety of socialism, he would in the end draw his support from rural property owners and the petty bourgeoisie – much, in fact, like the Nazis would do. The landholding elite never really turned to Mussolini in droves; landlords had long had alternative means of enforcement, the mafia itself having its origins as a protection racket in the rural South. However, building on his wartime network of fellow war hawk nationalists, the *Fasci d'Azione Rivoluzionaria*, in 1919 Mussolini gathered together bands of mostly unemployed veterans into a paramilitary organization called the *Fasci di Combattimento*, which would eventually compel his invitation to power. While the Fascists had local roots and local leaders, Mussolini was the only one of real national standing, and was able to leverage this to face down the incipient threat to his personal dominance over the movement. As an electoral vehicle, the Fascist Party was an abject failure. No Fascists won election in 1919, and though the party did better in 1921, winning 35 seats, it had no claims to power in the 535-member chamber. Although the violence of Fascist squads had grown to alarming proportions by 1921, Mussolini of all people knew that the armed route to power was a remote prospect. His strategy was instead to leverage his mediating role between this disruptive and violent gangsterism on the one hand and the conservative elite on the other.

Although never winning anything like the electoral support of Hitler, because of the shambolic performance of the parties in power, the widely perceived threat of domestic Communism, and a state of rural disorder in part caused by the Fascists themselves, Mussolini appeared to many to be the only viable figurehead to restore order. As a noted journalist, Mussolini was far more prominent and respectable than Hitler at that time. The March on Rome in late October 1922 pushed events along. Negotiations behind the scenes continued, but with the main contenders unable to agree among themselves, King Victor Emmanuel III was persuaded that Mussolini should be made prime minister. Reassuring parliamentarians that he would respect the constitution, Mussolini was given extraordinary powers, which in 1925, he used to establish a full-blown dictatorship. There was little if anything populist about Mussolini's initial path to power. Although never possessing the same level of organizational control over his more fragmented launching movement as Hitler, Mussolini in power would increasingly seek to enshrine a cult of personality that would give him more freedom of manoeuvre. Party fanatics – potential rivals – were pushed aside, and Italian fascism became in a sense, Italian Mussolinism. Repression remained a vital tool of Mussolini's dictatorship, but at least through to the Second World War, popular support, more so than the incomplete party organizational penetration of Italian corporatism, was its main complement. Mussolini, in other words, was more popular dictator than populist.

Aspiring populists elsewhere largely failed to replicate the success of Hitler. Even if not exposed to the American economy to the extent of Germany, France was hardly spared the pain of the worldwide depression, although its troubles didn't really begin until 1931. Inept economic management made matters worse than they needed to be. While unemployment doubled and industrial production plummeted, successive governments refused to devalue the franc, ushering in a painful period of deflation. As in Germany and Italy, the potential opening for populist mobilization came in the countryside. With the franc overvalued, export markets for its agricultural output, especially wheat, collapsed, dealing the peasantry a crushing blow. The son of a butcher, Henry Dorgères founded a veterans' association for peasants after the First World War. Taking up a career as a journalist, Dorgères built a minor reputation arguing for Brittany farmers' interests through the 1920s, exhorting his supporters to raise their pitchforks against "the tyranny of towns." His political breakthrough, however, required an external shock. The economic collapse of the 1930s made the peasantry amenable to Dorgères' message in a way they would not have been otherwise. Like Hitler after the failed Munich putsch, Dorgères was fully aware that power could not be taken through a frontal assault; elections, or at least popular pressure in the form of mass agitation and strikes, were the only way of challenging for power in a France that had been genuinely democratic for more than fifty years. With the local agrarian elite in disarray due to the depression and the left divided between reformers and socialists, Dorgères won a by-election at Blois in May 1935. Despite his personal popularity, however, he was unable to construct a political machine that was broad enough to mount a serious electoral threat beyond his Brittany

base. Another veterans' association, the Rhône–based *Croix de Feu* of Count
Francois de La Rocque, did somewhat better, obtaining an impressive membership roll of some half a million. Like the Greenshirts, the *Croix de Feu* was
grounded in rural France, picking up support where the conservative elite had
become especially fragmented. La Rocque's forte was organization rather than
oratory, but without the image of La Rocque himself as a distinguished officer
and patriot, it is unlikely that the *Croix de Feu* would have grown as quickly as
it did. Even reincarnated as a purely parliamentary party, the French Social
Party (PSF) remained authoritarian and personalistic in its internal structure.
Yet as the dismal electoral record of the PSF illustrates, charismatic mobilization in interwar France clearly had its limits.[30]

Ultimately, neither Dorgères nor La Rocque could make the transition from
populist agitator to popular dictator as did Hitler. Several factors stood in their
way. Neither was able extend to extend their appeal beyond their immediate
rural constituency. Moreover, even in rural France, both movements were
inhibited by the presence of a range of agricultural organizations, by the activity
of left-wing parties in the countryside that had no equivalent in Italy or Germany,
and by the continued presence of rural notables who could still turn to an
effective state in their fight against the strike activity of farm laborers. Lastly,
not only were French farmers less available than in Germany, but non-populist
parties of the left were at least temporarily better able to coordinate their
opposition – the Socialist–Communist collaboration of France's Popular Front
standing in stark contrast to the bitter division of Germany's SPD and KPD. Even
if most French political parties of the late Third Republic – especially on the
right – were still fragmented, because there was no means of controlling executive
office except through a cobbled-together majority in Parliament, satisfying
patronage-hungry deputies was the only way an ambitious leader might make
take up residence in the Hôtel de Matignon. Historian Eugen Weber proposed
that the absence of an autochthonous dictatorship in 1930s France was due to a
lack of charismatic leaders like Hitler or Mussolini; Dorgères, if not La Rocque,
suggest to the contrary. A better explanation is that populist mobilizers were
crowded out by the persistence of a dug-in, if not sclerotic, local elite in the
interwar French political marketplace. Fragmented as that elite was, in the
absence of a direct path to executive office – such as through an elected presidency – there was no cost-effective means of circumventing it.[31]

Although Britain experienced a sustained economic slump in the postwar
period, and although right-wing views were widely held, fascism as a political
movement never went beyond a marginal fringe. Indeed, even if the war and its
aftermath sounded the death knell for the Liberal Party, both the Conservative
Party and the nascent trades union–aligned Labour Party were strengthened in
the process, although the latter was not yet the second national party. Amid this
electoral realignment, Lloyd George's populist strategy kept him in office in the
Coupon election of 1918, with his Liberal faction comprising a minority of the
coalition with the Conservatives. The Tories preponderance, however, gave

party leader, Bonar Law, the confidence to drop Lloyd George in 1922, and seek an electoral majority of its own. The resulting Tory victory irrevocably split the Liberal Party, the radical branch hitching its wagon to the rising Labour Party, its centrist wing to the Tories. On Law's retirement, new prime minister, Stanley Baldwin, sought his own mandate but instead lost the majority in the general election in December 1923. With the Conservatives unable to form a stable government, Labour leader, Ramsey McDonald, became prime minister in January 1924 in a minority government with the Liberals' support. However, with the Liberals split over the party's alliance with Labour, its share of the seats in Westminster plummeted from 158 in December 1923 to just 40 in October 1924. Although the Liberals who remained with Lloyd George took some 27 percent of the vote in 1929, this translated into just 59 seats (18 percent of the total). The result was that the Tories ran home with a healthy majority, while Labour was now decidedly the second party. Although Labour suffered a stunning reverse in 1931, the Liberals had split into three distinct factions – one aligned with the Conservatives, one with Labour, and the other just about surviving in its own right. By the early 1930s, the party realignment was basically complete, with little of the electorate that was not firmly within the organizational orbit of either the Conservatives or Labour. There was little room for a populist third force.

Moreover, whatever opportunity Britain's economic crash of the 1930s might have created, there was no one ready to exploit the opening. The best-known populist of the period was Oswald Mosley. Mosely may have been one of the nation's most charismatic politicians, but once he withdrew first from the Conservative Party and then subsequently from the Labour Party, unlike Hitler he did not have the organizational apparatus in place to take advantage of the crisis. Mosley belatedly created the New Party in March 1931 with financial backing from Lord Nuffield, but all the party's candidates, including Mosley, lost their deposits on unsuccessful campaigns in the 1931 general election. Mosley set up the British Union of Fascists (BUF) in 1932, but by the time it had gotten its act together, Britain was on the road to economic recovery. The much greater organizational resources of the Conservative Party on the right and, already by the late 1920s, the Labour Party on the left, meant that the BUF had little empty space in which to grow. So socialized into the two parties did the British populace become that populism was banished to the margins as an uneconomical political strategy. At least this would remain the case until yet another crisis came along.

Popular as was the bombastic Winston Churchill in the interwar period, there was no way for him to gain power without a party. Having defected from the Conservative Party to the Liberals in 1904, Churchill would forever be viewed with suspicion by stalwarts of both parties. Although Churchill rose to the upper ranks of the Liberal cabinets that followed – heading the Board of Trade, the Home Office, and the Admiralty – many of his colleagues viewed him as an opportunist. At the same time, Conservatives, not least Bonar Law, had not forgotten his disloyalty. When Asquith was toppled in 1916, Law and the Tories acquiesced in Lloyd George's elevation to prime minister on the strict condition that Churchill be excluded from the War Cabinet. Lloyd George accepted the terms, earning the enduring wrath of Churchill's wife, Clementine, who called him the "direct descendant of Judas Iscariot." Although Churchill himself remained fond of Lloyd George and was restored to the cabinet by him in defiance of Unionist wishes in 1917, he continued to be excluded from the inner circle. After the war, Churchill retained a spot in government, but as neither a member of the majority Conservative part of the parliamentary majority nor with a following within the Liberal Party of his own; Churchill kept his position purely by hanging on to Lloyd George's mercurial coattails. The precarity of his situation was made clear when Lloyd George was brought down in 1922. Having recently undergone surgery, Churchill, as he put it, found himself "without an office, without a seat, without a party, and without an appendix." In 1924, Churchill again abandoned what was by then a sinking ship – the Liberal Party. He ran for Parliament in a by-election as an "anti-Socialist Constitutionalist." Although defeated by the official Conservative candidate, he overturned the result in the general election later that year. Even more surprising was what followed; Tory leader and new prime minister, Stanley Baldwin, appointed Churchill as Chancellor of the Exchequer following the Conservative victory in 1924, even though Churchill had still not officially rejoined the party. However, this was a decision that reflected Baldwin's efforts to close ranks against the left rather than a demonstration of Churchill's pulling power per se. If there was a populist bogeyman in 1924, it was still Lloyd George, not Churchill. Indeed, after dropping out of government following Labour's 1929 general election win and unnecessarily earning the ire of his Tory colleagues by his position on Indian reforms, Churchill was again easily and ignominiously excluded from the returned Tory-led National governments of Baldwin (1935–37) and Neville Chamberlain (1937–40).[32]

Not that Churchill took his medicine without complaint. A gifted writer and practiced orator, with sympathetic editors ready to keep his name in the papers, Churchill was a thorn in the side of the Tory leadership of the second half of the 1930s. His was not a lone voice, but it was by far the most prominent one opposed to the government's appeasement of Nazi Germany in the late 1930s. He famously characterized the spineless response of the Baldwin government to Germany's aggressiveness as "decided only to be undecided, resolved to be irresolute, adamant for drift, solid for fluidity, all powerful to be impotent." In a now historic speech on October 5, 1938, he trashed Chamberlain's Munich deal as "a total and unmitigated defeat." Churchill of course disclaimed any attempt to "court political popularity," but it was indeed popular opinion, rather than the opinion of his esteemed colleagues that he was seeking to mobilize. In fact, in late 1938, the local Conservative Association – the body that selects the party's candidate in a given constituency – contemplated dropping Churchill and forcing a by-election for his disloyalty. Churchill survived the vote, but he had resolved to take the battle out of doors anyway, putting out feelers to his Liberal friends to gauge his support among the broader electorate should he have to run again as an independent. When Britain had no choice but to declare war in September 1939, Chamberlain reluctantly recalled Churchill to the cabinet as First Lord of the Admiralty. When Labour withdrew its support from Chamberlain after a discouraging start to the war, the latter had no choice but to recommend Churchill as his replacement. Churchill had few friends in the Conservative Party. Despite his pedigree, he was by no means the establishment candidate. Rather, as biographer Roy Jenkins puts it, Churchill's "authority most stemmed from popular acclaim." Like Lloyd George in 1916, Churchill was popular among the masses, and this was the reason for his elevation to the prime ministership. However, in the British party–based system the populist route to Number 10 worked only under the most extenuating of circumstances. This time, unlike Lloyd George in 1918, with the war over, Churchill faced a strong and united opposition. Despite his outsized role in bringing victory to the Allies in Europe in May 1945, Churchill was defeated in the general election by Clement Attlee's Labour Party barely two months later. Much as Churchill remained a popular figurehead for the Conservative Party, and although the anticipated transfer of power to deputy leader, Anthony Eden, was excessively postponed by Churchill, the peacetime Tory party was never his personalist vehicle. Populism in the British programmatic party system had its limits.[33]

The Great Depression was a worldwide event, but its epicenter was America. That it weathered the storm with populism registering only a minor ripple is another good reminder that crisis conditions are not by themselves sufficient to make populism an effective strategy. The 1920s were a mini era of prosperity and optimism, its heady opulence – and ignorance – poignantly portrayed by F. Scott Fitzgerald in *The Great Gatsby*. With the return to hard money in the early 1920s, the economy had grown rapidly, giving birth to the "roaring twenties." The technocratic Republican Herbert Hoover won easy election to the presidency in 1928, promising in effect, more of the same after eight relatively prosperous years under his Republican predecessors Warren G. Harding and Calvin Coolidge. The period from 1927 through to mid-1929 had seen an astronomical rise in the stock market (in part, as we saw, as speculative money retreated from Europe). Coolidge and Hoover simply saw it as their duty to keep the band playing. When the reality of this speculative bubble became apparent, stock prices fell through the floor, and because much of this speculation had been funded on credit, thousands of banks crashing down with them. As the economy began to tank in the months after his inauguration, Hoover's initial response was orthodox. Yet over the next three and half years, he experimented with a wide range of fiscal reforms, including agricultural price supports. No matter what he did, however, the economy sank further into depression.

Unemployment in the United States increased sixfold between 1929 and 1932. That meant by 1933, 13 million, or one in every four workers, stood idle. By 1933, gross national product had fallen to half of its 1929 level. Although the stock market bubble and banking crisis that followed was certainly an important element of the Depression, most economists conclude that by the late 1920s, the fundamentals of the American economy were not good. At the same time that consumerism, the automobile, and electrification were transforming urban social life into something recognizably modern – this was after all the age known as Modernism – rural America was mired in a slow-burning crisis. With production and productivity both ramped up as a consequence of the First World War, American farms were producing more than could be consumed domestically, or given growing protectionism abroad, internationally. Farm incomes stagnated even as production increased. Farm income fell from the already lean figure of six billion dollars in 1929 to a paltry two billion in 1932. Even nature seemed to conspire against American farmers. In another epoch defining novel, *The Grapes of Wrath*, John Steinbeck writes of the desperation of small-time farmers in the cotton production complex of Texas and Oklahoma, where, after years of excessive exploitation of the region's light soils, a drop in precipitation turned the region into a dust bowl. This was an ecological and economic disaster of epic scale.

By 1932 New York Governor Franklin Delano Roosevelt was one of the leading members of the Democratic Party. Given the state of the economy, it was almost inevitable that the Democrats would sweep home. Indeed, once he won the nomination, winning the presidency itself was an almost simple matter. In spite of the state of the economy, in 1932 there was no hard populist push from either left or right within the Democratic Party. Roosevelt had won the governorship of New York in an off year for Democrats, which gave him a good stake to the nomination. He was opposed by Tammany Hall Catholic, Al Smith, the party's 1928 nominee, who hadn't given up hope of running again despite his comprehensive defeat the last time around. Roosevelt had the support of the Deep South and a good number of northern delegates, with the exceptions of some of the ethnic urban machines in New York, Chicago, and elsewhere, who went for Smith. The balance was held by John Garner of Texas and William McAdoo of California, both of whom had sizeable delegations but could not take the ticket. When they eventually rolled in behind FDR, the deed was done. There was little, in short, about FDR's rise to power that was in any way populist.

FDR, as we know, responded to the crisis with vigor. His first hundred days were some of the most active on Capitol Hill. For the most part though, FDR's early interventions were an intensification of those pursued by Hoover. The first order of business was to enact the legislation, mostly written by Hoover's aides, which restored confidence to the banks. FDR's approach was moderate rather than radical, which seems a reflection both of the possibilities of the time and of his own inclinations. In spite of all of the legislative activity of his first administration, unemployment remained stubbornly high, never dropping below 20 percent. But two years of incessant activity and renewed optimism – "freedom from fear" – hadn't done much to restore the economy. Inevitable as FDR's long reign seems in retrospect, the president was not without challengers, the most serious of whom was Huey P. Long Jr. With the economy still deep in crisis, as governor and then senator for Louisiana, in 1936, Long seemed poised to mount a credible, or at least highly disruptive assault on the presidency.

If Hitler's early exploits taught him that he could "talk," Long's taught him that he could "sell." In four years as a salesman, the Louisianan developed all the skills of the consummate retail politician, calling politics "the sport of kings." He knew what his audience needed to hear, and how they wanted to hear it. On one occasion, a long-time enemy of Long was seen slipping away from a meeting at which Huey was speaking; when asked why the next day, he said "I left because I was afraid. That guy was convincing me. I had to get out." Huey was the quintessential charismatic leader. As one Louisiana Old Regular put it, "[o]thers had power in their organization, but he had power in himself." This is not to say that Long neglected the use of patronage; far from it. Long built his base slowly, always styling himself as being against the political establishment, which in Louisiana, primarily meant the Old Regulars' New Orleans machine and its wealthy backers. Long promised the moon, and when he won the governorship in 1928, he delivered on some of his high-profile measures, including the provision of free schoolbooks and increased corporate taxes. Long gathered power in the executive mansion, accumulating massive patronage resources to dispense to his allies and to control the state legislature. He ruled the state in large part through the distribution of jobs and the careful allocation of infrastructural and other state funds. Yet Long kept his organization loose, never allowing rival factions to develop around prominent secondary leaders. To the extent that there was an organization, it was the *Long Organization*.[34]

However much he lavished funds on it, the city of Baton Rouge could not satisfy his ambitions. Although Long had backed Al Smith, for whom Roosevelt acted as campaign manager, in 1928, and then FDR himself in 1932 – in fact playing an instrumental role in the Chicago Convention that nominated Roosevelt – he continued to plot his own populist assault on the presidency. He knew that he did not have the national organization to threaten a popular incumbent like FDR directly. The patronage-based party machine that kept Theodore Roosevelt from the Republican nomination in 1912 would almost certainly do the same for FDR as leader of the Democratic Party organization in 1936. Long sought to go outside of party channels, playing a dangerous, long populist game. His voice was heard on radio in the 1930s more than any other national politician bar FDR. Pushing a radical scheme to redistribute wealth from rich to poor, Long gained a reputation among the generally cautious national political elite as a dangerous demagogue. Although initially a supporter of FDR, by the mid-1930s, Long had turned against him. Fiercely ambitious but politically realistic, Long recognized the challenge of taking on the popular FDR. Roosevelt nevertheless appreciated the threat, calling Long one of the two most dangerous men in America – the other was

General Douglas MacArthur. What Long seems to have wanted to do in 1936 was to entice a liberal into the race who might split FDRs vote and allow a weak Republican into power, whom Long would then be "called" to challenge in 1940. Had Long somehow managed to engineer a Roosevelt defeat to the Republicans in 1936, there is a chance his combination of strongarming and populism could have delivered him a wartime victory. However, Long was assassinated in 1935 before he could put his plans into motion, so we will never know if they would have had the desired effect. Yet given the political skills of his opponent, it seems unlikely.FDR wasn't infallible, but But as of 1936 he had enormous personal appeal. Moreover, much more so than his cousin and fellow upstate New Yorker, Theodore Roosevelt, FDR was a party politician. Although the progressive in him chaffed at dealing with the corrupt New York City Tammany machine, in the end, he learned to play the game, giving the city's Irish bosses their due share of patronage in return for their support on his rise to the governorship. The cocky Long himself even admitted after a meeting that he thought the president was "as smart as I am.".[35]

The American party system survived intact, and in some respects, strengthened. Indeed, while there was no absence of short sellers hoping to profit from the disaster of the Second World War, the nation's basic political configuration remained stable until demographic change, economic crisis, war and a corruption scandal finally broke apart the consensus in the 1970s – events we'll explore in Chapter 7. As this chapter has shown, when voters are deeply embedded into bureaucratic party networks, they are hard to mobilize, even for the most charismatic of leaders. Hitler could never make serious inroads into the base of the SDP, the Communist Party, or even the Catholic Center Party. These constraints on the populist strategy would remain after the war. Where party–voter ties were strong, populism was would be virtually absent. Where voters were available, populists would again emerge successful.

6

Survival of the Fittest

This preservation of favorable variations and the rejection of injurious variations, I call natural selection or the survival of the fittest.

Charles Darwin[1]

Democracy doesn't have a price but it has a cost.

Emmanuel Macron[2]

CREATIVE DESTRUCTION

At the same time that new technologies, from rail to refrigeration, from television to the Internet, make some business models redundant, they also open up profitable new markets. In a process that Austrian political economist, Joseph Schumpeter, christened *creative destruction*, technological change "continuously revolutionizes the economic structure from within, incessantly destroying the old one, incessantly creating a new one." That is, simply by its operation, the structure of the economy is relentlessly changing; some sectors and niches become obsolete while new ones are created. Just as changing technology disrupts the economic marketplace, it powerfully affects the costs and benefits of different types of political organization. To adapt the famous aphorism of Charles Darwin quoted in the epigraph, those organizations most suited to the changing environment will live and thrive; others will fail and die. Focusing on Western Europe in the years since the Second World War, this chapter is about adaptation, and the failure of adaptation, in the face of technological – or environmental – change.[3]

Most research on populism has tended to focus on how technological change affects the demand side. Unskilled workers, under pressure from automation, outsourcing, and immigration, have become increasingly resentful of the economic and political elite. As a result, they have embraced the nationalist nostalgia of populists like Nigel Farage and Marine Le Pen in their millions. However, technological change also affects the supply side. From an economist's point of view, with technological change comes a shift in the relative prices of labor and capital; of modes of work, transport, and domestic life; of social networks; of tastes and wants. Technological change determines whether people will work in mines or in factories; remotely from coffee shops or in their apartments. The means of transport and communication determine how societies are physically organized, whether they are urbanized, suburbanized, or subterranean. Technology says whether people will live in villages or in cities, whether they'll live in one place, or whether they'll move, maybe multiple times. As a result, technological changes in the areas of production and consumption indirectly but powerfully affect the costs and benefits of different types of political organization.[4]

For a long time, the bureaucratic political party seemed to have a certain inevitability about it. For much of the twentieth century, it was hard to imagine Britain without the perennial Conservative Party, Ireland without Fianna Fáil, or Sweden without the Social Democrats. Yet when examined over the longer run, the creation of parties such as these was a historical aberration. They emerged during quite unusual circumstances and as a result have organizational structures that are historically distinctive. Industrialization, urbanization, and, in some cases, imperialism together created both opportunities and incentives for the elite to organize and incorporate the masses. Labour and Social Democratic parties developed to represent industrial workers – the proletariat – on the left; Liberal, Conservative, and Christian Democratic parties emerged to represent the proprietary classes – farm owners and the *petite bourgeoisie* – on the right. There was, during this period, a cost advantage in building and maintaining bureaucratic political organizations that kept populism on the margins.

However, as the social and economic context that gave birth to these organizations began to change in the 1970s, the basis on which these parties were constructed also became eroded. On the left, several developments came together to weaken the links between voters and social democratic and labor parties. First, between the 1940s and the 1980s, unprecedented levels of social mobility meant that many from the working class became middle class, with all of the implications this had for their preferences on taxes and redistribution. Second, automation, digitization, and economic globalization reduced demand for workers without an advanced education, leading to persistent unemployment and underemployment of a population that once formed the core membership of labor unions and their associated political parties. Third, new low-income jobs were increasingly to be found in the nonunionized service sector. Unlike the urban proletariat of the first half of the twentieth century, in the post-industrial economy, low-income workers therefore ceased to be bound together by a dense network of cultural and social organizations. As a result, by the 1990s, parties on the left could no longer rely on their traditional strategies to mobilize voters at low marginal cost.

On the right, parties have fared somewhat better. In the 1970s and 1980s, Conservative parties inherited many of the voters who had benefited from the economic growth of the postwar period to make it into the middle class. As the steam ran out of Keynesian economic policies, conservative calls for a reduction in the size of the state – and the taxes used to fund it – became increasingly popular among such voters. However, while conservative parties' suburban followings were growing, their traditional rural bases were in demographic decline. Moreover, the growth in inequality in more recent decades has had the effect of eroding the relative position of the right's middle-class base. As a further indirect consequence of economic development, creeping secularization has also mitigated the role of religious organizations in building communal social networks for parties on the conservative end of the spectrum. In many places, the right has fragmented into an urban, professional elite that is socially liberal but economically conservative, and a lower middle class that is socially traditional but increasingly likely to be economically dependent on the state.

Scholars and pundits have been grappling with the political effects of these structural transformations for a long time. People in Western Europe do still vote distinctively by church and class, in part through a legacy effect, but these cleavages don't matter nearly as much as they used to. Rather, as the once distinctive parties of the left and right saw their distinctive social bases decline, they each first moved toward the center, becoming what Otto Kirchheimer, the German Jewish émigré scholar, called "catchall parties." With the emergence in the 1990s of the so-called Third Way – that is, neither left nor right – parties became virtually indistinguishable in terms of political economic policy. Summing up this situation, the late Irish political scientist Peter Mair wrote that modern parties "compete with one another for votes," but they "find themselves sharing the same broad commitments in government and confining themselves to the same ever-narrowing repertoire of policy-making." Allegedly dissatisfied with this anaemic, professionalized, perhaps even corrupt brand of politics, people became even more alienated from the traditionally dominant parties, and some have argued, even democracy itself. The result of this voter disenfranchisement with the political establishment was a rise in *demand* for populism.[5]

There is considerable truth to the claim that the political cleavages of the past based on class had substantially weakened by the 1990s. It is also the case that populists have sought to exploit the political realignment emerging from these trends. However, there is no reason that bureaucratic parties should not have adapted to this changing social environment. Indeed, Schumpeter was quite clear that *individual* firms could adapt in the face of technological change. Some firms fail to move with the times and die. Others, however, adapt and thrive; as so often, what goes for business goes for politics. In reality, party decline has been far from uniform, both within and across countries. Many parties on the old center right have remade themselves as culturally conservative or nationalist parties, while those on the on the left have embraced environmentalism and other progressive causes. In turn, the extent of populist success in Western Europe has been very mixed. In some countries, especially where the party system has become highly fragmented – with a large number of parties commanding small vote and seat shares – populists have won significant shares of the vote. However, despite hysterical headlines about looming populist assaults on Western democracy, the reality is that many, indeed most established parties, have adapted. Although populism has proved to be an effective, low-cost strategy in making initial political breakthroughs, the size and complexity of most administrative states in Western Europe has meant that unless populists adopt the organizational depth of more typical bureaucratic parties, they cannot sustain their political momentum. Forging an enduring political presence in the states of Western Europe is an expensive activity, less because of the cost of participating in elections than because of the need to recruit and retain political talent and to deliver services to constituents across multiple levels of government.[6]

As a result, for the most part, the old bureaucratic parties have endured. As of early 2022, when I was completing this book, the heads of government in Germany, Switzerland, Luxembourg, Britain, Ireland, Sweden, Norway, and Finland come from parties that had their origins in the mid-twentieth century at the latest, and most dated much further back than that. In the Netherlands, the governing People's Party for Freedom and Democracy (VVD) is nominally a new conservative-liberal party, but is, in effect, just a reincarnation of the Liberal State Party (LSP) that was founded after the First World War. The Christian Democratic Appeal (CDA), and its forerunner, the Catholic Party, participated in every Dutch government between 1917 and 1994, and again has been represented in every cabinet from 2002 to today. Similarly, in Belgium, the Open Flemish Liberals and Democrats Party has its organizational roots in the Liberal Party, which was founded in the 1840s. It is true that parties of the old union-aligned left have, in general, found the going harder over recent decades. Once electorally powerful parties like Germany's SPD, the Dutch Labour Party, and the Communist Party of France are shadows of their former selves. The Italian Communist Party, long the second largest party in Italy behind the Christian Democratic Party, formally dissolved in 1991. In terms of vote share, the British Labour Party has fared better, but it too has endured a long spell in opposition. In contrast, Spain's governing party, the Spanish Socialist Workers' Party (PSOE) founded in 1879, has been in power longer than any other party since the end of Franco's dictatorship. Similarly, Portugal's ruling party, the Socialist Party (PS), has rotated in government with parties on the right since the fall of the authoritarian Estado Novo regime in 1974. All in all, many old parties, including those on the left, have adapted successfully.

These long-established political parties and their modern offshoots – both left and right – look different than they used to. But that they now emphasize cultural issues as much as economic ones makes them no less bureaucratic than before. More pertinently, these parties have modified their organizational structures and approaches to getting out the vote in order to target voters in a radically changed electorate. They have changed substantially over time in membership size, leadership style, and electoral tactics. Political scientist, Angelo Panebianco, called this new party form the "electoral-professional party." These parties are much less the mass membership parties that they used to be. However, organizationally, most of these parties remain structured as bureaucracies. The best adapters have retained their internal organizational cohesion even as they have had to change the way in which they get out the vote. These parties continue to nurture and recruit talent, providing clear career paths to those with political ambitions. They maintain links with surviving civil society organizations, which are themselves increasingly professionalized. Critically, they still have a widely dispersed geographical presence and are deeply embedded in local and national government bureaucracies and agencies. These bureaucratic parties retain collective, not personalistic, leadership structures. Although this makes them somewhat old fashioned in appearance and style, it gives them an endurance that leader-centric parties typically lack. Bureaucratic parties have had to economize, but they still provide the most reliable route to power for the aspiring leader in the Western world's oldest democracies.[7]

This kind of adaptation is exactly what we should expect of functional organizations. Survival, even more than profit, is a powerful motive. However, because there been significant divergence from country to country in the degree to which parties have successfully adapted to economic and social change, there is also a large range in the proportion of voters who are *available* for political mobilization. Even then, however, not all of the political leaders looking to mobilize these newly available voters are populists. Some new parties have built bureaucratic organizations on the remains of old parties or existing civil society groups. Across most of Western Europe, such new parties have been incorporated into the political system as regular programmatic organizations. For example, Ireland's Sinn Féin and Germany's Die Linke may place themselves on the far left, but there's nothing inherently populist about this approach. Sinn Féin, itself more than a century old but long politically untouchable in the Republic (the South) due to its association with the terrorist violence of the Irish Republican Army (IRA), has grown rapidly in recent years by forging strong links with voters by service provision at the local government level, and through cultural institutions such as the Gaelic Athletic Association. At the same time, with the retirement of its longtime influential leader, Gerry Adams, the party's internal structures have become increasingly bureaucratized and democratic. Party leader, Mary Lou McDonald, is no populist. Germany's Die Linke too has a rich organizational heritage, being formed in 2007 out of a union of long-established socialist parties in the partitioned East and West Germany. Even if its policies are out of the mainstream, its political strategy is not.

Although anti-immigrant Eurosceptic parties have had notable successes in recent years, again this does not actually say anything about populism per se. Nationalism, nativism, or ethnic chauvinism, call it what you will, is not the same as populism. This is an important caveat to keep in mind when interpreting Brexit or the rise of the nationalist right more broadly. For instance, the

Alternative for Germany (AfD), a Euroskeptic and anti-immigrant party, which has done well at the polls over the last decade, is often termed a populist party. Its nationalism and nativism, and its appeals to the people, are used to make that classification. But if you recall the argument of Chapter 1, these kinds of policy appeals are not a particularly useful way of distinguishing populism from its alternatives. The AfD is not a leader-centric party – indeed, it has a unique co-leadership structure. It may be a new party, but as with Die Linke on the other side of the political spectrum, its organizational structure is increasingly bureaucratic, if still lacking in depth.

The coverage of the Western European experience in this chapter is necessarily selective. The aim is to tease out how varied environmental, or technological, conditions affect the relative cost of the populist strategy. Shortly I'll survey how bureaucratic party systems took root in Western Europe after 1945, before turning to the rise of populism in the 1990s. I briefly consider the Dutch case, where genuine populists have been able to consistently win significant pluralities in recent decades, and also examine the role of populism as a strategy in Brexit-era Britain. My main focus is, however, on the cases of recurrent populist success.

Within Western Europe, the populist strategy has been most prevalent in France, Greece, and Italy, each of which has seen a populist come to outright power more than once since the Second World War, and in Austria, where they have come extremely close on a few occasions (joining government as a junior coalition partner in 1999). However, although geographically these states are in located in the industrialized and bureaucratized core of Western Europe, it turns out that Greece, Italy, and Austria each fit much more closely with the patronage-party dominant systems of the nineteenth century explored in Chapter 4 than they do the bureaucratic parties that have dominated elsewhere on the continent in the postwar era. That populists have been most successful here should come as no surprise. As we saw, patronage-based incorporation often has a cost advantage in the early years after mass democracy is introduced, but as brokers become entrenched, the system becomes more expensive to maintain. Populism then becomes a cost-effective alternative. These cases of course have their own distinct characteristics, but a lack of space prevents me from analyzing each of their trajectories in depth. Italy has to serve as exemplar.

In France the story is sufficiently different – and underexplored in contemporary writing on populism – to warrant a fuller account. French parties were not clientelistic to the same degree as those in Greece, Italy, or Austria, yet political alignments were typically based on coalitions of prominent local elites – notables – built through higher level patronage than on a bureaucratic party strategy. Hero of the Second World War, Charles de Gaulle attempted to reform the system, but the parties of what would become the French Fourth Republic remained every bit as organizationally weak and personalized as those of the Third, and de Gaulle soon "retired" in disgust. However, with the squabbling party satraps unable to resolve the Algerian crisis, De Gaulle was recalled from political exile in 1958. Using his fresh mandate, De Gaulle introduced a strong and eventually directly elected presidency. This institution compensated for France's personalist and weak parties, providing for a decade of relative political stability, but with De Gaulle's second and final retirement in 1968, it became clear that the predominance of the executive over the legislature would effectively make parties the tools of presidential candidates, rather than the other way around. Henceforth, charismatic politicians who could directly appeal to the people had the opportunity to win power without having to build a political party. In no case has this been clearer than with the election of Emmanuel Macron in 2017. If French parties failed to adapt to the sociological changes of recent decades, this result was a long time in the making. Whatever their longevity, postwar French parties were not the well-organized bureaucratic machines of their Western European neighbors. The weakness and fragmentation of France's personalistic parties and the existence of a directly elected executive office has meant that populism has been a cost-effective strategy in Fifth Republic France.

BUILDING BUREAUCRATIC PARTIES

It is worth recalling here what is distinctive about the bureaucratic party. Bureaucratic parties provide a vehicle through which individuals can pursue power according to certain accepted rules of the game. These rules both constrain the ambitious and provide a vehicle for their advancement. Men and women, in their pursuit of power (and of whatever additional goals they may have), agree to abide by rules that limit their autonomy because these same rules also limit the autonomy of their potential rivals. Party rules dictate the accepted means of advancement. Seniority rules, for instance, reserve the most prestigious government positions for the longest standing party members. This, of course, blocks younger members from power, but these individuals know that due course, they will hold those positions of authority in turn. Factionalism and favoritism are not absent in the bureaucratic party, but they are deviations from the ideal type in which norms of party loyalty and professionalism predominate. Moreover, even if party leadership contests are often bitter, rival cliques typically agree to work together once the result is known. Ultimately, party factions derive their power from their ability to organize members – often parliamentary party members – around supporting interest groups and the votes these imply both in determining the party leadership and in mobilizing support on Election Day.[8]

To the extent that party members must work together in the pursuit of power, they typically share some ideological and policy commitments. However, it is unclear whether those shared views precede or follow party membership. Summing up decades of his research on political parties, Peter Mair wrote that bureaucratic parties built "strong organizational networks on the basis of shared social experiences." You could no more choose your party, wrote Mair, than you could choose to go to a Catholic or Anglican church on Sunday. Bureaucratic parties were typically social as well as political entities. They were deeply embedded in their communities. People knew each other and they knew their political representatives. It is worth quoting at length what Mair wrote of the social foundations of the bureaucratic party during its heyday:

[P]olitical communities were built on a foundation of closed social communities, in which large collectivities of citizens shared distinct social experiences, whether these were defined in terms of occupation, working and living conditions, religious practices, to name the most important. These social collectivities were in their turn cemented by the existence of vibrant and effective social institutions, including trade unions, churches, social clubs and so on. In other words, the closure of political communities usually derived from, or was based on, social closure, which, in a variety of European countries, tended to create a pattern of widespread segmentation, dividing social groups from one another while uniting their own individual "members" and adherents.

Parties, in short, were wholly communal things, with shared beliefs being in part a consequence of shared experiences.[9]

Put another way, political parties have deep social foundations; something that has made them seem almost inevitable. Yet their development was a deeply contextual, or we might say, historical process. Although many of Europe's modern, bureaucratic political parties had their origins in the late nineteenth century, their heyday came almost a century later, in the 1950s and 1960s. The three decades from 1945, which the French call *Les Trente Glorieuse*, birthed not only sustained economic growth but also stable bureaucratic party systems across most of Western Europe. Social Democratic and Labour parties on the left, and even more so, Christian Democratic and Conservative parties on the right dominated the political space. One of these two party groups formed the first postwar governments in every Western European democracy. In contrast to the interwar period, populism was conspicuous mostly by its absence. What explains this long period of bureaucratic party–dominated political stability?

There are a few viable explanations that we need to consider. Some scholars argue that it was the very totality of the Second World War that laid the conditions for the period of democratic stability and economic growth that followed. Between 50 and 80 million people, about two thirds of them civilians, died between 1939 and 1945. Europe's thriving industrial heart-lands were reduced to rubble. Millions of people, especially but not only Jews, were evicted from their homelands and repatriated across the continent. As Churchill rhetorically asked in the wake of the War, "[w]hat is Europe now? A rubble heap, a charnel ground, a breeding ground of pestilence and hate." The discrediting of extremists on both the left and right deemed responsible for the war restricted the bounds of political legitimacy. By wiping away the old order, aspiring political leaders would not be able to build mass follow-ings on the basis of extreme ethnonationalism, or given the emerging contours of the Cold War, Communism.[10]

Although this "blank slate" explanation has a certain verisimilitude, in broader perspective, it seems a little puzzling. As the rise of the Nazi Party in

Germany illustrated, military and economic catastrophe can provide just the conditions for an extremist alternative. The state of Europe after the Second World War hardly seemed propitious either for the bureaucratic party or for liberal democracy more generally. Even as the liberal democratic West – especially America and Britain – had been victorious over Germany and its authoritarian allies, the Soviet Union was at least as big a winner out of the war, installing sympathetic regimes across the eastern half of the continent. Socialism, as an economic system, and even Communism as a political one, were hardly discredited. In the late 1940s, the Communist Party of Italy (PCI) was that country's biggest and best-organized political group. The French Communist Party (PCF) was one of the leading parties in France in 1945, even forming part of the governing Triple Alliance until being pushed out in 1947. Even then, as late as 1956, it was the largest party in the Assembly. In Germany, the Communist Party (KPD) exceeded the threshold for representation in the Bundestag in the first postwar elections in 1949, although it faded into insignificance thereafter until it was banned in 1956. Moreover, even though they remained committed to democracy, socialist parties like the French Social Party (PSF) and Germany's Social Democratic Party (SPD) still advocated radical Marxist ideas concerning nationalization and redistribution. It was only in 1995 that the British Labour Party finally removed its commitment to establish the "common ownership of the means of production" from Clause IV of its constitution.

On the other side of the spectrum, large pockets of far right, nationalist support remained, not least in Germany. Many in Germany reacted to defeat and occupation, not with moderation but with the same sense of humiliation and revanchism that accompanied the settlement at Versailles in 1919. In fact, between 1945 and 1949, polls showed that a majority of Germans still believed that "Nazism was a good idea, badly applied." As late as 1952, a quarter of West Germans admitted to holding a "good opinion" of Hitler. Although West Germany's first premier, Konrad Adenauer, was a victim of Nazi repression – finding himself imprisoned at the age of 70 in the roundups conducted after the failed 1944 assassination plot against Hitler – he nevertheless proved to be comfortable with incorporating former Nazis into his administration. Nor was the new center-right Christian Democratic Union (CDU) the only place Nazi members and sympathizers could find themselves. Remarkably, many former Nazis became supporters of the KPD. For supporters of the collaborationist Vichy regime in France, including the many bureaucrats who had served the state between 1940 and 1944, it was mostly a case of business as usual after the war. De Gaulle had little interest in purges. In Italy too, plans to cleanse the administration of former Fascists was an abysmal failure. There the Common Man's Party, essentially a gang of unreconstructed Fascists, gained over a million votes (out of 25 million cast) in 1946 – more or less the same level of support as Mussolini had obtained in 1921. In local elections in 1951, the far right gained control over the government in Naples, Bari, and Foggia. The national elections of June 1953 saw Monarchists and a new neo-Fascist party, the Movimento

Sociale Italiano (MSI), win 13 percent between them. In short, there was hardly an absence of political extremism in Europe after 1945.[11]

A second explanation is that the descending Cold War provided a strong motivation to make democracy work in Western Europe. Anti-Communism provided the glue to moderate political demands on the one hand, and a stimulus to the continent's badly broken economies on the other. As the harshness of conditions on the eastern side of the Iron Curtain became clear, not least with the very public repression of dissent in Hungary in 1956, the radical left option had basically vanished in the West. Again, however, there is no reason that the emerging international conflict between East and West, Communism and capitalism, had to lead to the consolidation of liberal democracy and bureaucratic party domination on the western side of the Iron Curtain. Britain and America were more than prepared to support dictators as long as they kept the Soviet Union at bay. As FDR is supposed to have said about right-wing Nicaraguan dictator Anastasio "Tachito" Somoza, "he may be a bastard, but he's our bastard." Domestically, the commitment to democracy of many Europeans was half-hearted at best. Democracy, after all, had led to Hitler, Mussolini, and war. What the people of Western Europe wanted most of all were bread and peace. In other words, if the choice was between democratically elected Communist governments or merely ineffective liberal ones on the one hand, and efficient authoritarian free market ones on the other, there's no reason the latter could not have come to predominate in the West. Europe could have become a continent of Singapores and Chiles. Indeed, in Francoist Spain, something along these lines occurred.

Both the legacy of the Second World War and the emerging Cold War were likely instrumental in creating conditions suitable for democracy in the 1950s, but not in the ways usually suggested. We might want to believe that the success of postwar European democracy was the result of a popular rejection of Fascism and Communism as political ideologies. Instead, however, it may be more productive to see it as an economic problem. That is, we can think about how the events of the 1940s affected the costs and likely payoffs of different types of political strategy. By weakening the organizational bases of far right and far left, the war had made the supporters of these parties temporarily available for mobilization by others. In most cases, bureaucratic and patronage-based parties had a cost advantage over populists in incorporating these voters.

First, the non-Communist political groups with the most intact organizations after the war were those on the Christian right. The Catholic Church had, after all, lost no love for Communists over the course of the War. Although Pope Pius XII encouraged Italy's new center-right Christian Democratic party (DC) to enter an alliance with former Fascists to prevent the Communists from coming to power, the notion of a grand coalition on the right was rejected. As a result, the church began to swing its substantial organizational support behind Christian Democratic parties across the continent. Christian Democratic parties, both Catholic and Protestant, stressed family, responsibility, and community. They were avowedly nonradical, but they could tolerate a substantial role for the state in the economy in a way that traditional liberal parties could not. Being able to draw not just on the moral legitimacy of the church, but also on its social networks, drove down the cost of political mobilization faced by these parties. Historian Peter Pulzer observes of Germany, "[w]hat tipped the balance in favor of Christian Democracy as opposed to the revival of Weimar parties was the support of the churches."[12]

Second, with de facto control over the hypertrophied states of the immediate postwar period, bureaucratic parties – most of them on the center right – had ample resources to incorporate available voters into their networks in the years after the war. Driven largely by the mobilization of redundant human and physical capital, postwar economies benefited from easy gains. These favorable conditions allowed incumbent bureaucratic parties to use government resources to build loyal bases of support through corporatist economic policies, in which almost every group could gain something. Unionized workers benefited from growing employment and improved conditions. Farmers secured price supports for their outputs. Small businesses did well on the back of rising consumer purchasing power.

Third, having gained de facto control over the levers of government, bureaucratic parties set about introducing institutions that would keep them in power. Most states adopted a high threshold for parliamentary representation of around 5 percent, which would eliminate the entrance of many personalistic, demagogic politicians. A threshold of this sort, for instance, would have prevented the Nazis from gaining a foothold in parliament in the 1920s. Britain also encouraged the continent's leaders to adopt an electoral system like its own, which would have tended to produce a moderate two-party system. A tradition of proportional representation on the continent made this unpalatable, but European leaders adopted other rules that would keep populists at bay. In Germany, the role of the presidency was downgraded to a ceremonial position, and it became more difficult to remove a sitting chancellor. By adopting party list systems, voters were required to select parties rather than individuals, giving party leaderships significant disciplinary control over aspiring politicos in their ranks. Political advancement would henceforth mean a slow march through the bureaucratic quagmire of a rule-bound party. In all of these respects, institutions furthered the ability of well-organized parties to dominate politically.

In Germany, for example, the newly established CDU (and its Bavarian ally, the Christian Solidary Union or CSU), quickly forged a majority based on the supporters of the former Catholic Center Party with the Protestant rural conservatives who had formed a large part of the Nazis' base. In the British occupied zone, chambers of commerce and business associations were encouraged to form, giving a substantial organizational advantage to conservative forces made up of the CDU. There were extremists further to the right, but what the system now possessed was a large conservative bloc committed to compromise with some social democratic principles in a way that wasn't true of the interwar period. Then, conservative parties had been only one of many forces on the right. Now these groups had strong incentives to merge and form an organized bulwark against extremism or what Adenauer called "experimentation." Conservative elites like Adenauer agreed to bureaucratic party constraints on their autonomy in return for a controlling share of power. After the war, obtaining pluralities in early elections, Christian Democrats demonstrated that they were the best bet for the middle and upper classes against socialism, and eventually swallowed up most of those to their right. For any German with political ambitions the sine qua non of advancement was membership in the CDU-CSU, or perhaps if prepared to play the long game, the SPD. In postwar Europe, parties were in; populism was out.[13]

THE DECLINE OF THE WEST?

In his pre–World War I magnum opus, *The Decline of the West*, German philosopher and historian Oswald Spengler argued that all previous high cultures went through a similar life cycle, beginning with the most primitive rural social structures and ending with the development and decay of complex urbanized societies. Spengler saw in the decline of once dominant civilizations like the Classical Mediterranean and Islamic Arabia the impending doom of the West. Dominance leads to decadence and thence to degeneration. What goes up must come down. Echoing Spengler, some scholars have implied that the very success of the postwar European recovery sowed the seeds of its demise. Success bred contempt, with parties taking voters' support for granted. In most existing economic interpretations of the rise of populism in the West, the decade beginning in the late 1960s is a key turning point.

As productivity and profitability gains tapered off, the headlong growth of the postwar decades slowed down. Developed economies like France struggled to provide the opportunities demanded by its increasingly educated workforce, culminating in the student-led civil unrest of 1968. The American abandonment of the gold standard in 1971 and the oil crises of 1973 and 1979 added fuel to the fire. Inflation took off, but, contrary to conventional economic theory, unemployment remained high; the novel disease of *stagflation* gripped Western economies. The Keynesian remedy of fiscal stimulus seemed to have run its course. European governments began to retrench, privatizing and deregulating industries it had controlled since the war. However, the economic recovery of the 1980s and 1990s in many cases failed to generate much new employment, especially for the unskilled, thereby exacerbating the growth in economic inequality precipitated by tax and regulatory reforms of center-right governments. Related to these economic tribulations were growing ethnic tensions. Immigrants from the South – southern Europe, Turkey, and African and Caribbean colonies – who had been encouraged to come temporarily in order fill jobs during boom times stayed, often in new urban and peri-urban ghettos. Never fully integrated, either economically or politically, when economic growth slowed, immigrant and guest workers were the first to be let go, leaving in place impoverished and often segregated ethnic minorities. Incumbent parties, which had almost all converged on the same set of economic and social policies, appeared to have no response to the malaise.

Voter apathy, if not yet resentment, set in. Peter Mair showed that across Europe voter turnout became more erratic and electoral volatility – a measure of the continuity of party support from one election to the next – increased substantially. People were less inclined to support the same parties election in, election out. They either didn't bother to vote, or when they did, they did so more on spur of the moment. Party membership also went into a sustained decline. In the 1960s, for those European democracies with available data, party membership averaged 14 percent. By the 1980s this had fallen to 10 percent, and by the 1990s, to 5 percent. Membership numbers continued to fall into the 2000s. In turn, according to the prevailing wisdom, the decline of the programmatic party in these years set the stage for the era of populism in the 2010s. Voters unhappy with the establishment were primed for the emergence of the populist challenge.[14]

No case supposedly supports this proposed argument better than that of Britain. Undergoing much the same boom and bust cycle as the rest of Western Europe, by the late 1970s, the British economy was in deep crisis. With the election of Margaret Thatcher in 1979, Britain made the most concerted change of economic direction in Europe. Promoting a set of policies that has become known as neoliberalism, Thatcher declared that "[t]here's no such thing as society," that individual effort, not government assistance, would determine a person's success. Despite the limited effect of the Conservative Party's reforms on jobs and growth, the party repeatedly flattened Labour in the polls through the 1980s and early 1990s. It was only when Labour leaders Neil Kinnock and Tony Blair adopted much of the Conservative Party's platform, reorienting the party toward the middle class that it regained power in 1997. These so-called Third Way policies may have brought the Labour Party back into office, but an unintended consequence, so the story goes, was to leave poorer and older voters who leaned to the left with nowhere to go. The Conservative Party, back in power under David Cameron in 2010, presented a fresh face but not a radical departure of policy. His government's austerity measures following the Global Financial Crisis further enraged voters at the bottom of the income distribution who could justifiably feel that no party represented their interests. Voters turned away from both Labour and the Conservative Party. Stressing the threat that immigration posed to the British welfare state and to British workers, the "fruitcakes, loonies, and closet racists" of UKIP, as Cameron described them, made significant inroads among the working class. By the early 2010s, UKIP had replaced the Liberal Democrats as Britain's third most popular party. The *demand* for populism – so the story goes – brought Britain out of the European Union, allowed a radical like Jeremy Corbyn to take over the Labour Party, and made the controversial former mayor of London, Boris Johnson, prime minister.

However, popular demand tells only a small part of the story. First consider Corbyn's rise to the Labour leadership. Corbyn's message of a fairer, more equal economy appealed to a lot of the new or previously abstaining voters who were disenchanted by years of socioeconomic stagnation. Yet these voters had been unhappy for a long time, while Corbyn had been propounding essentially the same socialist message for years. That is, there was no great change in the demand or supply of left-wing policy remedies. Rather, the critical element in Corbyn's success in the 2015 leadership race was the novel strategy he employed. The defeat of Labour in the 2010 general election led the party leadership to embrace key procedural reforms as part of its 2014 review. The reforms ultimately weakened the power of the Parliamentary Labour Party, but this was not their intention. The party introduced the policy of one member one vote (OMOV) primarily to shift influence away from the increasingly radical and unrepresentative unions, toward the moderate mass membership (in part), and mainly toward the parliamentary party itself. Prior to 2015, parliamentary party members' votes counted for thousands of member votes, but now all members and registered supporters could also vote, for a fee of three pounds. The belief was that the organizational resources of the parliamentary party would allow it to monopolize those member and supporter votes, while the disciplined but numerically small unions would be weakened. Yet by allowing virtually open mass participation, the reformers inadvertently reduced the cost of the populist strategy vis-à-vis its programmatic alternative. Corbyn's main strategy to capture the leadership was to increase the party membership, bringing in new voters, especially the young who had never been a member of a party before. To connect with these former nonvoters, Corbyn launched a novel face-to-face campaign for the nomination, which included holding hundreds of meetings across the country. In addition, Corbyn had little if any backing from the traditional media, so he turned largely to social media, which allowed more direct communication with potential supporters; 57 percent of Corbyn supporters used social media as their main source of news. Corbyn's offer to these disaffected voters, as sympathetic observer, Richard Seymour, puts it:

> was simple and unique. In joining the Labour Party or registering as supporters, they could bypass the need to patiently build an alternative party or start a new one. Instead, they could take the leadership in an existing mass party with union backing, money, and a record of electoral success far greater than any of its rivals, and drive it to the left.

Corbyn would win 84 percent of the new three-pound members' votes.[15]

Corbyn's success, however, also depended on the factional dynamics of the British Labour Party, which lowered the winning threshold, and hence, the relative cost of the populist strategy. Before he could even appeal to new voters to be Labour Party leader, he had to gain a position on the ballot. Even in 2015, any candidate for the leadership still needed the support of 15 percent of the parliamentary party to feature on the ballot. For those on the far left of the party, even if Corbyn lost, his candidature held out the potential to pull the party's center of gravity in their direction. However, although the unions on which Labour relies had moved to the left, because they were now smaller and more narrowly focused in their membership than the corporatist organizations of the 1970s, this 15 percent threshold exceeded the share of the far left wing of the parliamentary party of which Corbyn was the most extreme avatar. He could not have gained a place on the ballot had he not gained further support from an unlikely source. Paradoxically, Corbyn's nomination also served the purpose of another major group in the parliamentary party. For those on the right, Corbyn's extremism made him seem like far less of a threat than a more electable candidate just left of the party's mainstream. However, when the leadership ballot came, the center right of the party couldn't coordinate behind an opponent to Corbyn, remaining divided between three candidates: Andy Burnham, Yvette Cooper, and Liz Kendall. In this highly divided field, and with his substantial backing among newly recruited supporters, Corbyn swept home. With little support among the parliamentary party, in the wake of Labour's lackluster contribution to the Brexit Remain campaign, Corbyn was subjected to a leadership challenge. Although he couldn't even muster the requisite support of fifty-one members of the parliamentary party, as leader, he was automatically entitled to appear on the ballot of the broader membership that would settle the issue. With a Facebook following of over 1 million, compared to the mere 3,000 of his opponent, Owen Smith, Corbyn crushed the revolt. As long as direct appeals to voters were sufficient to win and retain control of the party, Corbyn's position appeared unassailable. However, when Corby again presided over another general election defeat in 2019, despite the civil war then ongoing in the Tory ranks, he was so isolated within the parliamentary party ranks that he had no choice but to cede leadership of the party.[16]

Corbyn's rise to the Labour leadership showed that a combination of greater voter availability along with new communication technologies had made populism a viable strategy, at least under favorable institutional rules. Similar conditions would result in Boris Johnson's selection as Conservative Party leader some four years later. Like Labour, the Conservative Party had traditionally kept the choice of party leader firmly within the parliamentary party's control. The massive disruption of Brexit, however, forced an opening. Like Churchill in the 1940s, Johnson needed crisis conditions to weaken the cohesion of the party elite. Only then would a low-cost populist strategy based on his considerable celebrity succeed.

Boris Johnson had the background of any respectable member of the Conservative Party leadership – Eton, Oxford, a former Tory MEP for a father, and a background in Conservative student politics. Yet Johnson paints a stark

contrast to prior leaders of what is the quintessential establishment, bureaucratic party. From his earliest days, Johnson was enamored of power.
Intellectually gifted but ill-disciplined, in the words of one fellow Oxford
student, he had an "electrifying, charismatic presence" that drew others into
his orbit. However, as charming and charismatic as he was, Johnson struggled
to keep political friends for long. Never a team player, Johnson was anathema
to virtually the whole of the Tory leadership. "Boris was always about Boris,"
as one-time party leader, Ian Duncan Smith, put it. Johnson's rise was never
going to be based on the assiduous accumulation of favors and factional
backing; the path followed by Thatcher, John Major, Cameron, and others.[17]

Well known as the conservative *Telegraph*'s leading provocateur, *Spectator*
editor, and as a celebrity from his days as guest and then host of the popular
television political satire, *Have I Got News for You*, Johnson had tremendous
name (and face) recognition. It was this celebrity that brought him the local
Conservative Party Association's nomination for Michael Heseltine's vacant
Henley seat in 2001. Johnson though, in spite of his reputation as a formidable
college debater, was a nonentity in the Labour-dominated Commons, doing
more to win the distrust of Duncan Smith, Michael Howard, and other party
leaders than to burnish his own leadership credentials. When Howard resigned
as leader after the party's general election defeat in 2005, Johnson astutely
backed David Cameron for the leadership. There was no immediate quid pro
quo, however, as Cameron still justifiably distrusted Johnson. However, given
Johnson's undoubted fame, then Prime Minister Cameron had little choice but
to agree to his nomination as the Tory candidate for mayor of London in 2008.
Dislodging the seemingly impervious Ken Livingston, in part by pulling away
disaffected Labour voters, Johnson demonstrated his ability to mobilize voters
without the usual party-based machinery. With the pulpit of the mayor's office
from 2008 to 2016 and a weekly column in the *Telegraph*, Johnson had a
unique platform to cultivate his independent political persona.

As late as 2016, however, Johnson still had the chance to follow the bureaucratic route to power. In the lead up to Brexit, Cameron privately floated a quid
pro quo to Johnson. Back Remain, and I'll appoint you to a high posting in the
Cabinet. This, in turn, would allow Johnson to establish himself as a party
loyalist and rival with Chancellor George Osborne to succeed Cameron as
prime minister, whenever he stepped down. Even had he supported Remain,
however, suspicions over his loyalty to the party would have continued. Thus,
perhaps suspecting that the party elite would never willingly give him the
leadership, Johnson chose a different strategy. Johnson opposed his party's
leadership, becoming the most prominent voice of the Leave campaign in the
referendum on Britain's continued EU membership.[18]

With Prime Minister Cameron resigning in the wake of his government's
defeat in the Brexit referendum, the Conservative Party found itself suddenly
headless. As insiders like Osborne had feared, the Brexit campaign had exposed
severe factional tensions within the party. With little choice but to implement

some form of Brexit, the party was divided into hards and softs – those who favored withdrawal at any cost, and those who favored some kind of renegotiation with the European bloc. With the one-time heir apparent, Osborne, having resigned in the wake of the referendum defeat, the contest looked set to become a two-way race between then Secretary of State, Theresa May, and Johnson. Johnson appeared to have the support of the hards faction, including that of his longtime backer, Michael Gove. However, sensing an opportunity to grasp the crown for himself, Gove put his own name forward. Although Johnson had considerable support, a split in the hards bloc almost certainly spelled defeat. Rather than risk a loss on his record, Johnson pulled out. The Europhile wing of the party swung in behind May, who easily defeated Gove, along with Andrea Leadsom, the other moderate in the race. However, as prime minster, May failed to deliver a new deal with the EU, and, persistently dogged by the disputatious Leave faction within the party, she was eventually forced to resign in 2019. Johnson would have another shot, this time with the party even more fragmented than before.

Like Corbyn, Johnson was unintentionally aided by prior reforms to Tory party rules. Prior to 1965, the Tory leadership was decided by discussion among the parliamentary elite. With the reforms of party leader, Alec Douglas-Horne, leaders would henceforth need to be elected by a majority of Conservate MPs. To win on the first round, a candidate would need more than 50 percent of the vote and be more than 15 percent ahead of the next highest candidate. Failing this, balloting would continue until one candidate gained a sufficient majority of the votes. After the Conservatives' election defeat to New Labour in 1997, then leader William Hague further democratized the selection process. The new set of rules called for MPs to select the top two candidates, who would then proceed to a runoff election in which all party members have a single vote. With each round of the balloting of MPs, the lowest polling candidate, or those who receive fewer than seventeen votes, are eliminated until just two are remaining. Although ostensibly far more participatory than the former system, this process still afforded the party leadership a great deal of leverage in determining the outcome.

However, in 2019, persistent divisions among the leadership meant that the broader party membership would have more influence than ever. For Johnson, as with Corbyn, because of his celebrity status, the broader participation in the leadership selection process would be to his advantage but only if he could obtain a slot in the runoff. The field was wide open: Philip Hammond, Jacob-Reese Mogg, Sajid Javid, Amber Rudd, and Dominic Raab were all touted as possibilities. Bookmakers, however, soon installed the charismatic Johnson as their favorite. However much the party elite distrusted him, Boris was popular. His eventual opponent, Jeremy Hunt, utterly lacked either the charisma or the political machinery to win a mass popularity contest. While Johnson had won just 51 percent of Tory MPs on the fifth round of balloting, he won the support of almost two thirds of the voting party membership of nearly 140,000. Johnson's charisma won the day and he would shortly demonstrate that his ability to directly mobilize support went beyond the party membership. Johnson's outsider, politically incorrect reputation carried the Tories to a remarkable general election victory in December 2019. Yet, as is the case for most populists, governing proved a great deal more difficult than winning an election. His government's mishandling of the COVID-19 outbreak saw his popularity ebb away, and his utility to the party elite – his electoral coattails – receded with it.

What the British experience suggests is that the demand side provides at best a partial explanation for populism. Rather, supply-side factors play the main role in the kinds of leaders who can gain control of government. In the British case, changed party rules and internal factional divisions allowed charismatic leaders to appeal directly to voters to take leadership of their parties. In this period, it is Germany that presents the most illuminating contrast. In his satirical novel, *Look Who's Back*, Timur Vermes imagines what would happen if Adolf Hitler was to suddenly wake up in contemporary Germany. In Vermes' story, the reemerged Hitler, whom people assume to be a lookalike, becomes a Stephen Colbert–like television celebrity. Comically, liberals become his biggest fans, unwittingly taking Hitler's fascist rants for a parody. It's a darkly funny novel, but in reality, it seems highly improbable that comedic celebrity might be turned to a populist assault on political power in today's Germany. Like Britain, Germany was buffeted by a slowdown in growth in the 1970s and then had to cope with enormous budgetary pressure to pay for the integration of the laggard East after 1990. Yet, even in the enlarged Germany, long-established parties remain in government and populists are fringe players at best. Supply-side conditions never presented voters with a populist to elect, as bureaucratic party elites remain firmly in control of their leadership selection machinery.

In the postwar German context, for the politically ambitious there has been no alternative to the programmatic strategy. Angela Merkel's rise to power exemplifies that approach; she was, as one commentator puts it, the quintessential "party-manager." A physicist by training and profession, Merkel was a relatively late entrant to politics in her native East Germany. However, after experimenting with oppositional politics as the Communist GDR regime began to implode, Merkel quickly saw the benefits of joining the CDU – the party with the best political network in the East. As a corporatist party, the CDU constantly sought to promote to leadership position politicians who represented at least one – and ideally more – of its constituent groups. Fitting the bill of an eastern, female, Protestant, young, well-educated representative, who was untainted by any prior baggage, Merkel found herself rapidly promoted up the rungs of the CDU ladder by then Chancellor Helmut Kohl. Merkel, moreover, was ideally suited to retain power within the CDU's corporate party structure. As leader of the party from 2005, Merkel's initial electoral performances were modest at best, but with no core base of power in the party, she could credibly claim to be an unbiased arbiter of the party's existing factions or corporate groups.[19]

A small number of populists in the strategic sense have made serious inroads elsewhere in Western Europe, including in Denmark, Finland, the Netherlands, and to a lesser extent Switzerland and Iceland. These cases are worth pondering in a little detail, as in many respects their party systems resemble that of Germany, where populism has had little impact. What these cases suggest is that the populist strategy is made for a sprint not a marathon. Without the intervention of some extraordinary outside events – the 1848 revolution in Louis Napoleon's case or the Great Depression in Hitler's – unless populists come to power relatively quickly, they rarely have the resources to sustain the slow struggle for power. After initial breakthroughs, populist movements either tend to bureaucratize or to disappear. Without the resources of bureaucratic incumbents to occupy multiple lower levels of government and gradually build loyal bases of support, if populists fail to gain control of national government, this strategy fails to provide a good return on its investment.

Let's begin with the Netherlands. As in the other rich democracies of Western Europe, postwar political competition in the Netherlands was primarily between the Catholic (or Christian) center right and the Labour-based left, with the CDA being the main pillar of government throughout the latter half of the twentieth century. However, as the 1990s progressed, with church attendance in abeyance, the CDA began to bleed members. For a brief time, a new "purple" coalition filled the space, with Labour leader, Wim Koch, as the Third Way-Tony Blair equivalent, leading a multiparty coalition of left and right. Party allegiance remained critically weak, however, with each election from 1994 marking new highs of voter switching. It was in this context that European populism made a critical breakthrough. Just nine days after the assassination of its charismatic leader, the eponymous Pim Fortuyn List (LPF) won an impressive 17 percent of the vote in the 2002 Dutch general election. A sociology professor with a long record of anti-Islamic and anti-immigration punditry, Fortuyn planned a direct entry onto the national stage in the wake of the 9/11 attacks. Although the LPF was only formally created in February 2002, just three months before the elections, every television appearance made by Fortuyn swelled his party's approval ratings. Although rewarded with a junior share in government, the LPF quickly fragmented and fresh elections were called just a year later. Without its charismatic leader, the LPF's vote share plummeted to 5.7 percent, and by 2008 the party had disbanded.

This did not mean the end of the populist strategy in the Netherlands. The Party for Freedom (PVV), a party of similar ilk established by Geert Wilders, quickly occupied the space left by the LPF. Almost alone among major European parties, the PVV does not have members and remains very much the personal vehicle of the charismatic Wilders. The PVV is, as one expert has written, "a one-man party." Wilders entered the Dutch Parliament in 1998 as a member of the center-right VVD. However, in the Netherlands' party list electoral system – in which voters choose parties rather than individual candidates – being placed at number forty-six on the party's preference list, Wilders only just squeaked on to the backbenches because 1998 represented the party's best ever electoral performance. In other words, Wilders was well down the party pecking order and he knew it. Wilders tried and failed to push the VVD to take a harder line against immigration and Islamic terrorism, and when the party lost much of its support to the LPF in 2002, Wilders had basically had enough. In 2004, he left to set up the "Wilders Group." Although the name changed to the less personalistic sounding PVV in February 2006, it was still "far from being a properly organised party." The party remained a slim, personalized, low-cost organization: It had no administrative staff, office premises, party conferences, or even a newsletter. Wilders instead used the PVV's presence in parliament to develop his party's brand on the cheap, relying in particular on the use of often extreme, sometimes humorous statements and proposals to gain free publicity in the mainstream media. Winning 5.9 percent of the votes and 9 seats in parliament, the party's performance in the November 2006 elections far exceeded expectations. Since its breakthrough, the PVV went on to even greater success. Its vote share reached as high as 15.4 percent (2010), after which it agreed to support the government without taking office.[20]

Although the PVV remains the third largest party in the Dutch parliament, its vote share has steadily fallen – to 13.1 percent in 2017 and 10.8 percent in 2021. No doubt Wilders is one of Europe's most successful and enduring populists. Even still, however, Wilders remains far from the prime minister's office. The proportional quality of the Dutch electoral system – a setup shared by most states in Western Europe – has meant that the PVV remains just one party among many. It has never won a plurality, and even if it did, it would likely be opposed by a sufficiently broad coalition of other parties to prevent it forming a government. Although the opposition to the PVV remains fragmented into many political organizations, the proportion of voters available to the PVV is insufficient to win power in its own right. The result for Wilders and the PVV, as for many populists in Western Europe, is that they face strong pressures to bureaucratize after their initial breakthrough. Protest votes – votes for a party with no realistic chance of winning – may flow in for some time, but eventually voters want to see a favored set of policies implemented. To have policy impact in the complex and often decentralized administrations of Western European states demands a large, bureaucratic political entity. Charismatic individuals may make a breakthrough at the national level, but much governmental work is carried on at the subnational level. If they fail to develop national party offices at multiple levels, populist parties can quickly fade into irrelevance. Even the famously personalized PVV has had to institutionalize somewhat, participating in municipal elections from 2010 and Senate elections from 2012. At least part of the PVV's struggle to progress further has been Wilders' persistent personalization of the party, which has set a ceiling on its capacity to recruit and keep high-quality parliamentarians. One expert estimated that as late as 2012–14, the party had just 1,000 people performing paid or unpaid work for it in any capacity; this activity was full time for as few as 100 people. Organizationally, in other words, the PVV remained miniscule, a characteristic that is likely to prevent it from coming to power in the foreseeable future.

The Danish People's Party (DPP), formed by Pia Kjærsgaard in 1996 from a splinter faction of the Progress Party – itself a relatively new minority protest party – followed a similar initial trajectory to the PVV. Under Kjærsgaard's leadership, the party developed as a highly centralized and disciplined political organization, in which regular party members had little say on personnel or policy. Although the party's best electoral performance came in 2015, after leadership of the party had been handed over to Kristian Thulesen Dahl, its transition toward a regular bureaucratic party has been incomplete. At the top, with Kjærsgaard's departure, it remained highly factionalized, while its organizational development at the local level was limited. In 2019, the party lost 21 of its 37 seats in parliament before shedding more than half of its seats in local elections in 2021. A more successful transition toward the bureaucratic strategy appears to have been followed by the True Finns. Founded by Timo Soini, the True Finns gained a major electoral share following the party's institutionalization. As a junior party in government, the Finns increasingly developed into a bureaucratic organization with a presence at all levels. The leadership change in 2017 had a minimal effect on the party's support, with the Finns taking one more seat in 2019 than it had in 2015.

The charismatic appeal of a Pim Fortuyn or Geert Wilders may be sufficient to get a party started, but populist parties, being personalistic electoral vehicles, have a challenging time recruiting and retaining political talent. Often, such outsider parties are plagued by an influx of political wannabes with questionable records and temperaments. A more talented but unknown political hopeful may grab on to the coattails of a charismatic leader in the quest for political office. But eventually, the very terms of the personal, populist party become self-limiting, especially in Western Europe's proportional representation systems, which allow bureaucratic parties to form *cordons sanitaires* to exclude populists from power. Unless they gain a share in power very quickly, populists have little to offer the most capable members of their entourages. Moreover, the absence of rules governing the distribution of power and succession create inevitable tensions, especially if party subordinates begin to acquire reputations in their own right. Last, and perhaps most importantly, to function as parties of government, whether at the local, national, or supra-national (European Union) level, a great deal of organization is necessary. As a result, there are few cases of sustained populist success in Western Europe. In short, contrary to popular belief, the adaptation and survival of establishment bureaucratic parties remain the rule, with populists tending to occupy spaces on the margin. Where one-time populists have endured, it is by adopting the bureaucratic strategy for themselves.

FORZA

Although bureaucratic parties have been the rule in postwar Europe, they haven't had it all their own way. Superficially, the postwar Italian party system resembled that of the bureaucratic German or British ones. On the left was the

Communist Party (PCI), which under the leadership of Palmiro Togliatti in the late 1940s, moderated itself into a kind of social democratic party. On the center right was the Christian Democratic Party (DC), which drew primarily on the organizational capacity of the church, and promised a conservative but democratic counterpoint to the feared radicalism of the PCI. At the political level, voters' attachment to these (nominally) ideologically distinct parties – the DC and the PCI – has sometimes been identified as electoral support through *voto di appartenza* – a vote based on loyalty and affection. Yet the more important source of electoral support, particularly for the DC, was clientelism or the *voto di scambio* – vote-buying. As one DC worker described the system of the 1950s, "there were no political beliefs then. The only convictions were the packages of macaroni, sugar, flour, milk, etc. Moral convictions were of no use. The packages arrived and the packages convinced." In other words, although geographically in the bureaucratic party core of Western Europe, the Italian political system was dominated by patronage-based political groups.[21]

Created in September 1942 by former members of the defunct Catholic Popular Party, the DC was a minor political player in the anti-Fascist resistance. However, with Pope Pius XII's approval, the Italian Catholic Action Association shifted the support of its two million members to the DC as the main bulwark against the renewed threat of Communism. Already during the first years of the postwar Italian Republic, the DC had developed a capillary structure, typical of clientelist political organizations. At first, the DC's alliance with the Catholic Church gave it ready access to a fragmented population, but it quickly sought to outgrow a dependence on the church that had killed off its prewar predecessor, the Italian People's Party (PPI). The DC penetrated all kinds of social organizations and built up a substantial countrywide support network that had both an urban and rural presence. This in turn allowed local DC politicians to capture interest groups and establish a system of patronage, in which votes would be exchanged for access to government services or even jobs. Especially in the South, where its peasant society remained poor and atomized, this semi-feudal mode of political organization was both familiar and effective. DC leader Alcide De Gasperi would become one of Italy's longest serving leaders, commanding eight successive governments from 1945 to 1953. On the opposition side, the PCI was no organizational naïf. Although shut out of national office, at the local government level, like the DC, the PCI established support networks in which local party and local government were almost indistinguishable. This was the well-known "particracy" or *partitocrazia* at work.

The fuel for the *partitocrazia* was the payment of bribes to politicians by the private sector with the aim of receiving concessions for contracts in state-run enterprises, across all sectors of the economy, from construction to communications. Brokers in a position to control the distribution of these centralized funds to local communities became extremely powerful, eventually supplanting the supremacy of the old rural notables. This patronage system experienced rapid growth during the early postwar period and reached a peak in the 1980s as a third actor, the Socialist Party (PSI), emerged from its relative obscurity. The accession of the PSI to the premiership under the leadership of Benedetto Craxi saw a profusion of patronage, placing the system under increasing strain.[22]

Then, in 1992, the earth shook. Despite its longevity, the party system of the Italian First Republic came undone with remarkable speed. As anyone with a passing familiarity with Italy will know, along with the rise of patronage politics after the war came the resurgence of the mafia. Corruption pervaded the political system, with criminal organizations – the Cosa Nostra, the 'Ndragheta, the Camorra – occupying a pivotal, if shadowy role, turning force into cash, and cash into political influence. In the North, where mafia penetration was less pervasive, big business, the unions, and politicians had their own collusive networks. Reminiscent of the ratchet quality observed in America's nineteenth-century patronage democracy, or in the patronage-based political systems of Asia and Latin America I have analyzed elsewhere, beginning in the mid-1980s, the cost of running Italy's patronage party system had begun to skyrocket. In an increasingly competitive political environment, the cost of conducting election campaigns pushed politicians to squeeze businesses even harder for contributions. With the increased international economic competition that would follow passage of the 1992 Maastricht Treaty, business leaders felt they had no choice to but to push back. In the early 1990s, they lent their support to a concerted, if selective, effort by reformist judges to cleanse Italy's political system. A host of convictions of senior politicians and mafia bosses resulted from the *Mane Pulite*, or clean hands, investigation. In a little more than two years from 1992, all of the main parties, the DC, the PSI, the Liberal Party (PLI), the Republican Party (PRI), and the PCI had disappeared, although remnants of them would be incorporated into new parties, most notably the Democratic Party of the Left (PDS), which emerged from the wreckage of the PCI. Even if the investigations were themselves deeply politicized, the result was a near clean sweep of the old order: *Tangentopoli* – or "Bribe City" – was cleaned out. According to recent research, only a quarter of the deputies of legislature XI (1992–94) were reelected in legislature XII (1994–96). This was an unprecedented political rupture. With existing political attachments swept away by the mass of political prosecutions, there was a window of opportunity for new leaders and parties to connect directly with a public searching for political representation.[23]

The collapse of support for the traditional parties left a void in the political space that allowed the new political force led by media magnate, Silvio Berlusconi, to enter politics. A man of modest origins but great ambition, Berlusconi made his initial fortune in a number of major real estate deals in Milan in the 1970s. Through the 1980s, his fortune grew and his business empire diversified, most notably into television. As the municipal elections approached in November 1993,

Berlusconi endorsed Rome's Gianfranco Fini, leader of the neo-fascist MSI, but by the turn of the new year, it was clear that Berlusconi wanted power for himself. Presaging the rise of Trump some two decades later, Berlusconi exploited his media resources for all they were worth. Although a well-connected magnate himself, he was sufficiently distant from the old elite to adopt the image of an outsider, declaring "enough of these politicians." As owner of the famous AC Milan football club and piggybacking on Italians' love of football, he christened his new movement *Forza Italia*. His party quickly expanded across the country, establishing local "clubs" to provide some organizational footing, but the party's imagery and appeal remained very much on the charisma of the former crooner himself. Berlusconi's networks bombarded viewers with Forza Italia advertisements, and unsurprisingly, viewership of his channels was strongly positively associated with voting for his party. Forza Italia captured 21 percent of the vote in the March 1994 elections, making a party that hadn't existed just six months previously the largest in parliament. With his coalition partners, the nationalist and xenophobic Alleanza Nationale and the Northern League, and a few nominal independents, Berlusconi became the Second Republic's first prime minister. Berlusconi's first cabinet didn't last long. Deserted by the league, Berlusconi was forced to cede power to the economist, Lamberto Dini. In 1996, Berlusconi finished as runner-up to the leftist Olive Tree coalition (the former Communist PDS being the largest party), which backed former European Commission Bureaucrat Romano Prodi as prime minister. Just two years later, however, Berlusconi was back in the prime minister's office, this time with a larger majority.[24]

Although at the second time of asking, his government lasted for five years, a lifetime in Italian politics, his legacy was not to introduce any newfound political stability. Berlusconi's rule was characterized by rampant abuse of power, corruption, and sleaze. Indeed, most of his party's legislative efforts appear to have been dedicated to ensuring that Berlusconi's business interests continued to thrive and that Berlusconi and his allies remained out of prison. So disgraced had the Italian political establishment become after the scandals of the DC era and the two decades of Berlusconi predominance that the country was forced to turn to a sequence of essentially unelected or minority technocratic leaders to deal with the economic crisis of the late 2000s. In 2018, with not much place left for voters to go, a plurality of Italians turned to the Five Star Movement (M5S) of comedian and satirist, Beppe Grillo. With a conviction for manslaughter on his record, Grillo himself was unable to take parliamentary leadership, but he remained the charismatic face of the party through the election. Giuseppe Conte was chosen to lead successive governing coalitions backed by M5S, first with partners on the right and then on the left. Conte's style, like that of his recent predecessors, has been technocratic, relying little if at all on direct mass mobilization or party building. However competent, this lack of political institutionalization will continue to leave Italy susceptible to populist mobilization. Populism did not cause the collapse of the Italian party system; rather, populism was a political strategy that proved successful once the Italian party system had fallen apart under its own, hefty weight.

Clientelistic party systems have also proven more susceptible to populism elsewhere in Western Europe. Indeed, it is probably Greece where populism has had its most dramatic success in recent decades. Straddling the border between East and West, Greece resembles more than most the political forms found in southern Asia and Latin America. It has been recurrently susceptible to populist appeals, the figures of Eleftherios Venizelos and Andreas Papandreou towering over twentieth-century Greek history. If it seemed in the early 2000s that the demands of membership in Europe's exclusive economic club – the Euro – might have brought some technocratic stability to Greek politics, such appearances were deceiving. The dominant rival parties of PASOK and New Democracy were divided only by how generously they could promise to distribute the spoils of governing. When the collapse of international credit in 2008 precipitated a horrendous economic collapse and threatened to force the country to withdraw from the common European currency, the political consequences were sharply felt. SYRIZA, a coalition of left-wing opposition parties, eventually led by the charismatic Alexis Tsipras took nearly 27 percent in the election in 2012 on the basis of opposition to the austerity policies mandated by Greece's international creditors, thus making it the country's second largest party. In 2015, SYRIZA went one better. Although the party fell just shy of an absolute legislative majority, Tsipras became prime minister with the backing of the nationalist Independent Greeks (ANEL) party. What made Greece unusual was not just the depth of its economic crisis, but the vulnerability of the parties that had dominated the country since its democratization in the 1970s to such a crisis.

Like their Italian counterparts, Greek parties traditionally won support through the distribution of patronage; Greece's public sector payrolls were proportionally among the largest in Europe and its pensions and social services among the most generous. This, of course, left its economy susceptible to any weakening in the state's budgetary position, but it also meant that voters would be quick to abandon the parties if they failed to deliver on their end of the patron–client bargain. As newly unattached voters searched for another option, SYRIZA was there to pick up the pieces, and in Tsipras, they had a handsome, charismatic, and trustworthy leader. Adept at communication through traditional and social media, Tsipras quickly became a cult figure. The Italian and Greek cases more than illustrate that Western Europe is not immune from populism. Yet the unusual dependence on patronage in these cases suggests that the relevant characteristic in populist success is not geography but the prevailing form of linkage between parties and voters.[25]

ENCORE LA FRANCE

The French case complicates the story in some interesting ways. Even if France has lagged somewhat behind its Anglo-Saxon competitors in terms of economic modernization in recent decades, it has been and remains one of the world's major economies. Indeed, France's rapid economic development in the late nineteenth century gave rise to some of the world's earliest and best organized labor movements. In part for this reason, but also because of its strong tradition of anticlericalism, France's most institutionalized political organizations – that is, the ones most firmly based on rules, office-holding, managerial discipline, and so on – emerged on the left, not the Christian Democratic right as in much of the rest of Western Europe. After the Liberation of France in 1944, during which the Communists provided the most robust support to the Allies, the French Communist Party (PCF) had by far the most expansive network of support and was soon to become France's largest party, winning 28 percent of the vote in November 1946.

The successful organization of the Communist left might have precipitated emulation among other streams in French politics. However, the right never unified in postwar France as it did in Britain or Germany. Throughout the Third Republic, and into the Fourth, politics, especially on the right, remained the remit of individuals and factions, not parties. The Democratic Alliance (AD) and the Radicals survived from the Third Republic – to them were added the Christian Democratic Popular Republican Movement (MRP), and the party of Charles de Gaulle, the Rally of the French People (RPF). Historian David Hanley writes that Radicalism for one remained a "federation of locally based potentates." The small single-member constituencies elected with a second round runoff ballot that was favored by incumbents (who got to decide on the electoral system on an ongoing legislative basis) made politics exceedingly local; a member of parliament might have to know by name a large proportion of his voters. One study shows that two thirds of deputies were born in their constituency. Deputies had to cultivate and patronize their electorates, but these services were not put toward the construction of stable political parties. Unlike in Italy, because control over economic policy remained in the hands of the civil service, no clientelistic-minded conservative party could use state resources to entrench itself in national power as did the DC. Nor was this political atomization merely a feature of rural France, where local notables might still exert their influence over the peasantry. Hanley observes that if a candidate was "endorsed by a party organisation in Paris, the organisation would probably owe more to him than he to it."[26]

It is this context of party fragmentation that provides for the rise of Charles de Gaulle. A senior military commander, General De Gaulle was dismayed by the defeatism of his compatriots in 1940 – not least his former superior and the hero of France's stubborn defence in the First World War, Marshal Philippe Pétain. De Gaulle evacuated to North Africa before eventually decamping to London, where he proclaimed himself leader of the resistance, becoming famously the voice of Free France through the BBC's long-wave radio transmissions. De Gaulle indefatigably represented France's interests – and his own – pushing for a role alongside Britain and America in liberating Western Europe that had little justification in terms of Free France's capacities. Although De Gaulle was frustrated in his efforts at times, he was nevertheless able to stage events so that his role always seemed bigger than reality – the iconic victory march through Paris in August 1944 probably the greatest example. De Gaulle's Parisian procession was then repeated around the country, the goal being to establish his own "direct relationship with the population" as Julian Jackson, his biographer, puts it. Another historian writes that De Gaulle was "not only seen but physically touched by his people."[27]

After the liberation, De Gaulle became prime minister in the provisional government. From the time of his march through Paris until October 21, 1945, although nominally operating under the constitution of the Third Republic, the provisional government's authority was "purely charismatic." It depended fully on De Gaulle. On the one hand, he professed to be worried about the formation of a "populist government which would encircle my head with laurels, ask me to take a position which it would designate for me and pull all the strings ... until the day when the dictatorship of proletariat was established." On the other, De Gaulle felt that he "had to find support among the people rather than among the élites–they would tend to come between the people and me." Although much of the resistance from within occupied France had come from the Communists, De Gaulle loomed larger than anyone else as the savior of France in the popular psyche. De Gaulle disarmed the non-Communist resistance and tamed the Communists by promises of inclusion in the new government. Perceiving France's indecisive parties and hypertrophic parliament as to blame for France's defeatism, De Gaulle pushed for a new constitution that would empower an executive branch – occupied by himself of course – to stand above party and factional squabbles. Not a dictatorship but an institutional setup that would tilt heavily toward populist mobilization. De Gaulle's role as the charismatic leader of this direct form of democracy is best conveyed in his own words, "[b]eneath the cheers and behind the stares, I saw the image of the people's soul. For the great majority, what mattered was the emotion provoked by this spectacle, exalted by this presence, and expressed with smiles and tears by *Vive de Gaulle!*"[28]

De Gaulle's personalization of power did not go unopposed. The prewar left parties, the Communists and the Socialist Party (SFIO), were untainted by collaboration and retained their appeal after the war. Drawing on the radical republican tradition, the socialists were distrustful of personalist rule and wanted a system with a strong single-chamber parliament. The Communists, as noted, were the largest and most cohesive political party. They too favored a political system that would have kept power from De Gaulle. On the center right, unlike in Germany and the Low Countries, the Catholic church in France remained a deeply conservative, indeed reactionary, institution through the nineteenth and early twentieth century, associated more with royalism than with reformism. The MRP did follow the example set elsewhere in setting itself up as a Christian Democratic party in 1944. However, the historical absence of politicized church organizations in France meant that it was unable to command the kinds of electoral support that the DC and the CDU could in Italy and Germany, respectively. In the 1946 constituent assembly elections, the PCF won 26 percent, the MRP 24 percent, and the SFIO 24 percent. The three parties formed a unity government – the *Tripartisme* – largely based on the expedient of being able to influence the drafting of the new constitution.[29]

The narrowly adopted compromise constitution of the Fourth Republic of 1946 nominally sought to emulate the British system in fostering the development of disciplined political parties. In practice, though, the system was little altered from that of the Third Republic. The president would be a mere figurehead, while parties remained weak and deeply factionalized. Its function served, the tripartite coalition between the SFIO, the PCF, and the MRP lasted only a year before the Communists were thrown out. Disgusted at the rejection of his American-style presidential constitution, De Gaulle went into outright opposition, subsequently setting up the RPF as a party of the center right. Membership of the RPF took off, reaching upward of 400,000, putting the party second only to the PCF. The party's support was drawn "mainly from the mass of uncommitted French citizens" in "formerly unpoliticized social strata"; or to use this book's terminology, from *available* voters. Even as the RPF grew as an electoral force, it flouted one of the key rules of French politics, refusing to recruit its candidates from the *notables* – men of independent local esteem, lawyers, doctors, businessmen, and the like. De Gaulle wanted a personal mandate, not representatives with their own local agendas to push. He had little affection for the idea of a parliamentary party, preferring instead to forge a "direct bond" (*accord direct*) between himself and the people through mass communication. The RPF would remain a personalist electoral vehicle for the general. However, with De Gaulle refusing to outsource some of the costs of to local bosses mobilization to local bosses in this way, the RPF relied heavily on paid advertising and was perennially in debt. After a brief moment in the sun, it would disband.[30]

By not launching his party before the settlement of the constitution, De Gaulle had missed his shot. On his resignation, he had expected to be recalled by the people within a year. Even if that was what the people wanted, however, De Gaulle was now easily excluded by the institutional set up he had failed to prevent. The RPF subsequently performed strongly in municipal elections in 1947, commanding 40 percent of the vote, but this success came both too late and too early. Having missed the boat in 1946, he might have been better to wait until closer to the next general election to launch his campaign. De Gaulle could claim that he had popular support, but the MRP and the Socialists were under no compunction to call fresh elections for the national assembly until 1951, and so they let De Gaulle and the Gaullists stew. For the next two years, the RPF continued to hold mass rallies on a scale unmatched by any contemporaries, except perhaps the Communists. De Gaulle's opponents worried, sometimes genuinely, about a new Fascist movement. The Communists accused De Gaulle of seeking "a plebiscitary dictatorship." The RPF won the most seats of any party in 1951, but a coalition of center-left and liberal parties kept it out of power. De Gaulle's preference was to remain in dignified opposition, but the lure of office proved too much for many of those in his party who had won seats in parliament. Keeping the party united in opposition proved an insurmountable challenge. With his party broke and hemorrhaging support, De Gaulle effectively shuttered the RPF in 1953. The next five years would be among his quietist, as he remained in virtual exile in his modest country home some 150 miles east of Paris.[31]

Through the mid-1950s, as De Gaulle remained on the political margins, France sunk deeper into political crisis. The problem for France on this occasion was not economic. Rather the main issue was that just as the war against Germany ended, France was engulfed in a civil war of its own. While Britain swiftly withdrew from most of its colonial possessions after the war, France stubbornly sought to hold on to hers. In the wake of victory in Europe, uprisings were brutally put down in Algeria in 1945 (20,000 deaths) and in Madagascar in 1947 (80,000 deaths). Indochina presented an even more vexing problem. Leading domestic resistance to the Japanese occupation, the Vietminh had established a strong foothold in northern Vietnam (Tonkin), which Ho Chi Minh sought to leverage into independence. The French resisted, believing that independence for Vietnam would spark of the dissolution of its empire. At significant cost, France gradually began to retake control, but with its decisive defeat at the Battle of Dien Bien Phu in 1954, the war was lost. France's empire had begun to disintegrate and things would quickly get worse. Just three months after the International Geneva Conference had concluded, the Algerian National Liberation Front (FLN) launched a massive escalation of its resistance. With a tenth of its population of ten million being of French origin, the so-called *pied-noirs*, and formally part of the French republic, Algeria had a very different status to that of Indochina or anywhere else in the Empire. France itself was in crisis. The Army assumed de facto control of the Algerian government, in effective defiance of Paris. The prospect of a military overthrow of the government in France was very real. It was Algeria's descent into chaos that precipitated De Gaulle's recall, in March 1958 thousands taking to the streets chanting: "Let us call de Gaulle!" De Gaulle again relied heavily on direct communication with the masses rather than on any intermediaries or complex party organization. He was much better on radio than on television, but he understood the value of the medium for communicating directly with the people. Sensing the greater effectiveness of his direct approach after the Algerian crisis in contrast to 1946, he said that "in 1946 I did not have television."[32]

De Gaulle was made premier by acclamation for the second time. He tacitly accepted decolonization, removing a major political roadblock in France's political development and at the same time, reasserted France's pivotal position within Europe. Doctrinally, though, beyond the notion of French nationalism, "Gaullism was ... a black sheet." De Gaulle was guided simply by the notion that he alone had sufficiently selfless dedication to France to deserve to rule it. De Gaulle used his unique position to push through a new Constitution more to his liking. Institutionally, the presidency of the Fifth Republic Constitution was the fulfillment of his conception of a direct bond between him and the people. As he reflected later on, he believed he had created something like "a popular monarchy." The president was not chosen by parliament, but indirectly by a broad electoral college. The president alone formed the government – including its prime minister. De Gaulle, however, was still not satisfied, later pushing for an amendment that would have the president directly elected by the people. In large part, the direct election of the presidency was an attack on the parties, which De Gaulle once argued to his cabinet, "are beyond redemption." Although the president could call a referendum on any matter concerning the "organisation of the public authorities," this did not extend to referenda on constitutional amendments, which were supposed to be previously approved by both houses of parliament. Needless to say, the legislative parties refused to sign away their own power. De Gaulle faced them down, dissolving parliament and calling for fresh elections instead. The 1962 referendum on adopting direct presidential elections passed 62 to 38 percent and the Gaullists – this time as the Union for the New Republic (UNR) – won a handsome majority in the general election. That November, De Gaulle said of his victory, "I wanted to smash the parties. I was the only one who could do it and the only one to believe that it was possible at the time I chose. I've been proved right against everybody. I declared war on the parties. I shall refrain from declaring war on the party leaders. All they want is to regain a ministerial appointment." Much as the presidency created the possibility for party building through patronage, De Gaulle had little patience for this process. In a not untypical rage at the disappointing results of the municipal elections of 1965, De Gaulle criticized his erstwhile Gaullist party allies: "There you all are worrying about electoral questions, just thinking of political parties. But that is not the future; the future is the authority of the President."[33]

Despite the breakout of student protests in May 1968, De Gaulle remained popular across much of the country. Believing it was time to seek a fresh mandate, he forced through another referendum that would have emasculated the Senate and weakened the power of local *notables* in favor of a new regional level of government. Staking his presidency on the outcome of the 1969 referendum, defeat meant an end to his rule. Yet his institutionalization of a uniquely strong presidency would have implications for French politics for decades to come. Parties remained weak and, in effect, fragmented into personalist electoral vehicles designed to capture the presidency. De Gaulle's successor, George Pompidou, won election in 1969 almost by default as the inheritor of the still dominant Gaullist bloc. Without its charismatic leader, however, the Gaullist party, since renamed the Union for the Defense of the Republic (UDR), fractured. Valérie Giscard D'Estaing, a prominent aide of both De Gaulle and Pompidou, had already formed the Independent Republicans (RI) as his personal political vehicle. Although the RI remained in coalition with the UDR, the ambitious Giscard was positioning himself for a run at the presidency in 1974. Giscard won in large part thanks to the backing of the UDR leadership of Jacques Chirac. However, the election was perhaps most notable for the resurgence of the French left, led by François Mitterrand.[34]

Tactically astute but with the ideological consistency of a blancmange, Mitterrand wanted power above all else. Beginning on the right, accepting a position under the Vichy regime, getting elected to parliament though the backing of right and center-right parties, he then migrated to the left, in part simply because De Gaulle occupied the place he wanted on the right. Although the introduction of direct elections for the presidency raised the possibility of a personalistic candidate winning office, without De Gaulle's charisma, for most others this meant some kind of organizational backing. Mitterrand himself was terrible on television, although effective enough in public rallies. Although he pushed De Gaulle to a runoff for reelection at the head of a left coalition in 1965, he was prevented from running in 1969, when each of the small parties of the left ran their own candidates. Mitterrand came to the conclusion that neither he, nor the left in general, had any chance of success "without . . . big parties." Mitterrand's goal would not be ideological unity but identification of Mitterrand himself as the tool for the left to win. He accomplished his goal in 1981, but never the nationalist figure that De Gaulle was, his governing coalition soon fragmented, and he was forced to work with an opposition legislature again dominated by Chirac. Chirac had himself taken over leadership of the Gaullist UDR in 1974. Having supported Giscard for the presidency, Chirac was named prime minister. Serving from 1974 to 1976, however, he chafed under the domineering and pretentious Giscard. In 1976, Chirac in turn took his majority faction out of the UDR, creating a new organization – the Rally for the Republic (RPR) – which was "dedicated to promoting Chirac's presidential ambitions." The RPR put Chirac in the Parisian mayor's office in 1977 and it had a half-million members by 1978. As the dominant figure in the capital, Chirac finally succeeded Mitterrand to the presidency in 1995.[35]

The unwritten rule of French politics was that "control of a political party produces a natural advantage for a candidate seeking election to the presidency." A pattern thus seemed to be set, whereby prominent political leaders aiming for the presidency had to create or take over a political party and deal with its perennial factionalism. Emmanuel Macron would change this calculus. A precocious student, Macron throve in France's elitist educational system. With a degree from France's prestigious *Ecole Nationale d'Administration* (ENA) – a school he would shutter as president in 2021 – Macron was early marked out for success. Initially moving into the esteemed Finance Ministry and rising under the patronage of François Hollande, in 2007, Macron briefly registered as a member of the Socialist Party with the intention of running for the parliamentary region surrounding the holiday home belonging to his wife at Le Tourquet in Brittany. The party, however, refused to put Macron up. Macron then made the surprise decision to quit government and take up a position at the Rothschild & Co investment bank. He could not stay away from politics for long, however.[36]

When the 2016 French presidential election is discussed from the perspective of populism, it is usually the names of Marine Le Pen, leader of the nationalist Front National party, and Jean-Luc Mélanchon, head of the radical *France Insoumise* ("unbowed France") party, which come up. As political scientist Alastair Cole notes, however, a focus on policy or rhetoric doesn't get us very far in distinguishing the candidates. He writes "the theme of the 'people against the elites' is a constant of contemporary French ... politics." Certainly, both Le Pen and Mélanchon are the head of personalistic and antiestablishment political parties. Yet neither compares to the degree to which Macron pitched himself as an outsider to the political system. "I can reach voters who are outside of normal politics" insisted Macron when pitching the idea of En Marche! as a center-left movement to Hollande in early 2016. An internal Macron campaign poll suggested that people reported that the biggest problem in France was "the politicians." The political class was perceived as elitist and out of touch. This view may have had some truth to it, with one of the contenders in the Republican Party primary famously gaffing that he guessed the price of a *pan au chocolat* was about 10 or 15 cents – the real price being nearly ten times that. It was no great challenge for Macron to blame the country's problems on the vacuous "old two party system."[37]

Macron, somewhat of a scholar-politician himself, saw political leadership in Weberian terms. Eschewing parties altogether, he would be the charismatic leader par excellence. In an autumn 2016 interview, Macron said that he did not envision a "normal" presidency; this, for him, was Hollande's problem. Macron argued that the presidency should be "Jupiterian," evoking the Roman king of the gods. Also channeling De Gaulle, he felt the presidency should have a mystique that set it above petty political squabbles. Running outside of any of the main parties, and with just months between his formal decision to run and the election itself, even had he wanted to, there was no time to build a bureaucratic political organization. Macron's 2016 campaign was "constructed not according to a checklist of policies but around himself." According to journalist Adam Plowright, "Macron's movement was a highly centralised organisation built around him." One campaign worker described La République En Marche as a "ghost party." Marcon's campaign was quick and cheap. The manager of En Marche! organized the launch of the movement on a "shoestring budget." Macron traveled by second-class train. His whole campaign, as another journalist observed, had an "improvised low-cost feel to it." Macron frequently called his campaign workers "kids." In this, there was considerable learning from the Obama campaign of 2008 – in fact, one can't read about En Marche without thinking immediately of the strategy of Obama's political strategist, David Plouffe. Indeed, Plouffe and his successor on the campaign, Jim Messina, were consulted by Macron's team. Some of Macron's campaign managers were Harvard educated and themselves worked for Obama in 2008.[38]

The opposition that Macron faced was hopelessly fragmented. On the left, not long before the election, Hollande, the already unpopular incumbent

Socialist president saw his approval rating plummet to just 4 percent in the wake of a journalistic exposé of some of his gratuitously crass views; seven candidates stepped in for the Socialist nomination, the leader of the pack being Prime Minister Manuel Valls. He, however, eventually lost out to the unexceptional, Benoît Hamon, a moderate who was advised by the now famous French economist Thomas Piketty – on whom more shortly. On the right, former Prime Minister François Fillon won the Republican party nomination. His campaign was undone by revelations that he had put his wife and adult children on the government payroll. In spite of the weakness of his opponents, Macron barely made it into the runoff, winning less than a quarter of the first round vote, indicating just how fragile his own personalistic movement was.

Facing down the threat of the leader of the far-right, Marine Le Pen, Macron became in 2017 the hope of liberals worldwide. Macron's moderate, reformist, even technocratic approach to government may well be to the liking of many intellectuals (though not, perhaps, of the predominantly leftist French professoriate). Yet his strategy was thoroughly populist, no less so – in fact more so – than that of his supposed political antithesis, Donald Trump. What this suggests is not that we should expect Macron himself to all of a sudden start deporting immigrants or embracing protectionism. However, by fully sweeping away France's moderate, if moribund, political parties, he may inadvertently have made the populist strategy even more affordable for future populist candidates whom liberals may like altogether less. Macron retained power comfortably in 2022, but being ineligible for a third term, who or what will follow remains a troubling problem.

THE ECONOMICS OF RESENTMENT

Economist Thomas Piketty's 2014 book, *Capital in the Twenty First Century*, was a minor sensation. Through the painstaking collection and analysis of tax records, estate records, and other data from the United States and elsewhere, Piketty's surprise best seller confirmed what many people had come to feel: economic inequality has reached almost unprecedented levels. Although measurements of inequality have been around for a long time, Piketty's work was notable for its ability to show not just that the top 10 percent of the population were becoming increasingly better off than the rest, but also that the top 1 percent were accumulating wealth even faster than them, and that the top 0.1 percent was getting richer again. The slogan of the 2011 Occupy Wall Street movement, "[w]e are the 99 percent!" had a basis in fact. Contemporary inequality, Piketty showed, is approaching levels not seen since the noxiously corrupt Gilded Age or Belle Époque of the late nineteenth century. Moreover, with his coauthors, Piketty showed in the "elephant curve" that when looked at globally, the gains of recent economic growth had been distributed very unevenly. At the low end of the world's income distribution – making up the bulk of the elephant's hump – millions of people had begun to escape extreme poverty. At the opposite end of the distribution – those in the elephant's trunk – the already rich had become richer again. However, in the valley between hump and trunk, those in the middle of the global income distribution had seen nothing but stagnation. The working and lower middle classes in America and Europe have lost ground to the elite on the one hand and have seen their relative economic status eroded by the rise of once marginalized minorities and immigrants on the other. Could it be mere coincidence that these socioeconomic developments and the rise of populism occurred together?[39]

We may as well let Piketty answer. For him, as for many commentators, the answer is self-evident. In his follow-up 2020 book, *Capital and Ideology*, he argues that these interrelated economic changes – namely rising inequality and the stagnation of the middle class – have caused the success of populists in the West. The people, especially the once economically secure white working and lower middle class, are mad as hell – why shouldn't they be? Unhappy with the policies that have seen their relative living standards stagnate or decline, voters have abandoned the bureaucratic parties that delivered them, turning to the rabble rousers like France's Le Pen and Britain's Nigel Farage, who give voice to their anxieties. Promises to "take back control" speak to the nostalgia of people who have lost something – real or imagined – that they want back. The vote for Farage's UKIP, and later Brexit, coming primarily from older, less-educated, and less-cosmopolitan Britons is typically painted as a revolt of the left behind, of the traditional "somewheres" who identify with England and the Empire against the "anywheres" defined by their globalism and Europhilia. Populism is the additive result of these many, many individual disappointments with the status quo.[40]

Even though populists in Western Europe have had greater electoral success in the past decade than at any time since the Great Depression, great caution is required in asserting a causal relationship between economic distress and political outcomes. Populism has been completely absent in some of the countries hit worst by the Global Financial Crisis, such as Ireland and Portugal, while it has been a more successful strategy in states such as Denmark and Switzerland, which escaped the crisis relatively unscathed. The mediating factor, this chapter suggests, is how structural economic change – financialization, labor market opening, etc. – has affected political party organization over the longer term. In some cases, programmatic parties have successfully adapted to these changes; in others, they have not. Economic change affects populist success, therefore, but not in the way that existing approaches suggest.

Economic change matters because it has disrupted the networks of social ties in which people are embedded. Developments in the organization of productive economic activity, of transport, and of communications technology have radically altered people's social landscapes. People just don't work, socialize, or live in the same ways that they used to. It is these changes, rather than any alteration to people's value systems, that have most deeply affected how politics are organized. In those polities where people are no longer attached to bureaucratic political parties, they are available for mobilization through mass communication instead. Macroeconomics matters because of how it affects the availability of voters; because of how it affects the microeconomics of winning and keeping power. It is true that parties in much of Western Europe today are different kinds of organizations to those of their postwar predecessors. Certainly, they have fewer formal members. Yet for the most part, the old parties continue to dominate the political space across Western Europe. What explains this resilience?

I think there are two reasons. First, even as bureaucratic parties such as Britain's Labour Party and the Conservative Party, or Germany's SPD and the CDU have lost their multifaceted connections to voters through their mass party memberships, they remain internally effective and disciplined organizations. Like firms, they are organizations with a purpose; not to make a profit but to gain and keep power. In most countries, these professional organizations remain the only ones to have the capacity to win and control government at multiple levels and in multiple territories – the city and county councils, the landers, the departments, the regions. For sure, people care about national politics. But for many people, local government remains very significant. In a small country like Ireland, even national politics is decidedly local. The man who today represents the constituency where I'm from, grew up right around the corner. Members of parliament like him, councilors, aldermen, and so on perform the day-to-day tasks that link people and the state. This is not about providing corrupt, privatized goods to political clients. Rather, a major function of local politicians, and in some contexts even national ones, is to provide perfectly kosher minor interventions on behalf of constituents; letters of reference; advice on zoning laws; negotiating, legally, with a faceless bureaucracy on behalf of the regular citizen. The aldermen, councilors, state legislators – not to mention the student party leaders and volunteers – who perform this work are poorly compensated. This activity thus amounts to an indirect subsidy - a transaction cost - that bureaucratic parties can bear but that thinly staffed populist ones cannot. Populist political organizations, almost by definition, do not have the capacity to infiltrate government in this way. They lack these kinds of mundane but costly links between people and the state. Bureaucratic parties, in short, continue to serve important functions even as they have lost their mass memberships. To the extent that one-time personalized parties begin to do these things, to organize the pursuit of power in this way, they cease to be populist.

A second reason is that parties also continue to nurture intellectual and political talent. It took some time for parties to reorient themselves away from mass recruitment of members toward the recruitment of political professionals. Parties are not passive entities that simply wait for people to join. Parties, as I've said, are like firms competing in a marketplace. They need people with talent in order to beat their rivals. At one time, of course, politics was simply the occupation of the aristocracy. No one better encapsulated that aristocratic sense of noblesse oblige than Churchill, whose father was a noted Conservative cabinet member and whose ancestors include the Duke of Marlborough. Politics was a devotion. Many students at Harvard or Yale, Oxford or Cambridge want to get rich. But many more are already rich. For them, parties provide a route to power and status. Politics may still attract the idealistic amateur, for whom money doesn't matter, but for some time it has been increasingly professionalized. National politics pays well, even when that income is entirely legal. It can be a surprisingly stable career in its own right. Politics, even if it is a career with risks – all politicians lose elections – can also lead to opportunities in the legal, business, and journalistic fields. Parties can thus attract the talented and hardworking from all social classes. Extraordinary individuals might see a narrow path to power – a populist path – entirely outside the world of political parties. For most people in the West with political ambitions, however, there is a more straightforward route. Climb the party ladder, one rung at a time.

7

Parties, Factions, and Populism

> *In America the great moving forces are the parties. The government counts for less than in Europe, the parties count for more; and the fewer have become their principles and the fainter their interest in those principles, the more perfect has become their organization.*
>
> James Bryce[1]

> Donald Trump: *"I love that. That's what I am, a popularist."*
> Steve Bannon: *"No, no. It's populist."*
> Donald Trump: *"Yeah, yeah. A popularist."*[2]

BOARDROOM COUPS AND HOSTILE TAKEOVERS

Factionalism is a feature of almost all democratic party systems, but it is especially noteworthy in American politics. Readers well versed in political science will know that electoral systems shape patterns of party formation and competition. Electoral systems with proportional representation and multi-member districts, like those found in Western Europe, tend to produce multi-party systems. In contrast, in a first-past-the-post single-member district system like America's, the more stable equilibrium is for a two-party system with each party – like a multinational conglomerate – composed of multiple subunits. The legendary Democratic Speaker of the House, Tip O'Neill, once joked that if America was France, "the Democratic Party would be five parties." Only for relatively brief periods have more cohesive interest groups maintained their own parties, some of the best known being The People's Party, the Know-Nothing Party, the Free Soil Party, and the States' Rights Democrats. More commonly, in the United States, such groups have emerged and remained as internal party factions: Copperheads, Locofocos, Boll Weevils, Barnburners, and Blue Dogs; Mugwumps, Stalwarts, Half Breeds, and Tea Partiers, along with so many others. Within these semi-formal groupings there are often further factional divisions, with geography, religion, and even personality both dividing and uniting these various political camps. How does such party factionalism relate to the use of populism as a political strategy?[3]

Because of America's institutional setup – not just the first-past-the-post single-member district system but also its complex Electoral College – it is extremely difficult for a populist from outside the major parties to come to power. Not since Theodore Roosevelt's runnerup showing in 1912 has a third-party candidate threatened to break the hold of the famous duopoly. For all the interest they arouse, no third-party candidate – Robert La Follette in 1924 (16.6 percent of the vote), Strom Thurmond in 1948 (2.4 percent), George Wallace in 1968 (13.5 percent), John Anderson in 1980 (6.6. percent), or Ross Perot in 1992 (18.9 percent) – has come close. Rather, in modern America, it is more cost-effective for a populist to seek to take over an existing party, and then use it as a vehicle to capture power. This strategy was epitomized by Trump's "hostile takeover" of the GOP and subsequent march to the presidency in 2016. However, this populist strategy has only been successful under circumstances that have proven historically rare.

What exactly are these circumstances? We'll consider several frequently cited factors, including the structure of the nomination procedure, changes in communications technology, and shifts in campaign fundraising. In recent years, each of these developments has lowered the cost of mobilizing voters directly as compared with rival strategies; each helped Trump in his bid for power. However, when looked at over a longer period than just the 2016 election cycle, these factors alone are insufficient. Along with them must be considered the effect of party factionalism itself. Party factions compete fiercely for supremacy. Faction leaders wheel and deal, backstab and undermine. Factions compete for a share of the potential spoils, and the successful candidate is the one who can put together a winning coalition of a party's major groupings. Bitter as these factional contests can be, however, like the "boardroom coups" they resemble, they are usually insider fights among those with a shared goal: party victory. However, when a party's rival cliques fail to come to any sort of agreement, they are susceptible to take over from without. American populists appeal over the heads of the factional elite directly to party members (or primary voters). By lowering the threshold of victory to a smaller plurality, factionalism has been a critical ingredient in the success of the populist strategy in American politics.

THE RISE AND FALL OF THE PARTY FACTIONS

Both of America's major parties are large, often unwieldy amalgams. Never was this truer than with FDR's New Deal coalition, which relied on a carefully curated, though ideologically incongruous, grouping of northern ethnic urban machines, labor unions, growing northern black populations, and southern segregationists. As we saw in Chapter 4, however, power was a great salve to these factional divisions. FDR could use the party machinery to keep the factions quiescent and hold populist challengers like Huey Long at bay. The Republican Party was no more ideologically coherent, being riven by isolationist and internationalist wings. However, locked out of power after FDR's 1932 victory, it found factional reconciliation harder to achieve. It was this factional division, in fact, that allowed a true populist takeover of the GOP machinery for the first time in its existence.

Until just a year before the 1940 election, Wendell Willkie was a little-known utilities executive and registered Democrat. Never having held elective office, Willkie had a miniscule organization, with no clientele in the typical sense. He thus had no hope of gradually accumulating the support of delegates in party primaries. He concentrated instead on building up his political profile through public speaking events and magazine writings. Much as Willkie lacked a faction within the party, he had a genuine mass following, even if one wag could jest that his "grassroots" support was limited to the lawns of "the country clubs of America." We do know that his pro-business (anti–New Deal) and internationalist message pulled in a large number of liberal student volunteers, many of them from the Ivy League.[4]

Yet the main factor that allowed Willkie to become the party's candidate was the fragmentation of the GOP isolationist wing between several other candidates, including at that time, both Thomas Dewey and Robert Taft. With little competition on the internationalist flank of the party, Willkie could let the other candidates do most of the work eliminating one another. When the convention came, Wilkie could pose as the best choice for the internationalist faction. After the first ballot, Willkie had only 105 votes to Dewey's 360 and Taft's 189. However, Dewey and Taft still each believed they could take the top prize and so refused to work together to keep Willkie out. Willkie then had a stroke of luck. An unexpected death had put a Willkie supporter in charge of the allocation of tickets for the viewing gallery to convention. With the convention deadlocked, for want of a compromise candidate – former president Hoover wanted it but few wanted him – the crowds in the gallery chanting "[w]e want Willkie!" eventually got their way on a GOP–record sixth ballot. Like Bryan in 1896, Willkie boasted after the convention of his shoestring campaign – in this case costing him less than $4,000, which he declared he paid himself, so he was "under obligation to nobody except the people." Even after his nomination, Willkie remained an outsider, refusing the services of the GOP's "politically trained people."[5]

Despite a breathless presidential campaign that included covering some 18,789 miles by rail over just seven weeks, Willkie was resoundingly defeated. Although it is unlikely that any Republican would have unseated FDR in 1940, an important result of Willkie's failed campaign was that the GOP leadership tightened up control over its nomination process. This isn't to say that no one attempted to replicate Willkie's populist strategy. General Douglas MacArthur, hero of the Pacific War, repeatedly threatened to wield his enormous popularity to take the Republican ticket at some point between 1944 and 1952. FDR had long seen in the vainglorious general a potential Napoleon. In 1944, however, the year MacArthur came closest, the control of Dewey's New York machine over the GOP was unassailable, and the general's boomlet was over before it started. By 1948, much as MacArthur's star was still waxing, it seems that the people liked him better in the form of an imperial proconsul than as a democratically elected Caesar. MacArthur just could not escape his reputation as a cockalorum and a belligerent, a disposition ill-fitted to a nation exhausted from more than five years of all-out war.[6]

Defeated again in 1948, Dewey and his internationalist faction still retained control over the GOP machinery, and in 1952, secured the nomination of General Dwight D. Eisenhower over that of Taft and others. As the general who gained most credit for winning the Second World War, Eisenhower was immensely popular, of that there is no doubt. But Eisenhower never seems to have had any intention of taking his campaign directly to the people. Like General Grant in 1868, Eisenhower liked to believe that the presidency was a continuation of his service to the country: He would accept office if asked, but he would not overtly seek the privilege. His winning of the nomination was primarily the result of backroom deals, not public opinion. In fact, his narrow victory in the delegate count at the Republican National Convention in Chicago in July 1952 owed a significant debt to the machinations of the junior senator from California, a young Richard Nixon, who schemed to turn delegates away from both Taft and California's favorite son, Governor Earl Warren. Nixon was rewarded with the vice presidential slot. Although a five-star general and war hero like MacArthur, Eisenhower could not have been more different in temperament or appeal. Eisenhower too was a conservative, but he was also deeply practical. Much as he was cognizant of the Communist threat, he had no desire to risk a further devastating global conflagration. Domestically, he may not have agreed with some New Deal–Fair Deal policies on a philosophical level, but even by the 1950s, social security and other elements of the welfare state had become the new status quo. Rolling them back would have been, as Eisenhower himself saw it, the radical option.

In power, Eisenhower maintained a modest course. With the support of a majority of the party, he saw off the challenge of the firebrand senator from Wisconsin, Joseph McCarthy. McCarthy rose to prominence as an anti-Communist zealot, accusing hundreds of civil servants and prominent public figures of Red sympathies. At his peak, he was so popular as to be beyond criticism. But McCarthy was a bomb-thrower. He could be affable and was well-liked by many, but he was not a party man. Eisenhower was sure McCarthy was after his job. The president's strategy was to give McCarthy the rope to hang himself. When McCarthy took on the Army, public opinion of the senator caught up with that of the party leadership. The Senate moved to censure McCarthy and he quickly faded into drink, obscurity, and an early death. Even had McCarthy had the constitution to avoid this rash behavior, it is all but impossible to imagine how he might have ridden a populist strategy to the GOP nomination, never mind the White House. McCarthy's popularity was never so great as to threaten the party bosses' control. Whatever voters may have thought of him, powerful party factions who owed little or nothing to McCarthy still controlled the delegates needed for the nomination.

By the end of the 1950s, there was not much daylight between the parties on policy, which were respectively under the control of moderate office-seeking factions. As Richard Nixon would comment in a live television presidential debate with John F. Kennedy in September 1960, "our disagreement is not about the goals for America but only about the means to reach those goals." Yet so disruptive would the social turbulence of the next decade be that it is often viewed as the dawn of modern American populism. That conclusion is possibly correct but for the wrong reasons. On the Republican side, hardcore conservatives, still smarting from the purging of the Old Guard under the leadership of Dewey and Eisenhower in the 1950s, exploited the fracturing of the party's leadership in the wake of Nixon's 1960 defeat to make a renewed bid for power, eventually succeeding in nominating Arizona senator, Barry Goldwater, for president in 1964. Although no intellectual himself, Goldwater had become the voice of an improvised libertarian ideology that appealed to ideological conservatives. Goldwater could pack out massive speaking venues and acquired an almost messianic appeal for voters on the right. Yet Goldwater was no populist. Populism is not, as I've argued, just a synonym for conservativism or libertarianism. Goldwater appealed to "regular people," but this hardly made him distinctive. Moreover, Goldwater was not the reluctant "draftee" he made himself out to be. Rather, his nomination was the product of careful work by conservative operatives like Cliff White and community organizers like Phyllis Schlafly. Conservatives took over the GOP's youth wing, penetrated the party, and secured the supremacy of one faction over its rivals. In short, Goldwater did not win the nomination by appealing directly to the masses, but through a well-orchestrated conservative factional takeover of the Republican Party machinery.[7]

In fact, if anyone was a populist among the Republican presidential hopefuls in 1964, it was New York governor, Nelson A. Rockefeller. Scion of the Standard Oil family, the fabulously wealthy Rockefeller eschewed organization, relying instead on his own money and direct public appeals. As William Roberts, one of the men brought in to run his primary campaign in California, put it, they "went around the party apparatus" to appeal directly to "the general voter in the Republican Party." Yet for all his wealth Rocky, as he was known, could not compete with the party organization that Goldwater's would-be kingmakers then controlled. The gates were firmly closed to a populist takeover of the GOP. Insider networking and politicking remained the paths to power, as Nixon – the great accumulator of chits – would demonstrate in 1968. Ever since his vice presidency, Nixon had been an indefatigable campaigner for the Republican Party. Even out of office after his defeat to Kennedy in 1960,

Nixon didn't let up, stacking up political IOUs across the country. When Ronald Reagan, then governor of California, sought the nomination in 1964 over the heads of the predominant factions in the party, he found the door firmly shut; similarly, when he tried to turn the Mississippi delegation in his favor in the lead up to the 1968 Republican National Convention, the southern party chairman told him he "had better try where you have a few favors owing." In spite of his popularity in 1976, he was still unable to unseat then President Gerald Ford as the GOP's candidate. Ford, the former minority leader of the House, still held the organizational strings in the nominating process. Reagan finally concentrated on building up his support within the party, delivering speeches for candidates in obscure venues he called the "mashed potato circuit."[8]

For Democrats also, right through the 1950s and 60s, securing the presidential nomination meant gaining the support of state party brokers and bosses. Even in the 1950s, only around a dozen states held primary elections to choose convention delegates. At the convention itself, candidates' teams dangled vice presidential tickets, cabinet positions, and other sinecures to turn a state's delegates. However, events of the late 1960s would massively increase the direct role of voters in the nomination process. Controversy arose in 1968 when Lyndon Johnson, the consummate party insider, sought to secure the nomination of his vice president, Hubert Humphrey, to succeed him. Johnson's popularity had gone into steep decline as the Vietnam War was scaled up, and there was little enthusiasm for a Humphrey administration that would surely continue the same policies. Ironically, however, having so centralized power and patronage in the presidency, Johnson had substantially reduced the leverage of the old Democratic Party city and state machines. The result was that the contest for the election was thrown open to the influence of outside groups, especially those from the anti-war left. New York senator and brother of JFK, Robert Kennedy, still only forty-two, and Eugene McCarthy, the senator from Minnesota became the popular favorites of the peace movement. McCarthy won the early primaries but by May, Kennedy's campaign was gaining momentum. He won contested primaries in Indiana and Nebraska and then on June 4, the big prize of California. Tragically, however, on his way to the press room of the Ambassador Hotel in Los Angeles shortly after midnight on the day of his California triumph, Kennedy was shot dead by a Palestinian radical. Kennedy's devastated liberal supporters rolled in behind McCarthy, but when the delegates gathered at the Democratic National Convention in Chicago in late August, the party organization endorsed Humphrey as per Johnson's instructions, even though the vice president hadn't won a single primary. With only about a third of the convention delegates up for grabs in the primaries, Humphrey could dismiss them with confidence: "Any man who goes into a primary isn't fit to be president. You have to be crazy to go into a primary. A primary now is worse than the torture of the rack."[9]

The party bosses appeared to be in control, but all was not well. Given the near impossibility of winning a contested race against the wishes of the party hierarchy, the segregationist Democratic Alabama governor George Wallace had pulled out to contest the presidential race as a third-party candidate for The American Independent Party. A real populist, Wallace had little money and no organizational machinery outside of his home state to draw upon, but as one journalist at the time put it, Wallace was "the ablest demagogue of our time." Wallace won five states in the Deep South, netting 13.5 percent of the vote, the most of any third-party candidate since Robert La Follette in 1924. Wallace's campaign was most notable for the split in the Democratic Party that it represented. With white Southern voters abandoning the Democrats, there was to be a substantial rebalancing of factional forces within the party.[10]

It was in this context that Democratic Party activists' pressure for reform went through. After the debacle of Chicago, reformers insisted that voters should be free to select their desired candidate. Backroom deals, easily manipulated caucuses, unit rules, and other procedures all gave the party elite too much control. In 1969, the DNC created the Commission on Party Structure and Delegate Selection to review the party's nomination process. With the old Southern, segregationist wing now virtually excised from the party, the commission was controlled by Northern liberals, most notably, South Dakota senator, George McGovern. After two years of hearings and deliberations, the commission concluded that the selection process should be radically opened up in order to obtain greater representation of minorities, women, and young people (under thirty). In future, primary elections rather than state organizations would determine the selection of a majority of the party's convention delegates. However demographically unrepresentative the previous system was, to some contemporary critics of the reforms, the new order introduced in its place "quota democracy." Organized labor in particular was opposed to the change, which could only weaken its influence in the Democratic Party establishment. Historian Rick Perlstein dryly observes that the idealistic reformers of the McGovern-Fraser Commission couldn't imagine that the old system had any virtues at all, that there might be a disadvantage to selecting a presidential candidate in a forum in which "activists were overrepresented."[11]

As anticipated, the primary reforms substantially weakened the hold of party bosses over the nominating process. However, the result was not really majority rule. Rather, influence would instead devolve on "interest groups," most of which were defined by demographic criteria. Brown historian Robert Self writes that the first presidential candidate selection process to occur under the new rules unsurprisingly "descended nearly into incoherence." At the 1972 Democratic National Convention, feminist Shirley Chisolm, Black leader Jesse Jackson, and the returned segregationist George Wallace, incongruously took their turns at the podium. Excluded from any chance of victory in 1968, under the new open Democratic Party primary system in 1972, Wallace could now mount an insurgent campaign from within the party. However, on May 15, Wallace was shot multiple times by a deranged loner named Arthur Bremer. The shooting left Wallace paralyzed, which effectively ended his campaign. In any case, even though Wallace had won some 3.35 million votes compared to left-wing favorite McGovern, who obtained just 2.2 million, McGovern went into the convention with 410 delegates compared to Wallace's 325. That is, for far fewer votes, McGovern received more delegates. Other moderates, Hubert Humphrey and Henry "Scoop" Jackson, similarly fell by the wayside as did the pioneering Chisolm. It was telling of how devolved the selection process had become that Chicago Mayor Richard Daley, who had in effect chosen the winner in Chicago in 1968, was compelled to sit out the 1973 convention because his delegate slate was not deemed representative enough of Blacks and women. The "great broad middle" of the Democratic Party lost out to the representatives of the new social movements.[12]

BARBARIANS AT THE GATES

Although Wallace failed, not by coincidence it was another southerner who took advantage of the more open post-1972 nominating system to forge the first populist path to the presidency since Andrew Jackson. In 1975–76, Jimmy Carter knew the Northern liberal Democratic Party leadership was arrayed against him. One of his advisers aptly warned, "[m]y feeling is that unless we can put together a first ballot victory or damn close to it, this party will deny us the nomination ... Popular with the elites, we are not." Carter was no great orator, but he appreciated the need to connect directly with voters if he was going to have a chance. Running for governor of Georgia in 1970, Carter would arrive early at his rallies so he could shake hands with every person entering the room. He couldn't exactly replicate this strategy on a nationwide basis in 1976, but presaging the approach used to such effect by Obama in 2007–08, Carter went all-in in the early primary states. If prior to 1972 the main function of primaries had been to demonstrate viability (as was the case for Catholic candidate, John F. Kennedy, in winning Protestant West Virginia in 1960), Carter's campaign team recognized that this was the first time that primaries would have a decisive impact on the nomination. Wins in the early contests, especially in Iowa, could generate the necessary momentum – "the Big Mo" as George H. W. Bush would later call it – to maintain the long and expensive campaign ahead. A few early wins could both replenish his limited coffers and establish him as a credible candidate in later contests. Even if short on cash and factional backing, one advantage Carter did have over his primary opponents was time. Unlike most of his competitors for the Democratic nomination in 1975–76, Georgia's single-term limit on the governorship meant that he was free to campaign full time, while his main opponents were all occupied with official duties. Even before the primaries began, Carter had visited 250 cities in 46 states over 260 days.[13]

Critically, Iowa holds an open caucus rather than a primary. Caucuses are private events run by the parties, while primaries are run by state and local governments. Caucuses are less representative and have lower turnouts than primaries, meaning that even relatively small shifts can have an outsized impact.

Ostensibly favoring insider candidates, their relatively smaller scale means that they can provide access for well-organized grassroots campaigns like those of Carter and Obama. When Carter ran, the Democratic caucus was only 30,000 strong. They were the kinds of numbers that suited the personal, face-to-face, but low cost connections Carter liked to make with voters. Carter began campaigning in 1975, visiting small towns that most presidential candidates would have previously ignored. Carter won a plurality in the Iowa caucus, and by outperforming expectations, he had momentum that he could take to into future primaries. He lost Mississippi to Wallace as expected, but New Hampshire would be a better test of his viability. Ninety of Carter's Georgian friends and family, mostly self-financed, made the trip north, contacting some 10,000 primary voters in the state. Contact with a Carter family member or friend was one step removed from meeting the former governor himself, but this personal touch proved effective. Over the next month, Carter won in New Hampshire, Vermont, North Carolina, and more importantly, in Florida and Illinois. His campaign's direct approach, going around the party establishment gained Carter the nomination. Averell Harriman, an old Washington hand, was left bemused, "I don't even know Jimmy Carter," he said, "and as far as I know, none of my friends knows him, either." In the presidential race, despite being outspent by incumbent Gerald Ford, Carter still won, a feat which wouldn't be repeated until Donald Trump in 2016.[14]

Carter succeeded not only thanks to primary reforms, but because the factional alignments within the Democratic Party were still in flux in the mid-1970s. Southern whites had left the party in droves, but even in the North, the composition of the party's base was shifting rapidly. The northern part of the Democrat's New Deal coalition, the white working class, had also abandoned the party in large numbers in 1972. Remarkably, GOP stalwart Richard, Nixon won more union votes than McGovern. What was left inside the Democratic Party by 1976 was an array of interest groups organized by demography – especially minorities and feminists – who leaned much further to the left than the average former Democratic voter. Carter faced a field that was sharply divided. Democratic primary voters were split among Wallace (segregationists), Henry "Scoop" Jackson (Northern anti-bussers), Frank Church (libertarian westerners), Mo Udall (suburban liberals), and Pat Brown (environmentalists and liberals), allowing the ideologically ambiguous Cater to squeeze through the middle. Moreover, except for Wallace, they were all especially weak in the South, where the Georgian was relatively strong. It is worth noting, moreover, that Carter only won pluralities in the multicandidate primaries, taking just 39 percent of the primary ballots overall.

After Carter's crushing defeat to Reagan in 1980, the Democratic party organization tightened up its nomination rules, eliminating the requirement for delegations to be representative of gender and ethnicity. The 1981 Hunt Commission reforms front-loaded and clustered primaries together, making it more difficult for a poorly funded and little-known outsider to build momentum over the course of a long primary season. The result was to favor established, cashed-up candidates, who had the backing of the party and its massive organization. In 1984, leader of the left faction, Jesse Jackson, received more than three million votes in the primaries but could not muster a majority of the delegates. The strategy of the eventual winner, Walter Mondale, built on "organizational loyalties, institutional endorsements, and party identification." He received the backing of the AFL-CIO, the National Education Association, and many Democratic Party leaders. He was, one expert put it, the "quintessential Democratic insider." The decade from the late 1960s may have given the party machine a bruising, but by the 1980s it was recovering; it was proving that the programmatic strategy could survive in the era of primaries.[15]

For its part, the Republican Party was more united under Reagan in the 1980s than at any point in its postwar history. So popular was Reagan both inside and outside of the party organization that he could virtually choose as his successor his vice president, George H. W. Bush. By the time of Bush's reelection campaign in 1992, the establishment of both parties seemed to have all well in hand. In fact, it was in part the closure of both parties to outside influence that saw the 1992 race result in the highest third-party vote share since Roosevelt's failed run eighty years previously: that of IT business magnate, Ross Perot. Ever aware of the bottom line, even though Perot pledged $100 million of his own money to the campaign, he relied heavily on television and radio talk shows, where "the air time was free" to promote his campaign. Perot's campaign was mostly devoid of substance, with the exception of his opposition to NAFTA – the North American Free Trade Agreement – which would produce a "giant sucking sound" as jobs disappeared to Mexico. Perot's appeal was mostly just that he was not a politician associated with one of the major parties. Organizationally, his campaign was remarkably lean, with few professionals involved at all. One insider estimated that at its peak, the campaign had just a third of the number of staff of the Clinton and Bush teams. In spite of the cost to Perot himself, this was presidential campaigning on the cheap. Perot was completely skipping the process of building a political party organization.

Although the idea of a viable third-party candidate now seems improbable, it has to be acknowledged how popular Perot actually was. In May, his support hit 35 percent, putting him the lead. Remarkably, at the Democratic and Republican Party primaries in California – where nonparty members can vote for any candidate they please – Perot beat both Clinton and Bush. Yet frustrated with even the small degree of normalization – or bureaucratization – that his campaign acquired, Perot unexpectedly dropped out, leaving the field to Bush and Clinton. Although he reentered the race with a month to go, his support had now fallen to 7 percent. Americans might have been ready for an outsider but not one as flaky as this. In spite of his disastrous decision to temporarily withdraw from the race, Perot, the quintessential populist, garnered nearly a fifth of the popular vote. He did especially well, unsurprisingly, among the growing group of the electorate who described themselves as moderates and independents.[16]

The party elites were put on notice, but in the short term they rallied. Even though Clinton invested relatively little in the broader Democratic Party, it seemed that his coattails were strong enough to secure the succession of his vice president, Al Gore, as Reagan had done for Bush senior in 1988. However, in 2000, under the astute management of Karl Rove, George W. Bush built up a campaign organization to rival anything that Kennedy or Reagan had accomplished. In particular, Bush moved to court the backing of the Christian conservative right, which through the 1980s and 1990s had become an indispensable if unpredictable ally of the Republican Party. Johns Hopkins political scientist Daniel Schlozman writes that "[p]erson-to-person networks rooted in churches and linkages between elites and masses rooted in direct-mail lists survived the organizational tumult" of the 1980s and 1990s and were repurposed by Bush's wing of the party in the 2000s. Bush's 2000 presidential victory over Gore was notoriously close, but once in office, his team continued to build on its strong, if narrow, organizational foundations. Running for reelection in 2004, "[t]he Bush-Cheney campaign was a well-coordinated and tightly disciplined party organization." The RNC registered 3.4 million new voters between 2002 and 2004. Yet as the Afghanistan and Iraq wars dragged on and the economy crashed with the financial crisis of 2008, Bush's popularity ratings plummeted, and he dragged the party down with him. All the administration's key political figures, including Dick Cheney, Donald Rumsfeld, and Condoleezza Rice, were totally unviable candidates for the 2008 nomination. Perennial candidate John McCain, although hardly the favorite of the Bush wing of the party, was able to secure a relatively easy victory against his less experienced opponents. However, without access to the Bush-Rove religious-right network and only a weak organization of his own, McCain was thumped by the better funded and better organized Obama campaign.[17]

PAYING FOR THE PARTY

However, already by the time of the 2008 campaign, additional developments that lowered the cost of directly mobilizing voters were already well underway. First, consider the changes in communication technology. We've seen already that the means of mass communication available are an important constraint on the viability of the populist strategy. When the only way to communicate with the masses was through public speaking in an open forum, populism was limited to city states where large enough quorums could be physically assembled in one place. As democratic electorates grew in size, populists could draw on a combination of new technologies – the printing press, the post office, the rail network, and radio. Television, the Internet, and social networking technologies would eventually add further weapons to the populist armory. The spread of cable television, and in particular the need to generate content for 24/7 news networks provided politicians with an unprecedented medium for communicating directly with voters. All of these things massively drove down the cost of the populist strategy. As Macro Rubio observed, when he worked on Bob Dole's presidential campaign in 1996, "you needed some formal apparatus to conduct politics," whereas three decades later, "[y]ou don't need anything anymore. With social media and the [I]nternet, I can reach millions of people instantly without paying virtually anything." The upshot of this was that "[y]ou didn't *need* the party."[18]

In truth, technology was already undermining the cost advantage of the party before Rubio's political career had begun. Although television already had a place in political campaigning as early as Eisenhower's presidential run in 1952, the advent of dedicated news channels like CNN, and later Fox News, changed the equation. No longer were paid advertisements or "spots" the key means of communicating with voters. With so many more hours of coverage to fill and the competition between networks for ratings becoming ever more fierce, outspoken politicians had access to an increasingly powerful, and increasingly cheap, megaphone. Perot's campaign, kickstarted on CNN's *Larry King Live*, simply would not have happened before the age of cable television. According to journalist Peter Goldman and his colleagues in their analysis of the 1992 campaign, Perot became "the first serious candidate ever" to put himself in the race for the presidency "on a television show." For GOP leader of the House, Newt Gingrich, a few minutes on the evening news was worth more than many hours of paid advertisements. Not only was this coverage free, but it came with the imprimatur of journalistic endorsement. This meant that controversy was as important as substance. "Conflict equals exposure equals power" Gingrich would say. This "earned media" – that is, air time a politician doesn't pay for – has only become more important with time; a development Trump grasped intuitively.[19]

The exponential growth in internet usage has also benefited those who can exploit its network effects and use it as a low-cost mass communication channel. In some respects, the political effect of the Internet has been quite conventional. As Jennifer Stromer-Galley shows in her book, *Presidential Campaigning in the Internet Age*, the Internet is particularly effective as an advertisement delivery system. Google, Facebook, and Amazon collect inordinate amounts of data on their users; what websites you look at; how long you look at them; what things and groups you like; what you buy. This data can be packaged and paired with voting records (that you voted, not how you voted), tax records, credit history, supermarket loyalty cards, and multiple other databases. Voter profiles can be developed with extraordinary precision; single mothers, minority students, veterans. The likes of Google and Facebook can target these groups specifically with tailor made ads. Using these services isn't cheap, although the Trump 2016 campaign demonstrated that in a world of scarce resources, dollars could still be well spent here. In 2016, Trump devoted more than half his budget to social media, employing one consultancy firm, Cambridge Analytica, to run more than 5,000 individual ad campaigns with 10,000 modified iterations of each ad alone. In this respect, however, the

Internet is merely a more efficient advertisement tool than television. There is no inherent reason that it should favor the populist over the party.

However, the Internet works according to a different logic to that of television and other analog technologies. Being a network, it is subject to what are called "scale-free" dynamics. Put simply, this is the logic by which the rich get richer. When you do a search on Google, an algorithm determines the most suitable results based largely on the activity of countless other users. The most popular results get listed first, and in turn receive further clicks, and get even more popular. Facebook's newsfeed and other popular platforms work much the same way. With the advertising revenue of both content providers and platforms so dependent on traffic, the most contentious images and links are often the most profitable. It is in this context that Trump's flair for controversy comes into its own. A few heated – even offensive – statements are more likely to get "shared" or "promoted" than a boring policy-laden party platform. The effect is to exponentially increase the impact of any given controversy or conflict on a candidate's exposure.

The rich get richer effect is notable in another way. The already famous are far more likely to have their initial interventions read, shared, and liked. On the one hand, this network effect reinforces the formation of so-called filter bubbles – a process whereby users are linked to the like-minded and exposed to content that reinforces their existing biases. On the other hand, however, ostensibly nonpolitical celebrities can have networks that transcend these boundaries, which increases the probability that many non-partisans will be exposed to their image and message. As the longtime star of NBC's reality TV show, *The Apprentice*, Trump was instantly recognizable as the consummate "boss" to much of the population. Before his campaign officially began, he was already building his political profile as a regular guest on *Fox & Friends*. Before that, he'd made countless talk show appearances and movie cameos. This celebrity gave him an instant economic advantage in the battle for airtime.

Moreover, well in advance of his bid for office, Trump had access to an unprecedented direct and costless means of communicating with voters – his Twitter account. As Twitter allows for the regular free distribution of comment and content, the celebrity candidate Trump had an unprecedently inexpensive means of communicating with the masses. Not only could Trump connect with his base, but because he had a Twitter following that crossed partisan and even demographic cleavages, his Tweets could generate instant controversy. It is not mere coincidence that in the years prior to Trump's candidacy, Twitter usage in the United States exploded. While just one in three members of Congress had Twitter accounts in 2011, just two years later, every single representative had one. Trump's following grew from just 300,000 in 2011 to 4.3 million by the time he launched his candidacy in 2015. Moreover, the impact went well beyond his immediate followers, as his most outrageous Tweets were quickly repeated through mainstream media channels. Indeed, comparatively few Republican voters regularly consulted Twitter directly. Rather, as the 2016 election approached, it was the far greater extent of secondary sharing of Trump's initial Tweets by journalists that gave him such a massive advantage over his political rivals. Twitter is hardly a medium for a detailed policy debate. It is tailored to the soundbite, the slogan, the quip, the insult – precisely Trump's forte. With a massive, free assist from Russian hackers who stole terabytes of emails and other private data from the Democratic National Committee, Trump relentlessly propagated stories of alleged Clinton corruption. In the October before the election, he Tweeted 164 times about the WikiLeaks data dumps. This was cheap, dirty, and highly effective campaigning. *Washington Post* journalist Robert Costa wrote that "[a]rmed with a Twitter account and a phone, he believed he [Trump] could outmaneuver candidates who raised millions."[20]

Even if television and social media have provided cost-effective new channels for direct communication between leader and follower, the use of these media still require some resources. The use of conventional internet advertising, and of course other more nefarious techniques such as paid content providers, both cost a great deal of money. Contrary to much handwringing in the media, the mere requirement for money does not necessarily weaken parties over candidates and could in turn be a positive rather than a negative for democracy. At least since "Dollar" Mark Hanna's use of a massive campaign war chest to engineer William McKinley's defeat of the populist William Jennings Bryan in 1896, big money has played a big part in American elections. Of course, reformers have long argued that in order to preserve the independence of politicians from monied interests, donors should be limited in the amount they can give to any individual candidate. No single corporation, union, or individual should be able to buy access. Yet in spite of some modest campaign finance reform achieved during the Progressive Era, by the interwar period, the Republican Party's close ties with business had again given it a tremendous advantage in presidential campaigns. In 1952, it was oil men who stumped up the money for Eisenhower's pioneering television spots. In the 1956 rerun against Adlai Stevenson, Ike's team spent $2.9 million compared to Stevenson's $1.8 million. The Gilded Age funding gap had been partially closed by the alliance of the major labor unions and the Democratic Party from the 1930s, but with unions later classified as corporations, limits were also set on the amount they could contribute. After unions were prohibited from donating directly to candidates, in 1943 the Committee of Industrial Organizations (CIO) – an umbrella union for nonspecialist manual workers – formed the first Political Action Committee or PAC. PACs were unconstrained in the amount they could spend on advertising with respect to particular issues, allowing them enormous influence over elections, and of course, over the parties.

Whatever de jure funding limits that have been put in place have consistently come under pressure, with actual practice often skirting those legal constraints. In the wake of Watergate, which in part revealed the illegal political slush funds flowing through the system, Congress restricted individual contributions to just $1,000 for individuals and $5,000 for PACs.

However, a Supreme Court decision in 1976 declared that Federal Election Campaign Act (FECA) limits were in violation of the Constitution, thereby removing constraints on campaign spending. Congress responded by setting up the Federal Election Commission (FEC), establishing donation limits for individuals but not for parties, and repealing expenditure limits for candidates who didn't accept public funding. A candidate could always spend as much of her own money as she wanted. By this point, however, it would have been almost impossible for any but the very richest of outsiders – like a Perot or a Bloomberg – to self-finance a modern, media-intensive political campaign. These developments thus tended to strengthen party organizations.

Party elites continued to seek reforms that would favor organizations over individuals. However, reforms continued to have unintended consequences, perhaps best illustrated by the effects of the Bipartisan Campaign Reform Act (2001), otherwise known as the McCain-Feingold Act. The intent of the Act was to reduce the influence of "soft money" in politics, primarily by limiting corporate and union contributions to the parties. The end result, however, was to channel that money directly to the campaigns of individual candidates. With limited control over the purse strings, party leaders had few tools with which to discipline their members. McCain-Feingold opened the spigot for outsider candidates to challenge incumbents and party stalwarts in the primaries. Legislators with good access to outside funds could establish their own private fiefdoms within the party; supporting allies, threatening opponents. The factionalism that opened up especially in the Republican Party was not merely, or even, ideological, but personal.

The Supreme Court's *Citizens United* decision in 2010, which has allowed so-called Super PACs to raise and spend unlimited funds in support of a candidate (or against her opponent) as long as the PAC does not "coordinate" directly with the campaign, has exacerbated this trend, although the decision's effects are easily overemphasized or misunderstood. Certainly, with *Citizens United* a small number of big donors, what casinos would call whales, have been able to greatly increase their financial contributions, and hence their political leverage. The Koch brothers, Charles and David, in particular, through their Super PAC donations, have become an extremely important source of funds on the Republican side. As of 2016 the Kochs had an even larger machinery than the official RNC. The Mercers have become major donors too, sometimes collaborating with, and sometimes competing with the Kochs. In less costly "down-ticket" races – including Congressional primaries, state legislatures, and even governorships – these kinds of funds can tip the balance.

However, it is less clear that such mega-donors have had a decisive effect on presidential races. The Kochs, after all, had wanted almost anyone *but* Trump in 2016. The Mercers only belatedly supported Trump after their initial favorite, Ted Cruz, was eliminated. Trump triumphed in spite of the efforts of many of the Republican mega-rich donors, who each favored different candidates. In fact, it was likely because there were so many sufficiently well-funded candidates that primary delegates were widely shared across the field. Jeb Bush was easily the most cashed-up candidate, with his super PAC raising more than $100 million in its first six-months. Although Bush withdrew relatively early on, John Kasich and Ted Cruz stayed in the race as late as May. It's well known that Rubio and Cruz were more concerned with each other than they were with Trump. Trump triumphed because the flow of money was divided among others, not because it was united behind him. Indeed, Trump won the nomination on the basis of the lowest share of the ballot since primaries were introduced.[21]

THE COST OF FACTIONALISM

Changes in technology and campaign financing may have contributed to Trump's unlikely 2016 victory. However, even though the timing is coincidental, by themselves these factors were probably insufficient to have brought him to power. Previous technological and financial shocks had come and gone without opening the White House doors to a populist. Something else was going on to tip the scales in his favor. For most observers that something was the long-developing conservative, or even *paleoconservative*, ascendancy within the Republican Party, going back to Goldwater if not before. Trump's victory was the victory of a radical, deeply discontented, right wing in American politics. Trump has indeed become the chief avatar of the far right, but the latter's role in Trump's initial victory is often misunderstood. Trump was not initially the favored candidate of ultra-conservatives in the Republican Party. Indeed, if the GOP had indeed become so ideologically monolithic either at the level of the electorate or the party elite, as this perspective suggests, Trump would never have become president. Rather, the key to Trump's 2016 victory was the contemporaneous fragmentation of the Republican Party.[22]

After its 2008 defeat, the GOP was in a dire state. Looking at the scope of the Democrats' victory that November, Conservative commentators feared being returned to the minority for a generation. Just as the onset of economic stagflation, the debacle of Vietnam, and a surge of Black urban unrest discredited the Democratic establishment in the late 1960s, the onset of the Great Recession and the unending quagmires in Afghanistan and Iraq condemned the neoconservative core of the GOP to oblivion. In its wake, a different, more amorphous opposition to the Obama presidency arose in the form of the Tea Party. As several commentators have noted, the Tea Party was itself far from homogenous. Emerging at the end of the Bush presidency, in part in response to the bailouts of Wall Street, various libertarian and ultra-conservative groups, self-financed or backed by a range of right-wing donors, found a common identity in the Tea Party label. Almost all were already Republican sympathizers and voters, but the result was the influx from 2010 of a new generation of Republican office holders with few if any ties to the institutional GOP. The churn in the Congressional leadership sparked by this influx is indicative of how fractured the party became in the wake of 2008.

The Tea Party, and its Congressional counterpart, the Freedom Caucus, was just one faction among many in the GOP during the Obama presidency. The party establishment, led by RNC chairmen Michael Steele and Reince Priebus, argued that the party needed to broaden its appeal to an increasingly diverse population. Although Mitt Romney, a key figure in this wing of the party, lost to Obama in 2012, moderates remained in control of the party infrastructure. The "Autopsy" report that Priebus commissioned in the wake of the 2012 defeat called for Republicans to embrace immigration reform, a position that Jeb Bush – the former Florida governor – was well placed to do.

Trump, needless to say, was anathema to the party establishment. But he was also a poor match for the party's right wing. Trump was hardly a paragon of conservative moral values. By 2016, he was in his third marriage, had run a network of casinos, had previously been strongly pro-choice, and had donated large sums to Democratic Party candidates, including Hilary Clinton. In 2016, the right-wing faction's candidate of choice was Ted Cruz. Of all the primary candidates Trump squared off against, Cruz probably had the most formidable organization, grounded in the Evangelical, anti-immigrant, low-tax right. Cruz was determined to the point of truculence – GOP House Speaker John Boehner called Cruz "Lucifer in the flesh." But he had a well-oiled machine and a rich network of backers in the party, even if he held limited crossover appeal to moderates. What distinguished Trump in 2016 was the fact that he could win as a candidate *without* a faction. As political scientists Bryan Gervais and Irwin Morris conclude in their book on the Tea Party, Trump won the nomination "with little institutional support–Tea Party or otherwise." Trump was equally popular among all Republican subgroups. He sought available voters, whatever their beliefs. Trump gave reactionary voters plenty of red meat, but because he didn't depend on wealthy donors like the Kochs or Mercers, he could also support the popular if heterodox policy of strengthening Social Security and even raising taxes on the rich. Trump, in other words, was not the darling of the Republican right wing. Trump was free of dependence on a particular faction of the party. He could pursue his populist – or to use Trump's own malapropism, his "popularist" strategy – unencumbered.[23]

Populism, of course, is not free – otherwise it would be successful always and everywhere. Trump supposedly spent some $66 million of his own money on the campaign. But his populist approach was more cost-effective than Clinton's programmatic strategy. Just before the Republican convention, Clinton had raised $264 million in comparison to Trumps' $89 million. Clinton, following the operational playbook of previous elections, substantially outspent Trump on traditional forms of advertising. Some media outlets estimated that she had three times the number of field offices as the Trump campaign. Trump husbanded his resources. With limited cash for mass media, he concentrated on direct appeals through social media and public rallies where he could viscerally connect with, and energize, his base. Unlike his opponents, Trump also focused his attention on exurbs and rural areas, which traditional political machines find hard to reach. Trump held massive rallies in these areas during the primary, including in places like Mobile, Alabama. Although this mystified political experts, the value of these activities soon became clear as Trump swept primaries in the Deep South. This attention to rural and exurban areas continued to pay off in the presidential race itself. In total, Trump's campaign officially cost only $322 million compared to Clinton's $565 million. The *marginal cost* – or additional amount paid per unit – of each Trump vote was only half that of his rival. Officially, Tump spent about $5 per vote compared to Clinton's $10. He nearly repeated the feat in 2020, coming within a hair's breadth of reelection. Joe Biden won, but he only did so in part by outspending Trump by some $200 million. That may not seem like a lot, but as the last week of the campaign approached, Trump's campaign had only a third of the Biden team's cash on hand, money badly needed for last-minute advertising and an effective Election Day get-out-the-vote operation.[24]

Trump's path to the presidency suggests that he grasped the economic logic of populism on an intuitive level. His main qualification for office, as he enjoyed telling anyone who'd listen, was his experience as a businessman. And even though he's had a few bankruptcies along the way, he has been a fairly successful one. Even as his real estate, hotel, and casino businesses struggled, his image as a real-life Gordon Gecko proved to be an enormously marketable source of wealth. Trump's name could be put to profit on everything from steaks to hotels. When sizing up his Republican competitors in 2015, his sense was that none had the natural charisma for the current age of celebrity. Like many of his supporters, Trump understood political competition in terms of personality. Despite being among the country's richest men, for voters Trump was relatable. In 2016, Trump won the Republican primary in spite of being vastly out-fundraised, outspent, and out-advertised by his rivals, exploiting the news media to receive more earned media coverage than any other candidate. The more he outraged the establishment, the more attention he got. In terms of turning money into votes, the Trump strategy was staggeringly efficient. If, like Trump, you can "buy" a vote more cheaply than your opponents, spending fewer dollars per ballot received, you have obtained a crucial strategic edge. In 2016, Trump was able to convert cash into votes more effectively than his competitors, winning the Republican nomination in large part by relying on the comparatively cheap mass communication tools of public rallies and social media while avoiding the cost of building up a large independent political machine. The master of marketing and communication, we might say, with only a touch of exaggeration, drove down the marginal cost of winning a vote to the price of a Tweet.

In the same way that a fully integrated, publicly listed, multinational financial corporation has an advantage in some contexts while the nimble hedge fund with just a handful of owners and employees has advantages in others, different types of political organization are best suited to different types of environment. The evidence presented here is only suggestive. It calls out for further research. But Trump's success suggests the efficiency of populism as a political strategy where the technology of direct mass communication is relatively low cost – in Trump's case, Twitter, earned media coverage, small-town rallies. However, as much as these technological features affect the supply side of the equation, there is good reason to think that intra-party factionalism is the main driver of populist success in contemporary America. The two populists who have made it to the White House in the twentieth century did so when their *own* parties were rent by faction. The post-reform factionalism of the Democratic Party allowed the relatively unknown "peanut farmer," Jimmy Carter, to take the party's nomination with a bare plurality of delegates in 1977. It was in a similar context of party factionalism that Trump's use of free mass communication through earned media and Twitter gave him an edge over his opponents; none of them had a consistent nationwide advantage in organizational infrastructure. In the end, Republican factionalism made the calculus look good for Trump's populist strategy; he took over the GOP for a relative pittance. His GOP primary victory, for what it's worth, was less the result of a long-term conservative ascendancy than of a historically notable period of fragmentation with the party organization. Trump may be gone for now, but his signal lesson for success in the twenty-first century-political marketplace endures: Seek market share, and seek it cheaply.

8

Populism and Democracy

Make America Great Again.

Donald Trump Campaign Slogan

of those men who have overturned the liberties of republics, the greatest number have begun their career by paying an obsequious court to the people; commencing Demagogues, ending Tyrants.

Alexander Hamilton, Federalist no. 1

CAUSE OR COINCIDENCE?

In the months between Donald Trump's primary victory in June 2016 and the presidential election of November that year, the question of what happens to democracy under populist rule began to take on an urgent new relevance. Even if most observers, myself included, expected the Democratic Party's superior organization to deliver a win for Clinton, it appeared worthwhile to speculate on what might happen if the alternative scenario came to pass: What if Trump won? For all the research that had been done to that point on how and why populists came to power, we knew remarkably little about what they did when they got there. Some populists appeared to erode democratic institutions; others, in contrast, seemed to extend and deepen them. Faced with this conflicting evidence, it was hard to say what might happen to American democracy under Trump.

To answer this question, with my then colleague at Trinity College Dublin, Christian Houle, I constructed an original database of all populist and nonpopulist governments from 1980 to 2010 in Latin America, a region and time period where populist rule has been relatively common. We examined what happened to socioeconomic inequality, rates of popular participation, the rule of law, and the relationship between the executive, judicial, and legislative branches of government under populist rule. The results we obtained were unequivocal. Populist presidents were more likely to erode the independence of the judiciary, stack courts with their supporters, reduce legislative oversight, and generally aggrandize the powers of the executive over the other branches of government. Nor did we find any evidence of the supposed redeeming quality of populism. Populists, even those on the left, did not reduce inequality and did not increase democratic participation, putting off and excluding many former voters just as they mobilized new ones. In follow-up research, I found that the populist erosion of liberal democracy went beyond formal government institutions, with populist rule associated with notable drops in a range of indicators of press freedom and freedom of speech more broadly. These findings were also backed up by other research teams. Kirk Hawkins, a political scientist and specialist on Venezuela's Hugo Chávez, led a team that used a different methodology and different data to ours, but which produced remarkably similar findings.[1]

As the 2016 election approached and with my newfound statistical confidence, I reached out to Hawkins, and along with one of his coauthors, Saskia Ruth, we jointly penned an op-ed for the *Washington Post*'s Monkey Cage Blog. We predicted that a Trump victory could spell bad news for the famed autonomy of America's judicial branch, for Congressional constraints on the president, and for press freedom. The editors liked our article but thought we underestimated the formal and informal constraints that Trump would face if he attempted to erode democracy. Unlike in many of the Latin American democracies we had examined, the United States' political institutions, such as the Supreme Court, and informal norms such as accepting election results as inherently legitimate – what Harvard political scientists Steven Levitsky and Daniel Ziblatt call "the guardrails of democracy" – were too strong to permit an authoritarian reversal, and so insisted that we walk back our most bearish predictions [2]

Whether Trump's double impeachment, his flat-out denial of the legitimacy of his election loss in 2020, and his subsequent drumming up of a violent occupation of the Capitol Building tend to prove us right or wrong, the editors, to their credit, were right to be skeptical about inferring what might happen under a populist government in the United States from what had occurred under populist governments elsewhere. All we had shown in our original study was an association. True enough, we undertook many procedures in our analyses to suggest that the relationship was real rather than merely spurious. It was very unlikely that these associations were due to the possibility that countries that elected populists were just predisposed toward undergoing a decline in the quality of their democracy. It was not akin to jumping to the conclusion that swallows flying south *cause* the onset of winter. However, what our analysis was missing was what scientists call a *mechanism*.

Siddhartha Mukherjee, Columbia University professor and New York Presbyterian Hospital oncologist, writes about the enormous difficulties of proving a link between suspected carcinogens and cancer in *The Emperor of All Maladies*, his masterful, Pulizer Prize–winning history of cancer and the various treatments that doctors have developed to treat it. Even though researchers found overwhelming evidence that smokers were statistically more likely to have lung cancer, and that lung cancer patients were overwhelmingly smokers, correlation didn't mean causation. The tobacco industry famously obfuscated the science, calling for more research, knowing full well that the gold standard of empirical science, the randomized controlled trial (or RCT), could never be applied to test the link between smoking and cancer. No ethics review board, nor any but the most unscrupulous researcher, could randomly assign trial participants to a treatment – smoking – that they were almost certain would cause cancer. Without an understanding of the physiology through which a carcinogen – in the case of cigarettes, tar – caused cells to mutate uncontrollably, deniers could always deny. Just as importantly, without an understanding of the mechanism linking cause and effect, doctors seeking treatments were flying blind.

Simply knowing that there is an association between populism and democratic decline is not enough. We need to know *why* such an association exists. Here I think existing scholarship has brought mostly confusion, not least because of the predominance of the ideological approach to defining populism. Many scholars and pundits have argued that populism is equivalent to democracy without liberalism, or "democratic illiberalism" as one scholar has put it. Or as another writes, populists "are deeply democratic" but at the same time "they are also deeply illiberal." Populists hold and win elections but at the same time repress minorities and expand executive power. However, while ostensibly at pains to distinguish populism from authoritarianism per se, this approach runs into inevitable difficulties. In fact, it often leads to nonsensical propositions like the one that "populism is an authoritarian form of democracy." It may as well be a "wet form of dry" or a "down form of up." More generously, this approach might be said to place populism on a continuum between democracy and authoritarianism. This could in theory describe the often-noted grey area between democracy and authoritarianism (elsewhere called anocracy or semi-democracy). However, this ambiguity is then replaced by new grey areas between both populism and democracy and between populism and authoritarianism. Sharper distinctions between these regime types are both valid and needed. If democracy, at the very minimum, means the counting of heads, in order for that process to be anything other than a sham, people must be able to freely cast their vote and the opposition must be able to actually win. Either they can do this, or they can't. The state of being partially authoritarian is like that of being a little bit dead. The civil rights of minorities are not merely a liberal addendum to democracy; they are essential to it. An "anti-pluralist" democracy is a contradiction in terms. As we saw in the cases of Napoleon and Hitler once they had consolidated their hold on office, there have been, and still are, popular and even plebiscitary dictatorships, but there is no need to stretch the term populism to fit their regimes in their entirety. Populism is not a regime type between authoritarianism and democracy.[3]

Beginning with the alternative premise that populism is a political ideology that pits the people against the elite, we similarly end up with more questions than answers. Populist ideology, in this sense, gives no clear expectations about its effects on democracy. Just as it promises a remedy to domination by a minority by restoring power to "the people," it raises the specter of illiberal domination by a majority in its place. As we saw in Chapter 3, the American founding fathers – Jefferson and Madison included – were at least as concerned with the tyranny of the mob as they were the with tyranny of George III. There is nothing inherently democratic or authoritarian about populism as an ideology in this sense, an ambiguity revealed in the title of one recent book, which asks whether populism is "a threat or corrective" to democracy. Some proponents of the ideational approach have tried to provide clarity by dividing populists into *inclusionary* or *exclusionary* types. The former stands up for the poor against the rich; the latter for an ethnic majority against a minority. But this trick doesn't quite work, as it requires peeking at the answers before doing the test. A potentially interesting empirical puzzle is defined away: *good* (inclusionary) populists are good for democracy; *bad* (exclusionary) populists are bad for democracy.[4]

But what if we take ideology out of the equation? If we run with the idea that populism is more about strategy than substance, organization rather than ideology, how might populism *cause* the erosion of civil liberties under democracy? Surprisingly, perhaps, the negative implications of populist rule for democratic liberties flow directly from the way in which populists organize the pursuit of power. The definitive characteristic of populism as a type of strategy designed to gain and keep power is that it eschews the use of an institutionalized political party. Parties, it turns out, provide hidden constraints on political leaders that prevent them from undermining liberalism and even democracy itself. As political scientist E. E. Schattschneider aphoristically put it, although parties may be organizations selfishly geared toward the pursuit of power, "[d]emocracy is unthinkable save in terms of parties." In other words, democracy cannot survive without political parties. Why is this? What exactly is it that parties do?[5]

NECESSARY EVILS

The typical view of political parties – at least outside of political science – is resoundingly negative. Parties, as Harvard political theorist Nancy Rosenblum writes, were long viewed by political philosophers as degenerate and divisive entities organized "for public plunder." As America's founders believed, they were the creations of ambitious individuals and groups that sought to pursue their own narrow interests over the welfare of society. Washington famously warned against the "baneful effects" of party. France's democratic revolutionaries saw things no differently. Robespierre wrote that "[p]arties are fatal to the public good; it is in the national interest to crush them just as it is in every citizen's duty to unmask them." Marquis de Condorcet, polymath, and revolutionary politician, wrote of parties that "one of the primary needs of the French republic is to have none." Among political philosophers, only a few voices, such as that of Edmund Burke, claimed that parties were potentially valuable as bodies of men united for promoting a common purpose. Yet Burke's justification of parties was premised on the condition that they upheld "the national interest" rather than the concerns of some narrow faction or interest group.[6]

Today most people continue to see parties as interested only in power, as serving the interests of their members, and maybe even their silent financial backers, not society as a whole. In public opinion polls around the world, political parties are almost always the least trusted kinds of governmental (or quasi-governmental) institutions: the army, the police, courts; even detested bureaucracies like the department of motor vehicles sometimes command a higher level of public trust. Parties weren't always so unpopular. In the first half of the twentieth century they seemed almost to be equivalent to mass politics itself. Voters proudly identified with their local Labour Party or Conservative Party. Yet the gradual transformation of mass membership parties into more professionalized organizations in recent decades has eroded much of this popular empathy. The extent of anti-partyism is closer to the era of the American and French Revolutions than to that of just a few decades ago. With the emergence of technologies to make direct participation of the masses possible in the form of online plebiscites and the rise to prominence of so-called deliberative democracy theory, the prospect of doing away with parties altogether appears tempting. This, however, is a temptation we should resist.[7]

To most contemporary political economists, the notion that there exists anything so exalted as "the general will" is fanciful, if not deeply pernicious. Social choice theorists – most notably the political economists Kenneth Arrow and William Riker – formally demonstrated the intuition of Condorcet, that there could be no such thing as a general will. Once we have to choose among more than two options – say, no public health care, full public health care, and some public health care – there is no stable social preference. As a result, the idea sometimes put forward by advocates of participatory democracy that policies on many issues could be decided by plebiscite, perhaps even via mobile phone polls, is naive. The Italian party M5S and the German Pirate Party made headlines by allowing supporters to vote policies up or down via the Internet in developing their party platforms. However, the framing of any such policy options, not to mention the number of options given, becomes critical to any voting outcome. Had British voters been given a more nuanced option of "Hard" Brexit (i.e., with no deal on trade or migration), a "Soft" Brexit (something like Norway's arrangement), or the status quo, the outcome may have been very different. Democracy via the App Store is a non sequitur. The Internet is not a site of true debate.

Deliberative democratic theory acknowledges the plural nature of political preferences but suggests that rather than simply counting heads to determine a majority, we should instead aim at consensus. Drawing on the reasoning of German philosopher, Jürgen Habermas, deliberative democrats argue that by communicating with one another, groups of individuals can hash out their disagreements, eventually coming to a consensus. This approach too is not without its critics. As any number of Hollywood depictions suggest, juries of men and women appear to readily establish a consensus through deliberation, and if Sydney Lumet's *Twelve Angry Men* is to be credited, this is a a consensus in which justice prevails. However, probe a little deeper and some of this rosy story begins to lose its luster. Simon Garrod, a professor of psychology at Glasgow University, found that groups of more than seven find it very difficult to establish a genuine consensus. In larger groups, dissenters are not convinced or persuaded, but intimidated. Harking back to an era of voice voting, people vote not with their conscience but according to what will make others happy. Pluralism cannot be deliberated away. At its most pernicious, deliberative democracy on a larger scale, like that of the Ancient Athenian assembly, allows charismatic individuals to dominate its proceedings. Democracy – participatory, deliberative, or otherwise – is a method of aggregation, no more or less inherently legitimate than others.

Political parties are another way to resolve the inherent pluralism of social preferences. Motivated by the rewards of office, parties do have to pay attention to public opinion, even if it often feels like they ignore what people want. Some of this sense that parties fail to deliver on voter preferences is that they are instruments of aggregating many differing views in the population. In a system of recurring plebiscites, or of only populist political organizations, it would be virtually impossible to tie together the multiple issues that animate people's political beliefs. Parties, by necessity, must aggregate preferences across different issue domains. Even if we assign to individual politicians the very basest of motivations – power and money – to the extent that winning an election demands a political organization, they are compelled to do something for others. They must, as Alexis de Tocqueville wrote, find some set of interests shared by others and, ideally, give a label to them. Sometimes these labels are incongruous, but this is a feature not a bug of political parties. It is extraordinarily un likely that a large group of individuals will share exactly the same preferences along multiple domains: pro-trade, anti-abortion, pro-welfare, anti–gun control, and so on. It would be simply impossible to have a separate party that meets exactly every single preference of each individual in society – that, by definition, would lead to a party system with almost as many parties as voting citizens. In the real world, party politicians must trade off on interests, allowing each member to get a little but not all of what they want. Voters too then are forced to compromise, selecting the party with the combination of policies that most suits their preferences. Parties in competition will then stake out the combination of policies that will yield it the most votes. This kind of pluralistic compromise is the very stuff of liberal democracy, coming close to the reality of deliberation, if not the abstract ideal.

POPULISM, PARTIES, AND THE THREAT TO DEMOCRACY

Although this functionalist approach helps us to understand some of what parties do, it falls short of providing a full explanation of why the leaders of regular parties wouldn't also look to consolidate their power through nefarious means. Pluralistic "values" are insufficient in the face of powerful incentives to entrench oneself in power. Parties matter because they are instruments for navigating the Scylla of personal ambition and the Charybdis of public opinion. Parties filter and aggregate public opinion, but, critically, they also regulate competition between ambitious office seekers. A system based on political parties accepts the fact that politicians may be motivated primarily by office and its spoils. However, it structures the incentives in such a way as to prevent any one party or individual from becoming unilaterally dominant. Rather than relying on outside observers like journalists or voters to do this, a party-based system instead makes ambitious politicians act as a check on one another. The notion that the organized opposition functions as a check on the government began to gain currency in the latter part of the eighteenth century, and it has become a key pillar of contemporary democratic theory. However, this monitory function too requires a minimal acceptance of the liberal democratic rules of the game. It is part of the outcome to be explained, not the cause. Opposition parties are only able to perform this function if they are tolerated to do so. As the evidence cited indicates, opposition parties are tolerated to a much greater degree under programmatic party government than under populist government. Why?

To answer this question, we have to look at the constraining effect of the party on its own leaders, not on the leaders of other parties. Parties, once established, have a value to politicians embedded both in brand recognition and human capital. Party reputations or brands provide signals about candidates, thereby lowering the search costs for voters in making a decision at election time. Parties create partisans, which for the politician translates into low-cost votes. Parties also, as we have seen, have rich networks of agents, advisers, volunteers, and supporters that can be mobilized to win and keep power. This human capital needs fresh investment from time to time, but it is intrinsically valuable. Any rational party leader would be loath to sacrifice the votes that these networks provide.

As a result of the assets that programmatic parties possess, if a leader chooses to create or use one, he must then tie his own hands. Politicians as Napoleon noted, howsoever personally talented or ambitious, become at least partly kept by their parties. Even if parties are purely elite vehicles for capturing the spoils, politicians must nevertheless become invested in the fiction that the parties represent real sociological or ideological differences. If politicians were to continually switch parties, partisanship would collapse, and once again the cost of mobilizing voters would rise. As any politician knows, changing party is no easy task. John Quincy Adams, who left behind the National Republicans to become a Democrat, was continually dogged as a turncoat. Abraham Lincoln was accused of *really* being a Whig, even though the Republican Party he came to lead hadn't existed when his political career began. Politicians become invested in the survival and success of their parties. They may seek to maximize their own personal control over the party, but rival elites are doing the same thing. The result is that for party elites, the organization is bigger than any individual. This is essential as it implies a collective restraint on any individual leader. The programmatic party elite may exploit a leader's coattails, but the withdrawal of that consent is always a possibility in the background. To understand why populism tends to be so harmful to democracy, we have to look to the ability that parties have to restrain their leaders.[8]

Efficient economic markets depend on a series of formal institutions, such as enforceable property rights. But they also depend to a large extent on rules that have a somewhat less fixed but still critical status. Rules are different from laws. Unlike laws, they are not enforced by some external agency of the state. As we've seen too often in recent history, populists are all too willing to flout the law, or change it as needs be. Rules are instead procedures internal to an organization. Members enforce them on each other. Organizational rules are not just about having some people order and some people obey. Rules provide a way to guide all sorts of behavior. They limit what can be legitimately asked of subordinates. They set out the process of advancement up the organizational hierarchy. Critically, they set out the process by which a leader can be removed. Organizations facilitate the interests of the men and women who lead them. But, depending on an organization's rules, they also constrain those leaders from actions that would be damaging to the organization itself. Even if some members attempt to shift the rules in their favor, rivals will take the opposite view. As sociologist Robert Michels argued, it may be an "iron law" that political parties, like any complex organizations, become oligarchies no matter how egalitarian their founding principles. Yet an oligarchy is not a dictatorship. A programmatic party, or even a patronage party, is not a populist one.[9]

Although it sometimes feels like the leaders of deeply institutionalized bureaucratic parties tower above their parties – think of Angela Merkel and Germany's CDU or Tony Blair and the British Labour Party – such parties have traditionally had the ability to restrain, and even topple, their leaders. Between 2010 and 2018, in my adopted homeland of Australia, five prime ministers in a row were removed by their own parliamentary parties – Kevin Rudd, twice; Julia Gillard; Tony Abbott; and Malcolm Turnbull. Party members know that the popularity of their organizations depends in part on their leader. In their pomp, leaders like Blair are said to have a "coattails" effect, by which lesser known candidates can win office simply by being a member of the same party as a popular leader. But party members also know that the party is bigger than any one person. Party candidates expect to be able to run for office regardless of who occupies the leadership position. They value the party brand more than a leader per se, however popular he or she might be.

This gives party memberships a relatively long time-horizon, which in turn affects their willingness to maintain or undermine institutions like press freedom and judicial independence that protect the interests of minorities (i.e., the opposition). Parties work to constrain a leader from pursuing her own short-term interests at the organization's long-term expense. Even though bureaucratic parties aim to be in power continuously, they accept the risk that they may have to survive in opposition on occasion. Although any given party leader would seem to have an ostensible interest in suppressing the opposition – say by closing down opposed press outlets – the greater procedural constraints on leaders, such as confidence votes, that exist within programmatic parties mean that the behavior of these leaders adheres closely to the interests of the party elite (if not its full membership). Any erosion of the rights of the opposition while in power could lead to reciprocal repression if they themselves lose a future election. As American president Martin Van Buren put it, "[a]ll men of sense know that political parties are inseparable from free governments ... [and that] [t]he disposition to abuse power, so deeply planted in the human heart, can by no other means be effectively checked."[10]

That kind of restraining influence might be easy to accept in the deeply institutionalized and programmatic parties of Western Europe. But given the rarity of those systems, this may not be encouraging. Would the patronage-based parties common to much of the rest of the world have fewer scruples about allowing their leader to erode liberal democratic practices? If these kinds of parties are willing to effectively bribe voters for support, might they not also be willing to undermine other democratic norms? Even though patronage-based political systems allow for government jobs, including on the courts or in the military, to become part of what is called the spoils system, patronage parties do still constrain the behavior of their leaders. As with bureaucratic parties, patronage or clientelistic parties have an institutional life expectancy that extends beyond a single leader. The membership of clientelistic parties also accepts the principle that they may have to survive in opposition. In some cases, in fact, rival clientelistic parties have evolved implicit agreements to rotate power and patronage between them. The party elite, if not the rank and file, have an interest in restraining their leaders from undermining democratic norms too far, as they fear that they could in turn be mistreated once they lose power. The leadership of any clientelistic party depends to a significant degree on maintaining the support of its brokers – the governors, senators, and other regional and urban bosses who control the party's vote banks. If these party elites feel that a leader threatens the long-term survival of their party, they can mobilize their factions against her. These expectations are also borne out in the evidence. Patronage party rule sits somewhere between programmatic and populist government in terms of its effects on press freedom and other constraints on the executive branch.

The organizational resources and electoral incentives of populists furnish very different expectations about how they should behave in office. Populists do not have the local party offices, civil society associations, or extensive national patronage networks to get out the vote for them in the way that programmatic or patronage party leaders do. As a result, populists face a great temptation to secure their hold on power through other, more nefarious means. Even if we assume that both populist and non-populist leaders experience similar personal benefits from holding office and face a similar risk of prosecution if they lose office, a populist leader is interested in her own survival rather than in the continued prosperity of a party per se. Populists have short time-horizons, that of an individual lifetime, not multiple generations. Eschewing the building of political organizations that might in turn constrain them, populist rule remains un-institutionalized, and so populists are prone to sudden downturns in their popularity. As Max Weber eloquently put it, "[e]very charisma is on the road from a turbulently emotional life that knows no economic rationality to a slow death by suffocation under the weight of material interests: every hour of its existence brings it nearer to this end." Explaining the all-too-brief honeymoon period of one-term president Jimmy Carter, his biographer, Jonathan Alter, writes: "[T]he bond he established with voters was connected to a passing public mood, not deeply shared interests or long-standing political ties." When the mood shifts, populists can find themselves out of a job. As a result, we've seen that, on average, populists face a great temptation to erode the ability of the people who put them into office to later remove them. Populists tend toward the rollback, even if partial, of democracy, not because of any values they supposedly hold, but because this is the most efficient way for them to hold on to power. Although populists can and do have parties, they are personalistic to the extent that the interests of populist parties are equivalent to the interests of party leaders. Populist leaders are thus not constrained to act in the interests of an enduring political organization. Once a populist has gained power, she has a greater interest in suppressing any opposition in order to retain power for as long as she can. Hence a populist is less interested in preserving the autonomy of institutions that balance governmental authority, such as the press. The problem of populism, then, is that its personalization of authority eliminates effective political constraints. Institutions are important, but in the end, power is needed to counteract power.[11]

THE COSTS OF POPULISM

Parties are effective tools for winning elections, and perhaps the best institutional bulwark for liberal democracy, but they're not the first choice of the power-seeking politician if there is a cheaper option. Political strategists are engaged in a constant struggle. Populists are always looking for gaps, opportunities to quickly establish cheap links with voters. Party leaders must constantly adapt to keep voters loyal and engaged. At the same time, they must balance the added value of a popular leader to its party brand against the risk of the personalization of party rule. Historical context matters, for sure. When labor unions and churches were at their zenith, it reduced the cost of building parties around them. But circumstance is not destiny. To rework the famous aphorism of Karl Marx, men do not make history as they please, but neither are they mere robots who lack any agency. Real politics occur somewhere in the interaction between context and action.

As this chapter has described, populism has a price to be paid in terms of political and civil liberties. The main argument of this book, however, has been that populism also has a value as a political strategy. Populists, by relying on mass communication rather than party building or the distribution of patronage, may lower the transaction costs of winning and keeping power. But this strategy is not always and everywhere viable. Rather, as the historical cases outlined in this book show, populism is blocked where entrenched programmatic or patronage-based parties predominate. Ironically, if the period of "greatness" referred to in Trump's campaign slogan was the 1950s, an outsider like him would have had a slim chance of success. Only during moments of disruption to the systems is populism viable. I'm hardly the first to argue that crises appear to be propitious for opportunistic populist politicians. But to say that some kind of crisis tends to precede populist success is to name rather than explain the problem. What this book suggests is that voters are more likely to be available, and populists successful, not just where existing parties have suddenly lost support (e.g., after an economic crisis or a corruption scandal) but also in new democracies, in systems in which ties between voters and politicians are mostly based on patronage, and in cases where party–voter ties have become attenuated due to more gradual demographic and social changes (e.g., post-industrial decline of unions, secularization). Each of these conditions makes voters more likely to be available for mobilization through mass communication. They are leading indicators that populist success may follow.

These conditions are unlikely to be exhaustive. Technological change is a relentlessly disruptive force that will surely again rebalance the relative costs of programmatic, patronage, and populist strategies. However, in the shorter term, if we do indeed prefer to live under programmatic rather than populist government, if for nothing else than its better preservation of political liberties, then the more we understand how and why populists come to power, the better prepared we'll be. This book has shown that the viability of populism is dictated to a surprising degree by supply-side conditions; by the availability of voters for direct mobilization; by the costs of direct mass communication; and by political fragmentation. This doesn't mean, of course, that voters themselves are irrelevant. Indeed, a truly comprehensive explanation of the populist phenomenon, what economists would call a general equilibrium model, requires incorporating both supply and demand sides.

While some scholars in the "ideational" school already claim to examine both the demand and supply sides, this approach in fact lacks a price mechanism to bring the two into equilibrium. That is, in the approach of the ideational school, demands unrealistically have no cost to voters, while the supply of alternatives is determined by zeitgeist rather than the calculation of the costs and benefits of different political tactics. At best, in this approach the economic terminology of supply and demand is a loose descriptive metaphor, not an analytical tool. This book has shown that on the supply side, we have to appreciate that entering the marketplace – standing for election – is costly. Organized political parties, it has already been said, are tools for "reducing the transaction costs" of democracy. However, as we've seen in this book, whether bureaucratic parties have lower transaction costs than populists is very much contingent. In an immediate sense, political institutions affect the costs of different modes of incorporation. More deeply though, how society is itself structured affects the transaction costs of different types of political mobilization. The costs of different types of political strategy are affected by whether society is organized as a massive and diverse land empire like nineteenth-century America or as a city-state like Athens; or whether its economy is largely agrarian like late eighteenth-century France or post-industrial like contemporary Britain. We can't treat supply simply as a natural consequence of voters' preferences.[12]

Cost should also feature as part of our explanation of the demand side. One of political science's embarrassing trade secrets is that despite all the time spent explaining *how* people vote, we have no good explanation for *why* they do so. Demands in the traditional sense are insufficient to explain why voters vote. Voting has a cost in terms of time and effort. Given the small effect that an individual vote has on the outcome, why people bother to vote at all is a perennial question confronting political economists. Evidently, people extract some kind of value from the act of voting that is not directly instrumental. That is, people don't only vote because they expect a benefit in terms of an instant payoff or even a policy outcome. Instead of focusing solely on the substance of voters' beliefs or preferences – the demand side as usually understood – we might do well think more about the conditions that affect the cost to the individual of voting at all, or in economic terms, of people's willingness to pay to participate in the electoral process.[13]

Again, this is not to say that voter psychology per se is irrelevant. Rather, it is to say that we need to better understand the noninstrumental, or emotional side of voting. Much of that, I would suggest, is explained less by where voters stand than by where they sit. Political behavior, not least voting, is a social activity. In future, we need to go beyond the obvious voter characteristics such as education, wealth, and ethnicity, and explore how voters' social networks influence their political behavior. Political affiliations – Democratic or Republican, Labour or Conservative – are socially acquired and maintained. Where people live, what they work at, how they entertain themselves, and who they do all of these things with in turn affect the kinds of political networks of which they are a part. For instance, it should hardly come as a surprise that among British laborers, coal miners have often been able to undertake the most sustained and costly collective action. Miners traditionally lived and socialized in isolated towns that were themselves effective appendages of the mine where they worked. Every aspect of life was conditioned by this fact. Once the National Union of Mineworkers cast its lot in with the Labour Party, the allegiances of the vast majority of coal miners were set for generations to come. The transformation of the People's Party in America from the political front of the Farmers' Alliance into a cross-sectoral party of smallholder farmers and industrial workers was brought about largely by the peripatetic lifestyles of railway workers. As human conduits between farm and city, unionized railway workers were among the most likely to become People's Party voters. Understanding how people become and remain in their social and political networks – not just parties but also their factions – is complex, and requires going beyond the easily accessible data of nationally representative surveys. Traditional fieldwork, innovative field experiments, and other tools in the social scientist's kit are all likely to be needed to figure these things out. What I think such studies will reveal is that the perceived cost (and benefit) to the individual of voting for different *kinds* of parties – populist, patronage, and programmatic – will differ. The demand side, in other words, can likely also be understood through an economic approach.

Economics doesn't explain everything; nor, of course, does it claim to. What it does is reveal how incentives govern behavior. Even if we assume the worst of politicians, economics suggests that the better we align politicians' incentives with that of the general population, the better off we will be. The great contribution of liberalism has been to legitimize the notion that society is made up of a multitude of individuals with inherently conflicting and irreconcilable interests and preferences. These differences of interests and values doesn't mean that we need to be constantly at each other's throats. Rather, it means that we should design our political institutions for men and women, not as we wish them to be, but as we find them. As Alexander Hamilton wrote in one of his Federalist essays (no. 15), "the passions of man will not conform to the dictates of reason and justice without constraint." Politicians will use almost any and every means to get power. They will dole out bribes, they will inflame mobs. But, if necessary, they will also build up organizations over which their control is less than complete. The more we tailor our political institutions to favor bureaucratic parties over personalists and demagogues, the less likely will be the erosion of the civil liberties we most value. This is not a call for a return to the postwar heyday of the programmatic party. Technology and society are too different to rerun the past. Rather, it is a call for institutional adaptation. We don't yet know what changes will work best. Many efforts to strengthen political parties have backfired. But failure is the essence of the scientific method. Society best advances by marginal revolutions, improving things bit by bit. The building of the next generation of programmatic political parties is the great task facing today's democrats.

Notes

PREFACE

1 Alexander Hamilton, *Madison Debates*, June 18, 1787, https://avalon.law.yale.edu/18th_century/debates_618.asp.

2 "[He] who neglects," Niccolò Machiavelli, *The Prince*, trans. W. K. Marriott (Project Gutenberg eBook, 1998), ch. XV.

3 "Ambition" from "John Adams to John Quincy Adams, January 3, 1793," *Founders Online*, National Archives, https://founders.archives.gov/documents/Adams/04-10-02-0003, emphasis added. "First you must," quoted in T. Harry Williams, *Huey Long*, First Vintage Books ed. (New York: Vintage Books, 1981), 750.

4 "War without bloodshed," from a 1938 lecture, quoted in *Oxford Essential Quotations*, Susan Ratcliffe (ed.), 5th ed. (Oxford University Press, 2017).

5 "is simply political," E. E. Schattschneider, *Party Government: American Government in Action* (New Brunswick: Transaction Publishers, 2004 [1942]), 95, emphasis in original. "God" Napoleon did not coin the phrase – we know that Voltaire among others used it previously – but he certainly popularized it. On 2008 campaign spending, Tahman Bradley, "Final fundraising figure: Obama's $750m," *ABC News*, https://abcnews.go.com/Politics/Vote2008/story?id=6397572&page=1. On 1896, see R. Hal Williams, *Realigning America: McKinley, Bryan, and the Remarkable Election of 1896* (Lawrence: University Press of Kansas, 2010). Several incumbents have managed to win despite being outspent, Lyndon Johnson and FDR among them.

6 For a macroeconomic analysis of populism, see e.g., Dani Rodrik, "Populism and the economics of globalization." *Journal of International Business Policy* 1, no. 1 (2018): 12–33. "dismal science," Thomas Carlyle, "Occasional discourse on the negro question," *Fraser's Magazine for Town and Country*. v. 40 (1849): 531, emphasis in original. For one of the earliest elaborations of the idea that economics is the study of "human behaviour as a relationship between ends and scarce means which have alternative uses," see Lionel Robbins, *An Essay on the Nature and Significance of Human Science*, 2nd ed. (London: Macmillan & Co., 1935), 16; "science of" R. H.

Coase, *The Firm, the Market, and the Law* (Chicago: University of Chicago Press, 1988), 2.

7 Gary S. Becker, *The Economic Approach to Human Behavior* (Chicago: University of Chicago Press, 1976).

8 "going once more" quoted in Paul D. Kenny, *Populism and Patronage: Why Populists Win Elections in India, Asia, and Beyond* (Oxford: Oxford University Press, 2017), 1.

CHAPTER 1

1 Quoted in Steven Englund, *Napoleon: A Political Life* (Cambridge: Harvard University Press, 2004), 199.

2 The full video of Trump's announcement speech from which these quotes are taken can be found online.

3 "you're having," Daniella Diaz, "Trump's dramatic moments at the GOP debate," *CNN*, August 7, 2015; "they can say," Jennifer R. Mercieca, *Demagogue for President: The Rhetorical Genius of Donald Trump*, 1st ed. (College Station: Texas A&M University Press, 2020), 88.

4 "I don't, frankly," clip of the August 9, 2015, Fox News debate is available online.

5 Examples of this kind of explanation for Trump's success include: John L. Campbell, *American Discontent: The Rise of Donald Trump and Decline of the Golden Age* (New York: Oxford University Press, 2018); William G. Howell and Terry M. Moe, *Presidents, Populism, and the Crisis of Democracy* (Chicago: University of Chicago Press, 2020). For an application to populism over a longer period, see: Barry J. Eichengreen, *The Populist Temptation: Economic Grievance and Political Reaction in the Modern Era* (New York: Oxford University Press, 2018). For some valuable studies of how these macro-level social and economic developments may have resulted in mass resentment at the local level, see: Katherine J. Cramer, *The Politics of Resentment: Rural Consciousness in Wisconsin and the Rise of Scott Walker* (Chicago: University of Chicago Press, 2016); Arlie Russell Hochschild, *Strangers in Their Own Land: Anger and Mourning on the American Right* (New York: New Press, 2016). For the argument that declining liberal values in the electorate are behind the rise of populism globally, see: Edward Luce, *The Retreat of Western Liberalism* (London: Little Brown, 2017); Yascha Mounk, *The People vs. Democracy: Why Our Freedom Is in Danger and How to Save It* (Cambridge: Harvard University Press, 2018).

6 On the "product differentiation" idea of politics, see: Gary W. Cox, "Centripetal and centrifugal incentives in electoral systems," *American Journal of Political Science* 34, no. 4 (1990), 903–35. The classic account is Anthony Downs, *An Economic Theory of Democracy* (New York: Harper, 1957).

7 It would be impossible to cite all the literature taking this "demand side" approach here. In addition to those cited in fn. 5, notable examples include: Jan-Werner Müller, *What Is Populism?* (Philadelphia: University of Pennsylvania Press, 2016); John B. Judis, *The Populist Explosion: How the Great Recession Transformed American and European Politics* (New York: Columbia Global Reports, 2016); Roger Eatwell and Matthew Goodwin, *National Populism: The Revolt against Liberal Democracy* (London: Penguin UK, 2018); Pippa Norris and

Ronald Inglehart, *Cultural Backlash: Trump, Brexit, and the Rise of Authoritarian-Populism* (New York: Cambridge University Press, 2019).

8 On the tendency to equate populism with democratic politics, see: Ernesto Laclau, *On Populist Reason* (London: Verso, 2005); elsewhere, it might be noted, Laclau has equated populism with fascism, Ernesto Laclau, *Politics and Ideology in Marxist Theory: Capitalism, Fascism, Populism* (London: NLB, 1977); also on the blurring of the boundary between populism and authoritarianism, see: Müller, *What Is Populism*; Norris and Inglehart, *Cultural Backlash*; Federico Finchelstein, *From Fascism to Populism in History* (Berkeley: University of California Press, 2017); Takis Spyros Pappas, *Populism and Liberal Democracy: A Comparative and Theoretical Analysis*, (Oxford: Oxford University Press, 2019). On some of the difficulties of measuring populist attitudes and on the effect of these attitudes on political behavior, see: Paul D. Kenny and Boris Bizumic, "Is there a populist personality? Populist attitudes, personality, and voter preference in Australian public opinion," working paper, Australian Catholic University (2021); Fabian G. Neuner and Christopher Wratil, "The populist marketplace: Unpacking the role of 'thin' and 'thick' ideology." *Political Behavior* 44 (2022), 551–74.

9 The LSE collection is: Ghita Ionescu and Ernest Gellner, eds., *Populism: Its Meaning and National Characteristics* (New York: Macmillan, 1969). The chapter by Wiles is entitled "A Syndrome not a doctrine"; the recent best seller refers to Müller, *What Is Populism?*

10 On the "strategic" conceptualization of populism, see: Kurt Weyland, "Clarifying a contested concept: Populism in the study of Latin American politics," *Comparative Politics* 34, no. 1 (2001), 1–22; Robert S. Jansen, "Populist mobilization: A new theoretical approach to populism," *Sociological Theory* 29, no. 2 (2011), 75–96; Erik Jones, "Populism in Europe," *The SAIS Review of International Affairs* 27, no. 1 (2007), 37–47; Emilia Zankina, "Theorizing the new populism in Eastern Europe," *Politologický časopis-Czech Journal of Political Science* 23, no. 2 (2016), 182–99; Robert R. Barr, "Populism as a political strategy," in *Routledge Handbook of Global Populism*, ed. Carlos de la Torre (London: Routledge, 2018), 44–56; Kurt Weyland, "A political-strategic approach," *The Oxford Handbook of Populism*, eds., Cristóbal Rovira Kaltwasser, Paul A. Taggart, Paulina Ochoa Espejo, and Pierre Ostiguy (New York: Oxford University Press, 2017), 48–72; Paul D. Kenny, "The strategic approach to populism," in *Routledge Handbook of Populism in the Asia Pacific*, eds. D. B. Subedi, Alan Scott, Howard Brasted, and Tony Lynch (London: Routledge, 2023). For an interesting take by a political theorist on understanding of populism as a practice rather than mere set of beliefs, see: Nadia Urbinati, *Me the People: How Populism Transforms Democracy* (Cambridge: Harvard University Press, 2019). Although political "-isms" are usually associated with ideologies – liberal-*ism*, social-*ism*, conservat-*ism*, etc. – they can equally refer to practices or systems with little or no ideological content. Like clientel-*ism* – the buying of votes – popul-*ism* is a strategy to capture and keep power.

11 Max Weber, *Economy and Society: An Outline of Interpretive Sociology*, 2 vols. (Berkeley: University of California Press, 1978). For a more detailed application of Weber's typology to understanding populism, see Kenny, "The strategic approach to populism."

12 Nicos Mouzelis, "On the concept of populism: Populist and clientelist modes of incorporation in semiperipheral polities," *Politics & Society* 14, no. 3 (1985): 334.

13 Paul D. Kenny, *Populism in Southeast Asia* (Cambridge: Cambridge University Press, 2019), 12.

14 "simply impossible." Daniel Rueda, "Is populism a political strategy? A critique of an enduring approach," *Political Studies* 69, no. 2 (2020): 170.

15 "a dangerous ambition" Hamilton, Federalist, no. 1; "in a representative" John L. Brooke, *Columbia Rising: Civil Life on the Upper Hudson from the Revolution to the Age of Jackson* (Chapel Hill: Omohundro Institute and University of North Carolina Press, 2010), 112.

16 Martin P. Wattenberg, *The Decline of American Political Parties, 1952–1996* (Cambridge: Harvard University Press, 1998), 90.

17 R. H. Coase, "The nature of the firm," *Economica* 4, no. 16 (1937), 386–405. On search, bargaining, and enforcement costs, see: Carl J. Dahlman, "The problem of externality," *The Journal of Law and Economics* 22, no. 1 (1979), 141–62.

18 The story of Ford's misadventure in Brazil is told in Greg Grandin, *Fordlandia: The Rise and Fall of Henry Ford's Forgotten Jungle City* (London: Icon, 2010). The 70 percent outsourcing figure comes from Bartleby Research, www.bartleby.com/ essay/Ford-and-Its-Outsourcing-P3LU9SXH3GEZ.

19 "swilling the planters," Charles S. Sydnor, *Gentlemen Freeholders: Political Practices in Washington's Virginia* (Chapel Hill: Omohundro Institute and University of North Carolina Press, 1952): 51. On Johnson in Texas, see Robert A. Caro, *The Path to Power*, (New York: Vintage Books, 1981), 277.

20 On Louisiana, see Harry Williams, *Huey Long* (New York: Vintage, 1981), 184; for Texas, see Robert A. Caro, *Means of Ascent*, (New York: Vintage Books, 1991). On Murray, see Theodore Roosevelt, *Theodore Roosevelt: An Autobiography by Theodore Roosevelt* (New York: Charles Scribner's Sons, 1920; repr., Project Gutenberg, eBook, #3335), 70–2.

21 "disunited," Niccolò Machiavelli, *The Prince*, trans. W. K. Marriott (Project Gutenberg eBook, 1998), ch. XII. On some of the downsides of patronage as an election strategy, see Carolyn M. Warner, "Political parties and the opportunity costs of patronage," *Party Politics* 3, no. 4 (1997), 533–48.

22 For the 2016 election: "Cost of Election," OpenSecrets.org, www.opensecrets.org/ overview/cost.php; for Bloomberg, see Jason Lange, "Bloomberg bows out of presidential contest but his money will stay," *Reuters* March 5, 2020, www .reuters.com/article/us-usa-election-bloomberg/bloomberg-bows-out-of-presiden tial-contest-but-his-money-will-stay-idUSKBN20R2AJ.

23 For hours of party work in the nineteenth century, see Richard J. Jensen, Steven L. Piott, and Christopher C. Gibbs, *Grass Roots Politics: Parties, Issues, and Voters, 1854–1983* (Westport, CT: Greenwood Press, 1983), 31. On Obama's volunteers, see: Elizabeth McKenna and Hahrie Han, *Groundbreakers: How Obama's 2.2 Million Volunteers Transformed Campaigning in America* (New York: Oxford University Press, 2014).

24 Margit Tavits, *Post-Communist Democracies and Party Organization* (Cambridge: Cambridge University Press, 2013), 11. "To govern through a party," quoted in Englund, *Napoleon*, 199.

25 "affordable politics," Urbinati, *Me the People*, 178. In an unduly neglected article on populism in Bulgaria, Zankina argues that populists utilize "informal," leader-centric

institutions, rather than "formal," bureaucratic political parties, which lowers the transaction costs entailed in political mobilization. Although very much on the right track, the formal-informal distinction is perhaps overdrawn in her briefly outlined schema. Patronage too is a relatively low-cost informal institution, so we do not get a sense of why a political leader would choose populism over patronage. Zankina, "Theorizing the new populism in Eastern Europe." For a similar emphasis on populism as an "informal" institution, see Zoltán Ádám, "Explaining Orbán: A political transaction cost theory of authoritarian populism," *Problems of Post-Communism* 66, no. 6 (2019), 385–401.

26 On the importance of voter "availability" in explaining populist support, see esp. Weyland, "Clarifying a contested concept."

27 This short temporal focus is evident in some prominent works on populism in Europe: Judis, *Populist Explosion*; Cas Mudde, *Populist Radical Right Parties in Europe* (New York: Cambridge University Press, 2007). Longer time frames are much more common in research on populism in America, see: Michael Kazin, *The Populist Persuasion: An American History*, rev. ed. (Ithaca, NY: Cornell University Press, 1998); Laura Grattan, *Populism's Power: Radical Grassroots Democracy in America* (New York: Oxford University Press, 2016); Eichengreen, *The Populist Temptation* provides provides a comparative analysis of populism in twentieth-century Western Europe and America.

28 "Men do not go," *The Diary and Letters of Gouverneur Morris*, Vol I, ch. 8, https://oll.libertyfund.org/title/morris-the-diary-and-letters-of-gouverneur-morris-vol-1.

CHAPTER 2

1 Plutarch, *Pericles*, VII.1, in *The Parallel Lives*, vol. III, Loeb Classical Library edition (1916).

2 M. Tullius Cicero, *For Plancius, 4.11, in The Orations of Marcus Tullius Cicero*, trans. C. D. Yonge (London: George Bell & Sons, 1891).

3 "filth and shit," Cicero, Letters to Atticus, I.XVI.11; this colorful translation comes from Robert Morstein-Marx, *Mass Oratory and Political Power in the Late Roman Republic* (Cambridge: Cambridge University Press, 2004), 128. Although Antony may well have brandished Caesar's bloody shirt at the funeral oration, his main strategy was coercion, not populism; if anyone persued the latter strategy in the immediate aftermath of Caesar's death, it was his adopted heir, Octavian, in part because he initially lacked a military retinue of his own, see Jochen Bleicken, *Augustus: The Biography* (London: Penguin, 2016): 41–2.

4 "The people will follow," Aristotle, *The Constitution of Athens*, XII.2; "assiduous in cultivating," Thomas N. Mitchell, *Athens: A History of the World's First Democracy* (New Haven, CT: Yale University Press, 2015), 33; "properly and well," Herodotus, *The Histories*, I.59.

5 Fragment 111, Heraclitus, *Fragments: The Collected Wisdom of Heraclitus*, trans. Brooks Haxton (New York: Penguin, 2001), 110.

6 "government by the best," Plato, *Menexenus*, 238d; Donald Kagan, *The Archidamian War* (Ithaca, NY: Cornell University Press, 1974), 96. Xenophon, *Economics*.

7 "stirring up the people," "went beyond all men," "to humble his eminence," Plutarch, *Themistocles*, 3.2, 22.3.

8 "foremost among the Athenians," "in name a democracy," Thucydides, *Peloponnesian War*, 1.139.4, 2.65.9; Plato, *Phaedrus*, 269e; "popular" Plutarch, *Pericles*, VII.2.

9 Plague deaths, Robert J. Littman, "The plague of Athens: epidemiology and paleopathology." *Mount Sinai Journal of Medicine: A Journal of Translational and Personalized Medicine* 76, no. 5 (2009): 456–67. "Not much later," Thucydides, *Peloponnesian War*, 2.65.4.

10 "grasping at supremacy," "most persuasive," "fine speeches," "the people," Thucydides, *Peloponnesian War*, 2.65.10, 3.36, 3.38, 3.36–49. "the first to shout," Aristotle, *Athenian Politics*, XXVIII.3.

11 Aristophanes, *Knights*, 188–94; "subjected himself," Plutarch, *Moralia*, vol. X, 807, trans. H. N. Fowler (Cambridge: Loeb Classical Library edition, 1936). "the man who can persuade," Xenophon, *Memorabilia*, 1.2.11, trans. Robin Watterfield (London: Penguin, 1990); "a rapid way to power for the inexperienced," Walter Robert Connor, *The New Politicians of Fifth-Century Athens* (Princeton, NJ: Princeton University Press, 1971), 150.

12 "it cannot," Thucydides, *Peloponnesian War*, 5.26.2.

13 "For surely," Plato, *Protagoras*.

14 "What is the hope," Plato, *First Alcibiades*, 105a–c; see also, Plato, *Protagoras*; Xenophon, *Memorabilia*, 1.2.40–46.

15 "Nor is it unfair," Thucydides, *Peloponnesian War*, 6.16.4 Donald Kagan, *The Peace of Nicias and the Sicilian Expedition* (Ithaca, NY: Cornell University Press, 1981), ch. 7.

16 On the ostracism of Hyperbolos, see Plutarch, *Alcibiades*, XIII, Plutarch, *Nicias*, XI; Plutarch, *Aristides* VII.3; in one version, Alcibiades finds himself up against Phaeax (another prominent young noble) rather than Nicias; for a discussion of the evidence, see Connor, *The New Politicians of Fifth-Century Athens*, 79–84. Kagan, *Peace of Nicias*, 145–47.

17 "those most jealous," Thucydides, *Peloponnesian War*, 6.15.4. On the sacrilege, see David Stuttard, *Nemesis: Alcibiades and the Fall of Athens* (Cambridge, MA: Harvard University Press, 2018): 146–53.

18 "ran around and crowded," Plutarch, *Alcibiades*, XXX.4.

19 "the mob again," "the multitude," "do nothing," Xenophon, *Hellenika*, trans. John Marincola, ed. Robert B. Strassler (New York: Pantheon Books, 2009), 1.7.13., 1.7.12., 1.7.15.

20 "Athenian politicians," Jacqueline de Romilly, *The Life of Alcibiades: Dangerous Ambition and the Betrayal of Athens*, trans. Elizabeth Trapnell Rawlings (Ithaca, NY: Cornell University Press, 2019), 37.

21 "was an aristocrat," P. J. Rhodes, *Alcibiades* (Barnsley: Pen & Sword Military, 2011): 42. "there was an unbroken," Aristotle, *Athenian Politics*, XXVIII.4.

22 "master of our emotions," Longinus, *On the Sublime*, XII, 3–4; XVI, 2. "greatest," Quintilian, *Institutio Oratoria*, 10.1.76.

23 "Look at the politicians who are responsible for these things," Demosthenes, *Third Olympiac*, 3.29. On Demosthenes as a politician, see: Ian Worthington, *Demosthenes of Athens and the Fall of Classical Greece* (New York: Oxford University Press, 2013), esp. chs. 5–6.

24 "more important than his life," Julius Caesar, *The Civil War*, trans. John Carter (New York: Oxford University Press, 2008), 1.9. "cause lacks nothing," quoted in Christian Maier, *Julius Caesar*, (New York: Harper Collins, 1995), 5.

25 On political campaigning, Marcus Tullius Cicero, *Letters to Atticus*, I.I., I.XVI; "[a]nd it is our duty," Marcus Tullius Cicero, *For Plancius*, 4.11.

26 This characterization of the *comitia tributa* as a single entity is sufficient for our purposes, although some scholars prefer to further sub-divide it, for example, Lily Ross Taylor, *Roman Voting Assemblies: From the Hannibalic War to the Dictatorship of Caesar* (Ann Arbor: University of Michigan Press).

27 "appearance of liberty," Marcus Tullius Cicero, *On the Laws*, 3.38. "neither could kings," quoted in Marcus Tullius Cicero, *De Oratore*, 2.48/199, trans. J. S. Watson (1860). "acquire a distinct identity," E. P. Thompson, *Whigs and Hunters: The Origin of the Black Act* (New York: Pantheon Books, 1975), 266, 68.

28 In my interpretation of Tiberius' motivations, I'm siding with the likes of D. L. Stockton, *The Gracchi* (Oxford: Oxford University Press, 1979), 31, 37–8; Ernst Badian, *Tiberius Gracchus and the Beginning of the Roman Revolution* (Berlin: De Gruyter, 2016).

29 On the role of the Senate's rejection in the rise of Tiberius Gracchus, see Richard Alston, *Rome's Revolution: Death of the Republic and Birth of the Empire* (New York: Oxford University Press, 2015), 33–4; H. H. Scullard, *From the Gracchi to Nero: A History of Rome 133 BC to AD 68*, 5th ed. (London: Routledge, 2010), 21. Stockton, *The Gracchi*, 29. "hath not," "fame and influence," Plutarch, *Tiberius Gracchus*, 9. Appian, *Civil Wars*, 1.11.

30 "Let those," Appian, *Civil Wars*, 1.16.

31 "unprecedented," Appian, *Civil Wars*, 1.21. "incomparable," "appear to be." Plutarch, *Gaius Gracchus*, III.2, I.3.

32 Lily Ross Taylor, *Party Politics in the Age of Caesar* (Berkeley: University of California Press, 1971), 13.

33 Morstein-Marx, *Mass Oratory and Political Power in the Late Roman Republic*, 206. Henrik Mouritsen, *Politics in the Roman Republic* (Cambridge: Cambridge University Press, 2017), 112–23. The *ratio popularis* description was coined by Christian Meier, "Populares," *RE* suppl. 10, 549–615; it can be translated as a popular method or tactics. On intra-elite political competition, see also; Scullard, *From the Gracchi to Nero*, 5–6. "had no common cause," Maier, *Julius Caesar*, 39. "defending the rights," Sallust, *The War with Cataline* (Loeb Classical Library, 1931), 38.3. Richard Alston, *Rome's Revolution*.

34 On bribery and clientelism, see: John R. Patterson, *Political Life in the City of Rome*, (London: Bristol Classical, 2000), 60–3; Andrew Lintott, "Electoral bribery in the Roman Republic," *The Journal of Roman Studies* 80 (1990), 1–16; Alexander Yakobson, "Petitio et Largitio: Popular Participation in the Centuriate Assembly of the Late Republic," *The Journal of Roman Studies* 82 (1992), 32–52; Alexander Yakobson, *Elections and Electioneering in Rome: A Study in the Political System of the Late Republic* (Stuttgart: F. Steiner, 1999).

35 "Citizens," "a good reputation," quoted in Catherine E. W. Steel, *The End of the Roman Republic 146 to 44 BC: Conquest and Crisis* (Edinburgh: Edinburgh University Press, 2013), 54, 56; "deserter," Cassius Dio, *Roman History*, trans. Herbert Baldwin Foster (1905), 36.44.

36 "ambitious politicians," Erich S. Gruen, *The Last Generation of the Roman Republic* (Berkeley: University of California Press, 1995), 7. "technique," "method," W. Jeffrey Tatum, *The Patrician Tribune: Publius Clodius Pulcher* (Chapel Hill: The University of North Carolina Press, 1999), 16.

37 Some scholars have even characterized the contiones as democratic or quasi-democratic institutions: Fergus Millar, *The Crowd in Rome in the Late Republic* (Ann Arbor: University of Michigan Press, 1998), 225; Morstein-Marx, *Mass Oratory and Political Power in the Late Roman Republic*. This may going too far, given all of the other limitations on popular participation in the political process; for an assessment of this debate, see: Henrik Mouritsen, *Plebs and Politics in the Late Roman Republic* (New York: Cambridge University Press, 2001), ch. 3.

38 J. P. Toner, *The Day Commodus Killed a Rhino: Understanding the Roman Games* (Baltimore: Johns Hopkins University Press, 2014). "Bread and circuses," Juvenal, *Satire X*; "the popular feeling," Cicero, *Letters to Atticus* I.XIX; "worthless," Cicero, *Sestius*, 115.

39 "made for the amusement," "the consulship of Julius and Caesar," Seutonius, *The Lives of the Twelve Caesars* (trans. Alexander Thomson), X.8, XX.2.

40 I owe this interpretation to Steel, *End of the Roman Republic*, 123.

41 Henry Hansmann, Reinier Kraakman, and Richard Squire, "Incomplete organizations: Legal entities and asset partitioning in Roman commerce," in *Roman Law and Economics: Institutions and Organizations*, eds. Giuseppe Dari-Mattiacci and Dennis P. Kehoe (Oxford: Oxford University Press, 2020).

42 On Marius, see L. J. F. Keppie, *The Making of the Roman Army: From Republic to Empire* (Norman: University of Oklahoma Press, 1998), 43.

43 On the militarization of Roman politics, see: Arthur Keaveney, *The Army in the Roman Revolution* (New York: Routledge, 2007); Alston, *Rome's Revolution*.

CHAPTER 3

1 "Every party," quoted in R. R. Palmer, *Twelve Who Ruled: The Year of the Terror in the French Revolution*, 1st Princeton Classic ed. (Princeton, NJ: Princeton University Press, 2005), 291.

2 "Solicitations for office," Thomas Jefferson to James Sullivan, March 3, 1808. *The Writings of Thomas Jefferson*, Memorial ed., Lipscomb and Bergh (eds.), 12:3.

3 Vergniaud quoted in Jeremy Popkin, *A New World Begins: The History of the French Revolution* (New York: Basic, 2020), 372.

4 "the cutting off of heads," quoted in Ruth Scurr, *Fatal Purity: Robespierre and the French Revolution* (London: Vintage, 2006), 212. "My own affections," "From Thomas Jefferson to William Short, 3 January 1793," *Founders Online*, National Archives, https://founders.archives.gov/documents/Jefferson/01-25-02-0016; "[a] little rebellion," "From Thomas Jefferson to James Madison, 30 January 1787," *Founders Online*, National Archives, https://founders.archives.gov/documents/Jefferson/01-11-02-0095; Jefferson would later acknowledge in a letter to John Adams (dated January 11, 1816) that he grossly underestimated the violence of the French Revolution, not believing in 1789 that "they would have lasted so long, nor have cost so much blood," "Thomas Jefferson to John Adams, 11 January 1816," *Founders Online*, National

Archives, https://founders.archives.gov/documents/Jefferson/03-09-02-0219. In the American context, the phrase, "[g[ive me liberty or give me death" is usually attributed to a March 1777 speech by Virginia's Patrick Henry, https://avalon.law.yale.edu/18th_century/patrick.asp; there were numerous similar utterances in the French case, the radical Camille Demouilins, for instance, declaring at Paris's Café Foy on July 12, 1789 (two days before the fall of the Bastille), "I would rather die than submit to servitude," quoted in Simon Schama, *Citizens: A Chronicle of the French Revolution* (London: Penguin, 2004), 325; indeed, many French men and women took the oath to "[l]ive free or die!" quoted in Timothy Tackett, *The Coming of the Terror in the French Revolution* (Cambridge, MA: Harvard University Press, 2015), 63. Renowned historian of the Revolution, Tackett, is dismissive of the idea that the members of the Assembly were naive ideologues; see: Timothy Tackett, *Becoming a Revolutionary: The Deputies of the French National Assembly and the Emergence of a Revolutionary Culture (1789–1790)* (Princeton, NJ: Princeton University Press, 1996).

5   On patronage in Ancien Régime France, including this reference to Robespierre, see: Tackett, *The Coming of the Terror*, 20, 31.

6   "a blood sport," Popkin, *A New World Begins*, 328. Colin Jones, *The Great Nation: France from Louis XV to Napoleon 1715–99* (London: Penguin, 2002), 153–57.

7   On the press, see John Markoff, "Literacy and revolt: Some empirical notes on 1789 in France," *American Journal of Sociology* 92, no. 2 (1986).

8   "the people." David Lawday, *The Giant of the French Revolution: Danton, a Life* (London: Jonathan Cape, 2009), 37–8.

9   "Strike down," in Laura Auricchio, *The Marquis: Lafayette Reconsidered* (New York: Alfred A. Knopf, 2014), 259.

10 "We need a man," Lawday, *Danton*, 135.

11 "It's the people," "Il nous faut." Lawday, *Danton*, 13, 274; the English rendering of Danton's famous triplet as "Daring!" or "Audacity!" doesn't have the euphony of the French original.

12 "One cannot," Louis Antoine Saint-Just, speech to the Assembly, November 13, 1792, *Liberty, Equality, Fraternity: Exploring the French Revolution*, https://revolution.chnm.org/d/320. "I vote," Lawday, *Danton*, 169.

13 "the laws," Lawday, *Danton*, 148.

14 "dying six weeks," in Jones, *The Great Nation*, 493; "winding up," "it is hard," in Peter McPhee, *Robespierre: A Revolutionary Life* (New Haven, CT: Yale University Press, 2012), 59, 94. "obscure provincial advocates," Edmund Burke, *Reflections on the Revolution in France*, Selected Works of Edmund Burke, Vol. 2, Liberty Fund ed. (1999), 131.

15 On Robespierre as a speaker, see David P. Jordan, *The Revolutionary Career of Maximilien Robespierre* (Chicago: University of Chicago Press, 1985), 63–80.

16 This paragraph, and figures, draw on Michael L. Kennedy, *The Jacobin Clubs in the French Revolution: The First Years* (Princeton, NJ: Princeton University Press, 1982), 223.

17 On the fraught events of Thermidor itself, see Colin Jones, *The Fall of Robespierre: 24 hours in Revolutionary Paris* (New York: Oxford University Press, 2021).

18 "the inescapable," George Rudé, *The Crowd in the French Revolution* (Oxford: Clarendon, 1959), 208.

19 "I had," Popkin, *A New World Begins*, 481.

20 "whiff of," quoted in Adam Zamoyski, *Napoleon: A Life* (New York: Basic Books), 99.

21 Michael Broers, *Napoleon: Soldier of Destiny* (New York: Pegasus Books, 2015). "Do you believe that I triumph," in Philip G. Dwyer, *Napoleon: The Path to Power, 1769–1799* (London: Bloomsbury, 2007), 299. See also ch. 10 of Dwyer, *Napoleon* on the pillaging of Italy. "take up the plough," quoted in Zamoyski, *Napoleon*, 172.

22 On the dispatches, see Robert B. Holtman, Napoleonic Propaganda (Baton Rouge: Louisiana State University Press, 1950), 19–21. On Napoleon's newspapers, Philip Dwyer, *Napoleon*, 306–10.

23 "I shall arrive," "military government,"quoted in Patrice Gueniffey, *Bonaparte: 1769–1802*, trans. Steven Rendall (Cambridge, MA: Harvard University Press, 2015), 521, 363; "the people," "I have tasted command," "pear," quoted in Zamoyski, *Napoleon*, 58, 173, 168. "no other end," quoted in William Milligan Sloane, *Life of Napoleon Bonaparte*, vol. 2 (Ann Arbor: University of Michigan Press, 1896), 19. "If only Louis XVI," quoted in Steven Englund, *Napoleon* (Cambridge, MA: Harvard University Press, 2005), 51.

24 "There's your man," quoted in Englund, *Napoleon*, 158.

25 "politically opportunistic," Dwyer, *Napoleon*, 479.

26 "Have I heard you correctly?" quoted in Isser Woloch, *Napoleon and His Collaborators: The Making of a Dictatorship*, 1st ed. (New York: W.W. Norton, 2001), 30.

27 On the election results, although there was not the stark evidence of direct manipulation of the count as with the adoption of the Constitution of Year VIII that put him in power, as Alan Forest points out, it has to be kept in mind that voting was public and the police state kept a watchful eye; Alan Forest, *Napoleon* (London: Quercus, 2011); "confidence comes from," quoted in Englund, *Napoleon*, 169.

28 On Napoleonic propaganda, see Nina Martyris, "Napoleon's chamber pot: Propaganda and fake news," *The Paris Review*, February 26, 2018, www.theparisreview.org/blog/2018/02/26/napoleons-chamber-pot-propaganda-fake-news; M. K. Dziewanowski, "Napoleon: Legend and propaganda," *The Journal of Military History* 9 (1945). "first sovereign," Holtman, *Napoleonic Propaganda*, 246. On the dissemination of prints and engravings Andrew Roberts, *Napoleon the Great* (London: Penguin, 2014), 130–31; David O'Brien and Antoine-Jean baron Gros, *After the Revolution: Antoine-Jean Gros, Painting and Propaganda under Napoleon* (University Park: Pennsylvania State University Press, 2006). "forged his own legend," Jean Tulard, *Napoléon: Le Pouvoir, la Nation, la Légende* (Paris: LGF, 1997), 78–9. "bond between us," "in three years," quoted in Adam Zamoyski, *Napoleon*, 640, 326.

29 "to govern," quoted in Englund, *Napoleon*, 199. "I refused to be," quoted in Zamoyski, *Napoleon*, 241. "My power," quoted in Gueniffey, *Bonaparte*: 803.

30 "blustering ignorant men," quoted in Sean Wilentz, *The Rise of American Democracy: Jefferson to Lincoln* (New York: Norton, 2005), 29. "our rights," quoted in Woody Holton, *Unruly Americans and the Origins of the Constitution* (New York: Hill and Wang, 2007), 5. On paper money, see Roger H. Brown, *Redeeming the Republic: Federalists, Taxation, and the Origins of the Constitution* (London: Johns Hopkins University Press, 1993).

31 On the revolution's "unruly" elements, see: Holton, *Unruly Americans*. For an exhaustive treatment of this process in a single New York county, see John

Brooke, *Columbia Rising: Civil Life on the Upper Hudson from the Revolution to the Age of Jackson* (Chapel Hill: University of North Carolina Press, 2013). For the view that the Revolution's end was conservative, even reactionary, see Terry Bouton, *Taming Democracy: "The People," the Founders, and the Troubled Ending of the American Revolution* (Oxford: Oxford University Press, 2007); Brown, *Redeeming the Republic*. For the more traditional view that the American Revolution was truly "revolutionary" both in design and outcome, see Gordon S. Wood, *The Radicalism of the American Revolution*, 1st Vintage ed. (New York: Vintage, 1993); Edward Countryman, *A People in Revolution: The American Revolution and Political Society in New York, 1760–1790* (New York: W.W. Norton, 1989). On the continued salience of deference, patrimonialism, and faction as the building blocks of politics in the new nation, see Ronald P. Formisano, "Deferential-participant politics: the early republic's political culture, 1789–1840," *American Political Science Review* 68, no. 2 (1974), 473–87; Richard R. Beeman, *The Old Dominion and the New Nation, 1788–1801* (Lexington: University Press of Kentucky, 1972).

32 "every man will," in "From John Adams to James Sullivan, 26 May 1776," *Founders Online*, National Archives, https://founders.archives.gov/docu ments/Adams/06-04-02-0091; "rich will take advantage," quoted in John Keane, *The Life and Death of Democracy* (New York: W.W. Norton, 2009), 279; "disease," "poison," "Alexander Hamilton to Theodore Sedgwick, July 10, 1804," *Massachusetts Historical Society*, www.masshist.org/database/viewer.php?item_id=207. "excess of democracy," Alexander Hamilton, "Constitutional Convention Speech on a Plan of Government, June 18, 1787," *Founders Online*, https://founders.archives.gov/documents/Hamilton/01-04-02-0098-0004. On the persistent attachment to monarchical rule through the Revolution, see Eric Nelson, *The Royalist Revolution: Monarchy and the American Founding* (Cambridge, MA: Harvard University Press, 2014).

33 On Jefferson's elitism, see his one of his most thorough and admiring biographers: Dumas Malone, *Jefferson the Virginian*, 1st University of Virginia Pressed. (Charlottesville: University of Virginia Press, 2005). "An elective despotism," in Thomas Jefferson, *Notes on the State of Virginia*, Query 13, 120–21, https://press-pubs.uchicago.edu/founders/print_documents/v1ch10s9.html; "I have ever," and "any thing than," quoted in Merrill D. Peterson, *Thomas Jefferson and the New Nation: A Biography* (New York: Oxford University Press, 1970), 121–22; "disturbing the public," James Madison, February 5, 1788, Federalist No. 49; "the major number," quoted in Holton, *Unruly Americans and the Origins of the Constitution*, 7. "it would be the interest," "From James Madison to James Monroe, 5 October 1786," *Founders Online*, National Archives, https://founders.archives.gov/documents/Madison/01-09-02-0054.

34 Michael J. Klarman, *The Framers' Coup: The Making of the United States Constitution* (New York: Oxford University Press, 2016); Irwin H. Polishook, *Rhode Island and the Union, 1774–1795* (Evanston, IL: Northwestern University Press, 1969); Holton, *Unruly Americans*, 55–64. "only strengthened," Beeman, *The Old Dominion*, xii.

35 Robert A. Dahl, *How Democratic Is the American Constitution?* (New Haven, CT: Yale University Press, 2001); Michael J. Klarman, *The Framers' Coup*. On figures for the Electoral College, see James Roger Sharp, *The Deadlocked Election of 1800:*

Jefferson, Burr, and the Union in the Balance (Lawrence: University Press of Kansas, 2010), 116. "Ambition," Madison, Federalist no. 51. The perceived need to counteract state governments with the creation of a strong national executive do not preclude other motivations (e.g., foreign policy), see Max M. Edling, *A Revolution in Favor of Government: Origins of the U.S. Constitution and the Making of the American State* (New York: Oxford University Press, 2008).

36 Joanne B. Freeman, *Affairs of Honor: National Politics in the New Republic* (New Haven, CT: Yale University Press, 2001). "permanent electoral," Wilentz, *The Rise of American Democracy*, 50. "organizational development," "essential characteristic," Joel H. Silbey, *The American Political Nation, 1838–1893* (Stanford, CA: Stanford University Press, 1991), 15, 16. "If I could not go to heaven but with a party," in "From Thomas Jefferson to Francis Hopkinson, 13 March 1789," *Founders Online*, National Archives, https://founders.archives.gov/documents/Jefferson/01-14-02-0402.

37 Klarman, *The Framers' Coup*. Charles A. Beard, *An Economic Interpretation of the Constitution of the United States* (New York: The Macmillan Company, 1913). For research on the conflict between the sections, even at this early stage, see Robin L. Einhorn, *American Taxation, American Slavery* (Chicago: University of Chicago Press, 2006); Matthew Mason, *Slavery and Politics in the Early American Republic* (Chapel Hill: University of North Carolina Press, 2006). "subserviency" and "than to live under," quoted in James Roger Sharp, *American Politics in the Early Republic: The New Nation in Crisis* (New Haven, CT: Yale University Press, 1993), 36. "sole object," in "From Thomas Jefferson to James Madison, 27 April 1795," *Founders Online*, National Archives, https://founders.archives.gov/documents/Jefferson/01-28-02-0258; for a discussion of Jefferson's crossed-out letter, see James Roger Sharp, "Unraveling the mystery of Jefferson's letter of April 27, 1795," *Journal of the Early Republic* 6, no. 4 (1986), 411–18. On voting blocs in the early Congresses, see Mary P. Ryan, "Party formation in the United States Congress, 1789 to 1796: A quantitative analysis," *The William and Mary Quarterly: A Magazine of Early American History*, 28, no. 4 (1971), 523–42; John F. Hoadley, "The emergence of political parties in Congress, 1789–1803," *The American Political Science Review* 74, no. 3 (1980), 757–779.

38 On the use of gubernatorial patronage in colonial America, see Bernard Bailyn, *The Origins of American Politics* (New York: Vintage, 1968), esp. 107–24. Sydnor, *Gentlemen Freeholders: Political Practices in Washington's Virginia* (Chapel Hill: Omohundro Institute and University of North Carolina Press, 1952); Patricia U. Bonomi, *A Factious People: Politics and Society in Colonial New York* (Ithaca, NY: Cornell University Press, 2014); Jack P. Greene, *The Quest for Power: The Lower Houses of Assembly in the Southern Royal Colonies, 1689–1776* (New York: W. W. Norton, 1972).

39 "the only state," in Eric Foner, *Tom Paine and Revolutionary America* (New York: Oxford University Press, 1976), 108.

40 For a synthesis of the role of patronage in the American colonies, see Wood, *Radicalism*, 77–92. "controlled the federal," Noble E. Cunningham, *The Jeffersonian Republicans: The Formation of Party Organization, 1789–1801* (Chapel Hill: University of North Carolina Press, 1957), 148.

41 "professions of democracy," quoted in Charles Sellers, *The Market Revolution: Jacksonian America, 1815–1846* (New York: Oxford University Press, 1991), 35.

42 "killed themselves," quoted in John E. Ferling, *John Adams: A Life* (New York: Oxford University Press, 2010), 404.

43 Nancy Isenberg, *Fallen Founder: The Life of Aaron Burr* (New York: Penguin, 2007). On New York and South Carolina, respectively, see Cunningham, *The Jeffersonian Republicans*, 178, 238. On patronage after 1801, see. Noble E. Cunningham, *The Jeffersonian Republicans in Power: Party Operations, 1801–1809* (Chapel Hill: University of North Carolina Press, 1963), esp. chs. 2–3. Leonard L. Richards, *The Slave Power: The Free North and Southern Domination, 1780–1860* (Baton Rouge: Louisiana State University Press, 2000), 64–5. Carl E. Prince, *New Jersey's Jeffersonian Republicans: The Genesis of an Early Party Machine, 1789–1817* (Chapel Hill: University of North Carolina Press, 1967), 219–21.

44 "This expansion of popular politics," Wood, *Radicalism*, 173.

CHAPTER 4

1 "I never saw," quoted in John Steele Gordon, "An inauguration for the people," *The Wall Street Journal*, January 20, 2009, www.wsj.com/articles/SB123241405445996273.

2 George Dangerfield, *The Era of Good Feelings* (New York: Harcourt, 1952). For a recent overview, see Daniel Walker Howe, *What Hath God Wrought: The Transformation of America, 1815–1848* (New York: Oxford University Press, 2007).

3 "basis for a new organization," quoted in Charles Sellers, *The Market Revolution: Jacksonian America, 1815–1846* (New York: Oxford University Press, 1994), 131.

4 This account of Jackson's early career draws on Mark Renfred Cheathem, *Andrew Jackson, Southerner* (Baton Rouge: Louisiana State University Press, 2013); H. W. Brands, *Andrew Jackson, His Life and Times* (New York: Doubleday, 2005); Robert Vincent Remini, *Andrew Jackson and the Course of American Empire, 1767–1821* (Baltimore, MD: Johns Hopkins University Press, 1998).

5 "one motive," quoted in Remini, *Andrew Jackson and the Course of American Empire*, 418.

6 Charles Sellers, "Jackson men with feet of clay," *The American Historical Review* 62, no. 3 (1957): 537–51.

7 Donald J. Ratcliffe, *The One-Party Presidential Contest: Adams, Jackson, and 1824's Five-Horse Race* (Lawrence: University of Kansas Press, 2015).

8 "as hard as decency allowed," Robert Vincent Remini, *Andrew Jackson and the Course of American Freedom, 1822–1832* (Baltimore, MD: Johns Hopkins University Press, 1998), 61. On Pennsylvania, Kim T. Phillips, "The Pennsylvania origins of the Jackson movement," *Political Science Quarterly* 91, no. 3 (1976): 489–508; David S. Heidler and Jeanne T. Heidler, *The Rise of Andrew Jackson: Myth, Manipulation, and the Making of Modern Politics* (New York: Basic Books, 2018), 174–76.

9 The "corrupt bargain" interpretation, although obviously quite a self-serving one for Jackson, has been accepted rather uncritically by Jackson's most prominent biographer, Robert V. Remini. For more critical appraisals, see: Heidler and Heidler, *The Rise of Andrew Jackson*, 197, 215–33; Mary W. M. Hargreaves, *The Presidency of John Quincy Adams* (Lawrence: University Press of Kansas, 1985), 36–7; Ratcliffe,

The One Party Presidential Contest, 232–57. "I intermix with none," quoted in Remini, *Andrew Jackson and the Course of American Freedom*, 62. "the first principle of our system," quoted in Harry L. Watson, *Liberty and Power: The Politics of Jacksonian America* (New York: Hill and Wang, 2006), 97.

10 On the popular vote, see Ratcliffe, *The One-Party Presidential Contest*, appendix 1.

11 Lynn H. Parsons, *The Birth of Modern Politics: Andrew Jackson, John Quincy Adams, and the Election of 1828* (New York: Oxford University Press, 2009); Heidler and Heidler, *The Rise of Andrew Jackson*; Donald B. Cole, *Vindicating Andrew Jackson: The 1828 Election and the Rise of the Two-Party System* (Lawrence: University Press of Kansas, 2009). "personal popularity," in Donald B. Cole, *The Presidency of Andrew Jackson* (Lawrence: University Press of Kansas, 1993), 17.

12 "no portion of the Union," in Cole, *Vindicating Andrew Jackson*, 94.

13 "politics took precedence over ideology," Donald B. Cole, *Martin Van Buren and the American Political System* (Princeton, NJ: Princeton University Press, 1984). 115. "our money," in Lee Benson, *The Concept of Jacksonian Democracy: New York as a Test Case* (Princeton, NJ: Princeton University Press), 41.

14 "the goal was personal," Cole, *Vindicating Andrew Jackson*, 85.

15 Parsons, *Birth of Modern Politics*; Heidler and Heidler, *The Rise of Andrew Jackson*; "personal popularity," quoted in Hargreaves, *The Presidency of John Quincy Adams*, 300. "Don't back no losers," quoted in Milton Rakove, *Don't Make No Waves, Don't Back No Losers: An Insider's Analysis of the Daley Machine* (Bloomington: Indiana University Press, 1975), 11.

16 Sean Wilentz, *The Rise of American Democracy: Jefferson to Lincoln* (New York: Norton), 4.

17 "I wanted," "the fundamental vice," quoted in Alan Strauss-Schom, *The Shadow Emperor: A Biography of Napoleon III* (New York: St Martin's Press, 2018), 60.

18 Roger Price, *The French Second Empire: An Anatomy of Political Power* (New York: Cambridge University Press, 2001), 12–13.

19 "In the absence of organised parties," Roger Price, *A Concise History of France*, 2nd ed. (Cambridge: Cambridge University Press, 2005), 201. "dangerously fragmented," Roger Magraw, *France, 1815–1914: The Bourgeois Century* (New York: Oxford University Press, 1986), 139.

20 On Louis Napoleon's aborted return, see: Christopher Guyver, *The Second French Republic 1848–1852: A Political Reinterpretation* (Palgrave Macmillan, 2016), 91; "I'm going to Paris," quoted in Price, *The French Second Empire*, 15. "the earth [was] red," quoted in Price, *A Concise History of France*, 204.

21 "One day," quoted in Strauss-Schom, *The Shadow Emperor*, 139.

22 Replacement of officeholders, Jon Meacham, *American Lion: Andrew Jackson in the White House*, (New York: Random House, 2008), 82.

23 "We have taught them how to conquer us," quoted in Wilentz, *Rise of American Democracy*, 507.

24 Michael F. Holt, *The Political Crisis of the 1850s* (New York: John Wiley & Sons, Inc., 1978).

25 One of the few writings I've found to note the difference between the well-organized third-party movements of the mid-nineteenth century and the much more persona-listic, or populist, ones of the mid-twentieth is Michael F. Holt, "The primacy of

party reasserted," *The Journal of American History* 86, no. 1 (1999): 151–57. On the early development of the Republican Party atop these local political organizations, see: William E. Gienapp, *The Origins of the Republican Party, 1852–1856* (New York: Oxford University Press, 1987).

26 Richard L. McCormick, *The Party Period and Public Policy: American Politics from the Age of Jackson to the Progressive Era* (New York: Oxford University Press, 1986); Joel H. Silbey, *The American Political Nation, 1838–1893* (Stanford, CA: Stanford University Press, 1991).

27 The best general survey is Charles Postel, *The Populist Vision* (New York: Oxford University Press, 2007). Polk was undoubtedly the more popular and was a shoo-in for the 1892 nomination. However, he died just weeks before the nominating convention, leading to the selection of Weaver.

28 C. Vann Woodward, *Tom Watson: Agrarian Rebel* (New York: MacMillan, 1938), 238–41.

29 "frying the fat," Lewis L. Gould, *The Republicans: A History of the Grand Old Party*, 2nd ed. (New York: Oxford University Press, 2012), 81. "probably as small as anyone," quoted in Hal Williams, *Realigning America: McKinley, Bryan, and the Remarkable Election of 1896* (Lawrence: University of Kansas Press), 90–1. "last night," Robert W. Cherny and Oscar Handlin, *A Righteous Cause: The Life of William Jennings Bryan* (Boston: Little, Brown, 1985), 28. On the convention setting itself, see Richard Franklin Bensel, *Passion and Preferences: William Jennings Bryan and the 1986 Democratic Convention* (New York: Cambridge University Press). On Bryan, see esp. Michael Kazin, *A Godly Hero: The Life of William Jennings Bryan* (New York: Knopf, 2006).

30 "Our party," quoted in Matthew Hild, *Greenbackers, Knights of Labor, and Populists: Farmer-Labor Insurgency in the Late-Nineteenth-Century South* (Athens: University of Georgia Press, 2007), 201.

31 "more than he needed the party," from Minneapolis Journal November 9, 1904, quoted in Doris Kearns Goodwin, *The Bully Pulpit: Theodore Roosevelt, William Howard Taft, and the Golden Age of Journalism* (New York: Simon & Schuster, 2013), 406. "adopted the plan," Theodore Roosevelt, *Theodore Roosevelt: An Autobiography by Theodore Roosevelt* (New York: Charles Scribner's Sons, 1920; repr., Project Gutenberg, eBook, #3335), ch. 8.

32 "only certain people," quoted in Geoffrey Cowan, *Let the People Rule: Theodore Roosevelt and the Birth of the Presidential Primary*, 1st ed. (New York: W.W. Norton, 2016), 43; "I have absolutely no affiliation with any political party," quoted in Gould, *Republicans*, 139. "voice of the people," quoted in H. W. Brands, *T. R.: The Last Romantic* (New York: Basic Books, 1997), 170.

33 "As I never" and "Depend upon it" in Arthur H. Cash, *John Wilkes: The Scandalous Father of Civil Liberty* (New Haven, CT: Yale University Press, 2006), 41, 46.

34 On the Conservative Party and democratization, see Daniel Ziblatt, *Conservative Political Parties and the Birth of Modern Democracy in Europe* (New York: Cambridge University Press, 2017), chs. 3–4. On eighteenth-century England, Archibald S. Foord, "The waning of 'The Influence of the Crown,'," *The English Historical Review* 62, no. 245 (1947): 484–507; John A. Phillips, "The structure of electoral politics in unreformed England," *Journal of British Studies* 19, no. 1 (1979),

100–17. On the cost of votes in Victorian England, see K. Theodore Hoppen, *The Mid-Victorian Generation, 1846–1886* (New York: Oxford University Press, 1998), 257–58; William B. Gwyn, *Democracy and the Cost of Politics in Britain* (London: University of London, Athlone Press, 1962). On reform, see Cornelius O'Leary, *The Elimination of Corrupt Practices in British Elections, 1868–1911* (Oxford: Clarendon Press, 1962). Although not "eliminating" corruption, the Act did mark an important step forward toward more programmatic politics, see Kathryn Rix, "'The Elimination of Corrupt Practices in British Elections'? Reassessing the impact of the 1883 Corrupt Practices Act," *The English Historical Review* 123, no. 500 (2008): 65–97; Edward Porritt, "Political corruption in England," *The North American Review* 183, no. 603 (1906): 995–1004. "back the masses," quoted in David Cannadine, *The Rise & Fall of Class in Britain* (New York: Columbia University Press, 1999), 112.

35   "the rats desert," quoted in William Manchester, *The Last Lion: Winston Spencer Churchill: Visions of Glory, 1874–1932* (New York: Bantam Books, 2013), 148

36   On the elite under Bonapartism, see: Magraw, *France*, 164–67, 77–8. "There is only," quoted in William Shirer, *The Collapse of the Third Republic* (New York: Simon and Schuster, 1969), 35.

37   "effective republican," William D. Irvine, *The Boulanger Affair Reconsidered: Royalism, Boulangism, and the Origins of the Radical Right in France* (Oxford University Press, 1988), 53. "deputies were expected," Price, *A Concise History of France*, 229. "spent most of his time," D. L. Hanley, *Party, Society and Government: Republican Democracy in France* (New York: Berghahn Books, 2002), 40.

38   Michael Burns, *Rural Society and French Politics: Boulangism and the Dreyfus Affair, 1886–1900* (Princeton, NJ: Princeton University Press, 1984).

39   "Lloyd George was marked," in Simon Heffer, *Staring at God: Britain in the Great War* (London: Windmill Books, 2019), 476.

40   "the nearest thing," in Robert Blake, *The Conservative Party from Peel to Major* (London, Faber & Faber, 2010), 196–97; "if he wants to be dictator," quoted in Heffer, *Staring at God*, 481.

41   "I am preparing," quoted in Alan Hyman, *The Rise and Fall of Horatio Bottomley* (London: Cassell, 1972), 195.

CHAPTER 5

1   quoted in Ian Kershaw, *The 'Hitler Myth' Image and Reality in the Third Reich*, (New York: Oxford University Press, 1987), 91.

2   This aphorism is commonly attributed to Churchill towards the end of the Second World War, although its provenance is impossible to verify.

3   Barrington Moore, *Social Origins of Dictatorship and Democracy: Lord and Peasant in the Making of the Modern World* (Boston: Beacon Press, 1966), 418. There is a good case to be made for "co-discovery" of this idea with Ralf Dahrendorf, *Society and Democracy in Germany* (London: Weidenfeld & Nicolson, 1967).

4   Gregory M. Luebbert. *Liberalism, Fascism, or Social Democracy: Social Classes and the Origins of Regimes in Interwar Europe* (New York: Oxford University Press, 1991). Daniel Ziblatt, *Conservative Parties and the Birth of Democracy* (New York: Cambridge University Press, 2017).

5   On pre-WWI demagogy, see: David Blackbourn, *Populists and Patricians (Routledge Revivals): Essays in Modern German History* (Routledge, 2014).

6 "Gentlemen," quoted in Ian Kershaw, *Hitler: 1889–1936, Hubris* (London: Penguin, 2001), 266–67; "there, rolling," quoted in Peter Longerich, *Goebbels: A Biography* (New York: Vintage, 2016), 53.

7 "what before," Adolf Hitler, *Mein Kampf*, trans. Ralph Manheim (Hutchinson & Co., 1969), 323; "born popular speaker," "critical faculty," quoted in Kershaw, *Hubris*, 124, 186. "as a speaker," quoted in Longerich, *Goebbels*, 70. "extraordinary magnetism," quoted in Kurt Weyland, *Assault on Democracy: Communism, Fascism, and Authoritarianism during the Interwar Years* (New York: Cambridge University Press, 2021), 160, fn. 3.

8 Social conditions, see Michael H. Kater, "Hitler in a social context," *Central European History* 14, no. 3 (1981), 243–72; "the impact," Kershaw, *Hubris*, xxvi. "Our problems seemed," quoted in Juan J. Linz, *The Breakdown of Democratic Regimes: Crisis, Breakdown, and Reequilibration* (Baltimore, MD: John Hopkins University Press, 1978), 53–4.

9 Banning of unions, Barry Eichengreen, *The Populist Temptation: Economic Grievance and Political Reaction in the Modern Era* (New York: Oxford University Press, 2020), 51; on SPD membership, Luebbert, *Liberalism, Fascism, or Social Democracy*, 118.

10 On German conservative politics prior to the First World War, see Ziblatt, *Conservative Political Parties*, 172–214; Stanley Suval, *Electoral Politics in Wilhelmine Germany* (Chapel Hill: University of North Carolina Press, 1985); Geoff Eley, *Reshaping the German Right: Radical Nationalism and Political Change after Bismarck* (Ann Arbor: University of Michigan Press, 1990).

11 "nonsense," in William Manchester, *The Last Lion: Winston Spencer Churchill: Visions of Glory, 1874–1932* (New York: Bantam, 1984), 406. On the unanticipated nature of the war, see: Christopher M. Clark, *The Sleepwalkers: How Europe Went to War in 1914* (London: Allen Lane, 2012); Hew Strachan, *The First World War* (Oxford: Oxford University Press, 2001).

12 On the DNVP's early development, see Hermann Beck, *The Fateful Alliance: German Conservatives and Nazis in 1933: The Mactergreifung in a New Light* (New York: Berghahn Books, 2008).

13 "a nobody," Peter Longerich, *Hitler: A Life*, trans. Jeremy Noakes and Lesley Sharpe (Oxford: Oxford University Press, 2019), 1–45. "upraised," Peter Fritzsche, *Germans into Nazis* (Cambridge, MA: Harvard University Press, 1998), 5; "I saw a pale," historian Karl Alexander von Muller, quoted in Volker Ullrich, *Hitler: Volume 1, Ascent, 1889–1939*, trans. Jefferson S. Chase (New York: Vintage, 2018), 80. "a release," "many hundreds," Hitler, *Mein Kampf*, 161, 196. The authenticity of Hoffman's photograph has been disputed.

14 "Goodness," "post of chairman," Kershaw, *Hubris*, 126–27, 164; On Hitler's membership, Richard J. Evans, *The Coming of the Third Reich* (London: Allen Lane, 2003), 170; Longerich, *Goebbels*, 17, 74. "like a wet poodle," Hitler, *Mein Kampf*, 199.

15 mass meetings, "Hitler was the NSDAP" Kershaw, *Hubris*, 149, 56; "dictatorial powers," Evans, *The Coming of the Third Reich*, 180.

16 On Hitler's takeover, see Longerich, *Hitler*, 87. "The best organisation," Adolf Hitler, *Mein Kampf*, 314.

17 Frederick Taylor, *The Downfall of Money: Germany's Hyperinflation and the Destruction of the Middle Class* (London: Bloomsbury, 2013), 280.

18 "I must enter Berlin," quoted in Frank Diköttter, *How to Be a Dictator: The Cult of Personality in the Twentieth Century* (London: Bloomsbury, 2019), 36.

19 "brilliant"; "who is this man"; "people's tribune" in Longerich, *Goebbels*, 56, 63.

20 On the lack of enthusaism for war in Nazi Germany, see Ian Kershaw, The "Hitler Myth", ch. 5; Robert O. Paxton, *French Peasant Fascism: Henry Dorgères' Greenshirts and the Crises of French Agriculture, 1929–1939* (New York: Oxford University Press, 1997), 8; "ideas held no interest," Kershaw, *Hubris*, 137. "regular party worker," Michael H. Kater, *The Nazi Party: A Social Profile of Members and Leaders, 1919–1945* (Cambridge, MA: Harvard University Press, 1985), 212.

21 "the great popularity," "far beyond," "sick," "brilliant," Kershaw, The "Hitler Myth," 161, 187, 275, 277; Hermann Göring, "Aufbau einer Nation," 1934, *quoted in Laurence Rees*, The Dark Charisma of Adolf Hitler: Leading Millions into the Abyss (London: Ebury, 2012); "it doesn't matter," Longerich, *Goebbels*, 31.

22 "now we've finished," "supreme mastery," Kershaw, *Hubris*, 269, 276.

23 Longerich, *Goebbels*, 115; Tobias Straumann, *1931: Debt, Crisis, and the Rise of Hitler,* (Oxford: Oxford University Press, 2019), 40–1. On the decline of the DNVP see Ziblatt, *Conservative Parties*; Beck, *Fateful Alliance*.

24 "heap of special interests," Kershaw, *Hubris*, 329; "nothing worse," "Nazis did not take over," Fritzsche, *Germans into Nazis*, 180, 190. "catch all," Thomas Childers, "The social bases of the National Socialist vote," *Journal of Contemporary History* 11, no. 4 (1976), 25. See also Thomas Childers, *The Nazi Voter: The Social Foundations of Fascism in Germany, 1919–1933* (Chapel Hill: University of North Carolina Press, 1983).

25 1929 to 1932 fall in production, Tobias Straumann, *1931:*, 6 January 1930 unemployment; state election results, Kershaw, *Hubris*, 318, 355–68. Suicide figures, Robert Gellately, *Backing Hitler: Consent and Coercion in Nazi Germany* (New York: Oxford University Press, 2001), 10.

26 On Nazi propaganda techniques, see Nicholas O'Shaughnessy, *Selling Hitler: Propaganda & the Nazi Brand* (London: Hurst & Co., 2016). On the importance of mass rallies, public meetings, and technologies, see Longerich, *Goebbels*, 80, 133, 71, 82, 171. Speedway figures, twenty speeches, 34,000 meetings, Kershaw, *Hubris*, 330, 329, 363; Adolf Hitler, *Mein Kampf*, 111–69.

27 Jörg L. Spenkuch and Philipp Tillmann, "Elite influence? Religion and the electoral success of the Nazis," *American Journal of Political Science* 62, no. 1 (2018): 19–36. "penetrate the network," Kershaw, *Hubris*, 321; "the difficulty of winning over," quoted in Longerich, *Hitler*, 84. "a mile wide," Childers, *The Nazi Voter*, 268–69. "broad-based, not deeply rooted," quoted in Fritzsche, *Germans into Nazis*, 212. On this competitive mobilization more generally, see William Sheridan Allen, *The Nazi Seizure of Power: The Experience of a Single German Town, 1922–1945* (New York: F. Watts, 1984).

28 "genuinely charismatic ruler," "rests on the faith," Max Weber, *Economy and Society: An Outline of Interpretive Sociology* (Berkeley: University of California Press), 1114–15, and 1125.

29 "the bakeries," quoted in Alan Bullock, *Hitler and Stalin: Parallel Lives* (New York: Knopf, 1992), 225.

30 "Dorgères' strength," Paxton, *French Peasant Fascism*, 61. "the tyranny of towns," Eugen Weber, *The Hollow Years: France in the 1930s* (New York: Norton, 1994), 39.
31 Weber, *The Hollow Years*.
32 "without an office," in Roy Jenkins, *Churchill* (London: Macmillan, 2001), 376; "direct descendant," Simon Heffer, *Staring at God: Britain in the Great War* (London: Windmill Books, 2020), 300.
33 "authority," in Jenkins, *Churchill*, 591.
34 "I left because I was afraid"; "others had power," quoted in Harry Williams, *Huey Long* (New York: Vintage, 1981), 417–18; 737.
35 "sport of kings"; "as smart as I am," quoted in Williams, *Huey Long*, 108; 7.

CHAPTER 6

1 "This preservation," Charles Darwin. *The Origin of Species*, 6th ed. (1872), 65.
2 "democracy doesn't have a price," Adam Plowright, *The French Exception: Emmanuel Macron: The Extraordinary Rise and Risk*, fully updated ed. (London: Icon Books, 2018), 210.
3 Joseph A. Schumpeter, *Capitalism, Socialism, and Democracy* (London: G. Allen & Unwin Ltd., 1943).
4 For an excellent discussion of the political implications of technological change from the industrial revolution to today, see Carles Boix, *Democratic Capitalism at the Crossroads: Technological Change and the Future of Politics* (Princeton, NJ: Princeton University Press, 2019). Boix argues that "populism" lacks any consistent ideological or policy basis; it is instead the "creation of political entrepreneurs" who seek to inject some new political dimension or cleavage to "compete (and succeed) electorally," 166.
5 "compete with one another for votes," Peter Mair, *Ruling the Void: The Hollowing of Western Democracy* (London: Verso, 2013), 51. "catchall parties," Otto Kirchheimer "The transformation of the Western European Party system," in *Political Parties and Political Development*, eds. Joseph La Palombara and Myron Weiner, 177–200 (Princeton, NJ: Princeton University Press, 1966), 57.
6 On the globalization-based cleavage, see Boix, *Democratic Capitalism*; Pippa Norris and Ronald Inglehart. *Cultural backlash: Trump, Brexit, and authoritarian populism* (New York: Cambridge University Press, 2019).
7 On the emergence and persistence of the professionalized, nonmember party, see: Oscar Mazzoleni and Gerrit Voerman, "Memberless parties: Beyond the business-firm party model?," *Party Politics* 23, no. 6 (2017). See also Angelo Panebianco, *Political Parties: Organization and Power* (New York: Cambridge University Press, 1988).
8 Thomas Poguntke et al., "Party rules, party resources and the politics of parliamentary democracies: How parties organize in the 21st century," *Party Politics* 22, no. 6 (2016): 661–78.
9 Mair, *Ruling the Void*, 78–9.
10 "[w]hat is Europe" quoted in Sheri Berman, *Democracy and Dictatorship in Europe: From the Ancien régime to the Present Day* (New York: Oxford University Press, 2018), 286.

11   "Nazism was a good idea," quoted in Tony Judt, *Postwar: A History of Europe since 1945* (London: Vintage, 2010), 58.

12   On Christian Democracy in Europe in general, see Martin Conway, *Western Europe's Democratic Age, 1945–1968* (Princeton, NJ: Princeton University Press, 2020). "what tipped," Peter G. J. *Pulzer, German Politics, 1945–1995* (Oxford: Oxford University Press, 1995), 36.

13   Fulbrook, *A History of Germany, 1918–2014: The Divided Nation*, 4th ed., (Hoboken: Wiley Blackwell, 2014), 121; Arnold J. Heidenheimer, *Adenauer and the CDU* (The Hague: M. Nijhoff, 1960), 24–5. Charles Williams, *Adenauer: The Father of the New Germany* (New York: Wiley, 2000). On Italy, see Paul Ginsborg, *A History of Contemporary Italy, 1943–1988* (London: Penguin, 1990), 48–51.

14   Russell J. Dalton and Martin P. Wattenberg, *Parties without Partisans: Political Change in Advanced Industrial Democracies* (Oxford: Oxford University Press, 2000); Mair, *Ruling the Void*, 39. On membership figures, Peter Mair and Ingrid Van Biezen, "Party membership in twenty European democracies, 1980–2000," *Party Politics* 7, no. 1 (2001); Ingrid Van Biezen, Peter Mair, and Thomas Poguntke, "Going, going, ... gone? The decline of party membership in contemporary Europe," *European Journal of Political Research* 51, no. 1 (2012): 24–56.

15   Richard Seymour, *Corbyn: The Strange Rebirth of Radical Politics*, 2nd ed. (New York: Verso, 2017), 83.

16   Seymour, *Corbyn*; Alex Nunns, *The Candidate: Jeremy Corbyn's Improbable Path to Power* (New York: OR Books, 2016). On Labour in the aftermath of Brexit, see Tim Shipman, *All Out War: The Full Story of Brexit* (London: William Collins, 2017), ch. 27.

17   "electrifying," "Boris," in Tom Bower, *Boris Johnson: The Gambler* (London: Penguin, 2020), pp. 32, 77.

18   On this possible deal, see: Shipman, *All Out War*, 161.

19   "party-manager," Sarah Elise Wiliarty. "Angela Merkel's path to power: The role of internal party dynamics and Leadership," *German Politics* 17, no. 1 (2008): 83.

20   "a one-man party"; "far from being a properly," Koen Vossen, *The Power of Populism: Geert Wilders and the Party for Freedom in the Netherlands* (London: Routledge, 2016), 1, 20.

21   "there were no," Alan S. Zuckerman, *The Politics of Faction: Christian Democratic Rule in Italy* (New Haven, CT: Yale University Press, 1979), 53.

22   Paul D. Kenny and Michele Crepaz, "Corruption scandals and political crises: The 'free press' and democracy in Italy," unpublished paper, Australian National University, (2012). Ginsborg, *A History of Contemporary Italy*. Judith Chubb, *Patronage, Power, and Poverty in Southern Italy: A Tale of Two Cities* (New York: Cambridge University Press, 1982). Martin Bull and Martin Rhodes, *Crisis and Transition in Italian Politics* (London: Frank Cass & Company Ltd, 1997), 67; Zuckerman, *The Politics of Faction*.

23   Eric C. C. Chang, Miriam A. Golden, and Seth J. Hill, "Legislative malfeasance and political accountability," *World Politics* 62, no. 02 (2010), 177–220.

24   "enough of these politicians," in Stanton H. Burnett and Luca Mantovani, *The Italian Guillotine: Operation Clean Hands and the Overthrow of Italy's First Republic* (Lanham: Rowman & Littlefield, 1998), 160.

25   Cas Mudde, *Syriza: The Failure of the Populist Promise* (Cham: Palgrave Macmillan, 2017).

26 On the civil service and party building, see Sidney G. Tarrow, *Between Center and Periphery: Grassroots Politicians in Italy and France* (London: Yale University Press, 1977). Philip G. Nord, *France's New Deal: From the Thirties to the Postwar Era* (Princeton, NJ: Princeton University Press, 2010); "federation," "endorsed by a party organisation," David Hanley, *Party, Society and Government: Republican Democracy in France* (Oxford: Berghan Books, 2002), 20, 140; Mattei Dogan, "Les filières de la carrière politique en France," *Revue française de sociologie* (1967): 468–92.

27 "direct relationship," Jackson, *De Gaulle*, 336." "not only seen," Andrew Knapp, *Charles de Gaulle* (Abingdon: Routledge, 2021), 140.

28 "had to find support," quoted in Jean Lacoutre, *De Gaulle: The Ruler 1945–1970*, trans. Alan Sheridan (New York: Norton, 1993), 10. "populist government," quoted in Jonathan Fenby, *France: A Modern History from the Revolution to the War with Terror* (New York: St. Martin's Press, 2016), 312; "purely charismatic," Hanley, *Party, Society and Government*, 122, fn. 3. "Beneath the cheers," Knapp, *Charles de Gaulle*, 151.

29 Marc Lazar, "The French Communist Party," in *The Cambridge History of Communism: Volume 2: The Socialist Camp and World Power 1941–1960s*, eds. Norman Naimark, Silvio Pons, and Sophie Quinn-Judge, (Cambridge: Cambridge University Press, 2017). On the divergence of Christian Democracy in France, see Stathis N. Kalyvas, *The Rise of Christian Democracy in Europe* (Ithaca, NY: Cornell University Press, 1996).

30 "mainly from the mass," Jean Charlot, *Le gaullisme d'opposition, 1946–1958: histoire politique du gaullisme* (Paris: Fayard, 1983), 87–9. "formerly unpoliticized," Lacoutre, *The Ruler*, 142. "direct bond," quoted in Conway, *Western Europe's Democratic Age*, 266.

31 "plebiscitary dictatorship," quoted in Fenby, *France*, 328.

32 "in 1946 I did not have television," quoted in Jackson, *De Gaulle*, 622; Philip Short, *Mitterrand: A Study in Ambiguity* (London: Vintage, 2014), 191.

33 "popular monarchy," "Gaullism," "[t]here you are worrying," in Jackson, *De Gaulle*, 369, 619, 655. "I wanted to smash," quoted in Lacoutre, *The Ruler*, 494. "beyond redemption," in Short, *Mitterrand*, 221.

34 Philip Malcolm Waller Thody, *The Fifth French Republic: Presidents, Politics and Personalities* (New York: Routledge, 1998); William R. Nester, *De Gaulle's legacy: The Art of Power in France's Fifth Republic* (New York: Palgrave Macmillan, 2014).

35 "dedicated to promoting," David S. Bell, *Parties and Democracy in France: Parties under Presidentialism* (Brookfield, VT: Ashgate, 2000), 49. "without … big parties," in Short, *Mitterrand*, 274.

36 "control of a political," Alistair Cole, *Emmanuel Macron and the Two Years That Changed France* (Manchester: Manchester University Press, 2019), 32.

37 "old two party system," "the politicians," Plowright, *Emmanuel Macron*, 207, 225–26. "the theme," Cole, *Emmanuel Macron*, 7.

38 "normal" in "Macron ne croit pas 'au président normal, cela déstabilise les Français,'" *Challenges*, October 16, 2016, www.challenges.fr/election-presiden tielle-2017/interview-exclusive-d-emmanuel-macron-je-ne-crois-pas-au-president-normal_432886. "constructed not according," "improvised," Sophie Pedder,

Revolution Française: Emmanuel Macron and the Quest to Reinvent a Nation (London: Bloomsbury, 2018), 123, 124; "Macron's movement," Plowright, *Emmanuel Macron,* 196–97, 269, 388.

39 Alvaredo, Facundo, Lucas Chancel, Thomas Piketty, Emmanuel Saez, and Gabriel Zucman, "The elephant curve of global inequality and growth." *AEA Papers and Proceedings,* 108 (2008): 103–8.

40 "anywheres" and "somewheres" from David Goodhart, *The Road to Somewhere: The Populist Revolt and the Future of Politics* (London: Hurst & Company, 2017).

CHAPTER 7

1 James Bryce, *The American Commonwealth,* new ed., vol. II (New York: The Macmillan Company, 1914), part III, ch. 53.

2 Conversation between Donald Trump and Steve Bannon, quoted in Bob Woodward, *Fear: Trump in the White House* (New York: Simon & Schuster, 2018), 4.

3 "the Democratic Party would be five parties," Steven M. Gillon, *The Democrats' Dilemma: Walter F. Mondale and the Liberal Legacy* (New York: Columbia University Press, 1992), 189.

4 The crack about Willkie's grassroots following is from Alice Roosevelt Longworth, daughter of Theodore Roosevelt. See David L. Lewis, *The Improbable Wendell Willkie: The Businessman Who Saved the Republican Party and His Country, and Conceived a New World Order* (New York: W. W. Norton & Company, 2018).

5 "under obligation," Steve Neal, *Dark Horse: A Biography of Wendell Willkie* (Lawrence: University Press of Kansas, 1989), 97; "politically trained people," Charles Peters, *Five Days in Philadelphia: The Amazing "We Want Wilkie!" Convention of 1940 and How It Freed FDR to Save the Western World* (New York: Public Affairs, 2005), 154. On the early postwar factionalism in the GOP, see Michael Bowen, *The Roots of Modern Conservatism: Dewey, Taft, and the Battle for the Soul of the Republican Party* (Chapel Hill: University of North Carolina Press, 2011).

6 For insights into MacArthur's failed political ambitions, see William Manchester, *American Caesar: Douglas MacArthur 1880–1964* (New York: Arrow Books, 1979).

7 "our disagreement is not," in Theodore H. White, *The Making of the President 1960,* reissue ed. (New York: HarperPerennial, 2010), 287. On the Goldwater campaign, Rick Perlstein, *Before the Storm: Barry Goldwater and the Unmaking of the American Consensus,* 1st ed. (New York: Hill and Wang, 2001).

8 "went around the party," quoted in Geoffrey Kabaservice, *Rule and Ruin: The Downfall of Moderation and the Destruction of the Republican Party, from Eisenhower to the Tea Party* (New York: Oxford, 2012), 93. "had better try where you have a few favors owing," John A. Farrell, *Richard Nixon: The Life* (New York: Vintage, 2018), 333.

9 On Johnson's weakening of the party machine, see Doris Kearns Goodwin, *Lyndon Johnson and the American Dream* (New York: Harper & Row, 1976). "Any man," quoted in Elaine C. Kamarck, *Primary Politics: How Presidential Candidates Have Shaped the Modern Nominating System* (Washington, DC: Brookings Institution Press, 2009), 14.

10 "ablest demagogue," Richard Strout quoted in Frank Rich, "After Trump," *New York Magazine*, November 13, 2017, https://nymag.com/intelligencer/2017/11/frank-rich-trumpism-after-trump.html.

11 On party reforms, see Byron E. Shafer, *Quiet Revolution: The Struggle for the Democratic Party and the Shaping of Post-reform Politics* (New York: Russell Sage Foundation, 1983). "Quota democracy" is from the *New York Post*'s Max Lerner, quoted in Robert O. Self, *All in the Family: The Realignment of American Democracy since the 1960s* (New York: Hill and Wang, 2012), 250. "activists were," Rick Perlstein, *Nixonland: The Rise of a President and the Fracturing of America* (London: Scribner, 2008), 512.

12 Perlstein argues that the Nixon campaign even sought to ensure a McGovern win, Rick Perlstein, *The Invisible Bridge: The Fall of Nixon and the Rise of Reagan* (New York: Simon & Schuster, 2014). "great broad middle," quoted in Self, *All in the Family*, 259. The realignment of the Democratic Party away from its unionized white working-class base toward a more descriptively and ideologically diverse coalition in the late 1960s has been extensively covered: see Ronald Radosh, *Divided They Fell: The Demise of the Democratic Party, 1964–1996* (New York: Free Press, 1996); Adam Hilton, *True Blues: The Contentious Transformation of the Democratic Party* (Philadelphia: University of Pennsylvania Press, 2021).

13 "my feeling," Daniel K. Williams, *The Election of the Evangelical: Jimmy Carter, Gerald Ford, and the Presidential Contest of 1976* (Lawrence: University Press of Kansas, 2020), 166.

14 "I don't even know Jimmy Carter," in Jonathan Alter, *His Very Best: Jimmy Carter, a Life* (New York: Simon & Schuster, 2020), 233.

15 On Mondale, see Gillon, *Democrats' Dilemma*, esp. ch. 14. "quintessential Democratic insider," Kenneth S. Baer, *Reinventing Democrats: The Politics of Liberalism from Reagan to Clinton* (Lawrence: University Press of Kansas, 2000), 52.

16 "the first serious"; "the air time was free," Peter Louis Goldman, *Quest for the Presidency, 1992* (College Station: Texas A&M University Press, 1994), 423, 29.

17 "Bush-Cheney campaign," Donald T. Critchlow, *The Conservative Ascendancy: How the Republican Right Rose to Power in Modern America*, 2nd ed. (Lawrence: University Press of Kansas, 2011), 274.

18 "you needed," quoted in Tim Alberta, *American Carnage: On the Front Lines of the Republican Civil War and the Rise of President Trump* (New York: Harper, 2019), 66.

19 "Conflict equals exposure equals power," in Julian Zelizer, *Burning Down the House: Newt Gingrich, the Fall of a Speaker, and the Rise of the New Republican Party* (New York: Penguin, 2021), 67.

20 Jennifer Stromer-Galley, *Presidential Campaigning in the Internet Age*, 2nd ed. (New York: Oxford University Press, 2019). "Armed with a Twitter," Robert Costa, "Donald Trump and a GOP primary race like no other," in *Trumped: The 2016 Election That Broke All the Rules*, eds. Larry Sabato, Kyle Kondik, and Geoffrey Skelley (Lanham, MD: Rowman & Littlefield Publishers, 2017), 107.

21 Theda Skocpol and Alexander Hertel-Fernandez, "The Koch network and republican party extremism," *Perspectives on Politics* 14, no. 3 (2016). Hans Noel, "Why can't the GOP stop Trump?" *The New York Times*, March 1, 2016, www.nytimes.com/2016/03/

0;214; "with little institutional," Bryan T. Gervais and Irwin L. Morris, *Reactionary Republicanism: How the Tea Party in the House Paved the Way for Trump's Victory* (New York: Oxford University Press, 2018), 208.

22 In addition to those already cited, recent books that place Trump's rise in the context of the Republican Party's long lurch to the right include, Jeremy W. *Peters, Insurgency: How Republicans Lost Their Party and Got Everything They Ever Wanted* (New York: Crown, 2021); Dana Milbank, *The Destructionists: The Twenty-Five Year Crack-Up of the Republican Party* (New York: Doubleday Books, 2022); E. J. Dionne Jr., *Why the Right Went Wrong: Conservatism from Goldwater to Trump and Beyond* (New York: Simon & Schuster, 2016).

23 Tal Kopan, "Ted Cruz's Washington friends: The House Freedom Caucus," *CNN*, February 26, 2016, https://edition.cnn.com/2016/02/26/politics/ted-cruz-house-free dom-caucus/index.html. For the most insightful analysis of the role of Republican Party fragmentation in Trump's rise, see: Samuel L. Popkin, *Crackup: The Republican Implosion and the Future of Presidential Politics* (New York: Oxford University Press, 2021).

24 Hillary fundraising, Joshua Green, *Devil's Bargain: Steve Bannon, Donald Trump, and the Storming of the Presidency* (New York: Penguin, 2017), 194. Bill Allison, Mira Rojanasakul, Brittany Harris, and Cedric Sam. "Tracking the 2016 presidential money race," *Bloomberg Businessweek*, December 9, 2016, www.bloomberg .com/politics/graphics/2016-presidential-campaign-fundraising; E. Franklin Fowler, T. Ridout, and M. Franz, "Political advertising in 2016: The presidential election as outlier?" *The Forum*, 14(4), pp. 445–69. (2017). See also, John Sides, Michael Tessler, and Lynn Vavreck, *Identity Crisis: The 2016 Presidential Campaign and the Battle for the Meaning of America* (Princeton, NJ: Princeton University Press, 2018). Even if it is the case that Trump spent $66 million of his own money, we should also keep in mind that around $11 million of that went directly back into Trump businesses, and that in all likelihood, he's more than made his money back through the value added to brand Trump in the years since.

CHAPTER 8

1 Christian Houle and Paul D. Kenny, "The political and economic consequences of populist rule in Latin America," *Government and Opposition* 53, no. 2 (2016): 256–87. Paul D. Kenny, *Populism and Patronage: Why Populists Win Elections in India, Asia, and Beyond* (Oxford: Oxford University Press, 2017); Paul D. Kenny, "'The enemy of the people': Populists and press freedom," *Political Research Quarterly* 73, no. 2 (2020): 261–75.

2 Paul Kenny, Kirk Hawkins, and Saskia Ruth, "Populists undermine democracy in these four ways. Would a President Trump?" *Washington Post*, www.washingtonpost.com/ news/monkey-cage/wp/2016/08/18/populists-undermine-democracy-in-these-4-ways-would-president-trump; "guardrails," Steven Levitsky and Daniel Ziblatt, *How Democracies Die* (New York: Crown, 2018).

3 Jan-Werner Müller, *What Is Populism* (Philadelphia: University of Pennsylvania Press, 2016); William Galston, *Anti-Pluralism: The Populist Threat to Liberal Democracy* (New Haven, CT: Yale University Press, 2018); "deeply democratic," Yascha Mounk, *The People vs. Democracy: Why Our Freedom Is in Danger and How to Save It* (Cambridge, MA: Harvard University Press, 2018), 8; "democratic

illiberalism," Takis Pappas, *Populism and Liberal Democracy: A Comparative and Theoretical Analysis* (Oxford: Oxford University Press); "an authoritarian form," Federico Finchelstein, *From Fascism to Populism in History* (Berkely: University of California Press, 2019), xvii.

4 Cas Mudde and Cristobal Rovira Kaltwasser, eds., *Populism in Europe and the Americas: Threat or Corrective for Democracy?* (New York: Cambridge University Press, 2013); Cas Mudde and Cristóbal Rovira Kaltwasser, *Populism: A Very Short Introduction* (New York: Oxford University Press, 2017).

5 E. E. Schattschneider, *Party Government: American Government in Action* (New York: Routledge, 2003).

6 "for public plunder," quoted in Nany Rosenblum, *On the Side of the Angels: An Appreciation of Parties and Partisanship* (Princeton, NJ: Princeton University Press, 2010), 5. "[p]arties are fatal to the public good," quoted in David Hanley, *Party, Society and Government: Republican Democracy in France* (Oxford: Berghan Books), 1.

7 Frances McCall Rosenbluth and Ian Shapiro, *Responsible Parties: Saving Democracy from Itself* (New Haven, CT: Yale University Press, 2018).

8 John Herbert Aldrich, *Why Parties? A Second Look*, 2nd ed. (Chicago: University of Chicago Press, 2011).

9 Robert Michels, Political Parties: *A Sociological Study of the Oligarchical Tendencies of Modern Democracy* (New York: Free Press, 1966).

10 "all men of sense," Martin Van Buren, *The Autobiography of Martin Van Buren*, ed. John C. Fitzpatrick (Washington, DC: Government Printing Office, 1920), 125. On the party's time horizons, see the insightful essay by Jacob T. Levy, "The party declines," January 18, 2017, www.niskanencenter.org/the-party-declines.

11 Jonathan Alter, *His Very Best: Jimmer Carter, a Life* (New York: Simon & Schuster, 2021), 247. On populism as a threat to democracy due to its weak institutionalization, see: Zoltán Ádám, "Explaining Orbán: A political transaction cost theory of authoritarian populism," *Problems of Post-Communism* 66, no. 6 (2019): 385–401.

12 Philip Jones and John Hudson, "The role of political parties: An analysis based on transaction costs," *Public Choice* 94, no. 1/2 (1998): 175–89.

13 S. Erdem Aytaç and Susan Carol Stokes, *Why Bother? Rethinking Participation in Elections and Protests* (New York: Cambridge University Press, 2018).

Index